Core Science 1

2nd Edition

Stage 4 *Essential Content*

Marian Haire

Eileen Kennedy

Graeme Lofts

Merrin J. Evergreen

jacaranda

jaconline.com.au

Second edition published 2004 by
John Wiley & Sons Australia, Ltd
33 Park Road, Milton, Qld 4064

Offices also in Sydney and Melbourne

Typeset in 11/12.5 pt Garamond

© M. Haire, E. Kennedy, Clynton Educational
    Services and Evergreen Quest Pty Ltd 1999, 2004

First edition published 1999

National Library of Australia
Cataloguing-in-publication data

Core science. 1.

2nd edition.
Includes index.
For year 7 students.
ISBN 0 7314 0134 4

1. Science — Textbooks. I. Haire, Marian.

500

Illustrated by Paul Lennon, Stephen Francis,
Terry St Ledger, Patrick Watson, Maria Loi,
Steven Hunter and the Wiley Art Department.

Cover photograph: photolibrary.com/Stefan Mokrzecki

Printed in China by
C & C Offset Printing Co., Ltd

10 9 8 7 6 5 4 3 2 1

All the experiments described in this book have
been written with the safety of both teacher and
student in mind. However, all care should be taken
and appropriate protective clothing should be worn
when carrying out any experiment. Neither the
publisher nor the authors can accept responsibility
for any injury that may be sustained when
conducting any of the experiments described in this
book.

CONTENTS

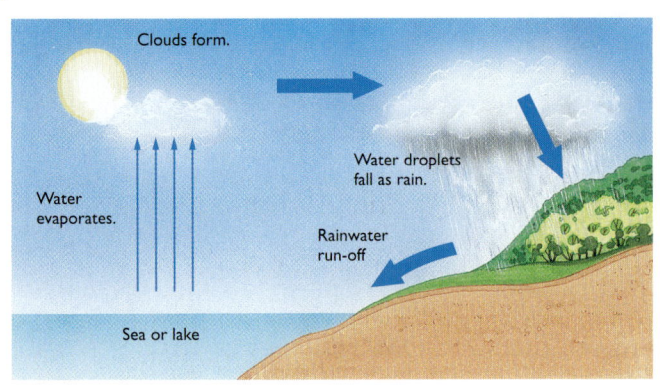

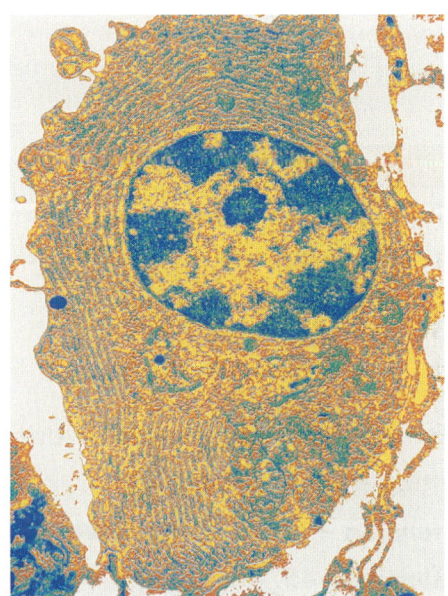

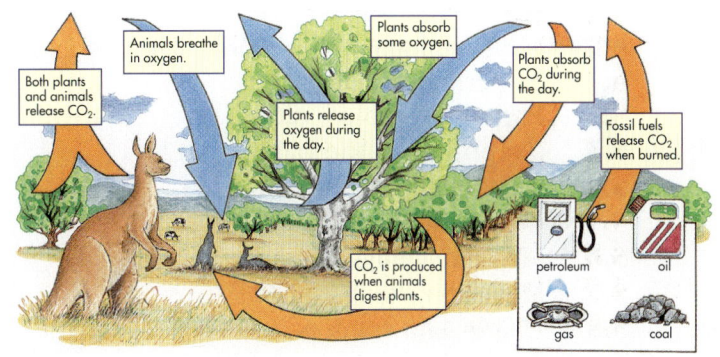

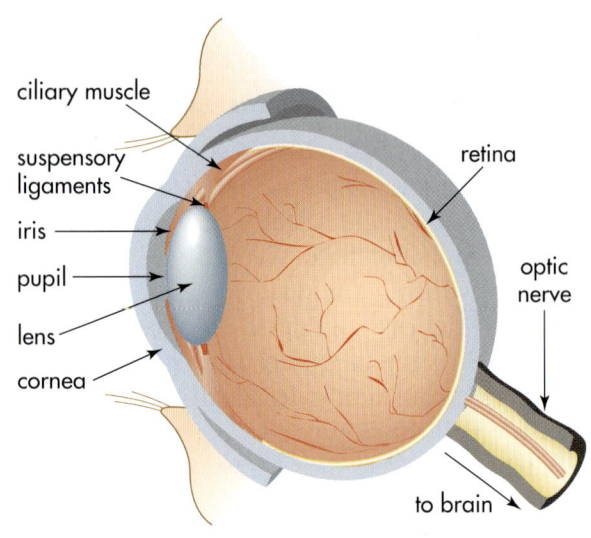

ACKNOWLEDGEMENTS

The authors would like to thank Marian Gauci, Yoka McCallum and Robyn Kronenberg for their contribution to this book. They would also like to thank Arthur, Brendan and Rebecca Haire, and Michael, John, Marcel and Conor Kennedy for their support, encouragement, advice and patience throughout the development of this book.

We would like to thank contributing author Peter Rozanski. In addition, we would like to acknowledge the friendly and professional advice of the many colleagues who have contributed ideas and provided constructive criticism. We would especially like to thank our publishing editor Angela Wong. Angela's patience, quiet determination and ideas were always a source of inspiration to us and encouraged us to continue when the task seemed overwhelming.

The publisher and authors would also like to thank the following copyright holders.

Images

• photolibrary.com: /SPL/Alfred Pasieka **iv** (bottom) and **97** (top right and bottom right); /Brett Allatt **30**; /SPL/David Scharf **83** (bottom); /SPL/Professors P.M. Motta, K.R. Porter and P.M. Andrews **92**; /SPL/Dr Jeremy Burgess **94** (left), **97** (bottom left) and **195** (top centre); /SPL/Andrew Syred **97** (top left); /SPL/Scott Cazamine **108** (left); /SPL/CNRI **108** (right); /Vaughan Fleming/SPL **122** (left); /SPL/NASA **129** (top right) and **173** (right); /SPL/TRL Ltd **135**; /Photo Researchers Inc. **138** (bottom); /SPL/Annabella Bluesky **194** (bottom left); /SPL/Geoff Tompkinson **202**; /SPL/J-L Charmet **219** • The Picture Source/Terry Oakley **194** (bottom centre) • ANT Photo Library: **86** (right); /N.H.P.A **iv** (centre) and **82**; /Ron and Valerie Taylor **66**; /Cyril Webster **71** and **84** (bottom right); /Ken Griffiths **74** (left) and **84** (centre right); /Peter McDonald **76** (top) and **84** (top right); /Kelvin Aitken **80** (right); /M. Cermak **80** (top); /G. & B. Cheers **84** (bottom left); /R. & D. Keller **85**; /Michael O'Connor **86** (centre); /Paddy Ryan **86** (left); /G.E. Schmida **75** and **124** (top); /Silvestris **138** (top); /Otto Rogge **84** (top left) and **146**; /Fredy Mercay **76** (bottom) and **152**; /Grant Dixon **159**; /Bill Bachman **171**; /Norbert Wu **180**; /Ted Mead **182** (right); /P. & M. Walton **185** (right); /J. Frazier **197** • Australian Picture Library: /Richard Martin/Agence Vandystadt **v** (top) and **126**; /CORBIS/Underwood & Underwood **26**; /Steve Vidler **50** and **114**; /CORBIS/Neal Preston **51**; /CORBIS/AFP/Patrick Hertzog **116**; /CORBIS **150** • © PhotoDisc, Inc. **v** (bottom), **28** (bottom), **80** (left), **87**, **124** (bottom), **134** (left), **140**, **161**, **165**, **166** (left and right), **167**, **168** (left and right), **169** (right), **177**, **193** (top right, bottom right and centre left), **196** (left and centre), **200**, **226** and **251** • © Butterfly Alphabet **2** (2 images) • Coo-ee Picture Library **6**, **13**, **15**, **20**, **38** (right), **40**, **49**, **56**, **77**, **182** (left), **185** (top left) and **249** • © imageaddict.com.au **28** (top), **39** (right) and **122** (right) • Courtesy of Sydney Water Corporation **34** • Photo courtesy Xstrata Copper **38** (left) • © Westfalia Separator Australia Pty Ltd **39** (bottom) • Fairfax Photo Library: /Dallas Kilponen **41**; /Rick Stevens **91**; /Brendan Esposito **195** (top right) • Reproduced with permission of Dr Emma L. Cooney **44** • © Digital Stock/Corbis Corporation **46** • Commonwealth Bureau of Meteorology **53** (8 images) • © CSR Bradford Insulation **60** (right) • © Viewfinder Australia Photo Library **74** (centre) • © Digital Vision **74** (right), **132**, **148** (top) and **193** (bottom left) • Newspix: **129** (bottom right); /Kelly Barnes **118**; /Gareth Morgan **129** (left); /Brian Condron **192** • Getty Images: /Shaun Botterill **128**; /AFP/Patrick Hertzog **191**; /Stone/Mike Severns **196** (right) • © Reebok www.reebok.com **134** (right) • © Denis Couch **148** (bottom) • Courtesy NASA/JPL–CALTECH **160** and **172** • NASA **169** (left), **170** (2 images) and **173** (left) • Metropolitan Ambulance Service Melbourne **183** • © Corbis Corporation **185** (bottom left) • Australia Telescope National Facility/ © CSIRO — Photo by J. Masterson **193** (top left) • Taronga Zoo **217** • National Measurement Laboratory, CSIRO **218** • Peter Rozanski **219** (2 images) • Vernier Software & Technology **220** • © John Wiley & Sons Australia: /Julie Stanton **225**; /Werner Langer **246** (2 images); /Narelle Kremmer **248** • CSIRO Education **255**.

Text

• Outcomes statements from Science, Stages 4–5 Syllabus © Board of Studies New South Wales, 2003 included with permission of the Board of Studies, New South Wales **viii–ix** • Reproduced from *The Slater Field Guide to Australian Birds*, by Peter Slater, Lansdowne Press, Sydney 1994 p. 218, New Holland Publishers **71** • © Taronga Zoo **217**.

Every effort has been made to trace the ownership of copyright material. Information that will enable the publisher to rectify any error or omission in subsequent editions will be welcome. If copyright holders in such instances contact the Publisher's Permissions Department, arrangements for the payment of the usual fee will be made.

PLANNING GRID

The content and activities in the following units of *Core Science 1*, second edition, and *Core Science 2*, second edition, support student achievement of the Stage 4 outcomes in the Science syllabus for Years 7–10.

The *Core Science Teacher Support Kit for Books 1 & 2*, second edition, includes a more detailed curriculum planning grid which provides essential and additional text references for Stage 4 Knowledge and Understanding content.

Note: I = introductory page
T = *Thinking about* page
E = *Extension* page
R = *Reflection* page

In *Core Science 1*: S = *Core Science Skills* units
SRP = *Student Research Project* units

In *Core Science 2*: SM = *Science Matters* units

Prescribed focus areas

Stage 4 outcomes	Core Science 1	Core Science 2
4.1 identifies historical examples of how scientific knowledge has changed people's understanding of the world	1.5, 1E, 1R, 2.4, 3.5, 4.1, 4.5, 4.6, 4.9, 5.1, 5.5, 5.8, 6.3, 6R, 7.1, 7.3, 7E, 8.1, 8.3–8.6, 8E, 9.7, S.1, S.6	2.1, 2.4–2.6, 2E, 3.2, 3R, 4.3, 4.6, 4E, 7.4, 9T, 9.2, 9.4–9.6, 9R, 10.8, SM.1, SM.2, SM.6–SM.8
4.2 uses examples to illustrate how models, theories and laws contribute to an understanding of phenomena	1.1, 3.4–3.6, 3R, 4.3, 4.8, 5.1, 6.1–6.10, 7.1, 7.4–7.7, 8T, 8.1, 8.2, 9.1, 9.2, 9R, S.14	1.2, 1.6, 2.1, 2.5, 2.7, 3.2, 3.6, 3.7, 7T, 7.1, 7.2, 7R, 8.1, 8.2, 9.2, 9.5, 9.6, 10.7, SM.1–SM.3, SM.5, SM.8
4.3 identifies areas of everyday life that have been affected by scientific developments	1T, 1.1, 2.2–2.6, 2E, 2R, 3.1–3.3, 3.5, 3.7, 5.2, 5.8, 5E, 6.4, 6.6, 6.7, 6.10, 6E, 7.1, 7.2, 7.4, 7.7, 7E, 8.5, 8.6, 8E, 9.3, 9.7, 9.8, 9E	1.6, 1.8, 2.6–2.9, 2E, 3.3–3.5, 3.8, 3E, 4.6, 4.9, 5.5, 5.12, 6.4–6.5, 6.7–6.10, 7.2, 7.4–7.8, 8T, 8.5, 8E, 9.3, SM.1, SM.2, SM.5, SM.6
4.4 identifies choices made by people with regard to scientific developments	2.3, 2.4, 2.6, 2R, 3.3, 3.7, 5.5, 7.1–7.3, 7.7, 7E	1.4, 1.8, 2.1, 2.4, 2.5, 2.8, 3.5, 3.8, 4.9, 5.5, 5.8, 6T, 6.1, 6.3, 6.5, 6.8, 7.8, 8.8, 9.4, SM.5
4.5 describes areas of current scientific research	1I, 1T, 1.1, 1E, 2.6, 2E, 2R, 4R, 5.1, 5E, 6.10, 6E, 7.2, 7.4, 7E, 8.3–8.6, 8E, 9.7	1.8, 3.4, 4.8, 4.9, 4E, 4R, 5.4, 6.11, 6E, 7.7, 7.8, 8.1, 8.3, 8.5, 8.8, 8E, 8R, 9.1–9.4, 10.5, 10.6, 10E, SM.1, SM.2, SM.5

Domain — knowledge and understanding

Stage 4 outcomes	Core Science 1	Core Science 2
4.6 identifies and describes energy changes and the action of forces in common situations	3.2–3.7, 3E, Chapter 6, 8.2, 9.1, 9.3, 9.7, 9E, S.14	3.5, 3.9, 5.1, 5.2, 5.5–5.8, 6.5, 6.6, 7.1–7.7, 8.2, 9E, SM.2, SM.7
4.7 describes observed properties of substances and theories using scientific models	Chapter 2, 3T, 3.1–3.6, 3E	2T, 2.2–2.4, 2.6, 2.7, 2E, 3T, 3.1–3.5, 3.9, 3E
4.8 describes features of living things	4.1–4.5, 4.7–4.10, 4E, 5.1, 5.2, 5.5–5.8, 5E, 8.1, 9.5, 9.6	1.1–1.3, 1.6–1.8, 5.10, 4.1–4.3, 4.5, 5.1, 5.6, 5.7, 5.9–5.12, 6.2, 6.4, 6.6, 6.7, Chapter 8, SM.6
4.9 describes the dynamic structure of Earth and its relationship to other parts of our solar system and the universe	3.3, 7.1–7.4, 7.6, 8.1–8.5, 8E, 9.7	2.8, 4.9, Chapter 9, 10.1–10.4
4.10 identifies factors affecting survival of organisms in an ecosystem		2.9, 6.1–6.9, 6E

Stage 4 outcomes	Core Science 1	Core Science 2
4.11 identifies where resources are found, and describes ways in which they are used by humans		2.8, 2.9, 3.9, 6.3, 10.2–10.4
4.12 identifies, using examples, common simple devices and explains why they are used	2.3–2.6, 2E, 3.5–3.7, 4.1–4.3, 6.3, 6.4, 6.7, 6.10, 6E, 7E, 8.3, 8.4, 8.6, 8E, 9.3, 9.6–9.8	5.6, 7.2–7.4, 7.7, 7.8, 8.2, 8.5, 10E, SM.2, SM.5

Domain — skills

Stage 4 outcomes	Core Science 1	Core Science 2
4.13 clarifies the purpose of an investigation and, with guidance, produces a plan to investigate a problem	all chapters	all chapters
4.14 follows a sequence of instructions to undertake a first-hand investigation	all chapters	all chapters
4.15 uses given criteria to gather first-hand data	all chapters	all chapters
4.16 accesses information from identified secondary sources	all chapters	all chapters
4.17 evaluates the relevance of data and information	all chapters	all chapters
4.18 with guidance, presents information to an audience to achieve a particular purpose	all chapters	all chapters
4.19 draws conclusions based on information available	all chapters	all chapters
4.20 uses an identified strategy to solve problems	all chapters	all chapters
4.21 uses creativity and imagination to suggest plausible solutions to familiar problems	all chapters	all chapters
4.22 undertakes a variety of individual and team tasks with guidance	all chapters	all chapters

Domain — values and attitudes

Stage 4 outcomes	Core Science 1	Core Science 2
4/5.23 demonstrates confidence and willingness to make decisions and to take responsible actions	Throughout the two books (and the series as a whole), students are continually given opportunities to develop these values and attitudes. This is achieved through the following features:	
4/5.24 respects different viewpoints on science issues and is honest, fair and ethical	• *Activities* (under the headings *Think, Create, Investigate* and *Imagine*) provide opportunities for students to consider both the beneficial and negative effects that science can have on their lives.	
4/5.25 recognises the relevance and importance of lifelong learning and acknowledges the continued impact of science in many aspects of everyday life	• *Science issues* are included throughout the text to provide a relevant context for the material in the chapters.	
4/5.26 recognises the role of science in providing information about issues being considered and in increasing understanding of the world around them	• Student activities in the *Thinking about* and *Reflection* pages emphasise discussion of issues and listening to the views of others. Their function is to develop student understanding of what they know and need to know.	
4/5.27 acknowledges their responsibility to conserve, protect and maintain the environment for the future	• The *Core Science skills* section in Book 1 focuses on both science skills and learning skills. Different learning strategies are described to enable students to develop an understanding of how they learn best.	

ABOUT THE CD-ROM

The CD-ROM accompanying this textbook includes the text in pdf format. The text is linked to the following features that are designed to assist learning and help students assess their own learning.

- *Learning objects* (see below) bring diagrams and other illustrations to life with the use of animation and provide a level of support for concept development that is not possible with a still picture.
- Each learning object is linked to an *e-tivity* (right) that tests understanding of the concept developed or reinforces the learning object.

Minimum system requirements

Windows 95/98 or NT
Processor: Pentium
CD-ROM drive speed: 4x
16Mb RAM
speakers

Macintosh
Macintosh OS 7.6
Processor: PowerPC
CD-ROM drive speed: 4x
6Mb RAM

Running the CD-ROM

To run this CD-ROM — on Windows 95/98 or NT, or Macintosh — simply place it in the CD-ROM drive.

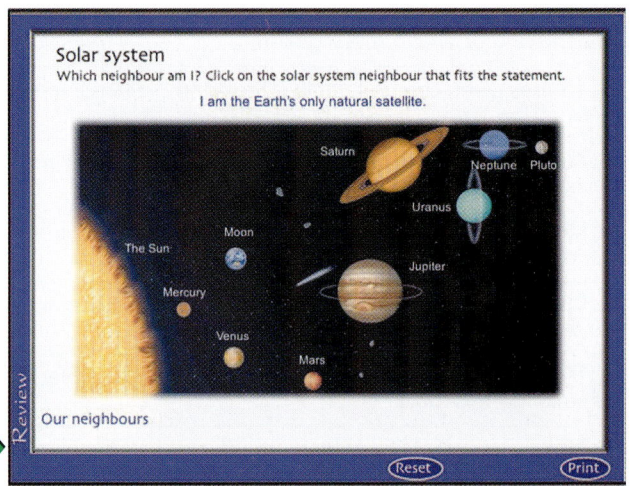

Troubleshooting

If you have problems with the operation of this CD-ROM:

- Check that you have the right equipment (see Minimum system requirements).
- Visit www.jaconline.com.au/contact_us/faqs.html to check if the answer to your problem is provided under 'Frequently Asked Questions'.
- Either e-mail or write to John Wiley & Sons Australia explaining the problem, and providing details of the type of computer and the amount of RAM you have, the processor type and the CD-ROM speed. If you return the disk, please package it appropriately to protect it during transit.

E-mail: multimedia@johnwiley.com.au

Address: Multimedia Assistant
John Wiley & Sons Australia, Ltd
PO Box 1226
MILTON QLD 4064

INTRODUCTION

The *Core Science* series has been developed to assist teachers to implement the revised Board of Studies Science Stages 4–5 syllabus in New South Wales.

TO THE STUDENT

Science is a study of the world around us in order to explain how it works. It includes knowledge and skills that humans have developed over a long period of time. It helps you to understand the substances around you, how machines work and why the stars seem to move in circles. Science explains how you see and hear, why it rains and why you need a skeleton. It even explains why elephants have big ears while polar bears have small ones! Scientific knowledge is all around you. Whenever you turn on a light, eat food, watch television or flush the toilet you are using the products of scientific knowledge.

Science helps you to understand why things behave in the way that they do. It helps you to find out how to swim faster through the water, whether life is possible on other planets, whether the Earth is flat or round and what makes plants grow faster. You are living in a period where knowledge is growing rapidly and technology is changing at an incredible rate. Learning how to learn is becoming just as important as learning itself. Learning is most effective when you build on what you already know and when you are motivated and take the time to reflect on your learning. *Core Science* has been designed to present you with opportunities to do all of this and to help you continue your own quest for scientific knowledge and tackle the challenges of the future. It will help you practise scientific skills that will help you continue to learn about science long after you leave school.

TO THE SCIENCE TEACHER

The Prescribed Focus Areas and Domains from the syllabus are presented in an integrated fashion in each chapter and are set in contexts that are relevant to young Australians. The grid at the beginning of the text will enable you to cross-reference the material in each chapter with the Stage 4 outcomes.

We have attempted to make the *Core Science* series easy to use, interesting and relevant to the students who are using it. As science teachers, we have designed *Core Science* to help you in your quest to teach science effectively.

The **key content** statements on the opening page of each chapter indicate the content included in the chapter that supports student achievement of outcomes for the Science Stages 4–5 syllabus.

The **key questions** on the opening page of each chapter are designed to stimulate student interest. They provide a starting point and the potential to begin a topic by finding out what students already know or what they would like to know.

The **Thinking about** section at the beginning of each chapter assists in identifying the current knowledge and views of your students. The activities are addressed to the student but it is intended that the teacher act as a facilitator and be actively involved in listening and detecting the thinking patterns of students.

The **activities** throughout each chapter demand different levels of skills. The names of the activities — using data, remember, think, create, imagine and investigate — are self explanatory.

The **Putting it all together**, **Summing up** and **Looking back** sections at the end of each chapter are designed to assist students to summarise the topic and apply the knowledge and skills introduced in the chapter. The **Reflection** section encourages students to reflect on their learning. It allows the teacher to discover how students have changed their views since the Thinking about section at the beginning of the chapter, and it also highlights any difficulties the students may have.

Each chapter includes an **extension**, which could be set as homework, as an extra activity for faster students or as an activity for the whole class. **Literacy skills** are developed throughout the text.

The **Student research project** is covered comprehensively on pages 239–55. The **Core Science skills** section on pages 202–38 will enable students to develop competencies that underpin the nature of science.

The **Core Science interactive CD-ROM** contains a wide variety of activities involving animation, video, audio and self-testing excercises that will engage students and promote learning with computer technology.

Core Science includes many examples of how the 'big ideas' of science were discovered and developed, and how scientists have worked, often over long periods of time, to develop the concepts, facts and theories that we now take for granted. This historical perspective encourages students to appreciate the contribution made by scientific achievements.

A teacher resource kit has been developed to help you make better use of the *Core Science* books.

We hope that you enjoy using *Core Science*.

Marian Haire and Eileen Kennedy

SCIENCE IS . . .

The word science comes from the Latin word **scientia,** *meaning knowledge. Science is a body of knowledge about the world around you. It is also a way of gathering knowledge.*

Science photographer Kjell Sandved spent 20 years searching for and photographing markings on butterfly wings that make the letters of the alphabet. He also found markings with the numbers 0 to 9. The inset photograph shows the letter 'E'.

KEY QUESTIONS

What do scientists do?

Do people other than scientists use science in their work or leisure activities?

How is a science laboratory different to other rooms?

Is the science laboratory a dangerous place?

Am I a good observer?

How are substances heated safely in the science laboratory?

Is it easy to shoot goals in basketball or netball with only one eye open?

KEY CONTENT

Select and use a range of scientific equipment with accuracy.

Identify hazards associated with particular procedures and equipment and adopt safe and responsible practices.

Integrate scientific understanding, personal observations and the ideas of others to suggest testable hypotheses.

Draw conclusions from data gathered and relate them to the aim of the investigation.

Organise data into tables and appropriate graphs, using correct units.

Use evidence to justify inferences.

Begin to recognise some limitations of equipment and the reliability of data and relate this to conclusions.

Report on the results of investigations in writing, orally or in drawings.

Identify problems that can be tested, and then design an investigation using variables to answer the problems.

Thinking about *Science*

A scientist taking samples 'out in the field' to monitor the effect of humans on the environment

A scientist teaching dolphins to communicate with humans using a keyboard

A scientist injecting silkworms with a virus to allow them to produce a human protein important to the immune system called interferon. This research may lead to a cure for AIDS.

A scientist using a replica of a pterosaur wing to learn about the aerodynamics of bird flight

Before you begin this chapter, take some time to think about what you already know about science.

A scientist checking the quality of a city's water supply

A scientist using water-sampling instruments on an Antarctic icefloe

1. Science is ...

GROUP WORK (a) In a group, make a list of all the words that come to mind when you think about the phrase 'Science is ...'. Now sort all the words that can be grouped together and place them under your own headings.

(b) Write a report using the words you have sorted. Instructions on how to go about starting your report are in the box on the right.

(c) Once you have finished you can read your report to the class. Practise reading it in front of your group first.

2. What does a scientist look like?

GROUP WORK Draw a picture to illustrate your group's description of a scientist. Present this to the class, explaining what you think a day in the life of a scientist might be like.

Paragraph 1 — Opening statement

Write a few sentences starting with the phrase 'Science is ...', making sure that you have included all your headings and words from the first part of this activity. This is the introduction to your report and tells the reader what the report is about.

Paragraphs following the introduction

You then need to write a paragraph for each of your headings. You can do this as a group or you might find it quicker if each student takes one or two headings. Write a few sentences about each heading and remember to include as many words as possible from the words that were grouped under each heading.

Science is ...

Branches *of* science

The science tree below shows six of the main areas of science. As our scientific knowledge increases, new branches develop, such as **acoustics** (the study of sound) and **biomechanics** (the study of animal or human movement).

The people *of* science

Not all scientists fall into one of the six areas of science listed below. Some scientists work in more than one area at a time. A **biochemist** works in biology and chemistry, studying the substances in living things. A **biophysicist** might study the small electrical signals that travel from your ear to your brain which enable you to hear. Scientists work in a variety of situations. They might work indoors or outdoors, in laboratories, in factories, on ships, in planes, underwater or even in outer space.

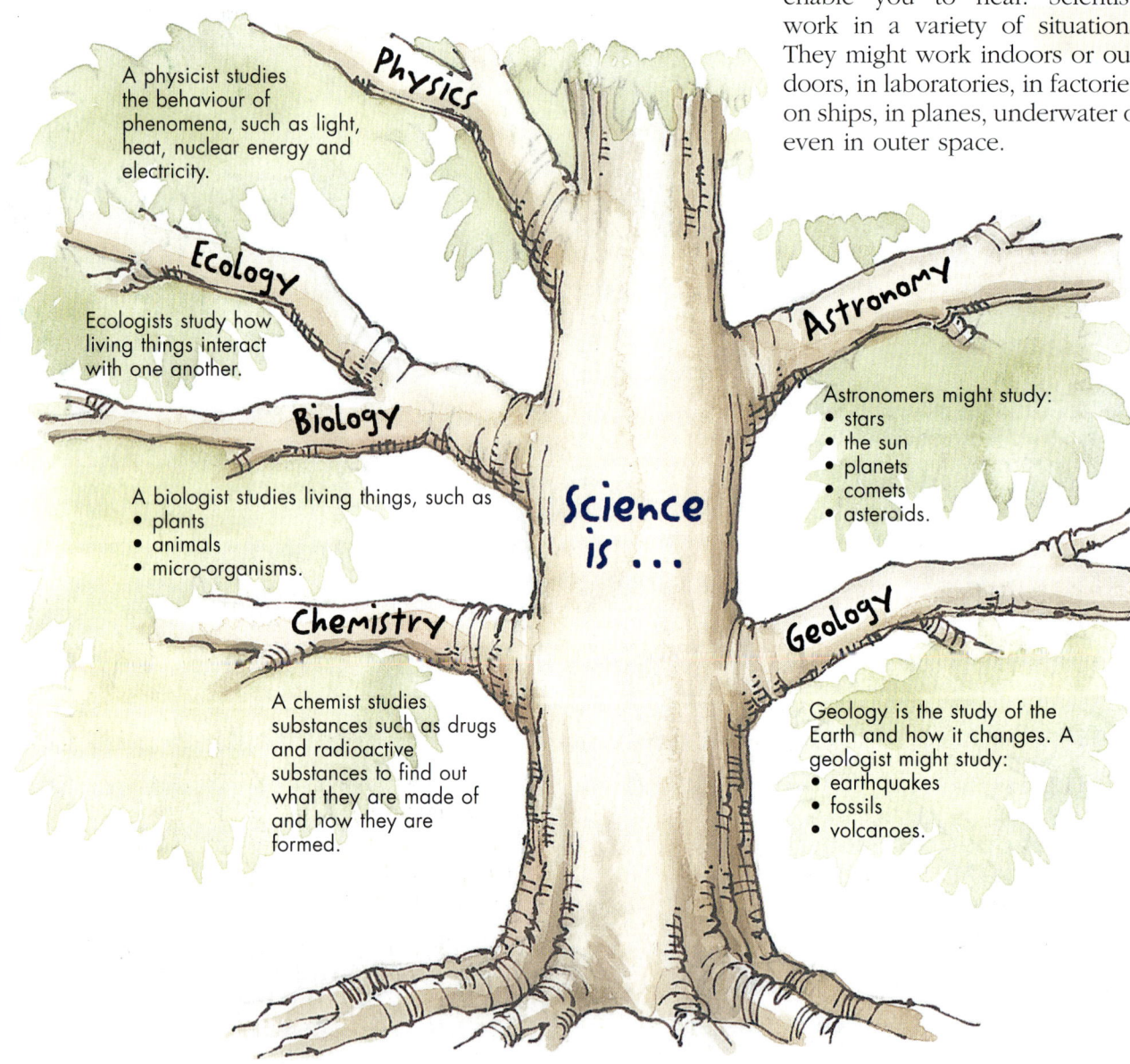

A physicist studies the behaviour of phenomena, such as light, heat, nuclear energy and electricity.

Physics

Ecology

Ecologists study how living things interact with one another.

Biology

A biologist studies living things, such as
• plants
• animals
• micro-organisms.

Astronomy

Astronomers might study:
• stars
• the sun
• planets
• comets
• asteroids.

Science is ...

Chemistry

A chemist studies substances such as drugs and radioactive substances to find out what they are made of and how they are formed.

Geology

Geology is the study of the Earth and how it changes. A geologist might study:
• earthquakes
• fossils
• volcanoes.

How scientists work

Scientists are curious about their surroundings. They look for patterns and trends to explain what they observe. When they think they know the reason for something, they design an experiment to prove or disprove their ideas. These experiments are repeated many times to ensure the results are accurate.

Sometimes concepts are difficult to understand or explain, so scientists develop a **model** to help understand their observations and ideas. For example, a physical model of the solar system is a useful way of demonstrating the relative size of each planet.

When an idea is first developed, it is called a **theory**. Much later, when many scientists have tested the theory and there is no evidence to contradict it, it is accepted as a **law**.

Since the beginning of time, scientists have made discoveries that have improved our quality of life. Once a scientific idea is used to make a device that makes life easier, it is called **technology**. The interaction of science and technology has been the driving force behind our modern technological world.

Science is ... *everywhere!*

Scientific knowledge is all around you. Whenever you turn on a light, eat food, watch television or flush the toilet you are using the products of scientific knowledge. People use scientific facts to solve everyday problems.

Nurses, police, vets, dietitians, teachers, doctors, mechanics, gardeners, stage designers and artists use scientific knowledge in their work. **Engineers**, for example, use scientific knowledge to design bridges, computers, factories, artificial limbs, sewerage systems and buildings.

You use scientific knowledge every day.

Activities

Think

1. Write down how people in each of the following occupations might use science in their daily work.

nurse	mechanic	gardener
chef	vet	architect
journalist	farmer	police officer

2. What would each of the following types of scientists be mainly concerned with?
   (a) biochemist
   (b) geophysicist
   (c) marine ecologist
   (d) seismologist
3. List five technological devices which you have used today that would not have been invented without scientific knowledge.
4. (a) 'Photos' means 'light'. List as many 'photo' words as you can.
   (b) 'Graphos' means 'written'. What do you think the words 'photograph', 'graphospasm' and 'graphology' mean?

Imagine

Imagine that you are given the chance to interview any scientist from the past or present.
   Who would you choose?
   Give reasons for your choice and prepare a list of questions that you would ask.

Investigate

1. Find out what the following scientists study.

vulcanologist	astrophysicist
entomologist	zoologist
taxonomist	pharmacologist
microbiologist	botanist
geneticist	palaeontologist

2. Make a list of any scientific theories or laws you can find.
3. Find out what you need to study to become a scientist or an engineer.

The science laboratory

Getting *to know* the science lab

- Sit quietly for a minute or two and look around the science laboratory.
- List as many differences as you can between the science laboratory and other general classrooms at your school.
- Draw a map of the science laboratory on a sheet of A4 paper, labelling each of the following items clearly.

  student tables and work
  benches
  teacher's desk or
  demonstration bench
  gas taps
  power points
  sinks
  fume cupboard
  eye wash
  fire extinguishers
  fire blanket
  sand bucket
  broken glass bin
  rubbish bin
  doors

Laboratory *equipment*

Some of the equipment that you are likely to use in the science laboratory is illustrated below.

- In your workbook, draw a table like the one on the opposite page. Use the illustrations to match each item of equipment with the list in the table. Write the relevant number in the middle column to show you have identified each piece of equipment. (You will complete the purpose column of the table during the 'Think' activity.)

A school science laboratory

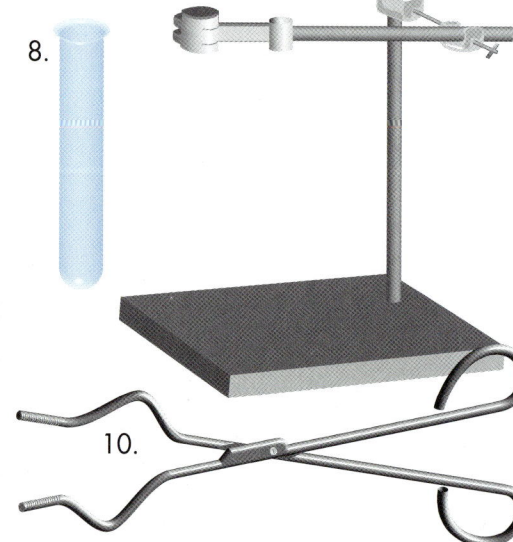

Some commonly used science equipment

Activities

Remember

1. What are the main differences between a science laboratory and a normal classroom?
2. List the items of science equipment that are made of glass.

Think

What is the purpose of each item of equipment? Complete the table in your workbook by selecting the correct statement from the list below.
- to pour liquids from one container into another; can be used with filter paper to separate some mixtures
- to hold liquids which need to be swirled around or filtered
- to hold small amounts of substances which need to be heated or mixed
- to pick up and hold small, solid objects, often while they are hot
- to move small amounts of solid substances from one container to another
- to protect eyes from sparks or splashes during experiments
- together with bossheads and clamps, to hold items of equipment at a suitable height
- to hold a test tube while it is being heated

Common laboratory equipment

Equipment checklist	Number	Purpose
heatproof mat		to protect the working surface
stirring rod		to stir
safety glasses		
beaker		to hold liquids or solids
thermometer		to measure the temperature of a substance
evaporating dish		to evaporate liquids
conical flask		
measuring cylinder		to measure quantities of liquids
test tube		
watchglass		to cover a beaker to stop evaporation
spatula		
test tube rack		to hold test tubes
retort stand		
bosshead		to hold the clamp on a retort stand
clamp		fits into the bosshead to hold items of equipment at a suitable height
filter funnel		
tongs		
test tube holder		

Investigate

Find out what the following items look like and how each one is used.
(a) crucible
(b) pipe-clay triangle
(c) separating funnel
(d) mortar and pestle
(e) pipette
(f) volumetric flask

11.

12.

13.

14.

15.

16.

SCIENCE *issues*

PLAYING IT SAFE

The science laboratory can be a dangerous place if you are not careful. Here are some rules for your safety and the safety of others. Can you add some more?

Do's *and* don'ts

Do

- Always follow your teacher's instructions carefully.
- Keep your notebooks and paper away from heating equipment, glassware, chemicals and flames.
- Tell your teacher immediately if you cut or burn yourself.
- Tell your teacher immediately if you break any glassware or spill chemicals. Spillages, even of water, need to be cleaned up without delay.
- Wait until hot equipment has had time to cool before putting it away.
- Leave all benches and tables clean and dry when you have completed your experiments.
- Wash your hands after you have handled any substances in the laboratory.
- Tie long hair back whenever you use a Bunsen burner.
- Point test tubes away from your eyes and your fellow students.
- Wear safety glasses while mixing or heating substances.

Don't

- Enter the laboratory without your teacher's permission.
- Run, push or behave roughly in the laboratory.
- Eat or drink in the laboratory.
- Smell or taste substances unless instructed to by your teacher. When you do need to smell substances, fan the odour to your nose with your hand.
- Put paper, matches or other solid objects in the sink.
- Pour substances down the sink. Follow your teacher's directions about the disposal of substances.
- Mix chemicals unless you have been instructed to by your teacher.
- Look directly into the top of a test tube, beaker or flask.
- Enter a preparation room without your teacher's permission.

Activities

Remember

1. What should you do if you cut or burn yourself in the laboratory?
2. If you are asked to smell a substance in a test tube, how should you do it?
3. What item of safety equipment should be worn while mixing or heating substances?

Think

1. In a group, take turns to give a reason for each rule on page 8.
2. Look around your science laboratory and locate any emergency equipment. When might they be useful?
3. Look carefully at the cartoons on the right and identify all the rules that are being followed correctly.
4. (a) On a map of your school, locate and mark the position of all fire extinguishers.
   (b) Survey five members of your school community to see if they know the location of their nearest fire extinguisher.

Create

Choose one of the laboratory safety rules that you have learnt and draw a poster that will illustrate the rule clearly.

1.4
Detective skills

Many skills that scientists use are the same as those used by detectives in solving a crime. Crimes are solved because someone makes careful **observations**. Observations are things or events that you notice. A footprint, the smell of perfume, the sour taste of a drink, an unusual sound or a warm log in a fireplace could provide clues to a crime. An observation can allow you to make an **inference**. You infer something when you use your observations and your previous knowledge to explain something. For example, if you recognised the smell of a perfume at the scene of a crime and you know that your prime suspect always wears that scent, you might make an inference that he or she is the culprit. But you would still need to prove this!

Observe the clues in the drawing below and write what you think has happened.

Normally you use all of your five senses to make observations. However, because you are trying to solve a mystery with just a drawing, you use only your sense of sight.

After making observations of the scene, you might be able to form a **hypothesis** about what happened. A hypothesis is an educated guess. It is a statement that you could investigate using all the available evidence. If your hypothesis was 'the thief left by the window', you would test this idea by looking for evidence to prove or disprove this hypothesis. Finding footprints in the garden outside would allow you to form a conclusion that the thief did leave by the window. A **conclusion** is the final outcome of an investigation; that is, what was found out.

Who or what did it?

Experiment 1.1 ARE YOU A GOOD OBSERVER?

YOU WILL NEED
candle and matches
jar lid

- Light a candle and place it on the lid of a jar. Write down as many observations as you can of the burning candle. Use all of your senses except the sense of taste. No chemicals should ever be tasted in the science laboratory!

CAUTION: Do not touch the flame of the candle.

1. Michael Faraday (1791–1867), a scientist famous for his discoveries in electricity and chemistry, made fifty-three observations of a burning candle. How many observations did you record?

- Use a table like the one below to record the number of observations made by the people in your class.

'Score' (number of observations made)	Number of people
0–7	
8–15	
16–23	
24–31	
32–39	
40–47	
more than 47	

- Construct a bar graph like the one shown below to display your class observations.

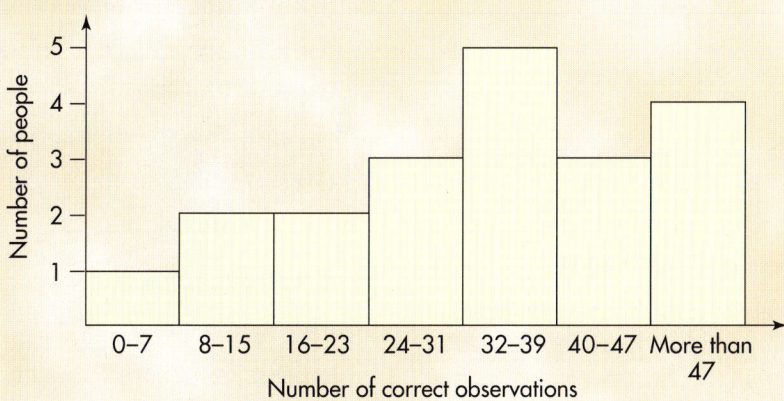

A bar graph can be used to display observations.

2. Which range of observations was most common?
3. Were the 'scores' evenly spread?
4. Is the bar graph more useful than the table? Why?
5. Answer the question 'What makes a good observer?'.

Activities

Remember

1. How is a scientist like a detective?
2. Explain the difference between a hypothesis and a conclusion.
3. Which of your five senses can be used to make observations?

Think

Read the following story and state whether each sentence is an observation, inference, hypothesis or conclusion.
(a) The dog in the house next door is barking.
(b) There are no lights on in the house.
(c) The owners must be asleep.
(d) There could be a prowler in the back yard.
(e) I heard the sound of breaking glass.
(f) The dog is still distressed.
(g) Someone is breaking into the house.

Investigate

Sit quietly in a nearby outdoor location and write down all of the things that you notice in two minutes. Use as many senses as you can apart from the sense of taste.
1. Which sense did you use the most?
2. Compare your observations with those of your friends. Which sense did they use the most?
3. Which other senses did you use?

Imagine

Imagine that you have lost your senses of sight and hearing. Write a description, giving as much detail as you can, about your favourite holiday or relaxation spot. Don't forget that your observations can be made only with your senses of touch, taste and smell.

1.5
Hot stuff

When you heat substances in the science laboratory, it is most likely that you will use a **Bunsen burner**. A Bunsen burner provides heat when a mixture of air and gas is lit.

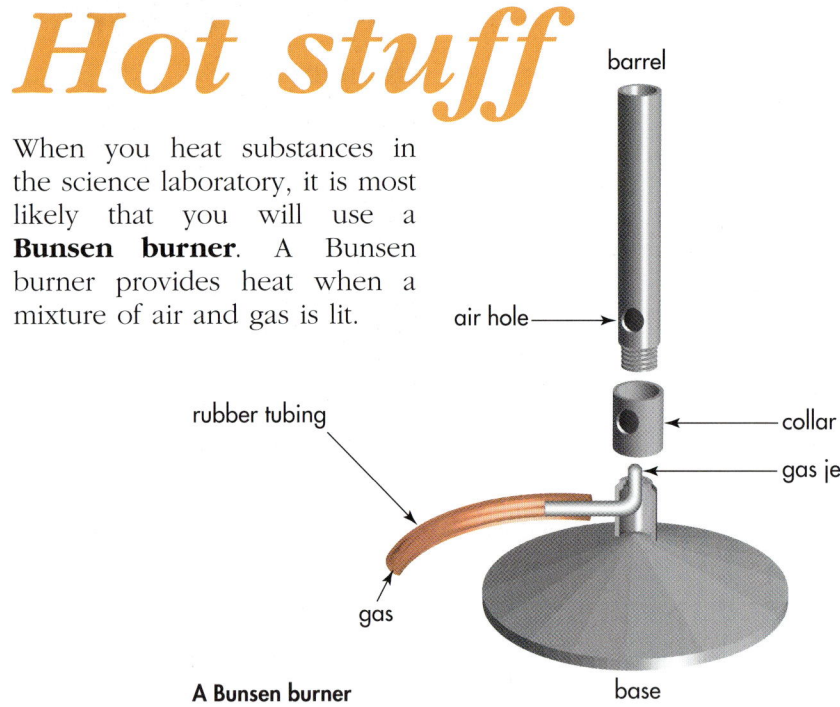

A Bunsen burner

Labels: barrel, air hole, collar, gas jet, rubber tubing, gas, base

Lighting a Bunsen burner

1. Place the burner on a heatproof mat.
2. Check that the rubber tubing is properly connected to the gas tap.
3. Ensure that the air hole is closed.
4. Light the match.
5. Open the gas tap.
6. Hold the burning match just above the top of the barrel.

The *two* flames

The yellow flame (safety flame) of a Bunsen burner is easily seen. So, when the Bunsen burner is not being used for heating, the yellow flame should be used. The blue flame of the Bunsen burner is much hotter and cleaner but is more difficult to see. The blue flame is used only for heating.

Experiment 1.2 INTRODUCING THE BUNSEN BURNER

YOU WILL NEED
Bunsen burner, heatproof mat and matches
safety glasses, tongs
several pieces of porcelain (from a broken evaporating dish or crucible)

- Examine a Bunsen burner and identify the parts labelled in the above diagram.
- Draw in pencil your own labelled diagram of the Bunsen burner.
- Put on your safety glasses and follow the steps in the box 'Lighting a Bunsen burner' to light your burner.

1. What colour is the flame?
2. Does the flame make any noise?

- Now turn the collar to open the air hole.

3. What colour is the flame?
4. Does the flame make any noise?
5. Is the flame easier to see with the air hole open or closed?

- Use tongs to hold a small piece of porcelain in the flame and record how long it takes the porcelain to become red hot. Place the porcelain on the heatproof mat to cool.
- Repeat this procedure with several other pieces of porcelain in different parts of the flame.

6. Which part of the flame appears to be the hottest?

- Close the air hole and heat one of the cooled pieces of porcelain.

7. Does it become red hot?
8. Describe any change in the appearance of the porcelain.

SCIFACTS

The Bunsen burner has been used in laboratories for about 150 years. It was invented by a German chemist, Robert Bunsen (1811–1899). The hottest part of a Bunsen burner flame has a temperature of about 1500°C which is higher than the temperature needed to melt gold! The inner blue flame contains some unburnt gas and is much cooler.

Experiment 1.3

HEATING A SUBSTANCE IN A TEST TUBE

YOU WILL NEED
100 mL beaker
Bunsen burner
heatproof mat
matches
test tube
test tube rack
test tube holder
food colouring

- Carefully pour water from a beaker into a test tube to a depth of about 2 cm as shown in the diagram below. Add a drop of food colouring to make it easier to see.

1. Why is the test tube placed in a test tube rack rather than in your hand?

- Light the Bunsen burner correctly and heat the test tube gently in the blue flame as shown in the photograph on the right. Remember that the open end of the test tube should be pointing away from you and your fellow students. The base of the test tube should be moved gently in and out of the flame. This prevents the water from splashing out of the tube.

2. Make a list of any changes that occur inside the test tube as you heat the water.

- Once the water has started boiling, stop heating and turn off the gas to the Bunsen burner. Place the test tube in the test tube rack. Leave it there until it has cooled before emptying it and cleaning up.

CAUTION: Before you start heating, check the following.
If you have long hair, is it tied back?
Are you wearing safety glasses?
Is the Bunsen burner on a heatproof mat?

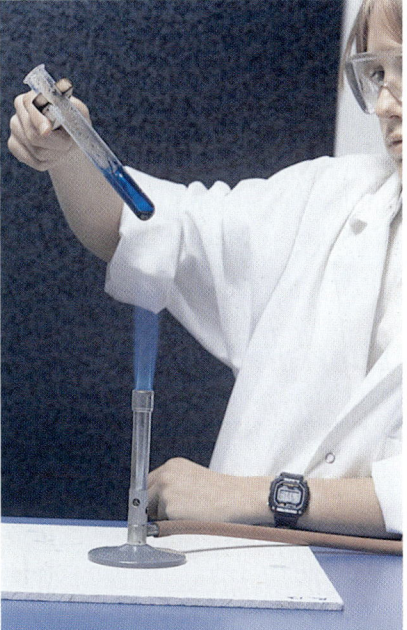
Heating a liquid in a test tube

Activities

Remember

1. Which flame of the Bunsen burner should be used for heating?
2. List the 6 steps that must be followed when lighting a Bunsen burner.
3. Which is the hottest part of the Bunsen burner flame?
4. Describe how a liquid should be poured into a test tube.
5. Explain the correct method for heating a liquid in a test tube over a Bunsen burner flame.
6. Why is it safer to use the yellow flame of the Bunsen burner while the burner is not being used for heating? Give two reasons.

Think

Why should you light the match before opening the gas tap when lighting a Bunsen burner?

Investigate

Find out more about Robert Bunsen. What were his achievements other than the invention of the Bunsen burner?

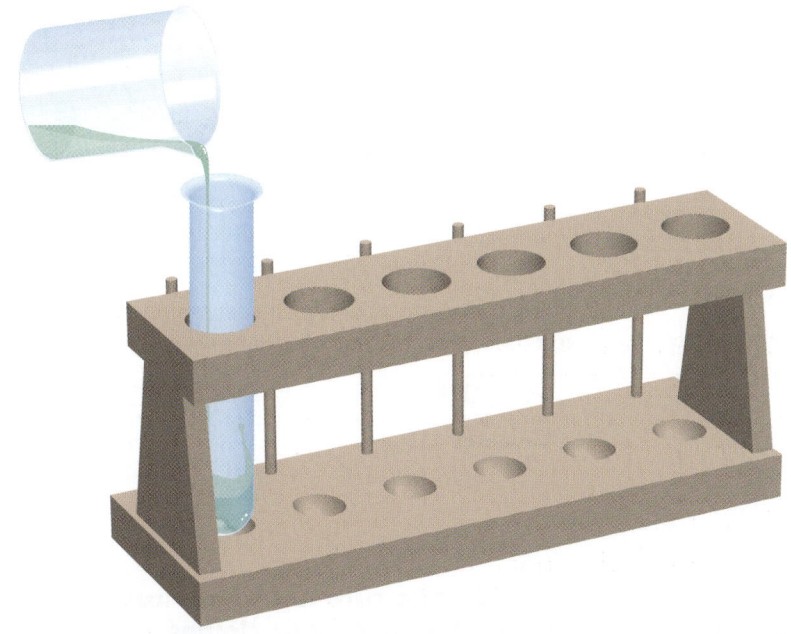
Pouring a liquid into a test tube

1.6 Observing & recording

When making a lot of observations, it is often helpful to organise them in a table. Observations and measurements which are organised in tables are easier to read. Tables also make it easier for you to draw graphs.

Experiment 1.4 RECORDING OBSERVATIONS IN A TABLE

YOU WILL NEED

test tubes	sodium carbonate
test tube rack	copper sulfate
50 mL beaker	methylated spirits
spatula	limewater
eye-dropper	starch suspension
drinking straw	iodine solution
vinegar	safety glasses
sodium bicarbonate	

CAUTION: Safety glasses should be worn while conducting these experiments.

- Draw a table like the one below in which to record your observations of each of the following activities.

What was done	Observations
1.	
2.	
3.	
4.	
5.	

1. Pour vinegar into a clean test tube to a depth of about 1 cm. Add a spatula full of sodium bicarbonate.

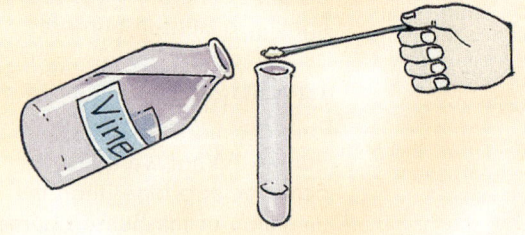

2. Quarter fill two clean test tubes with water. Add a dry spatula full of sodium carbonate to one test tube. Shake the tube until the sodium carbonate dissolves. Add a dry spatula full of copper sulfate to the other test tube and shake it until the crystals dissolve. Pour the contents of the second test tube into the first.

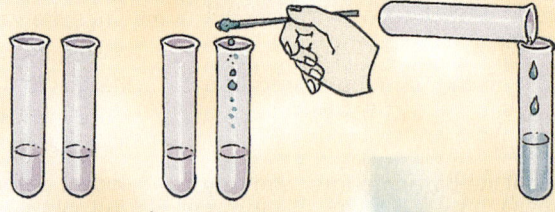

3. Use an eye-dropper to place one drop of methylated spirits onto the back of your hand. Blow air gently across the back of your hand.

4. Quarter fill a very small beaker with limewater. Gently blow out through a drinking straw into the limewater.

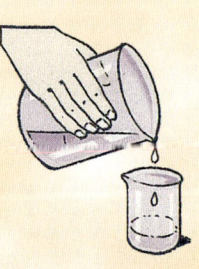 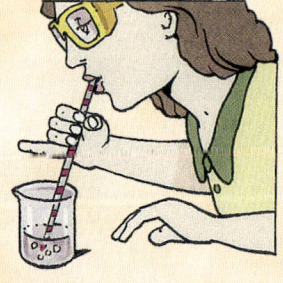

5. Place a few drops of starch suspension in a clean test tube. Add a drop of iodine solution.

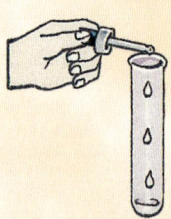 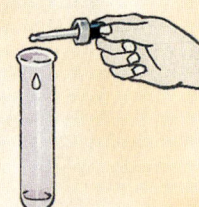

CAUTION: Take care not to get iodine solution on your skin or clothes.

Using *a thermometer*

A **thermometer** is used to measure temperature in degrees Celsius (°C). The thermometers used in most school laboratories contain alcohol with a red dye added. Thermometers are easily broken and need to be treated with care. Do not put your thermometer down in a place where it could roll off a table or bench. If you are using a thermometer containing mercury, a silver coloured liquid, extra care needs to be taken. Mercury is a poisonous substance.

CAUTION: If you break a thermometer, report it to your teacher immediately.

Some hints for using thermometers

1. Make sure that you are using the right thermometer. For example, a thermometer that reads only up to 50°C will not be suitable for measuring the temperature of boiling water (about 100°C).

2. Ensure that the whole of the bulb of the thermometer is in the substance that you are measuring the temperature of and not resting on the bottom of the container.

3. Wait until the column of liquid in the thermometer stops moving before you read the scale. For example, a thermometer that has been in the air will take a little while to reach the new temperature when placed in cold water.

4. When reading the thermometer you should have your eyes level with the top of the column of alcohol or mercury.

5. Record the temperature as soon as you have read it. Don't wait.

6. Never stir with a thermometer.

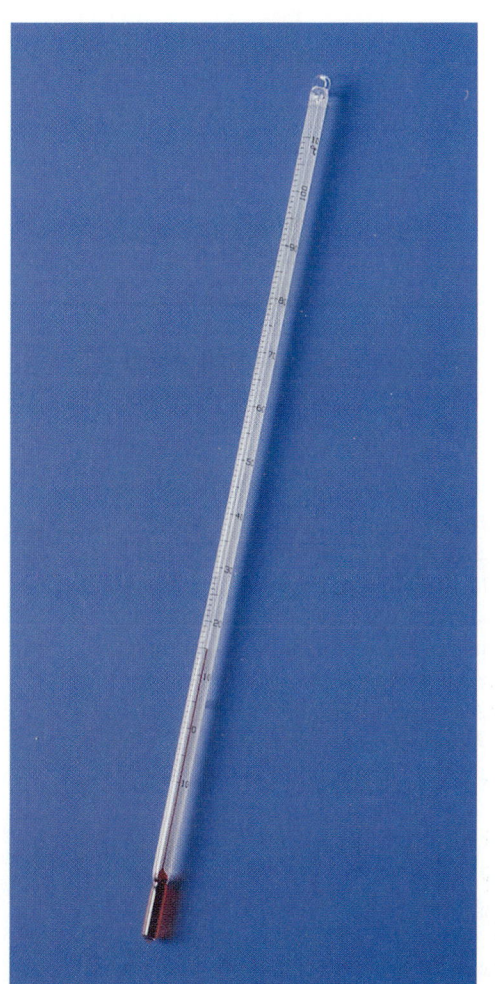

A school laboratory thermometer

Reading *the scale*

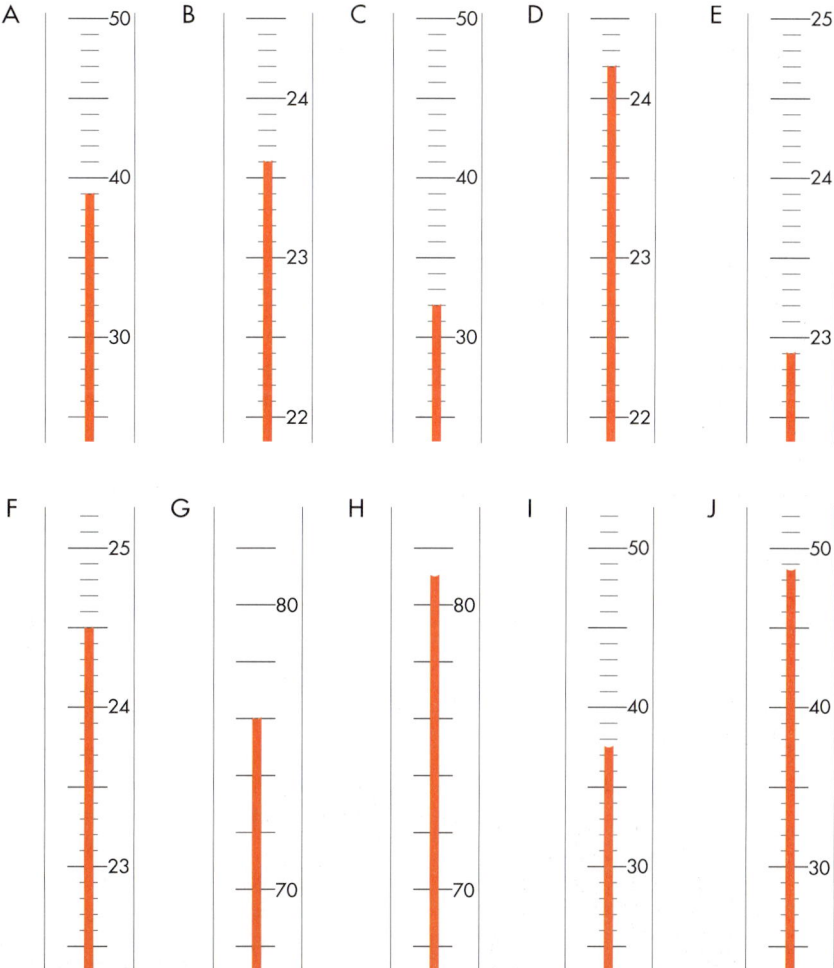

The temperatures measured by the thermometers A and B are 39°C and 23.6°C, respectively. What are the temperatures measured by thermometers C to J?

MEASURING TEMPERATURE

YOU WILL NEED

a thermometer

- Use a school laboratory thermometer to measure the temperature of:

  (a) air in the school laboratory
  (b) air outside the school laboratory
  (c) cold tap water
  (d) hot tap water
  (e) soil from a garden bed.

CAUTION:

Do not put the thermometer in your mouth!

- Copy and complete the following table so that you can record your measurements neatly.

Measuring temperature

Substance or location	Temperature (°C)
air inside the school laboratory	
air outside the school laboratory	
cold tap water	
hot tap water	
soil from a garden bed	

Heating *a liquid* in a beaker

A Bunsen burner is often used to heat liquids in a beaker. In the experiment below you will learn how to heat a liquid in a beaker. You will also take measurements of the temperature of the liquid and draw a graph to show how quickly the temperature changes.

Experiment 1.6 **HEATING A LIQUID IN A BEAKER**

YOU WILL NEED

Bunsen burner, heatproof mat and matches
tripod and gauze mat
250 mL beaker
100 mL measuring cylinder
retort stand, bosshead and clamp
thermometer
safety glasses

Copy the following table and use it to record your measurements.

Heating water in a beaker

Time (minutes)	Temperature (°C)	Time (minutes)	Temperature (°C)
0		6	
1		7	
2		8	
3		9	
4		10	
5			

- Set your equipment up as shown in the diagram at the top of page 17 and put on your safety glasses.
- Use a 100 mL measuring cylinder to measure out 100 mL of water and add it to the beaker without splashing. After a minute or two, measure the temperature of the water and record it in your table. This is the starting temperature. (time = 0 minutes)
1. Why is it better to wait a minute or two before taking the first temperature reading?
- Light your Bunsen burner and adjust the collar to produce a blue flame.
- Place it under the beaker and commence timing. You will need to quickly record the temperature every minute for ten minutes.
- After ten minutes, turn off the gas to the Bunsen burner. Wait a few minutes until your equipment has cooled before putting it away.

The measurements that you have made are called **data**. It is often helpful to display your data on a graph. Because the temperature of the water in this activity increased gradually, a line graph is appropriate.

- Copy the graph shown on page 17 and carefully plot your measurements on it. Plot each data point clearly and then join the points with a smooth curve.
2. Describe in words how the temperature increases.
3. Try to explain any unexpected results.
4. What happens to the temperature of the water when you heat it for another two minutes?
- If you have access to a computer and spreadsheet software, you could enter your data into a spreadsheet and print out a graph.

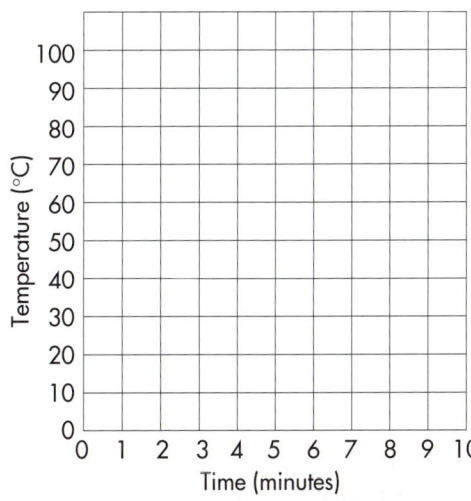

retort stand

bosshead

clamp

thermometer

beaker

gauze mat

tripod

Bunsen burner

box of matches

heatproof mat

The equipment needed for heating and measuring the temperature of a liquid in a beaker

Temperature of water heated in a beaker

Temperature (°C): 100, 90, 80, 70, 60, 50, 40, 30, 20, 10, 0
Time (minutes): 0 1 2 3 4 5 6 7 8 9 10

Activities

Remember

1. What unit is used to measure temperature?
2. There are two mistakes in the following drawing. What are they?

3. What are the temperatures measured by the thermometers below?

(a)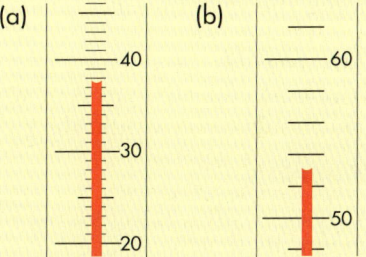

(b)

Think

1. You have three different thermometers X, Y and Z to choose from. Each has a different scale.
   X reads from 34°C to 42°C.
   Y reads from 0°C to 50°C.
   Z reads from −10°C to 110°C.
   Which of the thermometers X, Y and Z would be most suitable for measuring the temperatures of each of the following?
   (a) boiling water
   (b) sea water at the beach
   (c) your body
2. Explain why a bar graph is not appropriate for displaying your results in the second experiment (heating a liquid in a beaker).

Investigate

What is the lowest possible temperature in degrees Celsius? It is referred to as absolute zero.

Reporting investigations

When scientists conduct investigations they write reports to tell other people about their work. After conducting experiments you too should write a report that allows others to understand what you were trying to achieve, what steps you followed and what you found out. Your report should contain detailed **procedures** (aim, materials, method) so others can easily repeat your experiment.

Aim

A short statement about what you were trying to find out by doing the experiment.

Hypothesis

Your best educated guess of what you thought you would discover.

Materials

A list of the equipment and chemicals that were used.

Method

A set of steps outlining how to do the experiment. This will usually include a diagram showing how your equipment was set up. Include enough details to allow the reader to repeat your experiment.

Results and observations

A presentation of your data. This might include calculations, tables, graphs or a list of observations.

Discussion

An explanation of your results and a description of any difficulties that you had with the experiment. This might also include suggestions for improvements to the experiment.

Conclusion

A brief account of what you found out and how your findings relate to your aim. It is a good idea to read your 'aim' again before you write your conclusion.

Drawing science equipment

When reporting your experiments, a good simple diagram can make it much easier for the reader to understand what was done. Diagrams of science equipment are drawn in two dimensions (i.e. no depth) and are called line drawings. There are some rules to remember.

1. Diagrams in scientific reports must be drawn in pencil.
2. Straight lines should be drawn with a ruler.
3. Each item of equipment should be labelled.

The following diagrams show how some commonly used items of equipment should be drawn. In your workbook, practise drawing all the common items of laboratory equipment as line drawings.

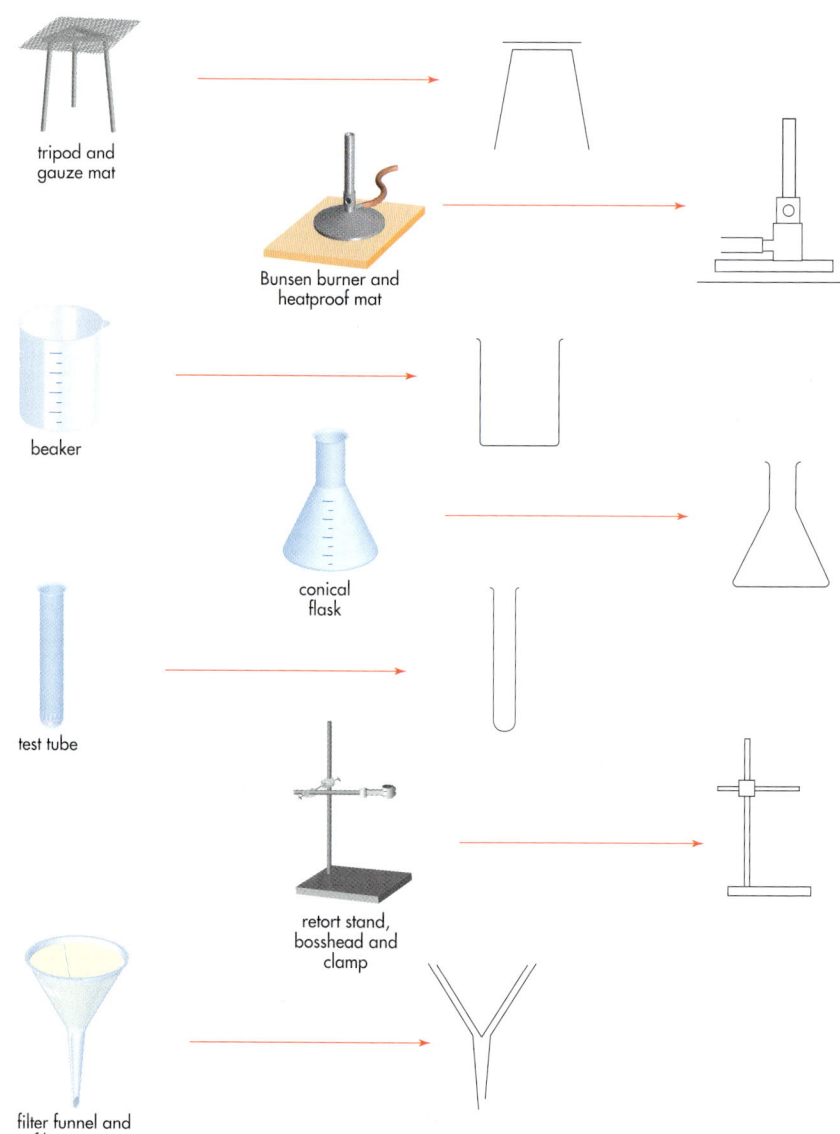

tripod and gauze mat

Bunsen burner and heatproof mat

beaker

conical flask

test tube

retort stand, bosshead and clamp

filter funnel and filter paper

Diagrams in scientific reports should be simple. In each case above the apparatus is shown on the left and the line drawing of this apparatus on the right.

Dissolving Sugar

Aim:
To compare how much sugar will dissolve in hot water compared to cold water.

Hypothesis:
Twice as much sugar will dissolve in hot water compared to cold water.

Materials:
Beaker, heatproof mat, Bunsen burner, tripod, gauze mat, matches, spatula, stirring rod, sugar, water.

Method:
1. A spatula was used to add sugar to 100 mL of cold water in a beaker. The sugar was stirred and more added until no more would dissolve. The number of spatulas of sugar that dissolved was recorded.
2. The mixture of sugar and water was heated with a Bunsen burner for 4 minutes and the extra amount of sugar that could be dissolved was recorded.

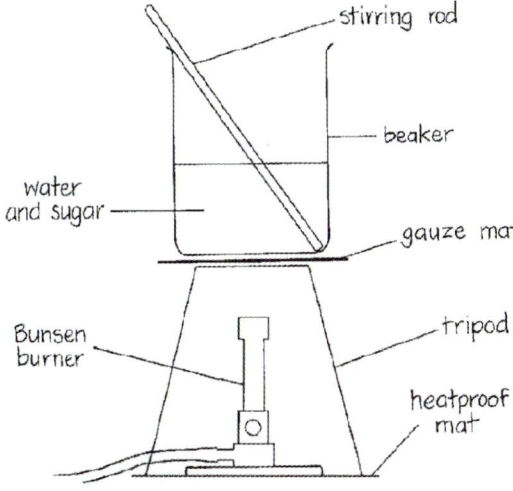

Results and observations:
Amount of sugar dissolved in cold water = 2 spatulas
Extra amount of sugar dissolved in hot water = 4 spatulas
Total amount of sugar dissolved in hot water = 6 spatulas

Discussion:
I was able to dissolve more sugar in the hot water than in the cold water. A thermometer could have been used to measure the temperature of the water. The amount of sugar could have been measured more accurately by adding smaller amounts at a time.

Conclusion:
Three times as much sugar dissolves in hot water as in cold water.

A good quality report of an experiment

Activities

Remember

1. Under which heading of your report of an experiment should the following information be included?
   (a) Suggestions for improvements to your experiment.
   (b) A reason for doing the experiment.
   (c) Graphs and tables.
   (d) A description of what you did.
   (e) A statement saying what you found out by doing the experiment.

2. Draw a neat, labelled scientific diagram of the following equipment. Water in a conical flask is being heated with a Bunsen burner. The conical flask is supported by a gauze mat on a tripod. The Bunsen burner is standing on a heatproof mat.

Think

1. Write a full scientific report on experiment 1.6 on page 16.

2. Draw a neat, labelled scientific diagram of the two sets of equipment that would be needed to safely perform the following activity.

   Part 1: Muddy salt water is being poured from a beaker into a filter funnel (with filter paper). The filter funnel is resting in the opening of a conical flask.

   Part 2: The filtered salt water, now in an evaporating dish is being heated by a Bunsen burner. The evaporating dish is supported by a gauze mat on a tripod.

3. Write a possible aim for the experiment described in part 1 and part 2 above.

4. Write three hypotheses and explain how you would go about testing them.

1.8 Measuring matter

Mass is a measure of how much matter there is in an object or substance. All substances have mass. Even air has mass! The standard unit of mass is the **kilogram**. Most substances and objects whose mass you will measure are quite small and light. You will therefore usually measure mass in grams (1 kg = 1000 grams). Mass is measured with a **balance**.

Electronic balances are easiest to use. All you need to do is place the object to be measured on the balance and read the digital display. In most school laboratories, however, you will measure mass using a multiple arm beam balance.

Many substances whose mass you want to measure cannot be placed in the pan of a balance. Liquids and substances such as salt should be placed in a container on the pan. To find the mass of such a substance you:

(a) measure and record the mass of the dry, empty container (often a watchglass or small beaker).
(b) measure and record the mass of the container with the substance in it.
(c) subtract the mass of the container (a) from the mass of the container with the substance in it (b).

Measuring *liquids*

Volume is a measure of the amount of space that an object or substance occupies. The standard unit of volume for liquids is the litre (L). If you are measuring small amounts of volume you would measure in millilitres (mL) (1 L = 1000 mL). Volume for liquids is measured using **calibrated** glassware. Calibrated means that it is marked with units of volume. Have a look at any measuring cylinder in your science laboratory — the lines are the calibration marks.

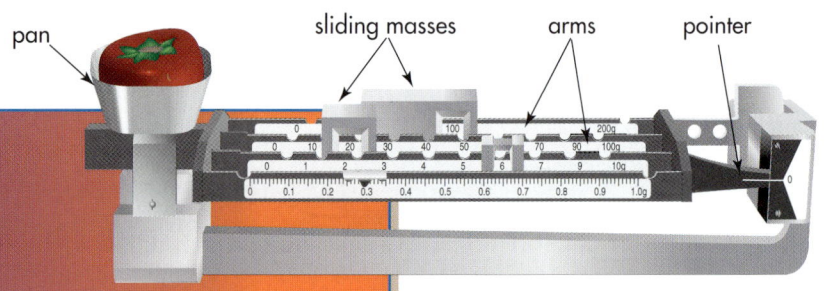

pan · sliding masses · arms · pointer

Using a multi-arm beam balance

Step 1: Move all sliding masses to the zero notch and check that the pointer on the arm of the balance lines up with the '0'. Consult your teacher if it doesn't line up as the balance will need adjusting.

Step 2: Place the object to be measured in the pan. The pointer will move upwards.

Step 3: Slide the heaviest sliding mass along its arm. When the arm overbalances, forcing the pointer to move below the '0', slide the mass back to rest in the nearest notch.

Step 4: Repeat step 3 for the other arms, ending with the arm with the smallest sliding mass. The arm with the smallest sliding mass does not have notches. Balance the arm as accurately as you can so that the pointer lines up with the '0'.

Step 5: Record the scale reading on each arm and add the readings to determine the mass of the object. The tomato in the figure above has a mass of 126.3 grams.

$$
\begin{aligned}
& 100 \quad \text{g} \\
+ & \ 20 \quad \text{g} \\
+ & \quad 6 \quad \text{g} \\
+ & \quad 0.3 \ \text{g} \\
\hline
= & 126.3 \ \text{g}
\end{aligned}
$$

Step 6: Move all of the sliding masses back to their '0' notch.

Step 7: If you are using a triple beam balance, you will have only three arms. Follow the same steps and add three readings to get the mass of the object.

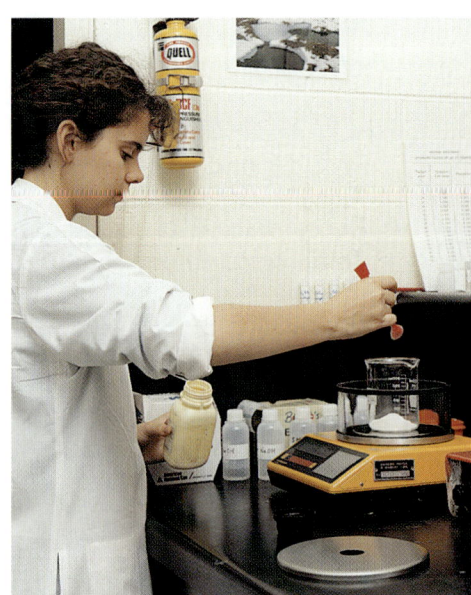

An electronic balance for measuring mass

When measuring the volume of liquids you need to make sure you are reading the volume correctly. The curved upper surface of a liquid is called the **meniscus**. Your eye should be level with the flat part in the centre of the meniscus. If your eye is not level with the meniscus, you will make an error called **parallax** error. (Parallax comes from the Greek word *parállaus*, which means 'change'.)

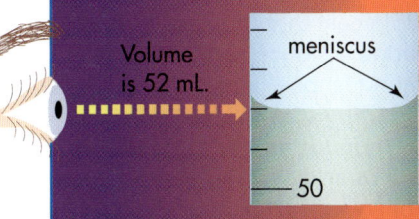

Volume is 52 mL.

Fill a measuring cylinder and see the difference for yourself. Remember, keeping your eye at liquid level will give you an accurate measurement.

Experiment 1.7

HOW WELL CAN YOU MEASURE MASS AND VOLUME?

YOU WILL NEED
beam balance or electronic balance
several small items, including
 100 mL of water and some salt
several different pieces of
 laboratory glassware, such as
 beakers, graduated cylinders
 and volumetric flasks

Part 1: Mass

- Estimate the mass of each object, then use the balance to measure the mass. (Think carefully about how you will measure the salt and water.)
- Draw up a table like the one below to record your results.

1. How close were your estimates to the actual masses?

2. Which items were hardest to measure? Why?
3. Write some rules for taking accurate measurements.

Part 2: Volume

- Measure the same 100 mL of water in as many different containers as possible.
- Write some observations about the accuracy of the glassware used.

1. Which piece of glassware is most accurate? Why?
2. What did you notice about the mass and volume of 100 mL of water?
3. Which piece of glassware produced the most obvious meniscus?

Estimating and measuring mass

Item	Estimated mass (g)	Measured mass (g)

Activities

Remember

1. What are mass and volume?
2. What are the standard units of mass and volume?
3. What do you use to measure the mass and volume of a liquid?

Think

1. The following diagram shows the arms of a four arm beam balance being used to measure the mass of two separate objects.

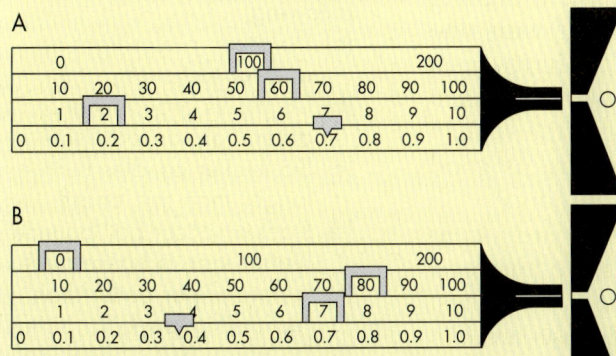

(a) What is the mass of object A?
(b) What is the mass of object B?
(c) What is the largest mass that could be measured on this beam balance?
2. A bag of potatoes at the supermarket is labelled 2.5 kg. How many grams is this?
3. Dean measured the mass of a beaker of water to be 235 grams. He then tipped out the water and measured the mass of the beaker to be 110 grams.
 (a) What was the mass of the water in grams?
 (b) What was the mass of the water in kilograms?
 (c) Genevieve claimed that Dean's measurement could have been more accurate. Is she right? If so, suggest how Dean could have improved his procedure.
 (d) What was the volume of water in Dean's beaker?
 (e) Make a list of some common errors people make when making measurements.

Investigate

1. Identify possible sources of error when making measurements and how best to avoid them.
2. Find out how to measure the volume of a solid.

1.9 Shooting for goal

Erin and Dean were in the driveway playing basketball. Erin is 15 years old and plays basketball for her team, Rebels, every Saturday and trains once a week. Dean, her younger brother, is 13 years old and doesn't play basketball with a team yet.

They decided to have a shooting competition. They agreed that they would each take 20 shots and that the best score out of twenty would win. They both shot from a distance of 5 metres.

Dean went first and scored 9 goals from his 20 attempts. Erin, being an experienced basketballer, said boastfully, 'I can do better than that with one eye closed!' Dean replied, 'I don't think you can. My science teacher says it's easier to judge distances with two eyes than just one. You won't be able to judge the distance and I'll win.'

Erin, annoyed at being challenged by her little brother, retorted, 'Your teacher is wrong! We'll prove it. If you win, your teacher is right. If I win with only one eye open your teacher is wrong.'

Erin proceeded with her 20 attempts with her right eye closed.

Who do you think won? Is it a **fair test** of Dean's teacher's statement? How could you conduct a fair test to answer the question 'Is it easier to judge distances with two eyes than just one?'

In a fair test all conditions, or **variables**, except the one being tested should be the same. Erin and Dean are different ages and different heights. They also have different levels of basketball shooting skills. Their competition was not a fair test of the question that they were arguing about. If Erin won it with one eye closed it could have been because of her greater height and experience rather than because one eye is just as good as two for judging distance.

When scientists are conducting experiments to answer a question they must do their best to ensure that their tests are fair. A fair scientific test is called a **controlled experiment**.

Activities

Remember

1. What is a fair test?
2. Erin and Dean's shooting competition was used to find out if Dean's science teacher's statement that 'it is easier to judge distance with two eyes than just one' was correct.
   (a) Why was the test conducted by Erin and Dean not a fair test?
   (b) What factors that were different should have been the same to make the test fair?

Think

1. Design a fair test of the question that Erin and Dean were trying to answer which involves only Erin and Dean shooting.
2. The story at the beginning of this page is true. Erin scored 11 goals from her 20 attempts with her right eye closed.
   (a) What conclusion would Erin and Dean have reached?
   (b) Write an account of how you would convince Erin and Dean that one eye was not really as good as two for judging distances.
3. Outline the procedure that you would use to investigate the following:
   (a) Do snails prefer light or dark conditions?
   (b) Do plants grow better in green light or red light?
   (c) Do thicker candles burn longer than thin ones?
   (d) Does a soccer ball bounce higher than a basketball?
   (e) Is new paper better than recycled paper?
   (f) Do plants grow better if you talk to them?

Experiment 1.8 ARE TWO EYES BETTER THAN ONE?

YOU WILL NEED

basketballs and at least one basketball goal

The aim of this experiment is to find out whether distances are easier to judge with two eyes than just one. You will do this by shooting for goal with a basketball from the foul line under three conditions.
- left eye closed
- right eye closed
- both eyes open

Remember that if the experiment is to be successful you must conduct a fair test. The following two questions need to be considered first.

Question 1. Will the results be reliable if only one person does the shooting test? Some people might be better than others at using one eye.

Question 2. Will the results be reliable if each person tested makes one attempt with the left eye closed, one with the right eye closed and one with both eyes open?

The answer to both of these questions is no. The results will be more reliable if many people are tested and an average score obtained. They will also be more reliable if each person makes a large number of attempts for each condition.

By considering the two questions above, you should be able to design a fair test. However, there are two problems that need to be solved first.

Problem 1: People who play basketball regularly will probably be able to use their experience to aim the ball and decide how hard to throw it. They might have to rely less on their sense of sight and might perform better than most people with only one eye open. The test would not be fair.

Problem 2: There is a 'practice effect'. That is, if you make ten attempts with the left eye closed, you might do better with the right eye closed because you have had some practice already. When you use both eyes you will already have had twenty attempts and may do better because of the practice. On the other hand, if you are not fit you might be tired by the time you do the test with both eyes. The test would not be fair.

Solving problem 1

Divide the class into two groups, one for regular players (regulars) and one for those who do not play basketball regularly (novices). Conduct a separate test for each group.

Solving problem 2

Jumble the order in which you perform the tests. For example, test yourself in a sequence like the following: left eye closed, right eye closed, both eyes open right eye closed, both eyes open, left eye closed both eyes open, left eye closed, right eye closed and keep going until you have completed a total of 30 shots. Now you should be ready to conduct a fair test. Conduct 30 trials yourself and record your own results in a table like the one below.

My own results

Scores out of ten		
Left eye closed	**Right eye closed**	**Both eyes open**

Use a copy of the following table to record the class results.

Class results

	Average score out of ten		
Type of player	**Left eye closed**	**Right eye closed**	**Both eyes open**
novices			
regulars			

1. The question to be answered by this experiment was 'Is it easier to judge distances with two eyes or just one?' What is your answer to this question for:
   (a) novices?   (b) regulars?
2. If the answer is different for the two groups tested, explain why there is a difference.
3. This experiment allows you to answer more questions than the original question. What two other questions can be answered? What are the answers to these questions according to your experiment?
4. Was this a fair test?
5. There were at least two variables that were deliberately ignored in this experiment. Name at least one of them.
6. Suggest how you might be able to improve this experiment.
7. Suggest another experiment that you might be able to conduct using the same equipment.
8. Write a formal report for this experiment.

Putting it all together

Summing up

Copy and complete the statements below to compile a summary of this unit.
The missing words can be found in the word list below.

1. The main branches of science are
   _____, chemistry, physics,
   _____, astronomy and ecology. There
   are many other smaller branches.

2. Nurses, police, dieticians, doctors, vets,
   mechanics and gardeners all use
   _____ knowledge.

3. The science _____ is very different to
   other classrooms and contains a lot of special
   equipment.

4. The science laboratory can be a _____
   place if you are not careful.

5. There are certain rules that must be followed in
   order to work _____ in the science
   laboratory. All students need to know the safety
   rules.

6. Scientists make _____, suggest
   hypotheses, perform _____ and draw
   conclusions.

7. Great care needs to be taken while
   _____ substances in a laboratory.

8. A _____ _____ is used to
   heat substances in test tubes and beakers in most
   school science laboratories.

9. A _____ is used to measure
   temperature in degrees _____.

10. _____ is often recorded in tables.

11. _____ can be drawn to make it easier
    to draw conclusions from data.

12. Scientific reports of experiments need to be
    organised in sections and include neat,
    _____ diagrams.

13. _____ can be measured accurately
    with a beam balance. The _____ of
    liquids can be measured using calibrated
    laboratory glassware.

14. It is important that scientific tests are
    _____. Variables need to be
    controlled

Word list

Bunsen burner	graphs	geology
biology	heating	experiments
laboratory	data	thermometer
fair	safely	dangerous
mass	observations	Celsius
scientific	labelled	volume

Looking back

1. The word puzzle below contains the names of twelve items of equipment that can be found in a school science laboratory. The names may be spelt across, down, diagonally or even backwards. Draw and label a diagram of each of the items and state what it is used for.

T	R	I	P	B	M	E	T	E	L	H	O
B	U	N	S	E	N	B	U	R	N	E	R
U	F	T	A	A	S	A	X	V	E	A	F
D	I	E	F	K	P	A	E	Z	N	T	W
N	L	S	E	E	A	C	L	A	M	P	F
A	T	T	T	R	T	D	O	P	I	R	T
T	E	U	Y	M	U	W	T	D	V	O	G
S	R	B	G	L	L	E	T	L	S	O	A
T	F	E	L	C	A	O	S	M	T	F	U
R	U	A	A	P	N	R	P	E	O	M	Z
O	N	K	S	G	A	U	Z	E	M	A	T
T	N	F	S	R	N	L	M	B	R	T	E
E	E	T	E	S	T	T	U	B	E	L	A
R	L	S	S	A	T	U	H	E	A	P	S

2. Indicate whether each of the following actions is a do or a don't in the science laboratory.
   • Wear safety glasses while mixing chemicals.
   • Pour all substances down the sink when finished with them.
   • Run in the science laboratory.
   • Drink water from the taps in the science laboratory.
   • Tie long hair back before using a Bunsen burner.
   • Wait until the end of the lesson to tell your teacher that you have burnt yourself.

3. Write a list of all of the equipment that you would need to boil water in a beaker in your science laboratory. Draw a labelled scientific diagram to show the equipment in use.

4. What item of equipment would you use to measure:
   (a) the temperature of hot water?
   (b) the mass of a small beaker of water?
   (c) the volume of a small quantity of water?

5. Kimberley and Glenn were walking past their neighbour's house when they noticed that a front window was broken. Glenn told Kimberley that somebody had probably thrown a ball through the window. They had a closer look and noticed clothes scattered all over the floor and drawers open. Kimberley noticed some blood on the broken glass. She told Glenn that the house had been burgled. Glenn agreed and they called the police.
   (a) List the observations that were made.
   (b) Who suggested a hypothesis?
   (c) What was the hypothesis and why was it suggested?
   (d) What conclusion was reached by Kimberley and Glenn?
   (e) Suggest a different conclusion based on the observations that were made.

6. Huang and Tina conduct an experiment to find out if radish plants grow better in the shade. They place three plants under a veranda at the back of the house and another three in a sunny place in the front yard. All plants were planted in the same soil. Huang and Tina watered each of the plants equally each day.
   (a) Did they conduct a fair test?
   (b) How could Huang and Tina improve the design of their experiment? List as many improvements as possible.

7. Name each of the following items of equipment.

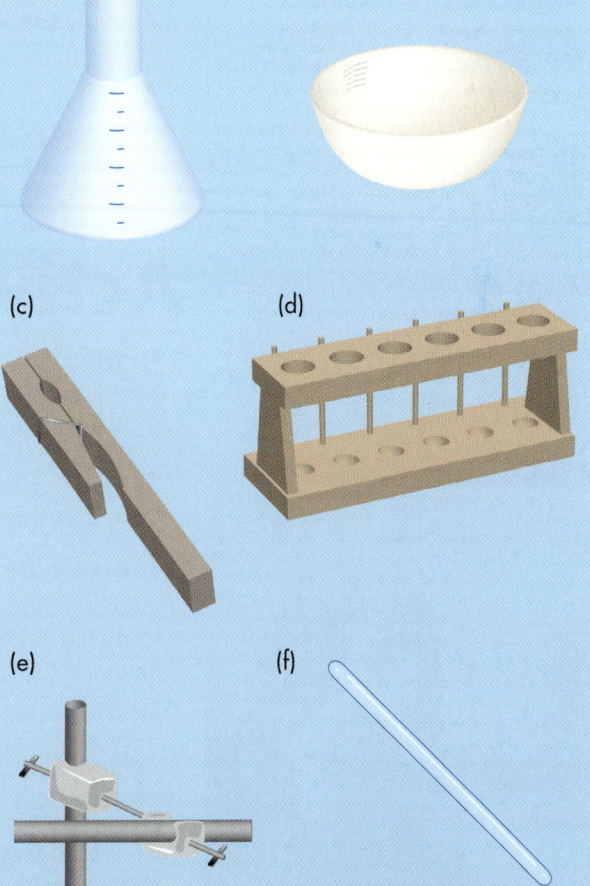

(a)   (b)

(c)   (d)

(e)   (f)

A family *affair*

Marie Curie (1867–1934) and her family are amongst the most well-known scientists of the past century. Marie married a French chemist, Pierre Curie, in 1895. Before they met, Pierre, with his brother Jacques, discovered how to produce electricity by heating crystals.

In 1903 Marie and Pierre were awarded the **Nobel Prize** in physics for their investigation of a rock called pitchblende and the mysterious radiation that it emitted. The radiation, called **radio-activity**, unlike light, was able to pass through almost any solid object. Pitchblende is the rock from which uranium is obtained.

Three years later, Pierre was killed in a Paris street by a speeding horse-drawn wagon. In 1911, Marie was awarded the Nobel Prize in chemistry for separating two new radioactive substances from pitch-blende. Marie became the first person to win two Nobel Prizes. One of the substances, radium, was later used in the treatment of cancer. The other substance, polonium was named after Marie's country of birth, Poland.

Marie devoted the last twenty years of her life to the application of her discoveries to medicine. Her constant exposure to high levels of radioactivity finally took its toll on Marie's health. She developed a type of cancer known as leukaemia and died in 1934.

Marie and Pierre's oldest daughter, Irene, continued her parents' work on radioactivity. Together with her husband, physicist Frederic Joliet, she showed that radioactive substances could be made artificially. For this work they were awarded the 1935 Nobel Prize in chemistry.

SCIFACTS

The Nobel Prize is probably the greatest award that an individual can obtain. Six Nobel Prizes are awarded each year — for chemistry, physics, physiology or medicine, literature, peace and economics. The first Nobel Prizes were awarded in 1901, being established by the Swedish inventor of dynamite, Alfred Nobel. He wanted to reward people whose work benefited humanity. The prizes include a medal and large cash award. Eight Australians have been awarded Nobel Prizes: Sir William Bragg and his son Lawrence (physics, 1915); Howard Florey (medicine, 1945); Sir Frank MacFarlane Burnet (medicine, 1960); Sir John Eccles (physiology, 1963); Patrick White (literature, 1973); Sir John Cornforth (chemistry, 1975); Peter Doherty (medicine, 1996).

Activities

Remember

1. For what achievements was Marie Curie awarded two Nobel Prizes?
2. What is pitchblende?

Think

Why was the discovery of radium so important?

Investigate

Working alone or in small groups, find out when and where one of the following scientists lived. List some positive and negative impacts of their work on society. Present a report to the rest of the class.

Sir MacFarlane Burnet	Albert Einstein	Barbara McClintock
Annie Jump Cannon	Howard Florey	Lise Meitner
Nicolaus Copernicus	Rosalind Franklin	Sir Isaac Newton
Gerty Cori	Galileo Galilei	Louis Pasteur
Charles Darwin	Caroline Herschel	Florence Sabin
Thomas Alva Edison	Irene Joliet-Curie	Sir William Bragg
Sir John Cornforth	Mary Leakey	Sir John Eccles
	Peter Doherty	Trofim Lysenko

Reflection

What I know about science

(a) Take some time to think about all you have learned while working through chapter 1 by completing the following two tasks.

   (i) Fill in a table like the one below in your workbook. You might find it useful to reflect on the key questions and key content statements at the start of the chapter on page 2.

Main ideas

Facts I have learned	Skills I have learned

   (ii) Make a list of skills that you think you need to practise more. Then make sure you take the time to improve in the areas you listed.

(b) Think about what you have just learned and what you knew before, and then write a story, poem or rap called 'Science is . . .'.

(c) You know a lot about what science is, but what makes a good scientist? List some skills that a scientist might need to develop. Suggest how you could further develop one of these skills yourself.

(d) Read the employment section of *The Sydney Morning Herald* to find job advertisements for people with a science background. Cut them out and use the relevant parts of these job advertisements to make a poster called 'Science is . . .'.

(e) Consider the picture of Kjell Sandved on page 2. He has worked on this project for 20 years. Why do you think he does this? Explain why you think this is or is not science.

(f) To make observations you need to train yourself to notice things. You should observe using all five senses.

Scientists recognise that our senses have limitations and have invented many instruments which extend our senses and allow us to make more detailed observations. Make a list of items that extend our senses, and indicate which senses are involved.

(g) Develop a parade of scientists! Individually, or in a group, dress up as a famous scientist who changed people's understanding of the world. Use whatever props you think are necessary. Find out which other scientists lived during the same time, knew one another or worked in the same scientific area. Each student or group can then present their report to the class, starting with the scientist who lived furthest back in time. The Internet may help you research this report.

(h) Decide which of the following statements are a conclusion, hypothesis or an observation. Copy the statements in your workbook and write C, H or O next to each statement and explain your choice.

   (i) The crystals were blue.
   (ii) Strong acids dissolve equal quantities of metals quickly.
   (iii) Iodine and starch react to make a black colour.
   (iv) John is taller than Patrick.
   (v) The gas released was carbon dioxide because it turned limewater milky.
   (vi) The oil floated on top of the water.
   (vii) Substances mixed together can produce new substances.
   (viii) The wax melted after three minutes of heating.
   (ix) The fish died from poisoning.
   (x) An asteroid impacting with the Earth caused the extinction of the dinosaurs.
   (xi) Listening to loud music will damage your hearing.
   (xii) More sugar dissolves in hot water than in cold.
   (xiii) Coffee contains more caffeine than cola soft drinks.
   (xiv) The candle burnt for 20 minutes.
   (xv) The hottest part of the Bunsen burner flame is the blue flame.
   (xvi) Vinegar and sodium bicarbonate fizz and produce a gas.
   (xvii) 1 mL of water has a mass equal to 1 g.

Did you notice some of these statements could be both hypotheses and conclusions? The 'correct' answer depends on your explanation. For example, conclusions need to follow from observations or results.

GROUP WORK Choose one section from experiment 1.4 that you wish to complete again. Decide on an aim, write a hypothesis, develop a plan and then discuss the experiment with your teacher before proceeding. Write up your results as a formal scientific report.

SEPARATING MIXTURES

Whether you are at home, at school, visiting the dentist, driving a car or even going to the bank, you would come across only a few products that are pure substances. Most of the products that you use consist of a mixture of two or more substances. The ground that you stand on, the air around you and the sea are all mixtures.

The dollar coins we call gold are actually made from a mixture of copper, aluminium and nickel.

KEY CONTENT

Demonstrate and devise methods of separating mixtures, including solutions, and use equipment correctly.

Describe how separation technologies are used in everyday life and recognise the work of Australian scientists in this field.

Solve problems from everyday life that involve separation techniques.

Distinguish between a physical and a chemical change.

KEY QUESTIONS

What makes a fizzy drink fizz?

Why does a car need an air filter?

How can you get fresh water from sea water?

What do a vacuum cleaner and tea strainer have in common?

What substances does your blood contain?

Where is the cream in homogenised milk?

How can magnets be used to treat sewage?

The air, sea and rocks are all mixtures of many substances.

Thinking about Mixtures

Words about mixtures

(a) Skim over the pages in this chapter and make a list of the words that you know the most about. Write down what you know about each word.

(b) Now skim over the pages again and make a list of all the words that you know very little about.

(c) Compare your lists in a class discussion or give them to your teacher.

(d) What does the word 'mixture' mean to you? Give some examples of mixtures that you know about.

(e) What does the word 'solvent' mean to you?

(f) Why is turps (turpentine) a solvent?

(g) Can you help Todd and Belinda in the cartoon below name other solvents besides water and turps, and explain what they do?

Experiment 2.1   FUN WITH CRYSTALS

This activity must be done in class with your teacher.

YOU WILL NEED
2 test tubes
solid copper sulfate (or alum)
a balance
150 mL beaker
3 glass stirring rods
hot water
string
test tube rack
forceps
microscope (optional)
piece of filter paper
filter funnel
conical flask or beaker
2 paperclips

- Weigh 28 g of the copper sulfate in the beaker.
- Prepare a hot concentrated solution of the copper sulfate by pouring 20 mL of hot water into the beaker. Stir the solution until no more solid will dissolve.
- Pour the blue copper sulfate solution through the filter paper into the conical flask or beaker. The undissolved copper sulfate will remain on the paper.
- Quickly pour equal volumes of the solution into two test tubes. Cool one test tube by putting it under cold running water.
- Tie the string to the glass rod. Attach the paperclip to the end of the string and arrange it as shown on the right. Do the same for the other test tube.
- Leave both test tubes to cool overnight in the test tube rack.
- Remove some crystals using forceps.

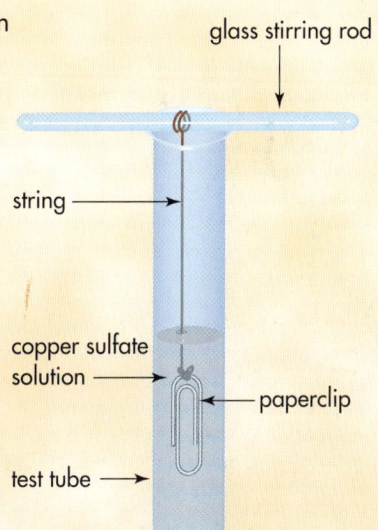

1. What can you see in the test tubes?
2. Compare the size of the crystals in the two test tubes.
3. How could you make bigger crystals?

- You may wish to view the crystals under a microscope.
- Crystals with interesting shapes can also be made using alum (potassium aluminium sulfate).

What's in a fizzy drink?

What puts the fizz in a fizzy drink? Like most substances, fizzy drinks are mixtures.

If you look at the label on a bottle or can of soft drink you will see that it contains sugar, food colouring, flavouring, preservative and carbon dioxide **dissolved** in water. A mixture of one substance dissolved in another is called a **solution**. The substance in which the chemicals can dissolve is called the **solvent**. The substances that dissolve in a solvent are called **solutes**.

Water is a good solvent because many chemicals can dissolve in it. A solute dissolved in water is an aqueous solution. There are other solvents that form non-aqueous solutions.

The preservatives in soft drink stop the drink from going bad. Flavourings make the drink taste more pleasant and food colouring makes the drink more attractive to look at.

The 'fizz' in fizzy drinks is carbon dioxide gas. The manufacturers pump the gas into the bottles or cans at high **pressure** and seal the containers. This keeps the gas dissolved in the solution. When you open the drink the pressure is reduced and the carbon dioxide gas bubbles out of the solution.

Mixtures and solutions

A mixture is a combination of substances that can be relatively easily separated from each other. In some mixtures, such as a mixture of salt and sand, the different substances can be seen. They are called **heterogeneous mixtures**. In other mixtures, such as a sugar and water solution, the different substances cannot be seen. They are called **homogeneous mixtures**. Solutions are homogeneous mixtures.

Creating the fizz

You can make carbon dioxide gas using two chemicals that are found in your kitchen — vinegar and bicarbonate of soda.

When vinegar and bicarbonate of soda are mixed, a **chemical reaction** takes place. The vinegar and bicarbonate of soda change into new substances. One of these new substances is the gas carbon dioxide, the same gas that is in fizzy drinks. In experiment 2.2 the rough surface of the sultanas allows the carbon dioxide bubbles to collect on the surface of the sultanas. The carbon dioxide bubbles rise, carrying the sultanas with them. When the bubbles reach the surface they break and the sultanas sink to the bottom.

Sticky fingers

Have you noticed how sticky your fingers get when you spill soft drink on them? This is caused by the sugar that is dissolved in it. You can separate this sugar from the water in the soft drink by **crystallisation**. When you heat the soft drink two things happen: the water **evaporates** and the sugar and other substances **crystallise**. This is *not* a chemical reaction: no new substances are being formed — the sugar is still present. The water has changed from a liquid to a gas (water vapour) and has moved from the soft drink into the air. This is called a **physical change**.

Chemical and physical changes

In a chemical reaction, new substances are formed. Chemical reactions are usually detected by colour changes, bubbles of gas, the formation of a precipitate (solid) or a change in the temperature of the mixture.

In a physical change, no new substances are formed. These changes are easily reversed by, for example, heating or cooling.

Experiment 2.2

FROTH AND BUBBLE

YOU WILL NEED

vinegar	stirring rod
bicarbonate of soda	gas jar
	sultanas
spatula	plastic tray

- Stand the gas jar on a plastic tray and pour the vinegar into the gas jar until it is 2 cm from the top.
- Add a spatula of bicarbonate of soda and several sultanas.
- Stir the vinegar and remove the stirring rod.
- Watch the sultanas as they rise and fall in the gas jar.

1. Explain how the sultanas rise to the surface.
2. When the sultanas get to the surface, why do they drop back to the bottom?
3. Try other things in the gas jar to see if they can be carried to the surface.
4. Repeat the experiment, adding different amounts of bicarbonate of soda. How does this affect the amount of carbon dioxide produced?
5. Try another experiment using vinegar diluted with water. Is carbon dioxide still produced?

Experiment 2.3 SEPARATING SUGAR FROM WATER BY CRYSTALLISATION

YOU WILL NEED
Bunsen burner
heatproof mat
matches
tripod and gauze mat
evaporating dish
10 mL measuring cylinder
soft drink
safety glasses

- Measure 10 mL of soft drink and pour it into the evaporating dish.
- Place the evaporating dish on the gauze mat.

CAUTION: Wear safety glasses during this experiment in case of spitting.

- Gently heat the soft drink until most of the water has evaporated. (Be careful not to burn the sugar.)
- Allow the dish to cool.
- Examine the product remaining in the dish.

1. Describe the product left in the evaporating dish.
2. The water has evaporated. Where is it now?

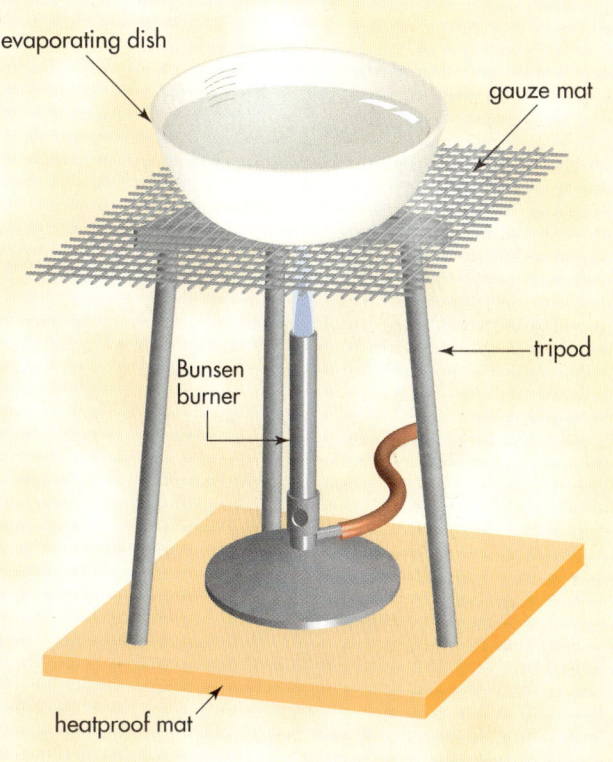

Equipment used to evaporate water from a solution

Activities

Remember

1. Specify the substances that are likely to be found in a bottle or can of fizzy soft drink.
2. Is fizzy soft drink a solution, solvent or solute?
3. Identify the substance that leaves a fizzy drink, causing it to go 'flat'.

Think

1. Copy and complete this table:

Solution	Solvent	Solute
soft drink		
sea water		
swimming pool water		
jelly		
cup of coffee		

2. Explain why a bottle of soft drink left lying in the sun will sometimes burst open.

Investigate

1. It is claimed that some washing powders work just as well in cold water as in hot water. Investigate washing powders to find out if they dissolve as well in cold water as they do in hot water.
2. Conduct a survey of food and drink products. Use their lists of ingredients to investigate what is in them. What are the most common chemicals added to food and drink products?
3. Design your own experiment to test whether the fizzy drink will go flat faster when it's cold or warm. Remember to use a **fair test**. You must keep everything the same except the one thing that you want to test.
4. Place an unopened can of soft drink and an unopened can of diet soft drink of the same type in a sink of water.
   (a) Which can floats?
   (b) Which can sinks?
   (c) What does this tell you about the sugar in soft drinks and diet soft drinks?

Sift and separate

What do a vacuum cleaner, tea strainer and protective face mask have in common? They are all devices for separating mixtures by **filtration**. In the laboratory, filtration is carried out using filter paper, but there are many other useful methods of filtration which are used in the home and in industry.

In filtration, solutions or gases pass through the filter but particles which cannot fit through the pores (holes) in the filter are trapped by it. **Insoluble** particles can be separated from a solution using filter paper in a funnel as shown below.

(a) A face mask filters dust from the air. (b) A car air filter removes dust particles from the air. (c) A vacuum cleaner contains a filter bag which traps the dust as air is sucked through it. (d) A food strainer separates the chips from the oil.

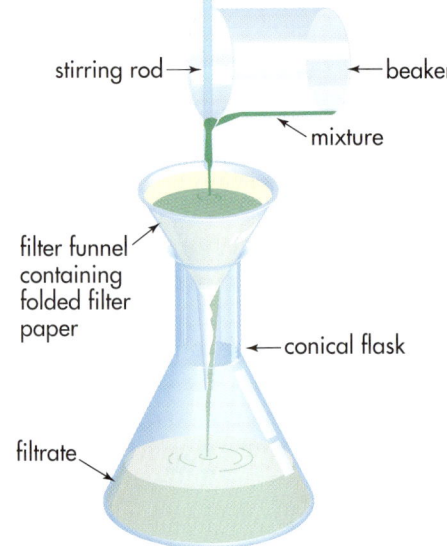

Equipment used to filter a solution

What's *the solution?*

When you begin to make toffee you have to stir sugar into water until it disappears into the water. The sugar is still there because you can taste it, but it has dissolved into the water. Substances which dissolve in a liquid are said to be **soluble** in that liquid. Sugar is soluble in water. When you make toffee the sugar is the solute and the water is the solvent. The particles of the sugar are very small and are mixed throughout the water. The clear (transparent) mixture is the solution.

A solid dissolved in a liquid is not the only type of solution. All types of solutions using solids, liquids and gases are possible, for example, a gas dissolved in a liquid (oxygen in water) and a solid dissolved in a solid (carbon dissolved in iron, forming steel).

When more solute is dissolved in a solvent the solution becomes more **concentrated**. When no more solute is able to be dissolved in the solvent the solution is **saturated**.

Substances which do not dissolve in a solvent are **insoluble** in that solvent. For example, sand is insoluble in water. The particles of the sand do not mix with the water. Instead the sand settles to the bottom of the water forming a **sediment**. Some insoluble substances such as clay can be seen to make the water appear cloudy. When the insoluble substance is dispersed (spread) throughout the liquid, making it cloudy, it is called a **suspension**. Some insoluble substances may even float on top of the liquid. Can you think of any?

(a) Solute is added to solvent.

(b) Solute dissolves, forming a solution.

(c) An insoluble substance may form a suspension.

(d) An insoluble substance may form a sediment.

(e) An insoluble substance may float on top of the liquid.

Experiment 2.4 FILTRATION IN THE LABORATORY

YOU WILL NEED
100 mL beaker
funnel
filter paper
glass stirring rod
conical flask
an insoluble substance, for example, soil, chalk dust, charcoal, wood chips

- Half fill your 100 mL beaker with water.
- Add your insoluble substance to the water and stir with the stirring rod.

1. Describe the appearance of your mixture in the beaker. Did it form a suspension, sediment or float on top?

- Set up the equipment for filtering as shown in the diagram on the right of page 32.
- Fold the filter paper as shown in the diagram on the right.
- Place the filter paper in the funnel and moisten with clean water to hold the filter paper in place.
- Pour your mixture into the filter paper.

2. The liquid passing through the filter into the conical flask is called the **filtrate**. Describe your filtrate.

3. Examine your filter paper. The material trapped by the filter paper is called the **residue**. Describe your residue.

4. Filter paper is like a sieve with small holes in it. Explain how the filter paper worked like a sieve in this experiment.

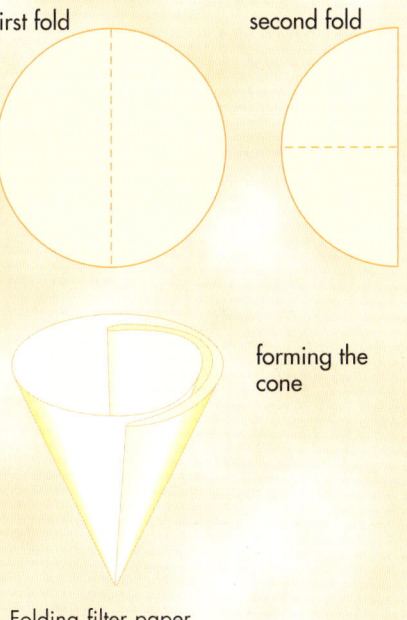
first fold   second fold

forming the cone

Folding filter paper

Activities

Remember

1. Replace each of the following sentences with a single word.
   (a) Liquid in which a substance dissolves
   (b) Insoluble particles dispersed in a liquid
   (c) When no more solute will dissolve in the solution
   (d) Liquid passing through the filter paper
   (e) Substance which dissolves in a liquid
   (f) Formed when a solute dissolves in a solvent
   (g) Material deposited on the filter
   (h) An insoluble substance which sinks to the bottom

2. What is a saturated solution?

Think

1. The drawing on page 32 shows a variety of commonly used filters. Think of some other filters used in the home. Construct a four-column table like the one at the top of the next column to describe the filters.

2. The air filter and oil filter in a car engine have to be replaced occasionally. Why do you think this is done?

Filter	Mixture	Residue	Filtrate
vacuum cleaner	air and dust	dust	air
food strainer	chips and hot oil	chips	oil

Imagine

You are out in the bush and the only water available to drink is in a muddy waterhole. You have an empty bottle and a cup. How would you remove the dirt from the muddy water so that you could drink the water?

Investigate

1. The kidneys act as filters to remove wastes from our blood. Find out more about how the kidneys filter wastes from the blood.

2. What types of paper can be used to filter a suspension? Design an experiment that tests a variety of different papers (such as newspaper, tissue paper, brown paper, kitchen paper, and so on) for their suitability as filter paper. Check the design with your teacher before carrying out the experiment. Record the results and write a report of your findings.

2.3
Parting ways

There are many ways of separating mixtures in a laboratory. Some methods are simple and quick to perform and others require expensive equipment or take more time.

Distillation

Some laboratory experiments require the use of pure water. This water is produced by a process called **distillation**.

Tap water is placed in the boiling flask (see the diagram below) and heated to the boiling temperature for water, 100°C. The water boils, evaporates and becomes steam. The steam travels along the **water condenser**. The steam inside the condenser is cooled to below 100°C and **condenses** to form liquid water. The condenser is kept cool by running cold water through its outer jacket. The pure water collected in the conical flask is called the **distillate** and can be rightly labelled **distilled water**. The impurities in the water are left behind in the boiling flask.

Distillation can be used to separate pure water from sea water. It can also be used to separate a mixture of two liquids as long as they boil at different temperatures.

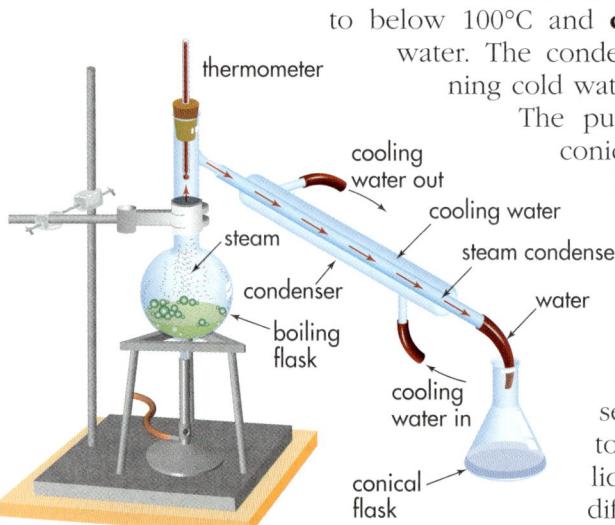

Equipment used for distillation in the laboratory

yams are boiled and placed into a dilly bag. The bag is squashed and the softer parts of the yam are strained through the bag into a can of water. The bag acts as a sieve, allowing some substances to pass through but not others. The skins and harder parts of the yam that are left in the bag are thrown away. The water is decanted from the can, and repeated washing with water removes more poison. The yam is then placed into another dilly bag and hung up overnight before being ready to eat.

Separation using a separating funnel

When one liquid does not mix with another but floats on top of it, a **separating funnel** can be used to separate the two liquids. Oil floats on water. This mixture can be separated using a separating funnel as shown below.

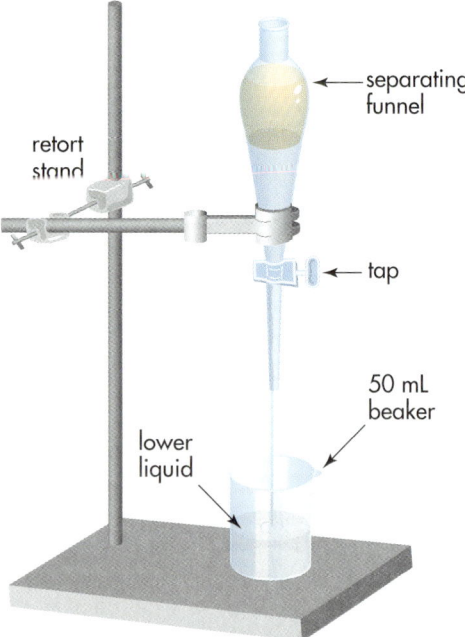

Using a separating funnel to separate oil from water

Experiment 2.5 DISTILLING PERFUMES

YOU WILL NEED
apparatus for distillation as shown in the diagram above
orange peel or sweet-smelling petals (eucalyptus leaves or lavender can also be used)
small knife
100 mL measuring cylinder

• Pour 30 mL of water into the boiling flask.

• Cut the orange peel (or petals) into small pieces and add them to the water in the boiling flask.

• Boil the water gently and collect a small volume of the distillate.

• Smell the distillate.

How does the odour compare to the original orange peel (or petals)?

Decanting

A simple method of separation for a mixture of a liquid and a sediment is **decanting**. The sediment is allowed to settle to the bottom of the container and then the liquid is carefully poured off the top.

Aboriginal Australians combine **sieving** (a type of filtration) and decanting to prepare native yams, which contain a poison. The

Centrifuging

A mixture can be separated by spinning it very quickly. This method is called **centrifuging**. The spin dry cycle of a washing machine acts as a centrifuge and a filter. As it spins, the clothes are forced to the sides of the tub and the water passes out through the holes in the tub. The clothes cannot fit through the holes and so much of the water is removed. In the laboratory, centrifuging is used to separate solid or liquid substances from liquids. The mixture is placed in special test tubes which are spun at high speeds. The heavier substances are forced to the bottom of the tube and the lighter substances are left near the top.

Experiment 2.6 CENTRIFUGING WITH A BILLY

YOU WILL NEED
a billy   tea leaves

- Half fill the billy with cold water and add a small handful of tea leaves.
- Spin the billy vertically with your outstretched arm. Make sure that you spin it quickly for 10 revolutions of your arm.

- When you stop spinning the billy make sure that you stop when the billy is up the right way or you will get a wet arm!
- Decant the liquid off the top.

1. Where are the tea leaves after spinning the billy?
2. Explain how this separation method works.

Chromatography

Paints, inks, dyes and food colourings are often mixtures of substances that have different colours. You can separate these substances in the mixture using **paper chromatography**.

In paper chromatography a liquid soaks through the paper, dissolving the substances on the paper and carrying them with it. Some substances in the mixture are carried through the paper faster than others. In this way the substances are separated along the paper.

Experiment 2.7 CHROMATOGRAPHY OF FOOD COLOURING

YOU WILL NEED
food colouring (that is made up of several colours — check the label on the bottle)
filter paper   watchglass
scissors   capillary tube
250 mL beaker   pencil

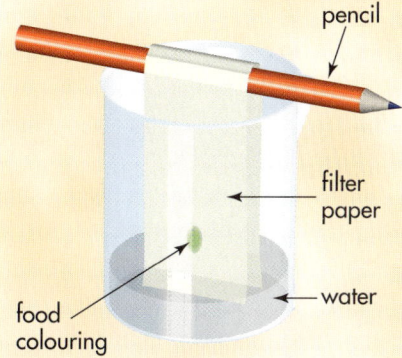

Paper chromatography separating the colours in food colouring

- Cut a piece of filter paper approximately 10 cm by 3 cm.
- Rule a line in pencil 2 cm from the end of the paper.
- Place some food colouring on a watchglass.

- Use a capillary tube to place one drop of food colouring on the centre of the pencil line on the filter paper.
- Pour tap water into the beaker to a depth of 1 cm.
- Stand the filter paper so that the end just dips into the water. Make sure that you keep the dot of food colouring out of the water.
- Fix the filter paper to a pencil to hold it in the water.
- Let the filter paper stand until the water has risen almost to the end of the filter paper.

1. What colours were in the food colouring?
2. Which colours were more soluble in water? How did you know?
3. Draw a labelled diagram of your results.

- You could repeat this experiment using Smarties instead of food colouring. (Mix a Smartie with one drop of water in a watchglass until the water is brightly coloured and place the drop on the filter paper.)

Activities

Think

1. In your own words, explain the term 'condensation' based on the information you have read about distillation on page 34.
2. Why is cool, running water passed through the distillation equipment shown on page 34?

Create

Design and build a separating machine that will separate a mixture of three substances. Create a brochure to advertise your machine which includes:
- the name of your machine and why it is useful
- a diagram of the machine
- information on what mixture your machine will separate
- instructions for how to use it
- an explanation of why it works.

Investigate

An oil spill at sea can ruin the local environment and kill wildlife. Find out when and where the worst oil spill disasters have occurred and how the oil was separated from the water.

Down the S-bend

The Tank Stream was Sydney's first water supply. It still flows beneath the city's streets.

Every time you flush the toilet, have a shower, wash the dishes or your clothes or even clean your teeth, the waste water travels into an underground **sewerage** drain.

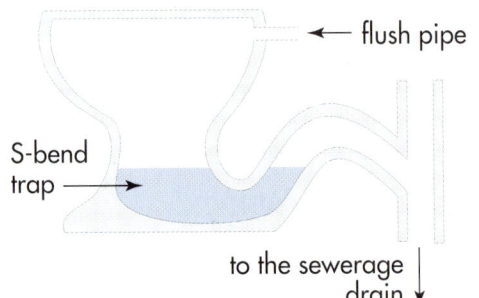

flush pipe

S-bend trap

to the sewerage drain

The S-bend trap in the toilet fills with clean water to prevent smelly gases from the sewer travelling back into the house.

The waste water is a mixture of human body waste flushed down the toilet, detergent, dirt, toothpaste, food scraps and other materials washed down the drains. The mixture, which is mostly water, is called **sewage**.

If you live in a major city, the sewage in the drain under your house flows into a larger drain under your street and travels through the sewerage system to a treatment plant. The waste water needs to be treated before it can be returned to the **environment**.

In country centres treatment plants are usually located on the edge of the town. If there is no local treatment plant, the waste water will flow into a personal sewage treatment system — a **septic tank** buried in the backyard.

A septic tank contains **bacteria** that break down the sewage. A thick, smelly sludge is formed. The sludge sinks to the bottom of the tank and clear water flows out into the surrounding area. The sludge needs to be removed from time to time.

SCIFACTS

The word 'sewage' describes the waste water carried away by drains. The word 'sewerage' describes the system of drains that carries the waste water away.

Old Sydney

As you turn on your tap for a glass of water or unplug your sink to let the waste water flow down the drain, it is hard to imagine the water supply in Sydney 200 years ago. When Governor Phillip founded the first colony at Sydney Cove (Circular Quay today), he did so because there was a constant source of water that was called the Tank Stream.

After 40 years the Tank Stream had become so polluted by the early settlers that another supply was necessary. John Busby, a mining surveyor, constructed an underground tunnel four kilometres long that supplied water from the lakes in (what is now) Centennial Park to Hyde Park. From there it was carried in water carts around the town. This system commenced in 1837 and was known as Busby's Bore. This in turn was replaced by a third water supply from Botany swamps. The water was pumped from the swamps to a reservoir in Crown Street.

The Upper Nepean System, which has been changed and updated over the years, commenced in 1888 and is the main water system for Sydney today. The reservoir for this purpose is Prospect Reservoir, which was completed in 1888. It is the main storage area for Sydney's water supply and receives water from the Warragamba Dam and the Upper Nepean River. Pumping stations at the reservoir deliver water to areas north, south, east and west of Sydney.

Being the world's driest continent, Australia stores a greater amount of water per person than any other comparable nation in the world.

Waste *water* treatment

Waste water contains **suspended** solids such as bacteria, grit and dirt as well as some large items like rags and sticks. It also contains many dissolved substances.

When the waste water arrives at the sewage treatment plant, it passes through a screen (a wire mesh **filter**) which removes the larger items. The sewage then flows into settling tanks where it is kept for about two hours. In the settling tanks suspended solids settle to form a sediment, and **floatables** such as oil and plastic collect on top of the sewage and are removed.

The watery part of the sewage flows from the settling tank into secondary treatment. This waste water still contains dissolved substances and bacteria. Secondary treatment takes place by filtering the water though soil and grass or by storing it in a series of one-metre-deep lagoons for two to four months. In the secondary treatment, the bacteria in the waste water break down the dissolved substances to purify the water further. In the lagoons, sedimentation also takes place. The treated water looks clear but it is still not safe to drink.

Experiment 2.8 — MAKING YOUR OWN WASTE WATER

YOU WILL NEED

large jar (500 mL capacity or larger) with lid
measuring cylinder or measuring jug
2 squares of toilet paper
5 mL cooking oil
1 teaspoon soil
1 teaspoon vegetable peelings
10 drops of detergent or shampoo
1 teaspoon grass cuttings
some small squares ($\frac{1}{2}$ cm × $\frac{1}{2}$ cm) plastic
$\frac{1}{2}$ teaspoon coffee grounds or tea leaves
some small sticks or twigs

- Measure out 500 mL of tap water and pour it into the jar.
- Add the substances suggested above to your water.
- Shake the jar vigorously.

1. Describe the appearance of the waste water.
2. Draw a flow chart showing the steps that you are going to take to clean your water.

Each box in your flow chart should contain the information for only one step of your method.

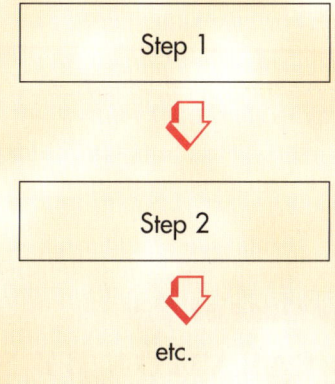

- Carry out your experiment to make your water as clean as possible.
3. Describe the appearance of your 'clean' water.
4. Is your water safe to drink? Give reasons for your answer.

- Measure the volume of water obtained from the original 500 mL.
5. Give reasons for the change in the volume of the water.

Activities

Remember

1. Read the history box, 'Old Sydney', and answer the following questions.
   (a) Why did Governor Phillip found the first colony at Sydney Cove?
   (b) How many water supplies has Sydney had? Name them and give the dates where possible.
   (c) What might be the difference between today's water supplies and those of Old Sydney?
2. What substances are in waste water?
3. How does a septic system work?

Think

1. Propose why disinfectants that kill bacteria cannot be poured down a septic system.
2. A certain type of shower provides water at a rate of 11 litres per minute.
   (a) If you have a five-minute shower, how much water do you use?
   (b) How much water would you use showering in a year?
   (c) How much water would your family use showering in a year?
3. (a) Make a list of the many ways that people use water in their homes.
   (b) Suggest ways to reduce water usage.

Investigate

1. Find out where your sewage goes. If you live in the country ask your local shire or locate your septic system.
2. Find out the kind of treatment (primary or secondary) that is used for Sydney's sewerage system. Where does the treated water go? Debate how suitable this system is for a large city like Sydney.
3. Find out if there is a tertiary treatment for water.

2.5 Essential separation

Separating the useful material from a mixture is often essential in industry. In mining, the mineral **ores** that are needed are mixed with useless rock called **gangue**. In the dairy industry, the cream has to be separated from the milk before it can be put into containers for sale. At the blood bank, plasma is separated from the blood for use in some transfusions.

Separating mixtures *in* mining

Copper

The metal copper is used in hot water pipes, electrical wiring and even in the coins we use. Copper is found in rocks in the Earth's crust in the form of mineral ores. Before the copper can be purified, the copper ore has to be separated from the gangue.

The **mixture** of gangue and copper ore which is dug out of the ground is in solid lumps. These have to be crushed to a fine powder before the copper ore and gangue can be separated. Crushing takes place in a ball mill. This is a long barrel containing lots of heavy steel balls. As the barrel is rotated, the steel balls crush the lumps into a fine powder.

Once the copper ore and gangue are crushed, the copper ore is separated from the gangue by a process called **froth flotation**. The crushed mixture is mixed with water and some special chemicals and stirred. Bubbles of air are blown into the bottom of the container and the copper ore is carried to the surface by the bubbles. The gangue sinks to the bottom of the tank and the copper ore is skimmed off the top of the liquid. The copper ore is then treated to extract the pure copper which can then be used to manufacture the many copper products we use.

Gold

Gold obtained from the ground is also mixed with unwanted rock. After grinding in a ball mill, the mixture of crushed rock and gold is mixed with water. The gold can be separated from the mixture using **gravity separation** because the gold is heavier than the rock. The mixture is spun and the gold sinks to the bottom.

In the same way, panning for gold by swirling the pan allows the heavier gold to settle in the pan while the lighter gravel and sand swirls out of the pan with the water.

Panning for gold at Sovereign Hill, Ballarat

Froth flotation separating the mineral ore from the gangue

Experiment 2.9

SEPARATION BY FLOTATION

YOU WILL NEED

jar and lid	sawdust
sand	teaspoon

- Half fill the jar with water.
- Add a teaspoon of sand and a teaspoon of sawdust.
- Place the lid on the jar firmly and shake vigorously.
- Allow the jar to stand.
- Use a spoon to remove the sawdust.

1. In this experiment, which substance represented the gangue?

2. Which substance represented the mineral ore?

3. How is the method of separation in this experiment different to the froth flotation method used to separate copper ore from the gangue?

Separation *at the* Blood Service

Blood is made of straw-coloured liquid called **plasma** in which are suspended many tiny living cells. These are mostly **red blood cells**, with some **white blood cells** and smaller cells called **platelets**.

Blood is collected at the Australian Red Cross Blood Service for use in blood transfusions. A blood transfusion transfers blood (or one of its parts) from one person (the donor) to another (the recipient).

Packed red blood cells are used mainly for transfusions. The whole blood is separated into packed red blood cells and plasma by centrifugation. Each donation of blood is collected into a sterile plastic pack with two or three satellite packs connected by plastic tubing. The pack of whole blood is spun in a centrifuge, separating the plasma from the red blood cells. The packs can be spun at various speeds to separate the different components of whole blood.

Blood donated to the Australian Red Cross Blood Service is separated by centrifuging.

Separation *in the* dairy industry

A centrifuge is used to separate cream from milk.

Cows' milk is a mixture of watery milk and fatty cream. If fresh milk straight from the cow is left to stand, the cream will float to the top of the milk. The milk that you buy as homogenised milk contains both the milk part and the cream mixed together. Milk is homogenised by forcing the cows' milk through a narrow pipe under pressure and spraying it onto a metal plate. This breaks the fatty cream into very fine droplets which disperse evenly throughout the watery milk.

However, skim milk is the watery milk part without the cream. Milk is separated from the cream at the dairy using a **centrifuge**. The cows' milk is fed continuously into the centrifuge at one end; as the milk is spun in the centrifuge, the lighter cream separates from the heavier skim milk and each part is continuously collected at the other end.

Skim milk powder is made by evaporating about half of the water from the skim milk. A fine mist of this skim milk is then sprayed into a stream of hot air, so that more water evaporates. The powdery dry milk is collected from the bottom of the chamber.

Activities

Remember

1. How is copper ore separated from unwanted rock?
2. How is gold separated from unwanted rock?
3. How are skim milk and skim milk powder separated from whole milk?
4. What are the main components of blood?
5. Describe how blood is separated into its components.

Think

1. What type of separation is used when panning for gold?
2. Does homogenised milk contain cream? Where is it?

Investigate

1. Find out how salt is obtained from sea water.
2. Crude oil is a mixture of many different chemicals. Research how crude oil is separated into the many different chemicals it contains.
3. Brandy is made from wine. Find out which separation method is used to make brandy from wine.

SCIENCE *issues*

FIT TO DRINK

Would you drink this water?

Would you like your water to come out of the tap looking like this? In a bath of this water you would get out of the bath dirtier than you got in. Imagine your clothes after washing them. Would you give your pets this water to drink? Would YOU drink this water? A clean water supply is taken for granted throughout most of Australia. Drinking water must be free of disease-causing **micro-organisms** and harmful chemicals.

Unwanted *substances*

Drinking water may be **contaminated** by dissolved substances or substances suspended in the water.

- Human and other animal body wastes contain disease-causing micro-organisms.
- Algal blooms cause the water to be cloudy and can release poisonous substances into the water. They can also affect the taste and cause odour problems.

- Pesticides or detergents can be washed into rivers from farms.
- Poisonous chemicals may also be washed into rivers from farms or industries.
- Salt dissolved in water can make it unfit for drinking.
- Iron dissolved in water can contaminate it. This is common in bore water.
- High levels of calcium and magnesium salts can cause water to be 'hard', making it difficult to lather. This causes problems in laundries, bathrooms and kitchens.

Sydney's *water*

The water supply for Sydney, the Blue Mountains and the Illawarra region comes from 14 different areas. In the water catchment areas surrounding the dams and reservoirs, human habitation is not allowed and public access is strictly controlled. This reduces contamination of the water.

There are also 13 water treatment plants, where the water is treated before it is considered safe for drinking and washing.

Chemicals

Some treatment plants treat the water slightly differently to others. Chlorine and fluoride are added to all water supplies, while lime or a small amount of ammonia is added to some supplies. If the water needs to be made clearer, iron chloride is added as a flocculant.

- The chlorine is added in very small amounts to kill any harmful micro-organisms which might cause diseases. Chlorine

keeps the water safe to drink right up until it reaches your tap.
- Fluoride is added to the water to prevent **tooth decay**.
- Lime (calcium hydroxide) is added to the water to balance the **acidity** caused by adding the chlorine and fluoride.
- Ammonia holds the chlorine in the system.

Country *water* supplies

If you live in a country town your water probably comes from a nearby river or lake. It is also quite likely that you would not want to drink the water from the river or lake unless it had been purified. In many country towns this water is pumped into water treatment plants. The cloudy water contains mud and other substances in suspension, which can be settled out of the water by a process called **flocculation**.

The suspended particles would take a long time to settle if the water were just left standing and so the chemical **alum** (potassium aluminium sulfate) is added to the cloudy water to make the small particles clump together. These clumps are called **floc**. The floc is heavy enough to settle to the bottom of the tank and form a sediment. The water above the sediment is clear and flows off to the filtering stage.

After flocculation the clear water is filtered through sand and gravel to remove any leftover suspended substances in the water. Chlorine is added to kill harmful bacteria. The purified water is then pumped to the local water tower which then supplies the town with drinking water.

Experiment 2.10 TREATING YOUR OWN DIRTY WATER

YOU WILL NEED

muddy water (muddy water made with clay is best)
alum (aluminium sulfate)
limewater
household bleach (5% solution) (use with care)

flower pot and tripod
sand
gravel
2 × 250 mL beakers
stirring rod

- Pour 150 mL muddy water into the beaker.
- Add half a teaspoon of alum and 10 drops of limewater.
- Stir the water to mix the chemicals and allow the floc to form.
- Once you can see the floc forming, allow the water to stand and the floc to settle to the bottom.
- Add gravel and sand to the flower pot to make the water filter as shown in the diagram on the right.
- Decant the water from the beaker into your water filter. Collect the filtrate in a clean beaker.
- Add two drops of bleach (which contains chlorine) to your filtrate.

muddy water mixture

flower pot → sand
← gravel
← tripod

beaker →

filtrate (water)

A flower pot water filter

1. Use a table like the one below to describe your water at each stage of the process. Include the appearance and odour of the water.

Treating dirty water

Treatment stage	Description of water
untreated water	
water after flocculation	
water after filtering	
water after chlorination	

2. Which separation techniques did you use to purify the water?
3. Prepare a series of picture diagrams to explain the steps you have taken to purify the water.
4. How useful is your treatment plant?

Activities

Remember

1. What chemicals are added to Sydney's water and why?
2. Why is chlorine added to water in such small amounts?
3. List five substances that can contaminate drinking water.

Think

1. If you live in a country town that does not fluoridate the water, how could you obtain your fluoride?
2. What natural method of separating mixtures takes place in reservoirs over a long period of time?
3. At the Taronga Park Zoo in Sydney, the seal pool's water is chlorinated to a maximum of 1 part per million, which is less than the amount in swimming pools. What is the reason for adding chlorine to the water?

Seal pool at a zoo

Investigate

1. In 1998, Taronga Park Zoo became the first zoo in the world to recycle its own waste water. The waste water is generated by:
   - hosing down animal exhibits
   - filling animal and ornamental moats
   - flushing toilets
   - irrigating lawns.
   Find out what methods are used to recycle the water.
2. Research the different brands of water filters available. Report on their cost, efficiency and ease of use. Why do people consider the use of these filters to be necessary?

Putting it all together

Summing up

Copy and complete the statements below to compile a summary of this unit. The missing words can be found in the word list below.

1. Most of the products we use consist of a _____ of two or more substances.

2. Mixtures may be _____ or _____ .

3. Changes in matter may be chemical or _____.

4. Fizzy soft drink is a mixture of sugar, food colouring, flavouring, preservative and _____ _____ gas dissolved in water.

5. When a substance (solute) dissolves in a liquid (solvent) a _____ is formed.

6. A suspension is an insoluble substance _____ throughout the liquid.

7. Filtration can be used to _____ mixtures of insoluble solids in liquids or solid particles in gases. The _____ traps the solids as the liquid or gas flows through it.

8. Sewage is treated by filtration, sedimentation and by natural breakdown of substances by _____ present in the sewage.

9. In mining the metal _____ is separated from the unwanted rock by crushing and then by froth flotation.

10. Centrifuging is a method of separating which involves spinning the mixture at high speeds. _____ substances are forced to the outside.

11. Small amounts of food colourings can be separated by _____ chromatography.

12. Panning for gold is called _____ separation because the gold is heavier than everything else in the mixture.

13. Separation techniques are used in the _____, in the laboratory and in industry.

14. There are other combinations that form solutions besides a solid dissolved in a liquid, such as a _____ dissolved in a liquid or a _____ dissolved in a solid.

Word list

ore	separate	solution
carbon dioxide	dispersed	paper
filter	physical	mixture
home	bacteria	heterogeneous
gas	gravity	homogeneous
heavier	solid	

Looking back

1. Copy and complete the table below to summarise what you know about separation techniques.

Method of separation	Description of how it works	An example of how it is used in the home or in industry
filtration		
distillation		
crystallisation		
flocculation		
decanting		
separating funnel		
centrifuging		
chromatography		

2. You have been asked to analyse some salt-contaminated soil. How would you separate the salt from the soil?
   (a) Write out the method that you would use to obtain pure dry salt and pure dry soil.
   (b) Draw a labelled diagram showing how your equipment would be set up for each stage of your separation.

3. Copy the following word puzzle into your workbook and complete it using the clues provided below.

```
         1.  S  __ __ __ __ __
        2. __  E  __ __ __ __ __ __
      3. __ __ __  D  __ __ __ __ __ __ __ __ __ __
    4. __ __ __ __ __  I  __ __ __ __
      5. __ __ __ __ __  M  __ __ __ __ __ __ __ __ __ __
  6. __ __ __ __ __ __  E  __ __ __ __
          7. __  N  __ __ __ __ __ __ __ __ __
        8. __ __ __  T  __ __ __ __ __ __ __
  9. __ __ __ __ __ __  A  __ __ __ __ __ __
 10. __ __ __ __ __ __ __  T  __ __ __ __
  11. __ __ __ __ __ __ __  I  __ __ __ __ __ __
          12. __  O  __ __ __ __ __ __
    13. __ __ __ __ __  N  __ __ __ __ __ __
```

1. A substance that dissolves in a solvent.
2. Refers to our body's waste products.
3. When steam changes to liquid water.
4. An instrument used to separate plasma from blood cells.
5. A method of separating mixtures of dyes or inks.
6. The material trapped by the filter paper.
7. When a substance does not dissolve in a liquid we say it is _____ .
8. A method of separation used to clean the air going in to a car engine.
9. A method of separation used to purify water.
10. A process used to obtain salt from sea water.
11. A process used to separate mineral ores from gangue.
12. A liquid in which a substance will dissolve.
13. Undissolved particles spread throughout a liquid.

Separating sewage

Emma Cooney, chemical engineer

Q.: Why did you become a chemical engineer?

Emma: I loved science at school, especially chemistry and physics, and I knew about engineering because I have a brother and a sister who are both engineers. I wanted a mixture of working experiences — I wanted to work in a laboratory and I wanted to work in industry where I could apply my knowledge to the whole process, starting with raw materials and designing the best way to achieve the final product.

Q.: What led you to work with sewage treatment?

Emma: My first job involved the extraction of edible oils from soybeans and sunflower seeds. This work gave me insight into the processing industry, including the need for effective waste water treatment. I was offered the opportunity to pursue this direction with CSIRO, working on the SIROFLOC process, and I couldn't resist!

Q.: What did your work on the SIROFLOC process involve?

Emma: When I started at CSIRO the SIROFLOC process had been shown to be a successful method of purifying sewage but some adjustments were needed. I worked on finding ways to recycle some of the chemicals used in the process and tested cheaper chemicals to make the process more economic. I used flotation and centrifuging to recover the chemicals.

Q.: What did you like about your job at CSIRO?

Emma: I enjoyed developing new processes. I feel that my work benefited the environment and the people living in it. My work was satisfying, challenging and has a useful purpose.

Q.: Did you get dirty during your work at CSIRO?

Emma: You had to wear protective clothing but most of the time it wasn't dirty work.

Q.: What would you actually do in a normal day's work at CSIRO?

Emma: At Lower Plenty there was a Research Station where I tested sewage treatment processes. When I arrived at work I started the plant operating and checked that the chemicals were ready to add to the sewage. I then let the sewage into the plant and started the treatment process. I took regular samples of the clear water coming out of the process to test how clean it was. I also checked the amount of magnetite to ensure that there was enough to clump all of the impurities. As I carried out my tests on different chemicals I made sure that I varied only one chemical at a time to test its effect on the treatment process.

Activities

Think

The SIROFLOC process uses the process of flocculation to remove the cloudy impurities in sewage.

(a) What is flocculation? (*Hint*: see 'Fit to drink' on page 40.)

(b) The substance added to impurities is called a flocculant. What is the flocculant used in SIROFLOC?

(c) After the impurities form clumps, the sewage is passed into settling tanks. Clean water is taken from the top of these tanks. What process of separation is taking place in the settling tanks?

Imagine

List the questions that you would like to ask Emma Cooney.

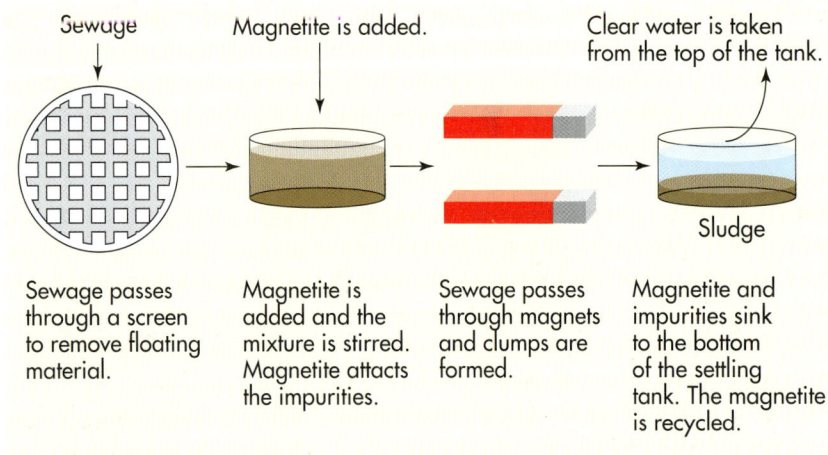

Sewage — Magnetite is added. — Clear water is taken from the top of the tank. — Sludge

Sewage passes through a screen to remove floating material.

Magnetite is added and the mixture is stirred. Magnetite attacts the impurities.

Sewage passes through magnets and clumps are formed.

Magnetite and impurities sink to the bottom of the settling tank. The magnetite is recycled.

The SIROFLOC process. Magnets are used to attract objects made from iron such as magnetite and the impurities attached to it.

Reflection

1. Separating mixtures — applications to everyday living

There are many situations in life where it is important to know how to separate mixtures. The table below outlines some problems relating to mixtures. The scientific description of the problem is also given. In your workbook write down the method that you would use to solve each problem. Simple terms may be used such as filtration or evaporation. This may be followed by a longer description if your teacher requires it.

Problem	Scientific description of the problem
Blue-green algae has grown in a lake. It forms a fine, green suspension in the water. The local council wants to make the water clear again so that fish and other living organisms can safely use the lake. 	A solid must be separated from a liquid. The solid does not dissolve in the liquid.
The inhabitants of a small arid town on the edge of the sea want to get their salt supply from the ocean and sell the surplus to other communities.	A solid must be separated from a liquid. The solid dissolves in the liquid.
The inhabitants of another small arid town not only want the salt from the ocean but also a fresh water supply.	A solid that dissolves in a liquid must be separated from the liquid. Both the solid and the liquid must be present after the separation.
An Australian bush camper discovers that the kerosene used for lighting the camping stove has become mixed with water. The kerosene must be separated from the water before it can be brought on the camping trip.	A liquid must be separated from a liquid. The liquids do not mix.

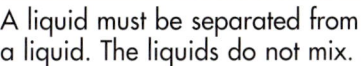

Try this

SEPARATE A MIXTURE

YOU WILL NEED
50 wooden toothpicks
50 straight pins
20 poppet beads
other equipment of your choosing

- Mix the toothpicks, pins and poppet beads into a small container (the size of a deep cereal bowl).
- Your task is to now separate the three components in only one minute. Plan your method carefully before you start (there is no time limit for planning!) All the methods you will need to accomplish the task in one minute have been described in this chapter. Write down your plan and the equipment needed. (*Hint*: pages 38 and 44 contain some useful information.)
- Obtain all the equipment, then start the job.

You could do this activity in a group, then have a race with other groups in the class!

2. Changing text into diagrams

Construct a flow diagram for the treatment of country water supplies as explained on page 40. Label all the steps in your diagram. You may wish to write a few words of explanation as well as drawing the steps.

3. Debating issues with a science background

GROUP WORK Participate in a debate entitled 'The water in our city is/is not fit to drink'. Use all the information you have learnt during your study of this chapter.

SOLIDS, LIQUIDS AND GASES

Properties are features that help to identify a material. For example, steel is strong, and glass is transparent. Materials become useful because of their properties. Steel is used in bridges because of its strength, while glass is used in windows because it can be seen through and will allow light into a room.

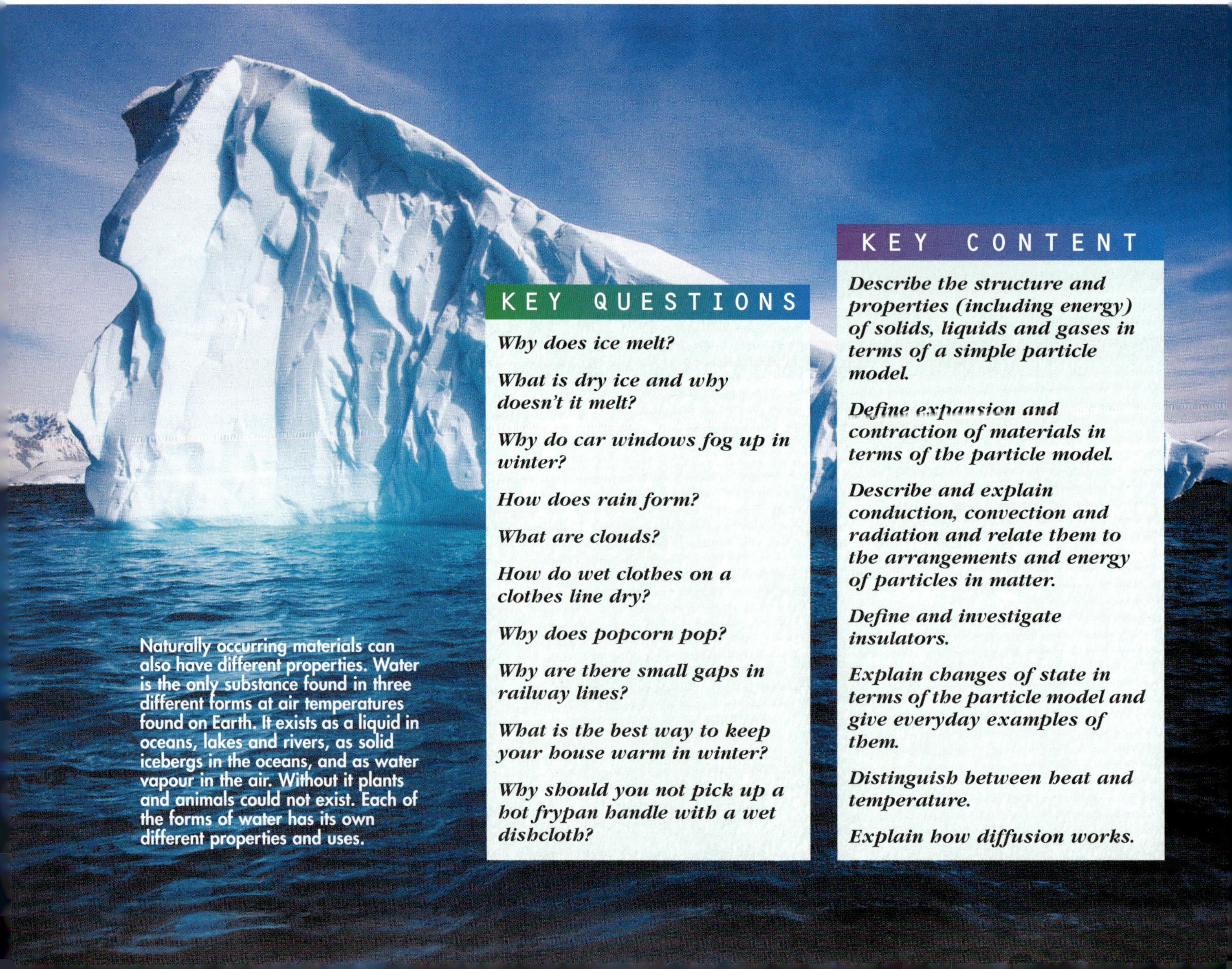

Naturally occurring materials can also have different properties. Water is the only substance found in three different forms at air temperatures found on Earth. It exists as a liquid in oceans, lakes and rivers, as solid icebergs in the oceans, and as water vapour in the air. Without it plants and animals could not exist. Each of the forms of water has its own different properties and uses.

KEY QUESTIONS

Why does ice melt?

What is dry ice and why doesn't it melt?

Why do car windows fog up in winter?

How does rain form?

What are clouds?

How do wet clothes on a clothes line dry?

Why does popcorn pop?

Why are there small gaps in railway lines?

What is the best way to keep your house warm in winter?

Why should you not pick up a hot frypan handle with a wet dishcloth?

KEY CONTENT

Describe the structure and properties (including energy) of solids, liquids and gases in terms of a simple particle model.

Define expansion and contraction of materials in terms of the particle model.

Describe and explain conduction, convection and radiation and relate them to the arrangements and energy of particles in matter.

Define and investigate insulators.

Explain changes of state in terms of the particle model and give everyday examples of them.

Distinguish between heat and temperature.

Explain how diffusion works.

Thinking about
Solids, liquids and gases

1. A survey

Complete the following survey before you start reading this chapter.

(a) Draw a table on a blank sheet of paper which is labelled with your name. Make the table large enough to fill up the whole page.

(b) Read the survey below which lists everyday events that you experience. Explain in your own words what you think has happened in each situation and write your explanations in your survey table. Note: use a blue or black pen, not a red pen.

(c) Give your table to your teacher, who will make a photocopy of it and return the original to you. Then paste the survey into your workbook, as you will need to refer to it later.

And remember — this is not a test!

Problem number	Question
1.	When a kettle boils, large bubbles rise to the surface of the water. What do you think the bubbles are made of?
2.	When you do the washing up, you leave the dishes on the sink. Suppose that you have a young brother or sister who later comes to the sink to dry the dishes and says 'The dishes are dry. See, the water has disappeared.' How would you explain this?

3.	When a thermometer is put into hot water, the liquid in the thermometer (usually mercury or alcohol) rises up the tube.
	    (a) What do you think happens when the liquid rises?
	    (b) Why does it happen?

4.	Most of the space in a room is filled with air. What do you think air is made up of?

5.	As a result of their observations and experiments, scientists think that all matter (solids, liquids and gases) consists of small particles. In your survey table, draw three squares and lines underneath the squares.
	    In the squares, draw diagrams showing how you think the particles are arranged in solids, liquids and gases and write an explanation of the diagram on the lines below.
	    Use ● or ○ or ✗ or another symbol you prefer to indicate a particle.

2. Making predictions

A prediction is a statement about what you think will happen based on previous observations or experiences. Below are two situations which will allow you to make and test predictions.

(a) Beaker A contains 100 mL of water at 80°C. Beaker B contains 100 mL of water at 40°C. Predict what the temperature will be when the water from the two beakers is combined. Write down your prediction, then carry out the test. Was your prediction supported by the test?

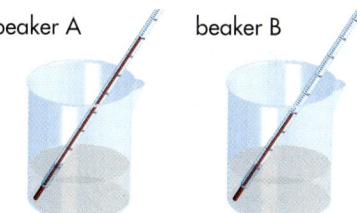

beaker A   beaker B

(b) A bimetallic strip is a thin strip comprised of two metals. When it is heated, the metals expand (become larger) by different amounts, causing the strip to bend.
    From the diagram below, which metal has expanded the most? Why do you think this?

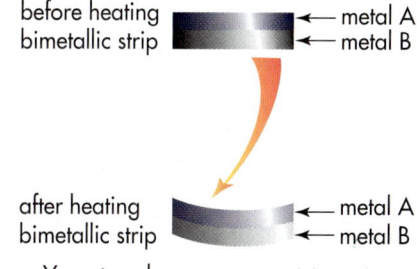

before heating bimetallic strip ← metal A / ← metal B

after heating bimetallic strip ← metal A / ← metal B

Your teacher may want to set up an experiment heating a bimetallic strip made of copper and tin. Predict which metal will expand the most. Then perform the experiment and check your prediction. Remember to follow your teacher's instructions and be careful when heating the strip.

States of matter

"Would you want to dive into a swimming pool if it contained only steam? Would you step into a bath filled with ice cubes? Steam and ice are two forms of water, but they do not look or feel the same. They have different **properties**.

Steam and ice have different properties because they are two **states** of water. The third state is liquid water. Most matter can be identified as being in one of three states: **solid**, **liquid** or **gas**. Ice is a solid, water is a liquid and steam is a gas.

Solids

Solids like ice have a very definite shape which cannot easily be changed.

They take up a fixed amount of space and are generally not able to be compressed.

Most solids cannot be poured, but there are some, like salt, sand and sugar, that can be poured.

Liquids

Water is a liquid and its shape changes to that of the container in which it is kept. Like solids, liquids take up a fixed amount of space.

If a liquid is poured into a glass, it will take up the shape of the glass. If you continue to pour, it will eventually overflow onto the bench or floor.

Gases

Gases spread out and will not stay in a container unless there is a lid. Gas particles move around, taking up all of the available space. This random movement is called **diffusion**, which can occur in gases and liquids. In the illustration below, iodine gas is being formed and is spreading, or diffusing, throughout the gas jar.

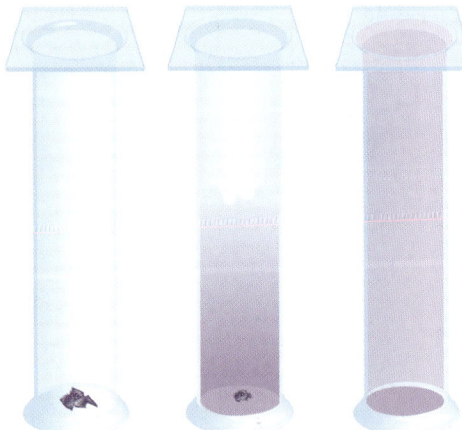

The purple iodine gas diffuses, taking up all of the available space. What will happen to the gas if the lid is removed?

Gases, unlike solids and liquids, are easily compressed, making them take up less space. An inflated balloon can be compressed by squeezing it.

Experiment 3.1 **COMPARING SOLIDS, LIQUIDS AND GASES**

YOU WILL NEED
ice cube
spatula
beaker of water
plastic syringe
balloon

- Pick up an ice cube and place it on the bench. Using a spatula, try to squash it or compress it to make it smaller.
- Take the beaker of water and draw a small amount up into the syringe. Place your finger over the opening at the end of the syringe and press down on the plunger.
- Partially inflate a balloon with air and hold the opening tightly closed. Try to squeeze the balloon.
- Release your hold on the opening of the balloon.

1. Copy the table below and use your observations to complete it.

Properties of solids, liquids and gases

Substance	State of substance	Can the shape be changed easily?	Does it take up space?	Can it be compressed?
ice	solid			
water	liquid			
air	gas			

2. Where did the air in the balloon go when you released the opening?

How *much* space?

The amount of space taken up by a solid, liquid or gas is called its **volume**.

The volume of solids and some other substances is measured in cubic metres (m³) or cubic centimetres (cm³).

A volume of $1\,cm^3$ occupies as much space as the cube below. This is also the same amount of space occupied by 1 millilitre (mL) of a **fluid**.

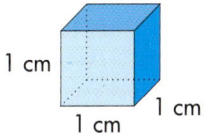

1 cm

1 cm

1 cm

This cube has a volume of one cubic centimetre and can hold 1 mL of a fluid.

Liquids and gases are fluids and their volume is usually measured in units of litres (L) or millilitres (mL). In a laboratory, volume is usually measured with a measuring cylinder.

Liquid products are sold by the litre or millilitre.

Experiment 3.2

MEASURING THE VOLUME OF AN IRREGULAR SHAPED SOLID

YOU WILL NEED
100 mL beaker
100 mL measuring cylinder
a stone or pebble that will fit into the measuring cylinder

- Half-fill (approximately) a 100 mL beaker with water.
- Carefully pour the water into the measuring cylinder.
- Read and record the volume of water in the measuring cylinder using the technique shown in the diagram.
- Carefully place the pebble into the measuring cylinder. Take care not to spill any water.
- Read and record the new volume.

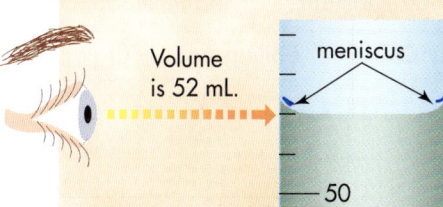

Volume is 52 mL.

meniscus

50

Reading the volume of a liquid in a measuring cylinder. The curved surface is called the **meniscus**. Your eye should be level with the flat part in the centre of the meniscus.

1. What was the volume of the solid in mL?
2. What was the volume of the solid in cm³?
3. Suggest another method of measuring the volume of the solid object.

Activities

Remember

1. List as many as you can remember of the solids, liquids and gases you came in contact with before leaving for school today. Organise them into a table under three headings: solids, liquids and gases.
2. (a) Write down three properties that most solids have in common.
   (b) Would liquids have the same three properties? If not, what differences might be expected?
3. Which properties of gases are different to those of liquids?
4. What is the unit used for measuring small volumes such as that of liquid medicines? How could you measure such a volume?

Think

1. Both steel and chalk are solids. Describe the properties of steel that make it more useful than chalk for building bridges.
2. Are plasticine and playdough solids or liquids? Explain why.
3. What is diffusion? Give two examples of this occurring around your house.
4. At the petrol station, the safety sign asks for the car engine to be switched off before you fill the tank. Why is this necessary?
5. Champagne contains a gas called carbon dioxide. When you open the bottle bubbles form, and the champagne must be drunk or it goes flat. Why does it go flat?

Imagine

You are designing a new type of armchair. It needs to be comfortable and capable of fitting in different positions or spaces around the room. What properties would you want in the chair? Would you need to develop a new material to match these properties? If so, would it be a solid or a liquid, or perhaps a combination of states?

Investigate

Different liquids pour or flow in different ways. Examine this by pouring honey, shampoo, cooking oil and water from one container to another. Time how long they take to pour. Make sure it is a fair test. Record your results in a table and make a conclusion based on your observations and results.

3.2
Changing states

Melting and freezing

The change from a solid to a liquid state is called **melting**. The ice sculpture in the photograph is melting as heat energy moves into it from the warmer air surrounding it. Ice usually melts at a temperature of about 0°C. The ice from which the sculpture was carved was made by **freezing** water. Freezing is the name given to a change of state from liquid to solid. Water freezes as heat moves away from it into colder surroundings. Water freezes at the same temperature (about 0°C) at which ice melts.

When the temperature is above 0°C, ice begins to melt as heat moves into it from the surrounding air. The higher the temperature, the faster the ice melts.

SCIFACTS

Why does popcorn pop **?**
Inside the corn there is some water. When this is heated it becomes a gas and takes up a lot more space as it expands. The gas builds up inside the corn and can only escape by bursting through the corn, making it pop.

Evaporation and condensation

Wet clothes hung out in the sun become crisp and dry. The heat from the sun has caused the liquid water in the clothes to change state to become **water vapour**. This change in state from liquid to vapour is called **evaporation**. The gas state of water is called water vapour if its temperature is below 100°C. It is called steam if its temperature is above 100°C. Steam is formed only after water has boiled.

Different liquids evaporate at different temperatures. When the top is removed from a bottle of perfume or aftershave, you can smell the scent throughout the room. This is because the perfume or aftershave evaporates at room temperature without any extra heat being added. It receives enough heat energy from the surrounding air.

When water in a saucepan is heated on a stove, evaporation takes place very slowly at first as some of the water begins to change state. As heating continues, evaporation takes place so fast that bubbles of water vapour form at the bottom and sides of the saucepan. They rise quickly to the surface. The water is then said to be boiling. The temperature at which evaporation takes place rapidly is called the **boiling point**. You will find the boiling point of water by doing experiment 3.3. The temperature remains constant while the water continues to boil. If the water is left on the stove for too long, all of the water will evaporate and the saucepan will be scorched.

The melting point of a substance is the temperature at which it changes from a solid into a liquid. The boiling point of a substance is the temperature at which a substance boils. Once boiling starts, evaporation takes place rapidly.

The melting and boiling points of some common substances are shown in the table below. Melting and boiling points change with the height above sea level. This is because the air gets thinner as you move away from the Earth's surface. If you were climbing Mt Everest, and made a cup of coffee, you would find that the water would boil at a temperature well below 100°C.

Melting and boiling points of some common substances at sea level

Substance	Melting point (°C)	Boiling point (°C)
water	0	100
table salt	804	1413
iron	1535	2750
aluminium	660	1800
oxygen	−218	−183
nitrogen	−210	−196

When steam from the kettle, or water vapour from the shower, hits cold wall tiles in the kitchen or bathroom, it quickly changes from a gas to a liquid state. This change of state is called **condensation**. Condensation is the opposite of evaporation. Condensation occurs when heat moves from a gas into its surroundings. This happens when you breathe onto cold glass. Water vapour breathed out condenses into liquid water as it loses heat. Evaporation occurs when heat moves into a liquid from its surroundings.

Experiment 3.3   HEATING WATER

YOU WILL NEED

Bunsen burner, heatproof mat and
    matches
tripod and gauze mat
thermometer (−10 to 110°C)

watch (with a second hand)
spoon
100 mL beaker
safety glasses

- Copy the table below into your workbook.
- Add about 50 mL of water to the beaker and place it on the tripod.
- Place the thermometer into the water and let it remain for a minute or so until the temperature stops changing. Take a reading and record this in your table under '0 minutes'.
- Light the Bunsen burner and begin heating the water. Record the temperature each minute. Continue heating until the temperature remains steady for three minutes.
- Hold the spoon in the vapour above the water and observe the effect.

CAUTION: Take care not to scald yourself with the hot water vapour.

Heating water

Time (minutes)	0	1	2	3	4	5	6	7	8	9	10
Temperature (°C)											

1. At what temperature did the liquid: (a) begin to bubble?   (b) boil?
2. What happened when the cold spoon was placed near the vapour?
3. What do you think was in the bubbles?
4. Draw a graph of your results. Explain the shape of your graph.
5. Write a conclusion based on your observations and results.

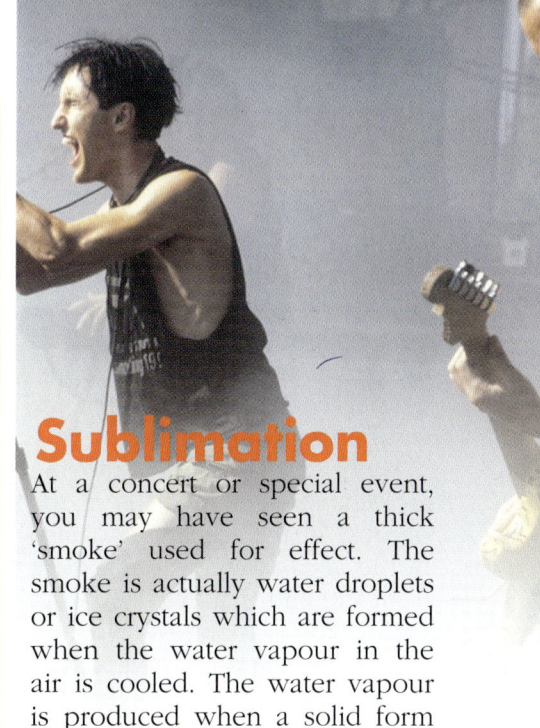

Sublimation

At a concert or special event, you may have seen a thick 'smoke' used for effect. The smoke is actually water droplets or ice crystals which are formed when the water vapour in the air is cooled. The water vapour is produced when a solid form of carbon dioxide called 'dry ice' is added to the air. Dry ice never melts or becomes a liquid. Instead it changes from the solid state directly to a gas. This very unusual change of state is called **sublimation**. Dry ice sublimes at a temperature of −78.5°C. Iodine also sublimes. Diamonds sublime at a temperature of 3550°C.

Activities

Using data

Use the table on page 50 to answer these questions.
1. At what temperature would you expect table salt to melt? At what temperature would it freeze?
2. Would you expect aluminium to be found as a solid, liquid or gas at:
   (a) 200°C?   (b) 680°C?
   (c) 1900°C?
3. Which substance — oxygen or nitrogen — would freeze first if the temperature were gradually lowered?

Think

1. What is the difference between evaporation and boiling?
2. Why is dry ice useful to produce a 'smoke' effect? What other uses are there for dry ice?

3. Why do solid blocks of air freshener disappear after a few weeks without a trace?
4. What is in the bubbles that you see when water is boiling?

Remember

1. Copy and complete the diagram on the right, labelling the changes of state.
2. Use a labelled arrow to add 'sublimation' to your diagram.
3. What is the name given to the change of state of liquid water to steam? What happens to make this occur?
4. What happens to liquid water when it is cooled below 0°C? Has heat moved into or out of the liquid?
5. Are changes of state physical or chemical changes? Explain.

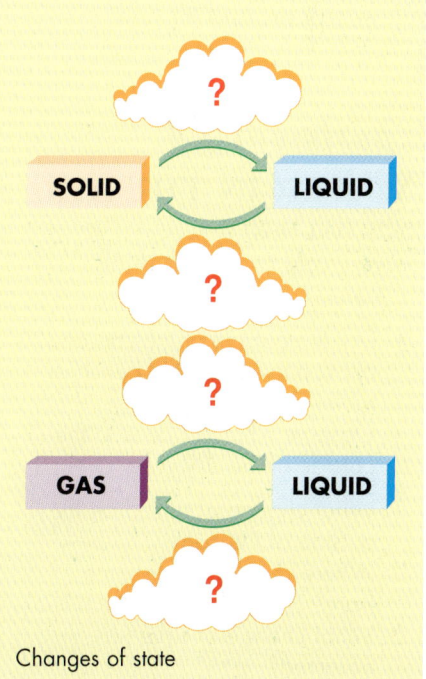

Changes of state

Water everywhere

Two-thirds of the Earth's surface is covered with water. Not all the water is in a liquid form. A significant amount exists as ice in the Arctic and Antarctic regions: 91 per cent of the world's ice can be found in Antarctica.

Water is constantly moving and changing states. It is in the oceans, in the icecaps and also in the air as water vapour. Heat from the sun makes water from the oceans evaporate slowly and form water vapour. The invisible water vapour rises with the warm air. When the water vapour becomes cold enough it condenses to form **clouds** of tiny water droplets. The clouds are visible and are kept up by the air moving around them. If a cloud is close enough to the ground it is known as **fog**.

At high altitudes the air is very cold. When thick clouds reach this very cold area, the water droplets in them join together to form larger droplets, which are too heavy to be held up by moving air. The large droplets fall to the ground as rain.

Rainwater falls into the sea or runs over the ground into rivers and streams, eventually reaching the sea. This constant movement of water between the various states is called the water cycle.

The amount of cloud cover and type of cloud affect how much sunlight will reach the Earth's surface.

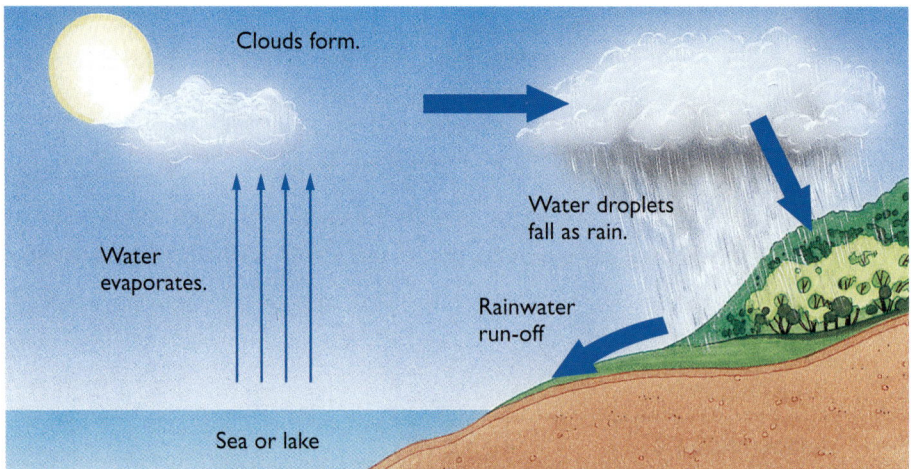

The water cycle carries water from Earth's hydrosphere (oceans, rivers and lakes) to the atmosphere (thin layer of gas surrounding the Earth) then to the lithosphere (land) and back to the hydrosphere as run-off.

Experiment 3.4

WATER IN THE AIR

YOU WILL NEED
a very cold can of soft drink
a towel

- Dry the outside of the can and allow it to stand on a bench or table.
- Observe what happens to the outside of the dry can.

1. What change occurred on the outside of the can?
2. Where did the water come from?
3. What change of state has occurred?

Experiment 3.5   FORMING CLOUDS

YOU WILL NEED
250 mL beaker
ice cubes
watchglass
heatproof mat, Bunsen burner and matches
tripod and gauze mat
safety glasses

- Half-fill the beaker with water and heat it until the water is boiling.
- Stop heating and cover the beaker carefully with a watchglass. Observe the bottom of the watchglass.

1. Describe what happens to the bottom of the watchglass.

- Remove the watchglass and heat the water again until it boils.
- Stop heating and turn off the gas supply. Quickly but carefully, cover the beaker with a watchglass containing ice cubes.

- Observe the area under the watchglass.

2. Describe what happens in the beaker just below the watchglass.
3. What change of state has taken place?
4. Write a conclusion about how clouds form.

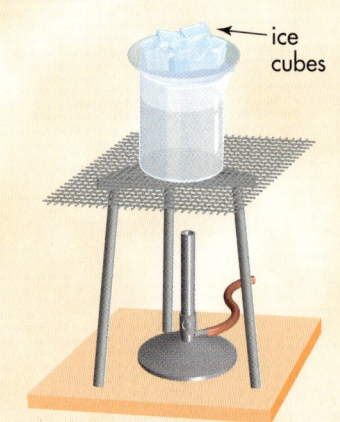

ice cubes

Forming clouds in a beaker

COMMON TYPES OF CLOUDS

Cumulus
Puffy clouds that look like cottonwool. They form at a low altitude but may get thicker and extend into higher levels. They may produce showers of rain.

Altocumulus
Middle-level clouds which are rippled and are mostly white. They produce light showers.

Stratocumulus
Low-level clouds that are generally white. They form groups or rolls of cloud. They produce drizzle.

Cirrus
Wispy, fine clouds found up in high altitudes. They consist of ice crystals. They do not produce rain.

Stratus
Low-level clouds that are found in layers, often grey in colour. They produce drizzle or fine rain. At very low levels they form fog.

Cumulonimbus
Low-level cumulus-type clouds but grey in colour. They produce thunderstorms with lightning. They may stretch from low levels up to 13 kilometres into the atmosphere.

Nimbostratus
Sheets of thicker, darker cloud at low altitudes. They produce heavy rain or snow.

Cirrocumulus
High-level clouds with many ripples. They do not produce rain.

Experiment 3.6 OBSERVING CLOUDS

- Before commencing your observations, design a table in which you can record them; but first read the observations to be made.
- Record the fraction of the sky covered by cloud for five consecutive days. Make your observations at the same time each day.
- Record whether or not there was any rain, hail or snow during the hour after your observations were made.
- If it did drizzle, rain, hail or snow, record the type of cloud that produced it.

1. Which types of clouds produced drizzle, rain, hail or snow?
2. Are your observations consistent with the descriptions in the captions for the photographs of clouds?
3. Does the likelihood of rain, hail or snow seem to depend more on the amount of cloud or the type of cloud?

Activities

Remember

1. Why does sea water evaporate?
2. What are clouds and how do they form?
3. Which groups of cloud produce rain?

Think

1. Why do some clouds pass over without producing rain?
2. What changes of state can be seen in the water cycle?
3. Why does the water vapour in clouds condense?
4. Why can we see clouds but not water vapour in the air?
5. Rain will be produced from very thick cumulus clouds, but not from thinner cumulus clouds. Why?
6. Discuss how humans could alter the water cycle.

Investigate

Research the importance of the Aboriginal rain dance.

Particular particles

How do you explain why ice has properties that are different from those of water or steam? Scientists use a model to explain the different properties of solids, liquids and gases. This model is called **the particle model**.

According to the particle model:
- all substances are made of tiny particles
- the particles are attracted towards other surrounding particles
- the particles are always moving or vibrating
- the hotter the substance is, the more energy the particles contain and the faster they move.

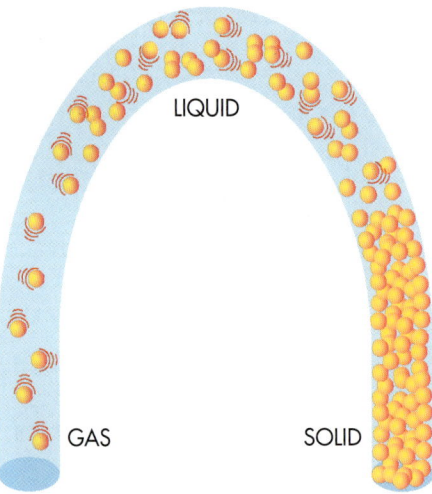

A particle model for different states

Getting *into* shape

In solids the particles are very close together, so they cannot be compressed. They can vibrate but remain in fixed positions, and there are strong attractions between the particles. For these reasons, solids usually have a fixed shape.

Two common types of solids are crystals and powders. Crystals have a regular shape due to the orderly arrangement of the particles in the solid. An example of a crystalline solid is sugar crystals. Powders, or amorphous (non-crystalline) solids, have particles that are close together but not organised into any particular order. An example is talcum powder.

In liquids the particles are held together by attraction, but it is not as strong as the attraction found in solids. The weak particle attraction allows the particles to move past one another so they can be rearranged and take a different shape. As in solids, the particles in liquids are still very close together, so they cannot be compressed into smaller spaces.

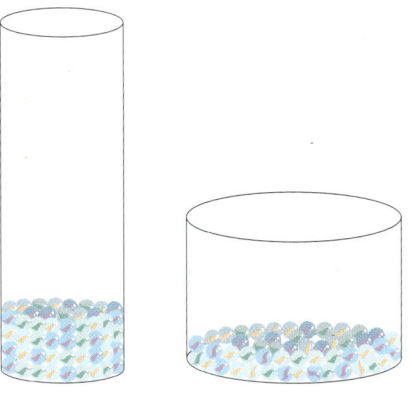

The same number of marbles poured into two different shaped containers shows what happens to particles in a liquid.

Changing state *and the* particle model

According to the particle model, as substances are heated, the particles move or vibrate faster because their energy increases. (As they are cooled, their energy decreases.) So when a solid becomes liquid, the strong attraction between the particles is reduced and the particles move more freely. Melting and boiling points are unique for each substance. This is because the amount of attraction between particles in each substance is different. Water boils at 100°C whereas aluminium boils at 1800°C. This is because the attraction between neighbouring particles is much stronger in aluminium than in water.

If the particles are hot enough they will break away from the other particles and move into the room as gas particles. When a liquid becomes a gas, the attractions between the particles are much weaker, so the particles are freer to move about.

The **densities** of solids, liquids and gases relate to how closely the particles are packed into a unit volume, as well as the mass of the particles. The more closely the particles are packed and the heavier the particles, the denser the substance. Density also changes with temperature. At higher temperatures, the particles have more energy and they can separate further from each other. (Data books listing densities of different substances usually quote their densities at 20°C.)

Spreading *out*

The particle model can be used to explain the behaviour of the air in the balloons. If particles are moving constantly, they will collide with each other and with the sides of the balloon, much like snooker balls moving all at once on a snooker table. Unlike the snooker table, the wall of the balloon can stretch as more particles of air are added or as faster particles push against it.

If the air is heated the particles have more energy. They move faster, collide more often and push the balloon wall with greater pressure. The balloon will get bigger or **expand**. If the air is cooled, the particles slow down and the balloon begins to grow smaller or **contract**.

The ability of gases and liquids to **diffuse** or spread around the room can also be explained using the particle model. For example, the particles in a gas are far apart so they are not attracted to each other very much. They are able to move freely or diffuse around the room. Because gas particles are so far apart, they can be easily compressed or pushed closer together.

Experiment 3.7   EXPLAINING GASES

YOU WILL NEED

balloons	small conical flask	ice cubes
piece of string	2 large beakers	hot and cold water
ruler		

- Copy the table below into your workbook.
- Inflate the balloon to a size slightly larger than an orange. Fit the neck of the balloon over the conical flask to seal it.
- Wrap the string once around the widest part of the balloon to find its circumference. Measure the length of the string that encircled the balloon with a ruler.
- Record the measurement in your table.
- Half-fill one of the beakers with ice cubes and a small amount of cold water.
- Place the conical flask in the ice-water beaker and observe the balloon. After a few minutes, use the string to measure the circumference of the balloon again. Record your measurement in a table like the one below.
- Put some hot water into the second beaker. Take the conical flask from the ice-water and place it into the hot water. Leave for a few minutes, then measure and record the balloon's circumference.

1. Was any air added to or removed from the balloon after it was placed over the conical flask?
2. After being in ice-water and hot water, were there any changes in the size of the balloon?
3. Using the particle model, try to explain what might have made the balloon contract and expand.
4. What quantity was varied or changed in this experiment? What things were kept the same?

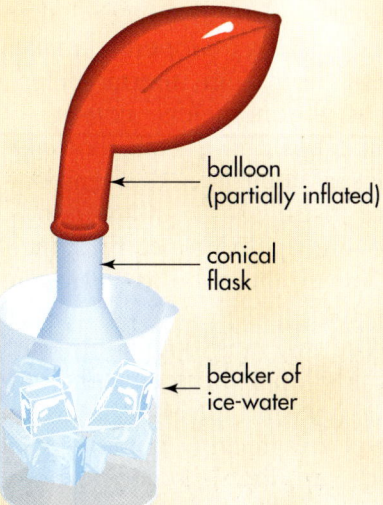

balloon (partially inflated)

conical flask

beaker of ice-water

What happens to the air in the balloon when it gets cold?

Effect of temperature on air

Temperature of surroundings	Circumference of balloon (cm)
room temperature	
cold (icy water)	
hot (hot water)	

Activities

Remember

1. What are the four main ideas of the particle model?
2. The following statements are incorrect. Rewrite them correctly.
   (a) To change a liquid to a solid you have to heat it.
   (b) Heating a liquid might make the particles stick closer together.
   (c) Solids do not have a definite shape because the particles are free to move around.
   (d) You can compress a gas because its particles are close together.
3. Explain why different substances boil at different temperatures.

Think

1. What happens to the particles in a gas when it becomes a liquid? What is this change of state called?
2. Use the particle model to explain why:
   (a) perfume can be smelt from a few metres away
   (b) steam can be compressed while ice cannot
   (c) an ice cube melts and changes shape when it is taken out of the freezer
   (d) water vapour takes up more space than the same amount of liquid
   (e) solids do not mix well, but gases and liquids mix easily in most cases.
3. Explain why wet clothes dry more quickly on a windy day than on a still day.
4. Use the particle model to predict what will happen to the length and width of a solid substance when it is heated (without melting).

Imagine

Imagine you are a particle of water. Beginning with the solid state of ice, describe the changes that you would encounter as you are heated to become a liquid and then a gas.

Bigger and smaller

The particle model can be used to explain changes in the size of substances as well as changes in state. When substances are heated, the particles have more energy, and so move faster, becoming further apart and taking up more space. The substance will expand.

The tyres on a moving car get quite hot. This heat energy makes the air inside expand. This may even cause a blowout in extreme circumstances. Gases usually expand much more than solids or liquids. Gases expand easily because the particles are spread out and not attracted to each other strongly. Solids, liquids and gases usually contract when they are cooled again because the particles slow down, need less space to move in and become more strongly attracted to each other.

Architects and engineers allow for expansion and contraction of materials when designing bridges and buildings. Bridges have gaps at each end of large sections so that in hot weather, when the metal and concrete expand, they will not buckle. Railway lines also have gaps to allow for expansion in hot weather. Electrical wires are hung from poles loosely so that when the weather cools, they will not become too tight and break as they contract. The amount by which each structure will expand or contract depends on the material it is made from; so when choosing a material for a special purpose, it is important to find out how much that material will expand or contract. The table on page 57 shows how much some commonly used materials expand when the temperature increases by 10°C.

> Temperature differs from heat. Temperature means the *level* of heat in a substance or body of matter. It relates to the average energy of the particles. The more particles there are, the more energy there is in an object. The sum of all the energy in all the particles is the *amount* of heat in the substance or body of matter. The heat content of a substance depends on the mass of the substance, but the temperature does not depend on the mass. For example, an adult and a baby may have the same temperature, but they have different amounts of heat in each of their bodies.

Thermometers

Liquids expand more than solids. This property makes them useful in thermometers. Most thermometers consist of thin tubes and a bulb that contains a liquid. As the temperature rises, the liquid expands, moving up the tube. In a thermometer the tube is sealed at the top.

The two most commonly used liquids for thermometers are mercury and alcohol. Mercury has a low freezing point (−39°C) and a high boiling point (357°C). Alcohol, however, is much more useful in very cold conditions because it does not freeze until the temperature drops to −117°C. Unfortunately alcohol boils at 79°C so it cannot be used for measuring higher temperatures.

Experiment 3.8

EXPANSION OF SOLIDS

YOU WILL NEED
metal ball and ring set
Bunsen burner and heatproof mat
tongs

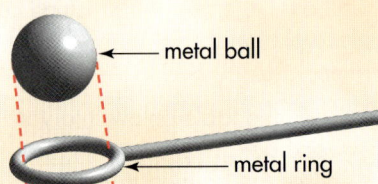

A ball and ring set

- Try to put the ball through the ring.
- Use the Bunsen burner to heat the ring and use tongs to try to put the ball through it. Take care not to touch the hot metal.
- Let the ring cool and try to put the ball through the ring again.
1. What has happened to change the size of the ring?
2. Use the particle model to explain the change that took place in the ring.

The temperature of the human body ranges between 34°C and 42°C; it is normally about 37°C. A clinical thermometer is especially designed to measure human body temperature. Look closely at the photo. There is a narrowing of the tube near the bulb. Once the mercury has expanded, this narrowing prevents the mercury contracting and moving back into the bulb before the temperature can be read. Once a reading has been taken, the mercury has to be shaken back into the bulb before the thermometer can be reused.

A clinical thermometer

Experiment 3.9

EXPANSION OF LIQUIDS

YOU WILL NEED
500 mL conical flask
narrow glass tube
rubber stopper with one hole to fit the tube
Bunsen burner, heatproof mat and matches
tripod and gauze mat
food colouring
eye-dropper
marking pen

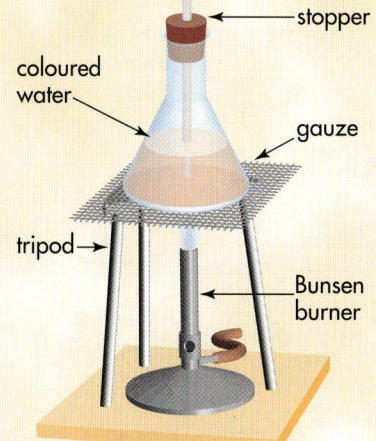

Investigating the expansion of liquids

- Use an eye-dropper to place two or three drops of food colouring in the flask and fill it with water right to the top.
- Place the stopper in the flask with the tube fitted. Some coloured water should rise into the tube. Mark the level of the liquid in the tube with the marking pen.
- Place the flask on the tripod and gauze mat, light the Bunsen burner and gently heat the liquid.
- After about five minutes of heating, turn off the Bunsen burner and watch what happens to the level of the liquid.

1. What happens to the level of the liquid while it is being heated?
2. What happens to the level of the liquid while it is cooling down?
3. Use the particle model to explain why liquids expand.

Activities

Using data

Expansion of materials

Substance	Expansion (mm) of 100 m length when temperature increased by 10°C
steel	11
iron	12
platinum	9
brass	19
concrete	11
glass — soda	9
glass — Pyrex	3
lead	29
tin	21
aluminium	23
bronze	18

Use the table above to answer the following questions.
1. If a steel rod of 10 metres in length were heated so that its temperature rose by 10°C, how long would the rod become?
2. Why is Pyrex, rather than soda glass, used in cooking glassware such as casserole dishes and vision saucepans?
3. Concrete is often reinforced with steel bars or mesh to make it stronger. Why is steel a better choice than another metal, such as aluminium or lead?

Remember

1. When a substance is heated its temperature increases. What happens to the energy of its particles?
2. (a) What change would you expect to see when hot metal objects are cooling?
   (b) Why does this happen? Explain, using the particle model.
3. Give two examples of structures that contain gaps to prevent them from buckling in hot weather.
4. Give one reason why overhead electric power lines are not hung tightly.
5. Why is there a narrow piece (a 'kink') in a clinical thermometer?

Think

1. A jar with the lid jammed on tightly can be hard to open. If you run hot water over the lid it becomes easier to open. Why?
2. Hot air balloons have a gas heater connected to them. The pilot can turn the heater on and the balloon will go higher. Why? How could the balloon be brought lower?
3. Discuss the conditions when you might use an alcohol thermometer rather than a mercury thermometer.

Investigate

1. The mercury thermometer was invented by a German named Gabriel Fahrenheit (1686–1736). A different scale is used for Fahrenheit thermometers. At what temperatures does water boil and freeze on this scale? How would you convert Celsius to Fahrenheit?
2. Why do icebergs float in the Arctic and Antarctic waters? Do you think there is much of the iceberg under the water, or is it mostly above? How could you test out your hypothesis? Design a suitable experiment.

Hot moves

Heat is a form of energy that moves from bodies at a higher temperature to those which are colder or at a lower temperature. If two bodies are at the same temperature, then there is no movement of heat from one to the other.

Heat can move from one substance to another in three different ways. What is between the hot and cold substances determines how the heat moves. Heat energy enables particles to move around or to vibrate more rapidly.

Conduction

If you have ever picked up a metal spoon that has been left in a hot saucepan you know that heat moves along the spoon until it reaches the handle. This is an example of **conduction** of heat. In solids the particles are packed very close together. When the particles are heated, they begin to vibrate more rapidly and begin to bump into one another. The vibrations are passed along the whole object and its temperature increases. The heat has moved along the object as a result of the colliding particles.

Not all solids conduct heat at the same rate. Metals, for example, are much better conductors than most other solids. Some solid substances are very poor conductors of heat. Glass, wood, rubber and plastic are all poor conductors of heat and are called **insulators**. Often metal saucepans will have a plastic or wooden handle. Suggest a reason for this.

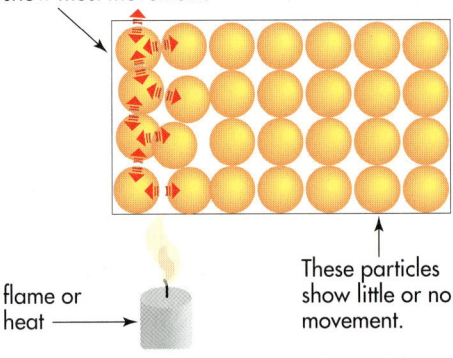

These particles show most movement.

flame or heat

These particles show little or no movement.

Conduction, using the particle model

Convection

Liquids generally do not conduct heat as well as solids because the particles in liquids are further apart than in solids. The vibrations cannot pass from particle to particle as easily as in solids. Gases such as air are very poor conductors of heat because of the greater distance between the particles.

Heat can move through liquids and gases by **convection**. The particles in liquids and gases are able to move around. When liquid water is heated, for example, the particles at the bottom of the container move more rapidly, and move further apart. In the levels above these warm water particles, there are colder water particles which are still close together. These cold particles move downwards or sink and the warm particles move up to replace them. This movement of particles is called a **convection current**.

Supermarket freezers are open at the top and supermarkets are very warm places. Why does the food remain frozen? Freezing coils around the sides and the base of the freezer produce cold air, but cold air is heavy and sinks so it remains in the freezer. Think about how your bare feet feel when you open the fridge door in summer.

Experiment 3.10

MOVING PARTICLES

YOU WILL NEED
250 mL beaker
single crystal of potassium permanganate
tweezers
Bunsen burner and heatproof mat
tripod and gauze mat
drinking straw

- Fill the beaker with water and place it on a gauze mat and tripod.
- Use the tweezers to drop a crystal of potassium permanganate down the drinking straw into the middle of the water at the bottom of the beaker.

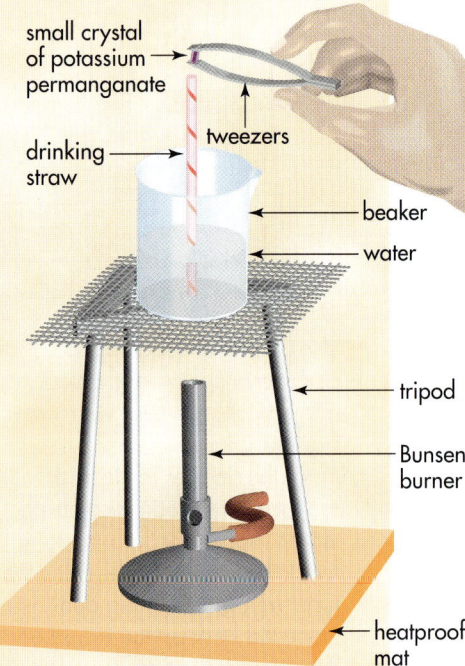

small crystal of potassium permanganate

tweezers

drinking straw

beaker

water

tripod

Bunsen burner

heatproof mat

Drop the coloured crystal down the drinking straw.

- Remove the straw and heat the beaker. Observe what happens to the crystal.

1. Draw a diagram to show the movement of colour through the beaker. This will show the currents within the beaker.
2. Where else would convection currents like these be found?

Radiation

When you put your hand just below a glowing electric light bulb, you feel heat from the globe as soon as it is switched on. The air between your hand and the bulb does not conduct heat quickly. Because your hand is below the bulb rather than above it, the heat is unlikely to have moved by convection. In addition, the heat is felt so quickly that there is not enough time for conduction or convection to occur. The heat from the bulb reaches your hand via rays of energy. This is called **radiation**, the third method of heat movement. Heat from the sun reaches Earth by radiation. The space between the sun and Earth is almost entirely empty (a vacuum). There are not enough particles for conduction or convection to occur. Radiated heat can travel through empty space.

When the sun's heat, or any other radiated heat, arrives at a surface it may be **transmitted**, **absorbed**, or **reflected**. The surface colour will determine what will happen to the heat. Light-coloured surfaces tend to reflect radiated heat. Black and other dark-coloured surfaces tend to absorb radiated heat.

If heat is absorbed, the temperature of the surface will rise. If it is reflected, very little change will occur.

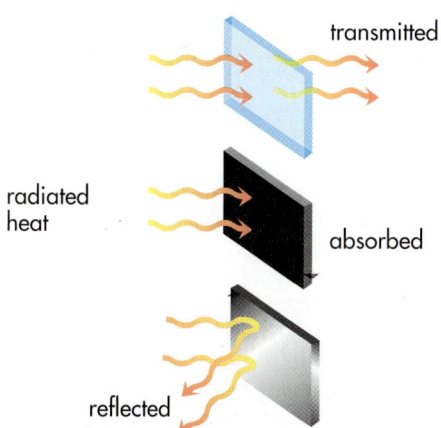

Radiated heat can be transmitted, absorbed or reflected.

Activities

Remember

1. Copy and complete the table below.

Type of heat movement	Describe briefly how heat moves	In which state or states would the heat move by this method?
conduction		
convection		
radiation		

2. What is an insulator? Name three different materials that can act as insulators.
3. Heat can travel through empty space: for example, between the sun and the Earth. How does the heat move?
4. What three things can happen to radiated heat when it arrives at any surface?

Think

1. Think about water as ice, liquid water and water vapour.
   (a) In which state of water does convection occur?
   (b) In which state of water does conduction occur?
   (c) In which state of water would you expect conduction to occur best?
2. Conduction is possible in solids but is not an effective means of heat transfer in liquids or gases. Use the particle model to explain why.
3. When you hold a mug of coffee or hot soup, your hands feel warm. How is the heat transferred?
4. When you put your hand on a metal surface and a wooden surface in the same room, one surface feels cooler even though both have the same temperature. Which surface feels cooler? Explain why. How would they feel if their temperatures were both 50°C? Why?
5. If you were to buy a black car and a white car, in which would it be hotter to sit during summer? Why?

Investigate

How quickly do things cool? The rate at which substances cool is determined by many factors. A cup of coffee will cool more rapidly than the same cup filled with thick vegetable soup. The material in the cup is one **variable** that affects how quickly cooling takes place. The size of the container, the temperature around the outside of the container, the temperature of the material inside the container and the type of container are other variables that affect the rate of cooling.

You have just made a cup of tea when the phone rings. You are expecting a phone call and know that you will be on the phone for 5 minutes. You want to have your tea as hot as possible after the phone call. Should you put in the milk before or after the conversation?
- Write down the aim of your investigation and state your hypothesis.
- List the set of steps that you will follow.
- Decide what equipment is needed and make a list of it. Remember that all variables must be kept the same except the variable you are testing.
- Decide how your results will be recorded and draw up any necessary tables.
- Check with your teacher before beginning.
- You may decide to work in small groups, brainstorm and produce a group plan.
- At the end of the investigation, discuss whether your hypothesis was supported. What evidence would you use in your discussion?

SCIENCE issues

A COSTLY ESCAPE

A knowledge of how heat moves from a warm place to a cooler place can help you to save energy, and therefore money, used to heat your home in winter. Using less energy for heating also conserves valuable resources such as coal (used to generate electricity) and natural gas.

Heat leaves the inside of a warm, cosy home by conduction, convection and radiation. New homes are designed to reduce heat losses by all three methods. However, there are also measures that occupants can take to reduce heat losses (and the bills that go with them).

Using *the sun*

The direction that a house faces, positioning of windows and skylights, and the type of trees planted around the house all affect the amount of sunlight and radiated heat that enter the home. **Deciduous** trees (trees that lose their leaves in winter) planted near north-facing windows allow radiated heat from the sun through in winter but block it out in summer.

Insulation

Heat loss by conduction occurs through the ceiling, walls, windows and floor. Since air is a very poor conductor of heat, materials containing air reduce heat loss. However, if the air is free to circulate it can move away, taking heat with it. The best insulators, therefore, are those that contain air that is restricted from moving. Woollen clothes, birds' feathers and animal fur are all good insulators because they restrict heat loss by both conduction and convection.

Some ways in which insulation is used in the home include:
- ceiling insulation such as fibreglass batts, and loose rockwool which can be blown in. These materials contain pockets of air that provide insulation, and reduce the loss of warm air from the roof by convection.
- cavity wall insulation, a foam that can be sprayed in between the inside and outside walls
- heavy curtains, which trap a still layer of air between them and windows
- double glazing — the use of two sheets of glass in windows with a narrow gap of air between them
- cavity bricks which have holes in them. The still air in the holes reduce heat loss by conduction and convection.

Heat can escape from many different places.

Labels on diagram: chimney, ceiling, walls, air vent, gaps in windows, gaps around doors, up unused chimney, floor, gaps where pipes penetrate walls

Air pockets within fibreglass batts reduce heat loss by conduction and convection.

Do you *feel a* draught?

Preventing draughts is the cheapest way to reduce heat loss in winter. There are many products available from hardware stores designed to seal small cracks and gaps to stop draughts. Draughts from chimneys and exhaust fans are difficult to control, but some exhaust fans have automatic shutters which close when the fan is not in use. Chimneys may have a metal plate to seal off air when there is no fire alight.

Radiation

A warm house radiates heat in all directions. Heat loss by radiation can be reduced with shiny foil that reflects radiated heat. Foil can be added to insulation in the ceiling and is also used in external walls.

Experiment 3.11

INVESTIGATING INSULATORS

YOU WILL NEED
6 empty soft drink cans
6 thermometers
newspaper

polystyrene foam and sticky tape or foam drink can holder
woollen cloth
cottonwool

foam rubber
hot water
measuring cylinder
sticky tape (to tape on the materials)

(a) plain (b) newspaper (a few layers) (c) woollen cloth (d) cotton-wool (e) foam drinking can holder (f) foam rubber

Investigating insulators

- Surround each can except one with a different material.
- Copy the table below into your workbook and use it to record your measurements.
- Measure out and pour 100 mL of hot water into each of the cans.
- Measure the temperature of the water in each can. Repeat the measurement of temperature every 5 minutes for 20 minutes.

1. Draw a bar graph that will allow you to compare the drop in temperature of the water in the cans after 20 minutes.
2. Which covering appears to be the most effective insulator?
3. Which one or more of the three methods of heat transfer does the most effective insulator reduce?
4. Use your data to suggest a good container for a mug of hot coffee.
5. Why was one can left without a covering?
6. Are your conclusions reliable? Discuss the difficulties encountered in making sure that the comparison of insulators was fair.

Temperature of water in cans (°C)

Can covering	Time (minutes)				
	0	5	10	15	20
none					
cottonwool					
woollen cloth					
foam rubber					
newspaper					
polystyrene					

Activities

Remember

1. What property makes a material a good insulator?
2. By installing insulation in the ceiling, which one (or more) method of heat transfer is being reduced?
3. What is the cheapest way of reducing heat losses from your home in cold weather?

Think

1. Foil placed in ceilings and walls is often referred to as 'insulation'. Is this term appropriate? Explain your answer.
2. Open fires were common before electric radiators were developed. But which radiates the most heat? Write a hypothesis and design an experiment to test it. Discuss your experimental design with your class group. Students who have open fires in their homes can carry out their experiment there. Electric radiators can be tested in the classroom.
3. Loose clothing is recommended on hot summer days as it allows heat from your body to escape. Explain why loose clothing is better than close-fitting clothing for this purpose.

Investigate

1. What features of a thermos flask reduce heat losses by:
   (a) conduction?
   (b) convection?
   (c) radiation?
2. Design a house to minimise heat loss in winter and heat gain in summer. Give reasons for each design feature.

Putting it all together

Summing up

Copy and complete the statements below to compile a summary of this unit.
The missing words can be found in the word list below.

1. Substances can exist in three different _____. The three states are solid, liquid and _____.

2. Changes between states can occur by adding or removing _____ from a substance.

3. Condensation, _____, melting, freezing and sublimation are all changes of state.

4. A substance has different _____ in different states.

5. Properties of substances can be explained using a simple _____ model.

6. The particle model of matter suggests that all substances consist of tiny particles which are _____ to each other. Particles are always moving and move faster as temperature _____.

7. Substances _____ when heated and contract when _____.

8. Expansion and contraction is greater in gases than in liquids and _____.

9. Heat moves in three ways — conduction, _____ and radiation.

10. _____ and convection can be explained in terms of the particle model.

11. Substances that are poor conductors of heat are called _____.

12. When radiated heat reaches a surface it can be absorbed, transmitted or _____.

13. Water on the Earth's surface and in the atmosphere continually changes state, existing as ice, liquid water and water _____.

14. Water vapour in the air may condense into small droplets and form _____.

Word list

solids	particle	states
cooled	increases	attracted
properties	clouds	heat
evaporation	conduction	insulators
gas	reflected	expand
convection	vapour	

Looking back

1. Complete the word puzzle below. Use the clues to find the nineteen hidden words. The words may be spelt across, down, diagonally or even backwards.

Clues

(a) You use a thermometer to measure this.
(b) Heat may travel through liquids and air by this method.
(c) Ice will do this if it is left out of the freezer.
(d) These must be left in railway lines to prevent buckling in hot weather.
(e) Clouds are called this when they are near the ground.
(f) Jack _____. Frozen water droplets on the grass.
(g) The three states of matter.
(h) Frozen water.

(i) Used in homes to reduce heat loss. The opposite of conduction.
(j) A visible form of condensed water vapour in the sky.
(k) The opposite of cold.
(l) All matter is made of these.
(m) Features of substances.
(n) A form of water that is wonderful to ski on.
(o) Heat from the sun travels to us by this method.
(p) If the droplets of water in clouds get too large, this is the result.
(q) Heat is moved through solids by this method.

T	C	O	N	D	U	C	T	I	O	N
E	L	O	F	S	N	O	W	C	R	R
M	O	I	N	O	W	A	R	E	A	A
P	U	H	Q	V	G	A	P	S	I	D
E	D	F	O	U	E	M	T	P	N	I
R	P	A	R	T	I	C	L	E	S	A
A	B	M	L	Q	Y	D	T	C	R	T
T	K	E	G	D	S	O	L	I	D	I
U	M	F	A	F	R	O	S	T	O	O
R	I	N	S	U	L	A	T	I	O	N
E	P	R	O	P	E	R	T	I	E	S

2. Use the particle model to explain why steam takes up more space than liquid water.
3. In which state are the forces of attraction between the particles likely to be greatest?
4. List all of the changes of state that take place in the water cycle.
5. Use the particle model to explain how heat travels along a metal spoon being used to stir hot soup.
6. Why does perfume or aftershave lotion evaporate more quickly than water?
7. Copy and label the three diagrams on the right to show which represent solids, liquids and gases. Make an improvement to each of the diagrams so that they describe the particle model more fully.

(a)   (b)   (c)

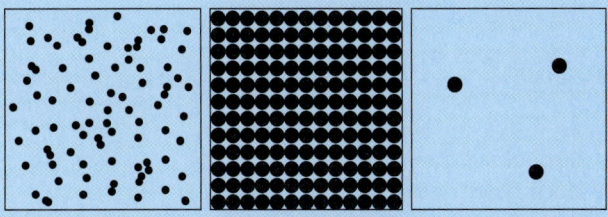

_____ _____ _____

Which states are represented by these diagrams?

Energy and particles

In this chapter you have learnt about the properties of solids, liquids and gases. In doing so, you have looked at the relationship between energy, particles and changes of state.

Energy

A simple definition of energy is that it is the ability to do work. Energy exists in many forms, such as heat, chemical, electrical and light energy. Energy can be transferred from one substance to another, and a common way of doing this is by heating.

Particles

All matter consists of particles that are constantly moving and have an attraction towards each other. They have energy because of their motion (kinetic energy). Non-moving particles have energy due to other properties such as their position (called potential energy).

Changes *of state*

Substances can exist in different states: solids, liquids and gases. In each state, the particles in the matter are at different distances from each other.

A change of state involves a change in the average distance of the particles from each other and in their freedom to move. Changes of state include melting, freezing, evaporation, boiling, condensation and sublimation.

Activities

Think

Look at the graph below. Use the graph and your understanding of the concepts of energy, particles and changes of state to complete the following activities.
(a) Write two short paragraphs describing what happens to the particles in the substance:
   (i) as they are heated   (ii) as they are cooled.
(b) Why doesn't the temperature rise continuously even though the heating occurs continuously? For example, why are there plateaus during melting and boiling? *Hint:* Think what might be happening to the particles:
   • while heat energy is being added to them without changing their state (the sloping parts of the graph)
   • while heat energy is being added to them and changing their state (the plateaus on the graph).
(c) Share your opinions on parts (a) and (b) in a class discussion.

Experiment 3.12

A HUMAN PARTICLE MODEL

Imagine that the students in your classroom are particles of a substance.

• Be a solid — all join hands to shoulders as in preparation for a march or parade.

1. Can you move freely?

• Be a liquid — join hands to shoulders but allow breaks in the rows every few students.

2. Can groups of students move freely?

• Be a gas — move freely throughout the room touching each other occasionally.

3. Why is it easier to move as a gas particle than as a liquid or solid?

4. In which state do the particles have the most kinetic (moving) energy? Why?

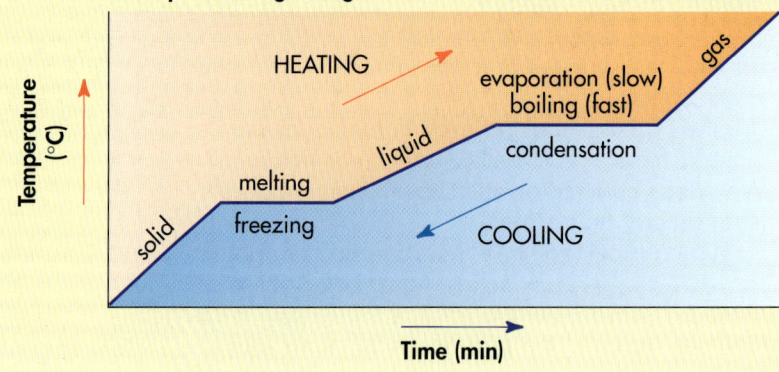
Graph showing changes when a substance is heated or cooled

Reflection

This is the time when you look back, decide if you want to change any of your original ideas on the topics in this chapter and use what you know to explain simple experiments. There are four things to do here. After discussion with your teacher, you might decide to do some or all of them.

1. Checking the survey

Revise the survey table that you completed at the beginning of the chapter. Check through it and *with a red pen* make any changes to your original responses. Also write a short note about why you made the changes.

Analyse your change of views — or your support for your original views — in a class discussion with your teacher.

2. Modelling the changes

The particle nature of solids, liquids and gases has been studied in this chapter. The exercise below will give you an opportunity to test your ideas and learn some more about the different states of matter.

Try this · A NEW USE FOR COINS

YOU WILL NEED
some 5c, 10c and 20c coins (or some small magnetic discs of different sizes)
overhead projector and a white screen (or a whiteboard)

- Students may wish to work in small groups with one member of the group presenting the group findings after the activity.
- Place your coins on the overhead projector (or magnetic discs on the whiteboard) to represent some particles packed together in a solid state.
- Now model what might happen at the particle level when the solid is heated and changes to a liquid and then to a gas.
- Present your model of the changes to the class by demonstrating what you did with the coins or discs. Use your model to explain all you know about solids, liquids and gases.
- When all groups or students have presented their models, summarise the activity by:
  (a) recording any differences of opinion among the class
  (b) recording what the teacher said to present the scientists' views
  (c) writing your own final conclusion about what happens when substances are heated, including a description of the changes that occur and any relationship between the changes and the size of the particles or the distance between the particles.

3. Using what you know

Do the two experiments on the right. (Experiment 3.13 may be done at home.) Suggest explanations for your results, then have a class discussion with your teacher. Finally, summarise the discussion and record the opinions and conclusions made in your workbook.

Experiment 3.13
FREEZING WATER

YOU WILL NEED
2 small, screw-top plastic bottles with lids

- Fill the plastic bottles with water. Put the lids on.
- Place one bottle in the freezer and the other in the refrigerator.
- After all the water in the bottle in the freezer has frozen, remove both bottles and record your observations. Does this match with what you know about substances that are cooled?
- Discuss with your teacher and the class. Try to find an explanation for what you observed.
- You may wish to try another simple experiment, in which you boil fresh water and salt water. Record the boiling temperatures for both samples and try to find an explanation for what you observed.

Experiment 3.14
MIXING WATER AND ALCOHOL

YOU WILL NEED
50 mL of water
50 mL of alcohol — ethanol
two 50 mL measuring cylinders
100 mL measuring cylinder

- Carefully measure 50 mL of water into one of the smaller measuring cylinders. (Make sure the cylinder is at eye level and measure the volume from the bottom of the meniscus.)
- In the other measuring cylinder, measure 50 mL of alcohol.
- Now take the 100 mL measuring cylinder and carefully pour both the alcohol and water into it.
- Record the final volume of liquid in the cylinder. Is it what you expected it to be? With your 'microscopic eyes' can you 'see' and explain what is happening?

CLASSIFICATION

Planet Earth has a great variety of different living things within it. Scientists classify these living things into groups on the basis of their characteristic features. In this chapter you will find keys to unlock the doors of classification and see how groups of living things have changed over time.

This photograph shows a colourful, graceful flatworm swimming through the warm waters of the Great Barrier Reef.

KEY QUESTIONS

Fire grows, moves and uses oxygen. Is it alive?

Why bother to classify living things?

How can you use a key to unlock the door to classification?

Are all living things either animals or plants?

Vertebrates are animals with backbones while invertebrates are animals without backbones. What percentage of animals are vertebrates?

Which animals have their skeletons on the outside?

Which animals have gills when young and lungs when adult?

Which two mammals lay eggs?

Which living animal is most like the extinct diprotodon?

Why do insects have a proboscis?

What did prehistoric pelycosaurs use their sail-like fins for?

KEY CONTENT

Classify living things into major groups using structural features.

Describe the changes in living things during an era of Earth's history.

Identify trends, patterns, relationships and contradictions in data and information.

Use keys to identify a range of plants and animals.

Describe why humans belong to the animal kingdom.

Thinking about Classification

This information is classified!

What does that mean? Usually, it means the information is available only to certain people who belong to a particular group, such as doctors, secret agents or government officials. When you group people or objects and give that group a name, you are classifying them.

Classification is a way of sorting or grouping. You use a rule to decide if something belongs to a group. For example, you could classify lollies according to colour.

A pile of lollies

Lollies classified using the following rule: Each lolly must be the same colour.

  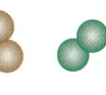

Classifying lollies

Think of two other ways you could classify lollies into different groups.

1. Classification — everyday examples

GROUP WORK ▶ Think about all the ways we classify information, objects and people. Complete a table like the one below to show as many examples as possible.

Example of classification	Rule
doctor	has medical degree
library numbering system	books on same subject placed together

2. Classification in science

GROUP WORK ▶ Classification is an important tool for scientists. Discuss the following questions.
(a) Why might a scientist want to use classification?
(b) What are some groups that scientists might use? (Also explain why it would be useful to use each grouping.)
(c) What do you think the following words mean?
(i) feature (ii) characteristic
(d) Now think only about living things. How does a scientist classify living things? Make a poster or mind map to show what your group already knows about classification.
(e) Make a mind map to show what you know about extinct animals.

3. Remembering new words

(a) The following words are scientific terms used in this chapter. In your workbook make a table like the one below to sort out the boxed words.

Words ending in:						
-don	-ene	-sperm	-phyte	-pod	-oic	Other

endothermic	nematodes	angiosperm
Eocene	porifera	arachnid
Cenozoic	xylem	dichotomous
Palaeozoic	pteridophyte	platyhelminths
procoptodon	amphibians	arthropod
proboscis	chilopod	echinoderm
gymnosperm	Oligocene	annelid
lichens	Palaeocene	phloem
diplopod	Mesozoic	bryophyte
ectothermic	epoch	crustacean
pharyngeal	mollusc	eutherian
cnidarian	vascular	

(i) Sort the words into the different columns based on their common endings.
(ii) Practise saying the words. Use the pronunciation guide at the back of the book to check any words that are new to you.
GROUP WORK ▶ (iii) In your group, take turns reading one of the columns of words you have listed.
(iv) Discuss what the words in each column might have in common.

(b) This chapter contains lots of scientific words that need to be learnt. While you read it, make a list of all the new scientific words you find and study your list every few days. You often need to see a word many times before your brain will remember it!

A useful tool for remembering new words is to write them on cards and hang them around your classroom or study area. It is usually easier to remember a word if you include its meaning and a symbol or illustration on the card, like the one below.

WORD	MEANING	SYMBOL/ILLUSTRATION
vertebrate	I have a backbone	

Is it alive?

While on a deep sea mission, you find a new form of life gliding along the sea floor. It is armour-plated, with multicoloured tentacles. How would you classify it?

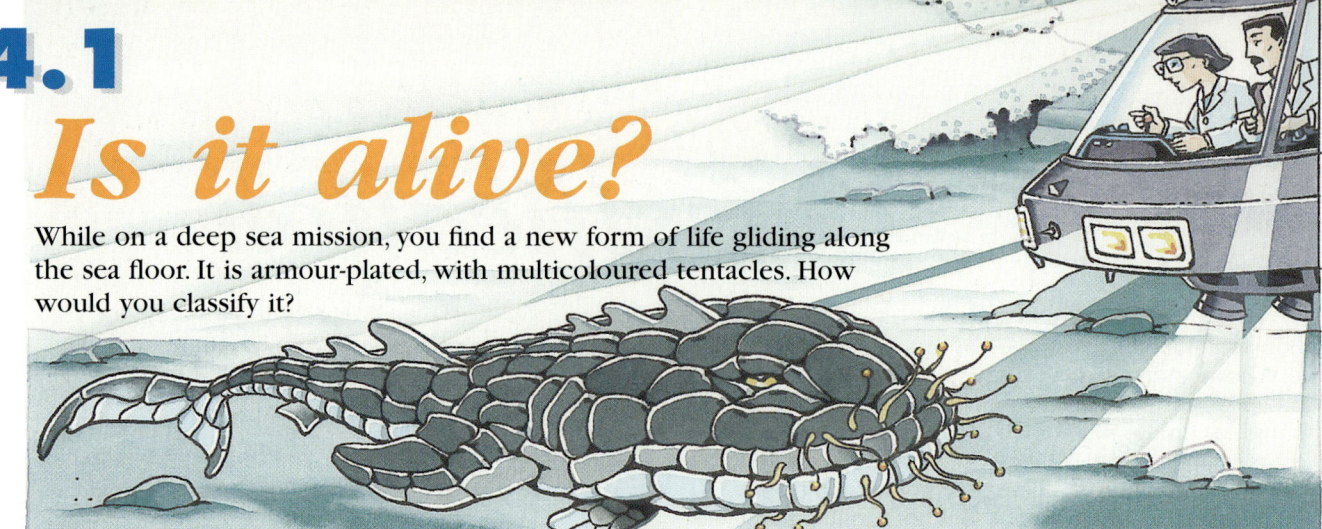

Why classify?

Classifying things into groups can make them easier to remember, and to describe and identify. For example, if you went to a supermarket to buy cornflakes, it would take you a very long time if the products were not classified into groups. Because cornflakes are classified as breakfast cereal, you know where to look.

As scientific curiosity led to the discovery of more and more living things, it became obvious that a system was needed to classify them. Scientists classify living things into groups. All living things are called **organisms**. If you were to find an unknown organism, you could describe it on the basis of the sorts of features that it shares with members of a particular group. For example, describing an organism using the word 'fish' would signify that the organism lives in water and has scales and a bony skeleton. The science of classifying organisms is called **taxonomy**. However, it is not always easy to decide into which group an organism fits. For example, a French poodle looks very different to a sheepdog but they are both dogs. A wolf looks very much like a dog, yet it is not a dog.

Today, almost two million living things have been classified by scientists. Back in the 18th century, as scientists were exploring new worlds and finding new examples to classify, they used a simple system — an organism was either in the plant kingdom or the animal kingdom. Eventually, living things were discovered that did not fit easily into these two groups. A new system was needed. Carl Linnaeus (1707–78), a Swedish biologist, came up with a system that is still used throughout the world today. This system allows all living things to be classified based on their structure. The original system developed by Linnaeus had three main kingdoms. Since then, scientists have learnt more and now use five kingdoms (see page 102), plus an extra group just for viruses. It is likely that this system will continue to evolve as new discoveries are made in the future.

Living, non-living or dead?

One of the features that can be used in forming groups is whether something is **living**, **non-living** (was never alive) or **dead**. If something is described as being dead, it means that it was once living, but no longer shows the features of something living. Some of the characteristics of living things are shown in the table on page 69.

Examples of living and non-living things

Think about this

LIVING, NON-LIVING OR DEAD

- Copy and complete the table below.

Characteristics	Robo-bilby (electronic toy)	Bilby	Bilby fossil
is able to move			
requires air			
requires water			
requires nutrition			
responds to changes in its environment			
produces waste and excretes it			
grows as it gets older			
reproduces itself			

1. Which of the three bilbies is non-living? Which characteristics does it have?
2. Which of the three bilbies is dead? Which characteristics does it have?
3. Which characteristics does the living bilby have?
- Construct another table the same as the one above but replace the bilbies with (a) paper (b) fire and (c) tree.
- Complete the table.
4. Which, of paper, fire and tree, are non-living?
5. Does the living thing have all of the characteristics listed?
6. Which characteristics does the living thing have that the non-living thing does not?

Activities

Remember

1. Why do scientists classify living things?
2. What are organisms?
3. List the characteristics that all living things have in common.
4. Which characteristics of living things are shared with non-living things?
5. How are dead things different from non-living things?

Think

1. Cave people were often only interested in two groups of living things — those that were useful to them and those that were dangerous. If you were to divide living things into groups, how many different groups would there be and what characteristics would you use?
2. Examine all the drawings of items on pages 68 and 69.
   (a) Without using the characteristics listed in the table, quickly make a list of the items in the drawings that are living, non-living and dead.
   (b) Which of the things were difficult to classify? Why?
   (c) Use the characteristics listed in the table to check that you classified each item correctly.
3. How are non-living things different from living things?
4. Use the drawings of living and non-living things on page 68 to complete the following activity.
   (a) Write down a description of each item. (Look for shape, size, colour etc.)
   (b) Divide the items into four groups. The items in each group must have some features in common. Use features other than living, non-living or dead to sort the items into groups.
   (c) Make up a name for each group.
   (d) Compare your groups with others in your class. How many different ways are there of grouping the items?
5. How are non-living things different from living and dead things?

Create

Create a list of as many living things as you can think of in 30 seconds. Create a second list of as many non-living things as you can think of in 30 seconds.
(a) Write down some differences between the two groups.
(b) Write down some similarities between the two groups.

Keys and field guides

Once the features of an organism have been noted, the information can be used to identify it using identification keys and field guides.

Dichotomous keys

The information that is used to classify organisms is sometimes put into a key. The key shown below is called a **dichotomous key**, because there are only *two* choices at each branch (dichotomous = 'cutting in two'). It shows how some foods may be divided on the basis of similarities and differences of their features.

Features such as size, colour, behaviour and habitat are not good for classification because they can change throughout the life of the organism. Using the structure of an organism is much better.

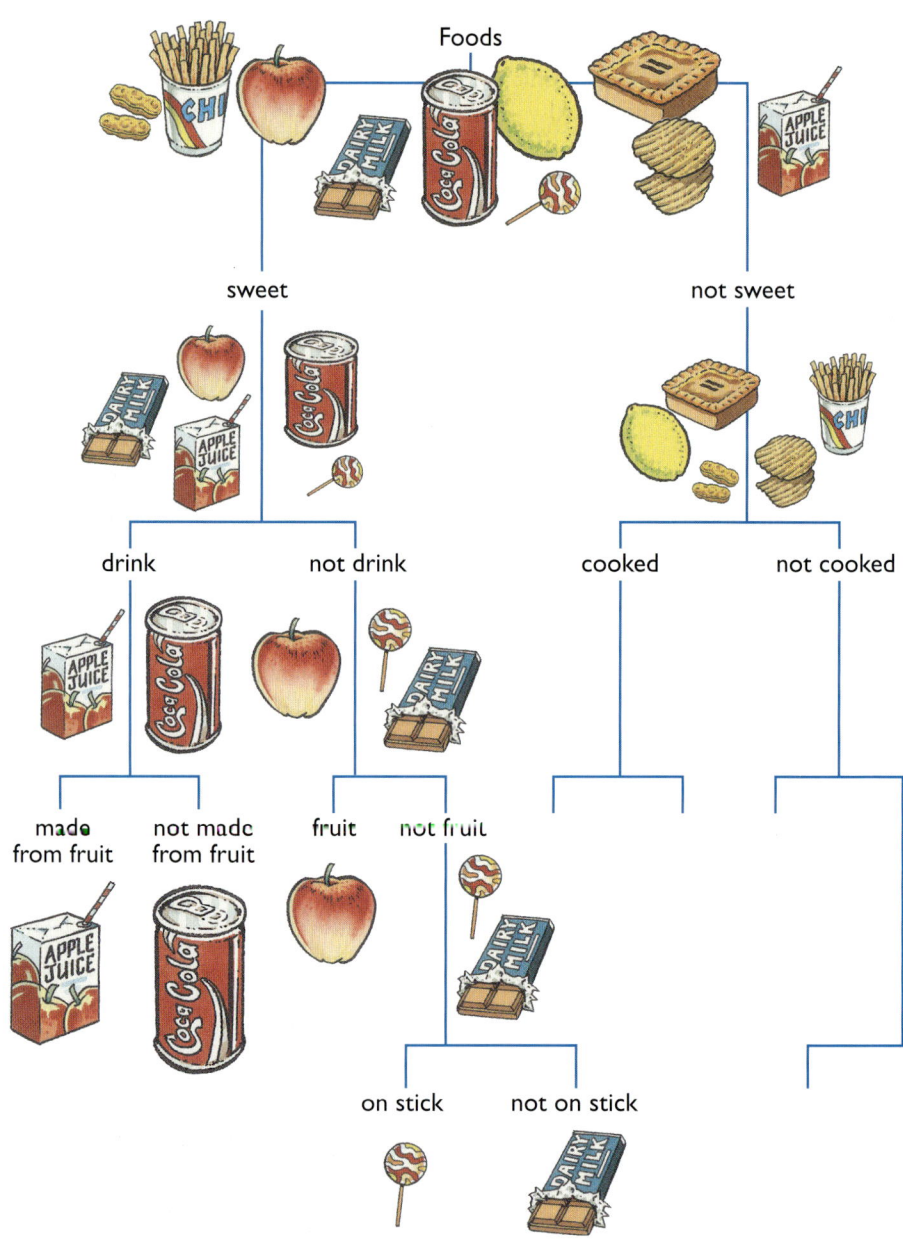

This key can be used to classify foods. The right side of the key is incomplete (see the 'Think' activity on page 71).

MAKING A CLASS FIELD GUIDE

YOU WILL NEED

paper, pencils

photograph or sketch of your partner

- Work in pairs. If there is an odd number of students in your class your teacher might agree to participate.

- Observe your partner and record data such as height, hair colour, eye colour etc.

- Interview your partner to find out some other details such as favourite music, movie, sport, colour, food etc.

- Allowing about half an A4 page for each class member, present the information and photo/sketch.

- Make the pages into a book or poster.

1. What are the benefits of a field guide?

2. Which features do you think would be most useful to include in a field guide to assist in identifying a class member? Why?

3. Which features would be most useful to include in a field guide for:
   (a) plants?
   (b) birds?
   (c) insects?

4. Describe any problems that you encountered when you were constructing the field guide.

- Use the class field guide (book or poster) see how easy it is to identify each student.

- Try making a field guide for the teachers in your school.

Field guides

Field guides are a commonly used type of reference book to help people identify organisms. These books are specially designed to assist you in 'on-the-spot' identification. They often contain brief written descriptions and pictures and are small enough to take outside when you are observing wildlife.

Eastern Yellow Robin   *Eopsaltria australis*   15 cm
Yellow-breasted robin with grey face, found in eastern and south-eastern Aust. *Juv:* dark brown streaked paler, moulting after several weeks into plumage like adult. Birds of north-east have rump bright yellow (race *chrysorrhoa*); south-eastern birds have rump olive (race *australis*). *Voice:* pre-dawn call whistle-like loud 'tewp tewp'; monotonous plaintive piping, particularly late afternoon. *Nesting:* bark cup with hanging strips of bark and/or lichen; 2–3 spotted light green eggs. *Range:* common forests, woodlands, well-planted gardens in eastern and south-eastern Aust. from about Cooktown, Qld, to Naracoorte, SA.

An entry from a field guide used to identify Australian birds

Activities

Using data

Not all keys are drawn like the one in the diagram on page 70. Use the following key to determine the identities of the dinosaurs labelled A, B, C, D and E.

KEY

1. Wings .... Pterosaur
   No wings .... *Go to 2*
2. Bony plates on back ..... Stegosaurus
   No bony plates on back ..... *Go to 3*
3. Horns .... Triceratops
   No horns .... *Go to 4*
4. Walks on two legs ... Tyrannosaurus
   Walks on four legs ...... Apatosaurus

Remember

1. What is a dichotomous key used for? Why is it called 'dichotomous'?
2. What is a field guide used for?

Think

In your workbook complete the right-hand side of the dichotomous key of foods shown on the opposite page.

4.3

Which animal?

Animals can be most easily grouped on the basis of whether they have an internal skeleton, an external skeleton, or no skeleton at all. Animals which have internal skeletons or backbones are grouped together and called **vertebrates**. Animals with external or no skeletons are referred to as **invertebrates**.

Only 5 per cent of animals are vertebrates whereas 95 per cent are invertebrates. Most of the invertebrates are insects.

Scientists classify humans as animals. Use this key to understand why.

ANIMALS

macroscopic (can be seen without a microscope) — microscopic

MICROSCOPIC ANIMALS

internal skeleton
VERTEBRATES

no internal skeleton
INVERTEBRATES

ectothermic (changing body temperature) — endothermic (constant body temperature)

feathers — hair/fur

AVES (e.g. birds)

MAMMALS (e.g. humans, dogs, possums, dolphins)

jointed legs — no legs

ARTHROPODS (e.g. insects, crabs)

external fertilisation (water required for reproduction) — internal fertilisation (no water required for reproduction)

moist, smooth skin — scaly skin

soft body usually with a shell or spiny skin — soft body, no shell

AMPHIBIANS (e.g. frogs and toads)

FISH (e.g. shark, goldfish)

REPTILES (e.g. snakes, lizards, turtles, crocodiles)

MOLLUSCS (e.g. snails, slugs) and **ECHINODERMS** (e.g. starfish)

WORMS (e.g. earthworms), **CNIDARIANS** (e.g. jelly fish) and **PORIFERA** (e.g. sponges)

Experiment 4.1   MODELLING MUSCLES AND BONES

YOU WILL NEED
2 cardboard tubes, each at least 30 cm long
sticky tape
rubber bands
large nail or other pointed object

- Cut each cardboard tube into two pieces about 15 cm long.
- Using the nail, make two holes on opposite sides of each tube. These should be about 5 cm from one end of each piece.
- Label two pieces 'Endo A' and 'Endo B' and the other two pieces 'Exo A' and 'Exo B'.
- Tape Endo A and Endo B together on one side, so that they form a hinge at the ends with the small holes.
- Cut two rubber bands and thread the cut ends through the holes from the outside.

- Tie knots so that the rubber bands can't pull back through the holes.

1. When one rubber band contracts, what happens to the one on the opposite side?

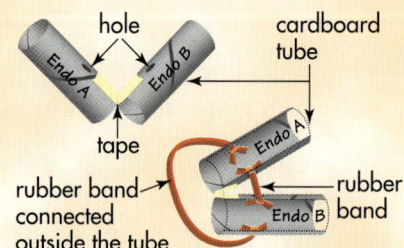

rubber band connected outside the tube

The rubber bands are like the muscles in your arm. They are attached to the bones on either side of your elbow. The arm bends at the joint, when the muscle contracts.

- Tape Exo A and Exo B together in the same way as Endo A and Endo B.

- Cut another two rubber bands and thread the cut ends through the holes so that they run *inside* the tube.
- Make sure that they are stretched very tightly, and then tie knots on the outside of the tubes.

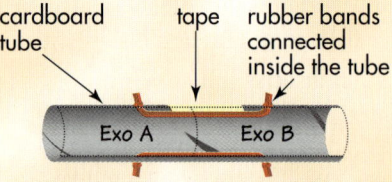

cardboard tube — tape — rubber bands connected inside the tube

The rubber bands are like the muscles in an insect's limb. When a muscle contracts, the joint on which it operates straightens.

2. Draw sketches of each and record your observations when the joint is moved.
3. Describe how the two skeletons are different.

Endoskeletons and *exoskeletons*

Did you know that 75 per cent of all animals in the world have a **skeleton** on the outside of the body? These external skeletons are called **exoskeletons**. They may be thick and hard like those of crabs and lobsters or thin and tough as those of ants and centipedes. As these animals grow they sometimes moult or discard their old exoskeleton before growing a bigger one.

Although exoskeletons are good for jumping and swimming, they do not allow flexibility for the twisting and turning actions that are possible for animals with an inside skeleton (**endoskeleton**). In an animal with an exoskeleton the muscles are attached inside the skeleton, whereas the muscles in an animal with an endoskeleton are connected onto the outside. Our endoskeleton is an internal skeleton which is made of bone or cartilage and clothed in muscle and skin.

No *skeleton* at all

Some animals, such as worms and jellyfish, have no skeleton at all. The body is supported by the pressure of fluid within it. What do you think would happen if a lot of fluid was lost? How can animals without skeletons move?

Earthworms expand and contract their bodies to burrow through the soil. They use two sets of muscles to do this. One set of muscles wraps around the body. When these contract, the body becomes long and thin, enabling the worm to poke into crevices in the soil. The second set of muscles runs along the length of the body. When these contract, the worm becomes short and fat. This helps to anchor the worm in place, pushing the soil apart to form a burrow. By shortening the rest of its body, the worm pulls itself up and moves through the soil.

Long and thin one moment, short and fat the next. A worm burrows through the soil.

CRASH DIVE!

Activities

Using data

Use the information provided in the animal classification key on page 72 to answer the following questions.

1. Which two groups of organisms (a) have the most in common and which (b) have the least in common?
   (i) fish and worms
   (ii) fish and amphibians
   (iii) reptiles and birds
   (iv) mammals and birds
   (v) molluscs and worms
2. Describe the characteristics of an organism that was classified as:
   (a) an arthropod
   (b) a reptile
   (c) a mammal
   (d) a fish
   (e) a cnidarian (formerly known as a coelenterate).
3. Explain why humans are classified as animals.

Remember

1. Which feature divides animals into two main groups?
2. Define the following terms: vertebrates, invertebrates, endoskeleton, exoskeleton.
3. Which are more common on Earth, vertebrates or invertebrates?
4. In which ways may invertebrates differ from each other?
5. (a) Give examples of three different vertebrates and three different invertebrates.
   (b) Construct a key to separate these animals.

6. Describe the difference between the way in which muscles are attached in animals with endoskeletons and in those with exoskeletons.
7. Worms have no skeleton and no legs. How do they move?

Think

1. On a bushwalk, Briana found two animals. The first animal had a backbone, no gills and scaly skin. The second animal did not have a backbone, a jointed covering or a shell.
   (a) Use the classification table to suggest which group each of the animals belonged to.
   (b) Was either animal difficult to classify? If so, explain why.
2. Consider the following animals: whale, shark, lizard, slug, snake, bat, kookaburra, possum and frog.
   (a) Design a key to classify these organisms into two groups.
   (b) Explain why you chose the characteristics you did.
   (c) Design a key to classify these organisms into three groups.
   (d) Explain why you chose the characteristics you did.
   (e) Look at the classification key and use these characteristics to classify the animals.
   (f) Compare your groupings in (a), (c) and (e). How were they different? What does this suggest about the nature of classifying organisms?

Vertebrates

Vertebrates are animals that have backbones made of bones called **vertebrae**. Members of this group also usually possess pairs of **pharyngeal slits** or gill-like openings in the neck region. These slits, however, may change or be lost during fetal development, as in the case of humans. Other features enable vertebrates to be further divided into seven subgroups: mammals, birds, amphibians, reptiles, cartilaginous fish, bony fish and jawless fish. Animals that can maintain a constant body temperature are called warm blooded or **endothermic**. Those animals whose body temperature changes are called cold blooded or **ectothermic**.

Mammals

Characteristics:
- skin with hair or fur
- females have mammary glands that secrete milk
- constant body temperature.

Examples: wallaby, possum, echidna, dog, human, dolphin, whale.

An echidna

Aves (birds)

Characteristics:
- skin with feathers
- eggs with hard shell
- beak for feeding
- constant body temperature.

Examples: kookaburra, emu, penguin, cockatoo, galah, parrot, seagull.

Reptiles

Characteristics:
- skin with scales
- membranous or leathery-shelled eggs laid on land
- lungs for breathing
- changing body temperature.

Examples: snake, lizard, tortoise, crocodile.

Amphibia

Characteristics:
- eggs without a shell, usually laid in water
- soft, moist skin without scales
- larvae usually live in water and have gills
- adults usually live on land and have lungs
- changing body temperature.

Examples: frog, toad, salamander.

A tree frog

Fish *with a cartilaginous* skeleton

Characteristics:
- found only in water
- skeleton made of cartilage
- visible pharyngeal slits
- skin with scales
- some have fins
- gills for breathing
- most lay eggs
- changing body temperature.

Examples: shark, stingray.

A stingray

Fish *with a bony* skeleton

Characteristics:
- found only in water
- skeleton made of bone
- covered pharyngeal slits
- skin with scales
- most have gills
- most have fins
- changing body temperature.

Examples: goldfish, barramundi, Murray cod, bream, flathead.

Jawless *fish*

Characteristics:
- found in water
- no paired fins
- gills for breathing.

Examples: lamprey, hagfish.

Lampreys

Dimetrodon was a meat-eating pelycosaur. The pelycosaurs were the most successful reptiles of the Permian period. They looked like big lizards with huge sail-like fins on their backs. The pelycosaurs used this 'sail' to regulate their body temperature. They could stand in the early morning sun with the sail arranged towards the sun to warm them up. To cool off they could turn it into the wind. It is thought that this fin arrangement was an early stage in the development of temperature regulation of mammals.

Dimetrodon —
a mammal-like reptile

Activities

Remember

1. What two features do most vertebrates have in common?
2. Summarise the information about each of the vertebrate groups in a table.
3. To which group of vertebrates do each of the following animals belong?
   (a) snake   (e) emu
   (b) cane toad   (f) shark
   (c) goldfish   (g) lamprey
   (d) whale   (h) turtle
4. What did pelycosaurs use their huge sail-like fins on their backs for?

Think

1. Who am I?
   Name the group to which each of the following animals belong.
   (a) I have lungs but no legs.
       My offspring are found in membranous-shelled eggs and use lungs to breathe.
   (b) I have moist skin but no scales, and two pairs of legs.
       Although I have lungs and live on land, my young usually live in water and use gills to breathe.
   (c) I have a constant body temperature, feathers, and lay eggs with a hard shell.
   (d) I have a changing body temperature, gills and fins, and a skeleton made of cartilage.
2. Goldfish and sharks are fish. Apart from their size, how are they different from each other?
3. Why is it thought that the pelycosaurs were a link between reptiles and mammals?
4. Match the translations to the scientific names.

English translation	Scientific name
(a) Greek: living a double life	(i) Reptilia
(b) Latin: creeping	(ii) Aves
(c) Latin: birds	(iii) Amphibia

5. Name five ectothermic and five endothermic animals.

Create

Design a dichotomous key to separate and classify the seven groups of vertebrates described on pages 74 and 75.

Mammals

There are three different types of mammals: the placentals, marsupials and monotremes. These groups differ from each other in the way that they give birth to their young.

Placental *mammals*

Placental (also known as eutherian) **mammals** are very well developed when they are born. They grow inside the body of their mother, attached by a cord to the **placenta**, which provides their food supply. After they are born the mother produces milk for them from mammary glands. Most mammals, including humans, are placental mammals. Other examples include horses, mice and cats.

Marsupials

Marsupials are mammals that give birth when their young are at a very early stage of development. Almost all marsupials have a pouch. Kangaroos, wombats, possums and koalas are all members of this group. The newborn marsupials, although blind and naked, crawl from the birth canal to their mother's pouch. They remain in the pouch, feeding on milk from the nipples inside, until they are ready to face the outside world. Two-thirds of the world's marsupials live in Australia — the rest are in North and South America.

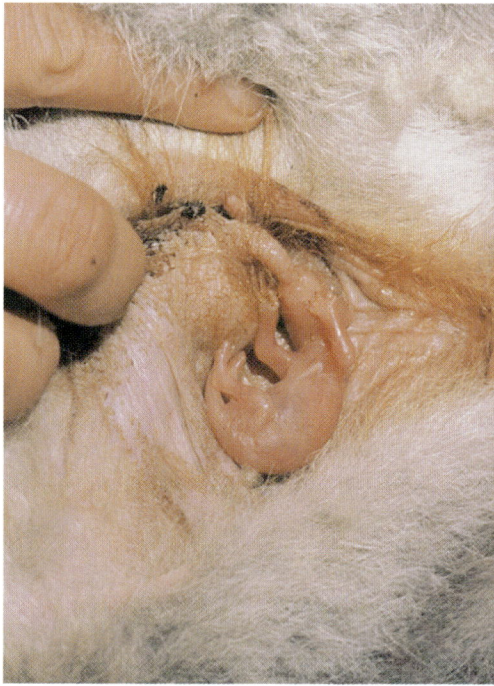

Kangaroo joey: 'When I was first born I looked just like a pink jelly bean. I climbed up into my mother's pouch and attached myself to a milk teat. I stayed there for 12 months. When I get too big to get into the pouch, mum says I can poke my head in for a drink until I am 18 months old.'

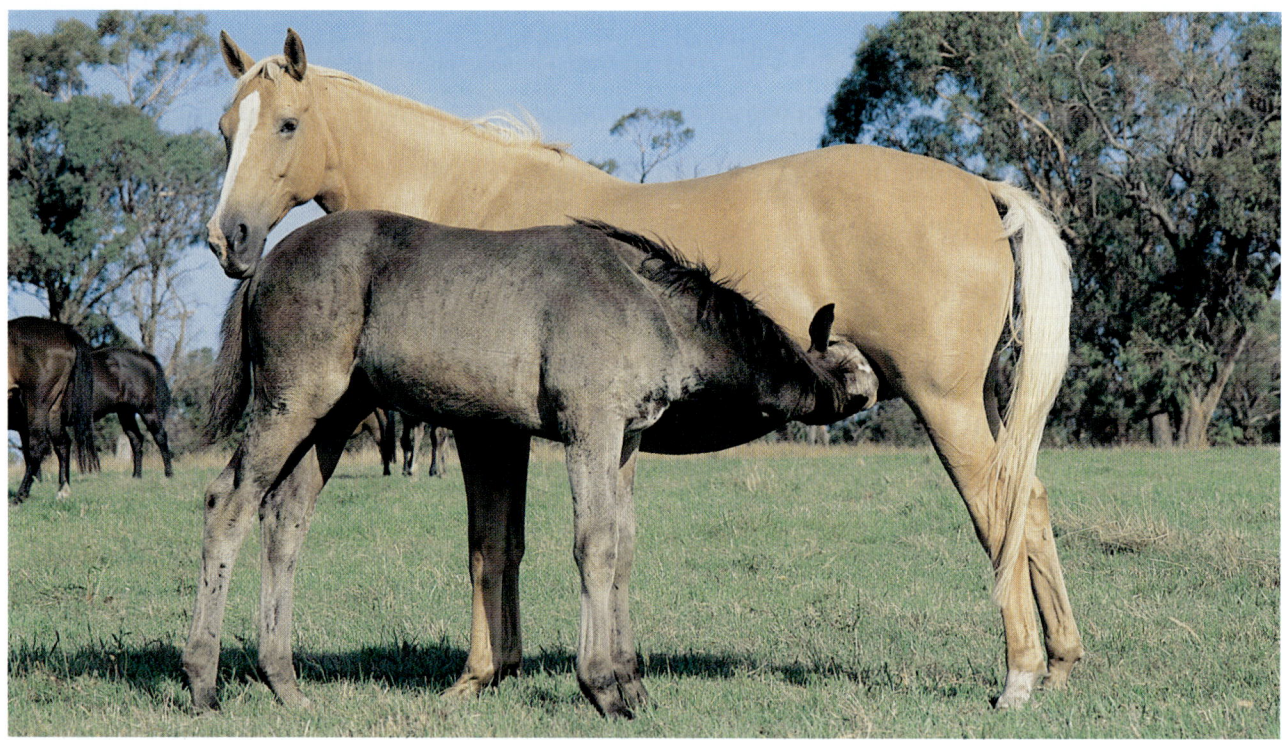

Foal: 'I am able to stand up within a few minutes of being born. I feed on my mother's milk for several months and although I can move about independently I like to stay close to her. After about six months I will move away from my mother to be with other horses of the same age.'

Monotremes

Monotremes are found only in Australia and some nearby islands. It is thought that they represent an early branch of primitive mammals that evolved in relative isolation on our island continent. There are only two types of living monotremes — the platypus and the echidna. Both lay leathery-shelled eggs and, after hatching, the young feed on milk like other mammals.

During spring, the female platypus makes a special nesting burrow, blocks the entrance and then lays up to three eggs. The eggs are held close to her body and about 10 days later they hatch. The young remain in the burrow for about four months, feeding on milk that oozes from the glands on the mother's abdomen.

Monotremes, such as the platypus, are the only mammals that lay eggs.

S C I F A C T S

The first platypus kept at the Bronx Zoo in New York ate 540 earthworms, 200 mealworms, 30 shrimps, 2 eggs and 2 frogs in just one day. Its own body weight was only 1.5 kg!

What kind *of creature is* this?

When European explorers returned from Australia with stories of 'strange' animals such as kangaroos, wallabies, koalas and wombats, people were surprised. Australian animals seemed so different from those common in Europe and other countries.

Imagine their disbelief when the platypus was first described to them. This strange animal had webbed feet and a bill like a duck, but it had no feathers. It laid leathery eggs like lizards and crocodiles, but it did not have scales on its skin. It also had fur and a large tail like that of an otter but, like a reptile, it had only one opening for ejecting faeces and urine.

In London in 1799, an Australian sailor presented a platypus specimen to Dr George Shaw, a prominent biologist of the time. It was so different that Shaw considered it a hoax and tried to cut off the duck-bill with scissors. The scissor-marks are still visible on the preserved platypus skin in the British Museum (Natural History) in London.

The reason for the existence of Australia's unique animals like the platypus is Australia's isolation from the other continents when they separated millions of years ago. The animals evolved over time to be well suited to the unique Australian environment.

Activities

Remember

1. Construct a three-column table and use it to summarise the main distinguishing characteristics of each of the three groups of mammals.
2. How are marsupials different from all other animals?
3. How did placental mammals get their name?
4. To which group of animals does the echidna belong? What other animal belongs to this group?

Create

Write a story, play or poem about the life of a placental, marsupial or monotreme baby.

Investigate

1. Find out more about one placental mammal, marsupial or monotreme and then present your information in a poster.
2. Find out about dugongs and why they are thought to be the basis of mermaid myths.
3. Elephant calves may drink 11.4 litres of milk a day. Find out:
   (a) whether an elephant baby uses its trunk or its mouth when suckling
   (b) how much milk some other mammals drink per day, and then summarise your results in a table or graph.
4. Did you know that adult hedgehogs have 5000 spines? So that the birth canal is not damaged when the mother is giving birth, the initial spines of a newborn are covered with a layer of skin. The spines pop through hours after birth. Although hedgehogs are mammals and they look a little like echidnas because of their spines, they are not classified as monotremes.
   (a) Find out whether hedgehogs are placental mammals or marsupials.
   (b) How do hedgehogs differ from echidnas?
   (c) A porcupine has spines as well. What type of mammal is a porcupine?
   (d) How are porcupines different from hedgehogs and echidnas?

4.6

Yesterday's marsupials

Marsupial mammals have existed in Australia for about 35 million years. Visiting Pleistocene Australia you would have seen large, stocky, wombat-like *Diprotodon*, fearsome lion-like *Thylacoleo* and wolf-like *Thylacinus*.

Giant kangaroo

The extinct giant kangaroo, *Procoptodon*, was heavily built and stood about 2.5 metres high. Procoptodons may have weighed about four times as much as the largest kangaroos of today. They had a short face and deep skull with huge molar teeth. Their molars may have helped them to eat tough plant foods. Procoptodons may have used their very long forelimbs to pull down the branches of trees and shrubs.

Diprotodons

The members of this group are all extinct. They were the largest of all the marsupials. *Diprotodon optatum*, often referred to as the diprotodon, was the largest known marsupial to have ever lived. The skeleton of the diprotodon suggests that the animal was about the size of a rhinoceros, being about 3 metres long and possibly weighing about 2 tonnes.

Timeline of the Cenozoic era — the age of mammals

Period	Epoch (millions of years ago)	Some marsupial fossil finds and major mammal events
QUATERNARY	HOLOCENE (recent) 0.01 mya–present	• Humans investigate Earth's history. • Fossil finds provide evidence of Earth's past history.
QUATERNARY	PLEISTOCENE 1.64–0.01 mya	• Most of the large Pleistocene marsupials became extinct about 15 000–30 000 years ago. • Aborigines arrive in Australia possibly about 55 000 years ago.
TERTIARY	PLIOCENE 5.2–1.64 mya	• Lots of diprotodons and grazing kangaroos. • Many giant grazing marsupials became extinct. • *Homo habilis*, the earliest known human, appears in East Africa.
TERTIARY	MIOCENE 23.5–5.2 mya	• Primitive marsupial 'mice' and 'tapirs' found at Lake Eyre, South Australia and diprotodons at Bullock Creek, Northern Territory. • Lots of marsupial mammals in Australia and South America.
TERTIARY	OLIGOCENE 35.5–23.5 mya	• Fossils of diprotodontids and a relative of pygmy possum found in Australia. • First marsupials appear in Australia about 23 million years ago. • First primates appear.
TERTIARY	EOCENE 56.5–35.5 mya	• Lots of marsupial fossils from this epoch found in North and South America. • Swimming and flying mammals appear.
TERTIARY	PALEOCENE 65–56.5 mya	• Dinosaurs became extinct about 65 million years ago. • More mammals around after dinosaurs became extinct.

The Cenozoic Era is one of the five eras used to describe the history of Earth.

short-faced kangaroo

giant wombat

diprotodon

flightless bird

diprotodon

This illustration shows some of the animals that inhabited Australia in the Tertiary period. Others included long-beaked echidnas (*Zaglossus*), marsupial lions, koalas, possums, wallabies, kangaroos and goannas. Much of the Australian landscape we recognise today was formed during this period. The Warrumbungle and Nandewar ranges were formed by volcanic activity during the Tertiary period. Mt Canobolas, Barrington Tops and the Liverpool Range were also centres of volcanic activity at this time.

Activities

Using data

1. Use the timeline to answer the following questions.
   (a) List the five epochs in the Tertiary period in order of most recent to least recent.
   (b) In which epoch did marsupials appear in Australia? How do we know this?
   (c) Earth's greatest ice age was in the Pliocene epoch. When was this, and what other events occurred during this time?
2. The first fish and amphibians appeared on the Earth in the Palaeozoic era (230–570 mya). Reptiles and mammals first walked the Earth in the Mesozoic era (65–230 mya). Draw a timeline to display this information.
3. Look up other sources to find what other important events occurred, and add these to your timeline.

Remember

1. Describe two features of the following animals:
   (a) *Diprotodon optatum*   (b) *Procoptodon*.
2. State the differences between *Procoptodon* and the largest of today's kangaroos. Suggest reasons for the differences.

Think

Look at the illustration of prehistoric animals above.
1. To which animals alive today are they most similar? Give reasons for your answers.
2. How are present-day wombats different from their ancient ancestors?

Investigate

1. Find out more about Australia's prehistoric marsupials and then present your information as a poster, poem, song or story.
2. Find out about the different climates, environments and organisms for one of the epochs in the Cenozoic era and then write a story about an imaginary journey back into Australia's past.
3. Besides the Cenozoic, what are the other four eras used to describe the history of Earth? Draw a timeline showing all five eras, including their periods, times in millions of years and any other information you can locate.

4.7
Invertebrates

Invertebrates are animals which do not have backbones. About 95 per cent of all animals are members of this group.

Platyhelminths
Characteristics:
- flat body with no segments
- head-like region
- mouth opening but no anus.

Examples: tapeworm, fluke, planarian.

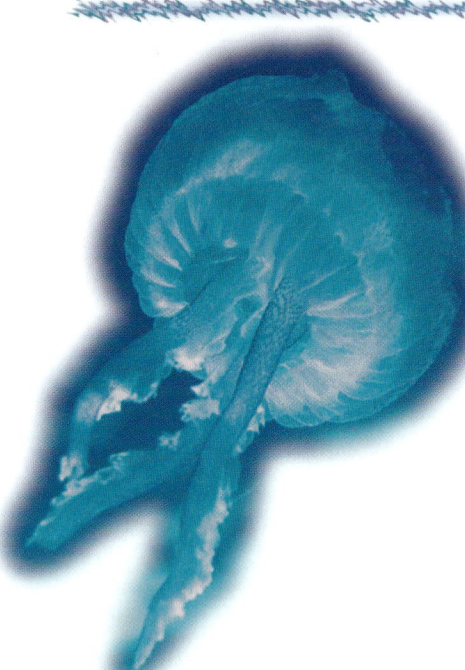

A jellyfish

Cnidarians
Characteristics:
- most live in the sea; a few in fresh water
- soft, hollow body
- only one body opening
- live singly or in colonies
- tentacles with stinging cells
- no body organs such as heart or lungs.

Examples: coral, sea anemone, hydra, bluebottle, jellyfish.

A trapdoor spider

Arthropods
Characteristics:
- found in land and in water
- segmented bodies
- exoskeleton
- jointed and paired legs
- most have antennae and compound eyes
- most that live on land use tubes (spiracles) in the side of the body to breathe
- most that live in water use gills to breathe.

Examples: tick, ant, silverfish, crayfish, scorpion, butterfly, millipede, centipede, spider, crab, fly, mosquito.

Nematodes
Characteristics:
- worm-like body with no segments
- mouth and anus
- found in water, soil, plants and animals.

Examples: threadworm, heartworm.

Echinoderms
Characteristics:
- found only in the sea
- spiny skin and arms that radiate from the centre of the body
- tube feet for movement
- mouth and anus
- body pattern based on five parts.

Examples: brittle-star, sea urchin, starfish, sea cucumber.

Poriferans
Characteristics:
- found in water
- spongy body with many holes
- food and water enter through tiny holes in body
- wastes go out through a single large opening
- usually fixed in one place to rocks or shells
- skeleton made of glassy or chalky needles, or spongy fibres.

Examples: bath sponge, glass sponge.

Annelids
Characteristics:
- most found in water; some in soil
- segmented worms
- round, soft-bodied
- take in air through moist skin.

Examples: leech, earthworm, beach worm.

A blue-ringed octopus

Molluscs
Characteristics:
- most found in water; some on seashore and land
- soft, unsegmented body
- usually covered with a protective shell
- well-formed head with eyes and/or tentacles
- mouth and anus
- muscular foot for movement.

Examples: snail, slug, octopus, limpet, clams, squid, oysters, mussels.

Activities

Remember

1. What is an invertebrate?
2. To which group of invertebrates does each of the animals in the photographs on page 80 belong?

Think

1. Use the dichotomous key to classify an octopus.
   (a) To which group does it appear to belong?
   (b) Check the lists of characteristics to see if the answer you gave to (a) was correct. If you find that you were incorrect, suggest a reason why.
   (c) Classification is not always straightforward. Use the lists of characteristics to design a dichotomous key of your own that will make it easier to classify an octopus.
   (d) Test your key by using it to classify a snail, a starfish and an earthworm. Does your key seem to work?
2. Compare the characteristics of slugs, earthworms and snails.
   (a) What features do all three animals have in common?
   (b) Which two appear to be most similar?
   (c) Which two are in the same group?
   (d) Do you agree with this classification? Explain.

Investigate

1. Cnidarians possess tentacles that can sting. Find out about the tentacles of three different cnidarians.
2. Echinoderms' bodies can usually be divided into five parts. Carefully examine pictures or specimens of any three animals from this group. How are their body plans similar and how are they different?
3. Carry out a dissection of a squid or octopus.

Using data

1. Use the lists of features of the invertebrate groups to state which group (or groups):
   (a) has jointed and paired legs
   (b) usually has a hard shell
   (c) can have tentacles
   (d) has a body with many holes.
2. Annelids, platyhelminths and nematodes are all worm-like in appearance. Describe how they are separated into different groups.
3. Use the dichotomous key below to classify each of the following invertebrates. As you work down from the top of the key, list the characteristics of the animal that enabled you to classify it.
   Example: snail: no legs, shell (usually), soft body, hard shell.
   (a) earthworm   (c) oyster
   (b) crab   (d) spider

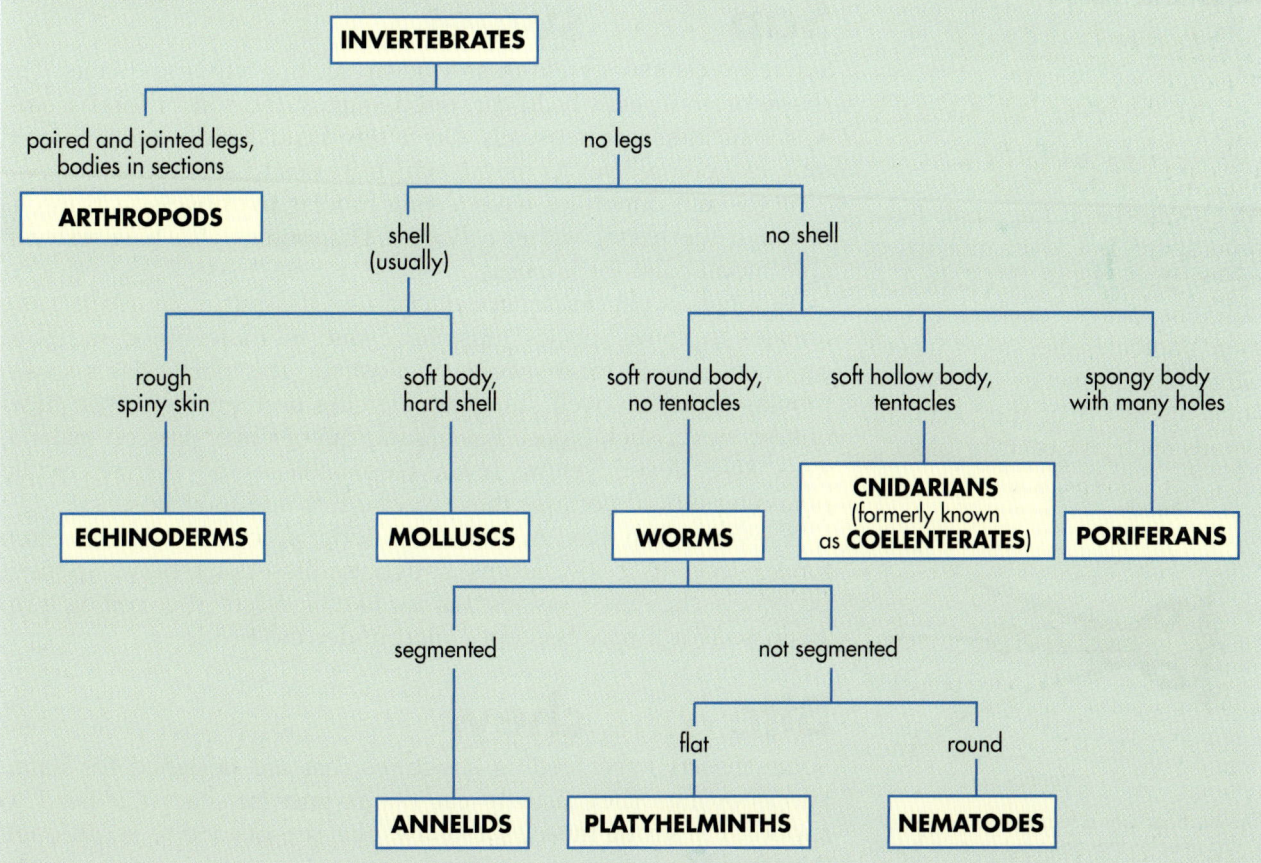

Buzz off

Feel a little itchy some mornings? Did you feel something bite you in your sleep? Was it an insect? All insects belong to the group known as arthropods.

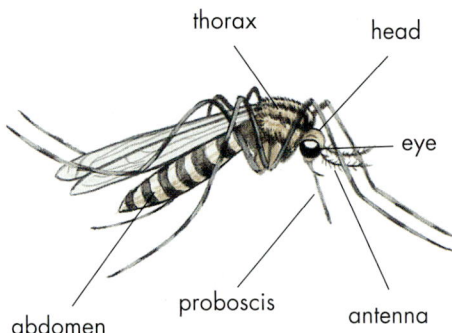

Insects' bodies are divided into three parts — the head, the thorax (chest) and the abdomen (stomach) — and have three pairs of legs attached. Most have either one or two pairs of wings, a characteristic that separates them from any other invertebrate animal.

Buzz off — keep that proboscis to yourself!

All insects have the same basic mouthparts but, over millions of years, these have developed in different ways depending on their particular diet. Most insects either bite off pieces of food and chew them up or they suck up liquids such as nectar or blood.

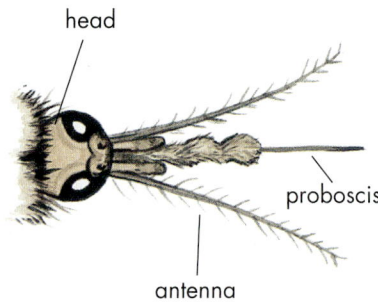

The proboscis of a female mosquito has sharp needles that poke out when a blood vessel in its victim is pierced.

A mosquito plunges its proboscis into a sleeping victim.

Sap *and* sweet *suckers*

Some insects may obtain their food by sucking sap from plants. The shape of an insect's head can often suggest the sort of food it eats. A sap-sucking insect usually has a tiny head with a long, pointed tube extending from its mouth which it uses to suck up sap.

Moths and butterflies have a long tubular **proboscis** that unrolls to reach the nectar within a flower. Dragonflies also have extendable mouthparts for hunting.

Although adult mosquitoes feed on the sugar in plants, the females in some species must have one or more blood meals to produce eggs. In most species of mosquito the female has a sharp, tubular proboscis well suited to piercing and sucking. Male mosquitoes never suck blood. Female mosquitoes may pass on malaria, Ross River fever, yellow fever, elephantiasis and filariasis while obtaining blood, because they inject saliva into their hosts.

A hawk moth has an unusually long proboscis — it is often longer than its body. Moths and butterflies don't blow up their proboscis; they use muscles that act like an elastic rod, coiling it up again so that it may be kept coiled under the head.

Bite *and* chew

Some insects have feeding structures that are designed for biting and chewing. They usually eat plants and have a large head to support the strong muscles and jaws that are needed to get through the tough plant tissue.

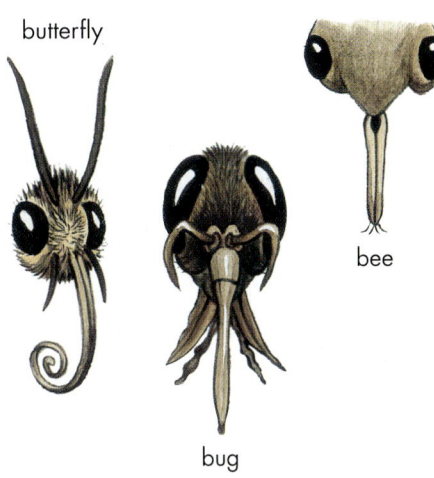

butterfly

bee

bug

Some different types of proboscis

Experiment 4.2 FLY FEEDING

Have you ever watched a fly feed? They have sponge-like feeding parts that are kept hidden when they are not eating. Flies don't just walk all over their food, they use their feet to taste it at the same time.

YOU WILL NEED
a glass jar with a lid or cover
teaspoon
1 teaspoon of sugar or honey
5 teaspoons of water
food colouring
a hand lens
a housefly in a jar

- Stir five teaspoons of water, one teaspoon of sugar or honey and a few drops of colouring until the sugar has dissolved.

- Using the tip of the spoon, place a few drops of the feeding solution on the inside wall of the glass jar.
- Gently transfer the housefly into your jar and put the lid on. You should not touch the fly. It can be transferred by tipping another jar over your feeding jar and carefully removing the lid.
- Use the hand lens to carefully watch what happens when the fly's feet touch the coloured feeding solution.

1. Draw a diagram showing the feeding parts of the fly.
2. Make a summary of your observations of the feeding fly.
3. Why do you think the food colouring was added to the feeding solution?

Activities

Remember

1. What is a proboscis used for?
2. Describe the mouthparts of the bedbug that enable it to feed on humans.
3. What do the shapes of the heads of insects tell you about the way they live?
4. Describe the types of heads and mouthparts of insects that obtain their food by sucking sap.
5. Describe how flies feed.
6. List some diseases that may be passed on by mosquitoes.
7. What special feeding characteristics do hawk moths have?

Think

Describe the likely diet of an insect with feeding structures designed for:
(a) sucking
(b) biting and chewing.

Investigate

1. Use a magnifying glass or stereo microscope to observe and sketch the heads of a range of insects. Pay special attention to the parts that may be involved in feeding. Suggest what types of food each of the insects might eat and how they might obtain these.
2. Find out more about how flies and other insects feed. Present your information in a poster.

Create

Make face masks to demonstrate the feeding parts of several different insects.

4.9
Which plant?

More than twenty-three centuries ago, a Greek philosopher by the name of Aristotle developed one of the first widely used classification schemes. He divided plants into groups on the basis of their type of stem. Although this is still a useful system, like most classification systems it has limitations.

The features used to classify plants today are generally structural ones such as seeds, roots, stems, flowers and leaves. The key below shows how these features may be used to divide plants into five groups.

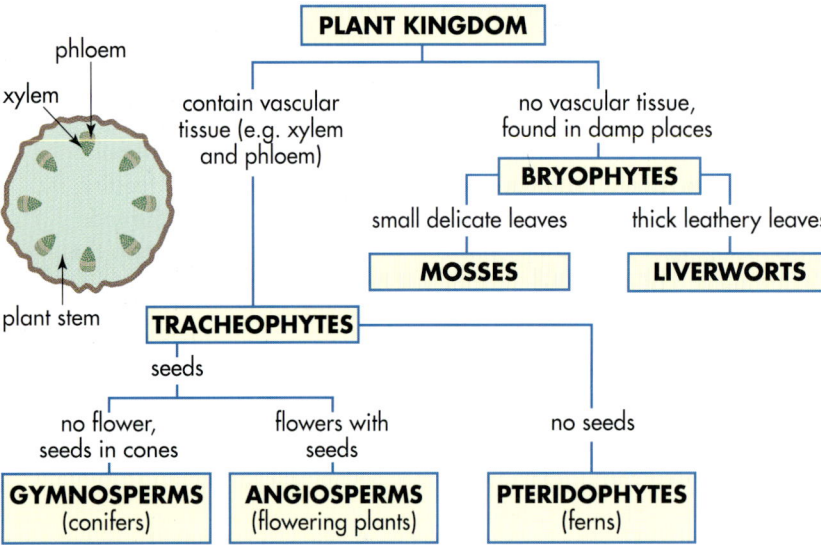

Plants that contain vascular tissue, such as ferns, conifers and flowering plants, belong to the group Tracheophyta (= 'windpipe' + 'plant') group. Vascular tissue consists of a system of cells making up tube structures that carry water and nutrients along the stem of a plant. Mosses and liverworts do not contain vascular tissue and are classified as Bryophyta (= 'moss' + 'plant').

Gymnosperm (*conifers*)

Characteristics:
- found on land
- have true roots, stems and leaves
- no flowers
- form seeds between scales of a woody cone
- most have fine, needle-like leaves.

Examples: cypress, pine, cedar.

The seed cone of the bristlecone pine

Angiosperms (*flowering plants*)

Characteristics:
- most found on land
- most common type of plant
- produce flowers, fruits and seeds
- have true roots, stems and leaves

A waratah flower

Examples: fruit trees, cereal crops, wattles, vegetables.

Pteridophytes (*ferns*)

Characteristics:
- found in moist, shaded areas
- no flowers, cones or seeds
- spores, rather than seeds, found on the underside of leaf-like fronds
- have proper roots and stems
- most less than a metre high (except tree ferns).

An Australian fern

Examples: maidenhair fern, tree fern, bracken.

Bryophytes (*mosses and liverworts*)

Characteristics:
- found mainly in damp places
- root-like structures very fine and hair-like
- simple leaves or leaf-like structures
- usually only several centimetres long
- spores are formed in a capsule.

Examples: mosses, liverworts.

An Australian moss (top) and liverwort (bottom)

The *language of* plants

Plants can be described using different words, depending on a person's purpose. For example, in describing a bottlebrush tree:

- a scientist would refer to its correct botanical name as *Callistemon citrinus* and say it belonged to the angiosperm or flowering plant group

A bottlebrush flower

- a gardener might say 'I planted a new tree called a bottlebrush'
- a horticulturist would tend to use both scientific and common names.

Words to describe groups of plants

Scientific terms	Common names
bryophytes	mosses and liverworts
pteridophytes	ferns
angiosperms	flowering plants
gymnosperms	conifers
tracheophytes	plants with stems

Gardeners use words like tree, shrub, herb and grass to describe groups of plants. To a scientist, a tree could belong to the angiosperm or gymnosperm group. A scientist would carefully examine the characteristics of the plant to find out if it had flowers, seeds and fruit, or cones containing seeds. The scientific names for individual plants and groups of plants are more specific than the common names.

Activities

Remember

Make a table to summarise the characteristics of bryophytes, pteridophytes, angiosperms and gymnosperms. Include these headings:

Name of group	Where found	Type of stem	Flowers or no flowers	Seeds or spores	Other information	Examples
bryophytes						

Think

1. Design a key which uses the following features, in the order in which they are shown, to separate ferns, mosses and liverworts, conifers and flowering plants.
   (a) seeds or no seeds
   (b) seeds in cones or seeds in flowers
   (c) stem or no stem
2. Make a list of ten plants you already know. To which plant group does each belong? Alternatively, walk around your school grounds and list some characteristics of the different plants. Then draw up a table or key to distinguish between them.

Investigate

1. Design a key which would help a gardener tell the difference between trees, shrubs, herbs and grasses. Ask at least five people to test your key.
2. (a) Find three examples of a tree, shrub, herb and grass. Observe and record five characteristics for each of these plants.
   (b) Using your observations, decide to which scientific plant group each example belongs.
   (c) Use field guides or keys to identify the plants you observed.

SCIENCE issues

PLANTS NO MORE

Algae, fungi and lichen were once considered as the most primitive plants on Earth. Not only did they not produce flowers or seeds, but they also did not have roots, stems or leaves, and some of them were unicellular (consisting of one cell). Based on current information, many biologists no longer consider them as part of the plant kingdom, but classify them within their own special group (see page 102).

Some of the characteristics of algae, fungi and lichens are outlined below.

Algae

Characteristics:
- all live in water
- often unicellular
- no true roots, stems, leaves or flowers
- no special tissue for transporting food or water
- divided into groups depending on their colour
- make their own food using photosynthesis.

Examples: diatoms, euglena, 'Neptune's necklace', sea lettuce.

Giant kelp (seaweed) is an alga.

Fungi

Characteristics:
- no true roots, stems, leaves or flowers
- usually multicellular; some unicellular
- no chlorophyll and unable to make their own food
- usually obtain their food from other living or dead organisms
- produce enzymes which break down food outside their cells
- broken-down food is absorbed through their cell walls.

Examples: yeasts, moulds, mushrooms, toadstools.

A maiden veil fungus

Lichens

Characteristics:
- found on bare rocks, bark of trees, in cold polar regions and on mountain tops
- no true roots, stems, leaves or flowers
- made up of two different organisms: an alga and a fungus
- algal cells live among tiny fungal threads
- algal cells photosynthesise and supply the fungus with food
- fungus provides protection and anchorage for the algal cells
- grow very slowly and are extremely long-lived
- often responsible for breaking down rocks, allowing other organisms to grow.

Several types of lichen may grow together.

The key below can be used to separate algae, fungi and lichens from plants.

1a	No roots, stems, leaves or flowers	**algae**, **fungi** and **lichens**
1b	Distinct leaves: with or without roots or flowers	go to 2
2a	No true roots or flowers	**bryophytes**
2b	True roots: with or without flowers	go to 3
3a	No flowers or seeds, reproduce by spores	**pteridophytes**
3b	Seed-bearing plants	go to 4
4a	Seeds in cones	**gymnosperms**
4b	Seeds produced in an ovary/flower	**angiosperms**

Experiment 4.3 CATCH THAT MOULD!

YOU WILL NEED
stereo microscope
variety of food moulds

Caution: Take care not to breathe in spores when handling moulds and wash your hands thoroughly immediately afterwards. Some moulds may trigger an asthma attack.

• Use the stereo microscope to observe at least three different food moulds.

1. Make a pencil sketch of what you observe.
2. Record, next to your sketch, as many details about the moulds as you can.
3. Describe how the moulds were different to each other.

Bread mould is a type of fungus.

Experiment 4.4

A LOOK AT LICHEN

YOU WILL NEED
a sample of lichen
stereo microscope

1. Sketch and describe your observations of lichen under a stereo microscope.
2. On your diagram, suggest and label which parts are algal or fungal features. Remember that the algal parts contain chlorophyll and the fungal parts may appear thread-like.

Activities

Remember

Construct a table that summarises the characteristics of lichens, algae and fungi.

Think

1. Construct a key to divide lichens, algae and fungi into separate groups.
2. Suggest reasons why lichen, algae and fungi are no longer classified as plants by some biologists.
3. Suggest reasons why lichen, algae and fungi were once classified as plants.
4. Which, if any, of these organisms do you think are most like plants? How?
5. If you were a biologist would you classify any of these as plants? Why?
6. Within a group, prepare and then present a debate to the class on whether 'Lichens, algae and fungi should be included in the plant kingdom'.

Investigate

1. Look up lichens, algae and fungi in at least three different biology books and record whether they are classified as belonging to the plant kingdom or to a different group. Try to find at least one biology book published before 1980. Why have ideas about the classification of lichens, algae and fungi changed? Use your data to complete a table like the one below.
2. Find out which features are used to classify fungi.
3. What are slime moulds? Describe their characteristics. Into which kingdom would you classify them?
4. Design an investigation, using slices of bread or another food, to find out which conditions are best suited to growing moulds.

Reference title	Date published	Lichen grouping	Fungi grouping	Algae grouping
e.g. Text A	1983	Plant kingdom	Plant kingdom	Plant kingdom
e.g. Text B	1990	Fungi kingdom	Fungi kingdom	Protista kingdom

Putting it all together

Summing up

Copy and complete the statements below to compile a summary of this chapter. The missing words can be found in the word list below.

1. Living things require oxygen, water and some form of nutrition and they produce and excrete _____. They also react to changes in their environment and can _____ themselves.

2. _____ things into groups can make them easier to remember, describe and identify.

3. Living things are often called _____.

4. Features of organisms, often structural ones which are easily observed, are noted and identification _____ and field guides are used to identify them.

5. Animals can be divided up on the basis of whether they have an _____, _____ or no skeleton at all.

6. Animals with a _____ are called vertebrates whereas those with an external skeleton or no skeleton at all are called invertebrates.

7. Mammals, birds, amphibians, reptiles, cartilaginous fish, bony fish and jawless fish are all _____.

8. _____ can be classified as monotremes, marsupials and placentals.

9. Arthropods, echinoderms, molluscs, cnidarians, annelids, platyhelminths and nematodes are groups made up of different types of _____.

10. Some insects have a _____ to help them obtain foods like sap, nectar or blood.

11. Some of the features used to classify plants include structural ones like _____, roots, stems, flowers, and the presence or absence of _____ tissue.

12. Ferns, _____ and flowering plants contain vascular tissue, whereas _____ and liverworts do not.

13. Algae, _____ and lichen are no longer considered by many biologists as plants.

Word list

conifers	classifying	mosses	vertebrates
endoskeleton	mammals	seeds	vascular
fungi	exoskeleton	invertebrates	wastes
reproduce	organisms	proboscis	keys
backbone			

Looking back

1. Which prehistoric creature is this? Match words 1–20 on the right with their clues. Write down the numbers of the correct words next to the clues. Then copy the puzzle and join the numbered dots in the order of the clues.

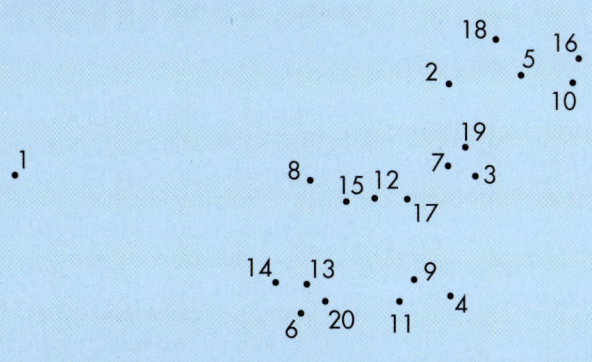

2. Unscramble the words to find the answers:
   (a) living things   ASMOGNIRS
   (b) key which allows only two   HOOTODICMUS
       choices at each branch
   (c) a mammal-like dinosaur   OMDODETIRN
   (d) a group of mammals with wings   ATBS
   (e) a prickly, egg-laying mammal   DCHINAE

3. Arthropods are the most abundant animals on the planet Earth. Use the arthropod key to classify the organisms below.

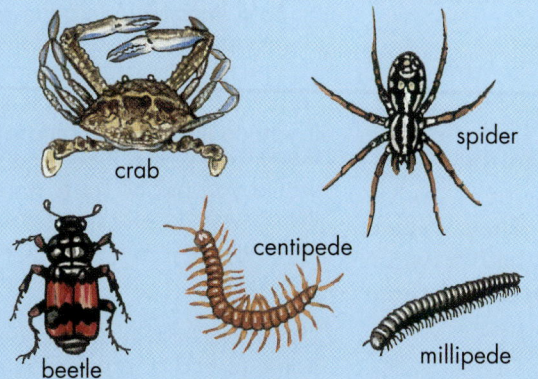

crab   spider

centipede

beetle   millipede

Clues	Words
(a) These animals have no backbone.	1. field guide
(b) The shark belongs to this group of vertebrates.	2. exoskeleton
(c) The goldfish belongs to this group of vertebrates.	3. invertebrates
(d) These mammals lay eggs.	4. marsupials
(e) These mammals have pouches.	5. proboscis
(f) Insects and spiders belong to this group.	6. porifera
(g) Flatworms belong to this group.	7. cartilaginous fish
(h) This group of invertebrates contains segmented worms.	8. reptiles
(i) An animal with a backbone.	9. monotremes
(j) Snails belong to this group of invertebrates.	10. key
(k) Sponges belong to this group of invertebrates.	11. arthropods
(l) These mammals have a placenta.	12. platyhelminths
(m) Snakes and lizards belong to this group.	13. vertebrate
(n) This is used to identify wildlife.	14. placentals
(o) The tough, external skeleton of insects.	15. annelids
(p) The internal skeleton of vertebrates.	16. platypus
(q) A monotreme with a duck-like bill.	17. bony fish
(r) Insects may have this to suck up nectar, sap and blood.	18. endoskeleton
(s) This unlocks the door to classification.	19. amphibian
(t) The adults have lungs and live on land, whereas the young have gills and live in water.	20. molluscs

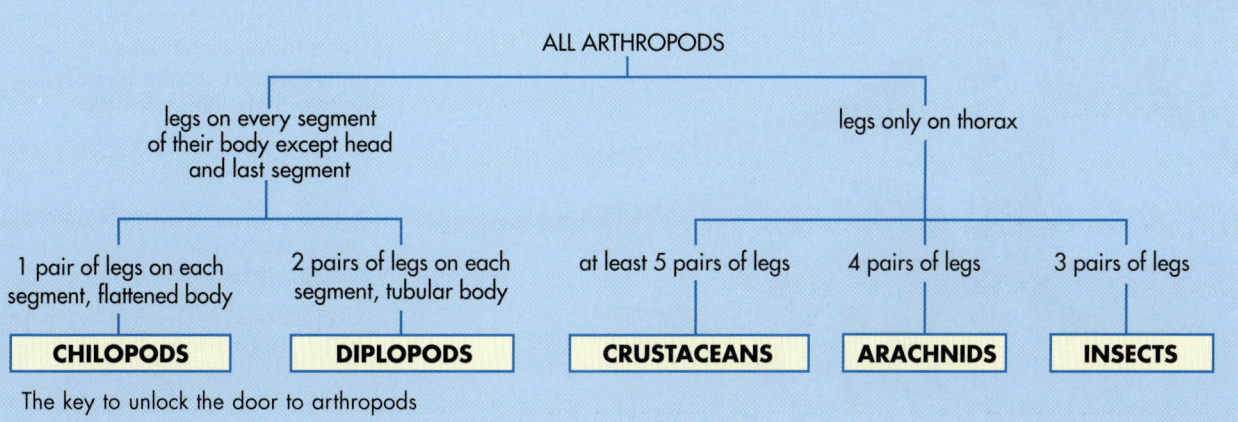

The key to unlock the door to arthropods

Walk like a dinosaur

Tell-tale *hip* bones

The shape of the hip bones of dinosaurs provides us with information on how they walked. Dinosaurs can be divided up into two groups, depending on the positions of their hip bones.

The **lizard-hipped** dinosaurs belonged to the saurischian group and had a hip which was arranged like that of a lizard. The first dinosaurs and all meat-eating dinosaurs had this hip arrangement. There were three kinds of lizard-hipped dinosaurs:

- *Prosauropods* were the first plant-eating dinosaurs. They could walk either on two legs or on four legs. ***Plateosaurus*** was a member of this group.
- *Sauropods*, the giant plant-eaters, had long necks and walked on four legs. ***Apatosaurus***, ***Diplodocus*** and ***Brachiosaurus*** were members of this group. *Brachiosaurus*, about 24 metres long and 12 metres tall, was the largest dinosaur of all.
- *Theropods* were meat-eaters. These dinosaurs, which included ***Tyrannosaurus*** and ***Allosaurus***, walked on two legs.

The **bird-hipped** dinosaurs belonged to the ornithischian group and were all plant eaters. They had a beak-like bone at the front of their heads. There were four kinds of bird-hipped dinosaurs:

- *Ornithopods*, including ***Iguanadon***, could walk on two or four legs. This was the earliest group of bird-hipped dinosaurs to appear on Earth.
- *Stegosaurs*, including ***Stegosaurus***, walked on four legs. They had a small head and big bony plates along their backs.
- *Ankylosaurs* were the armour-plated dinosaurs. They walked on four legs. ***Ankylosaurus*** fossils have been found in the Gippsland region of Victoria.
- *Ceratops* had a bony frill on the back of the head. They walked on four legs. All except one (***Protoceratops***) had between one and five horns on the face. ***Triceratops*** had three horns.

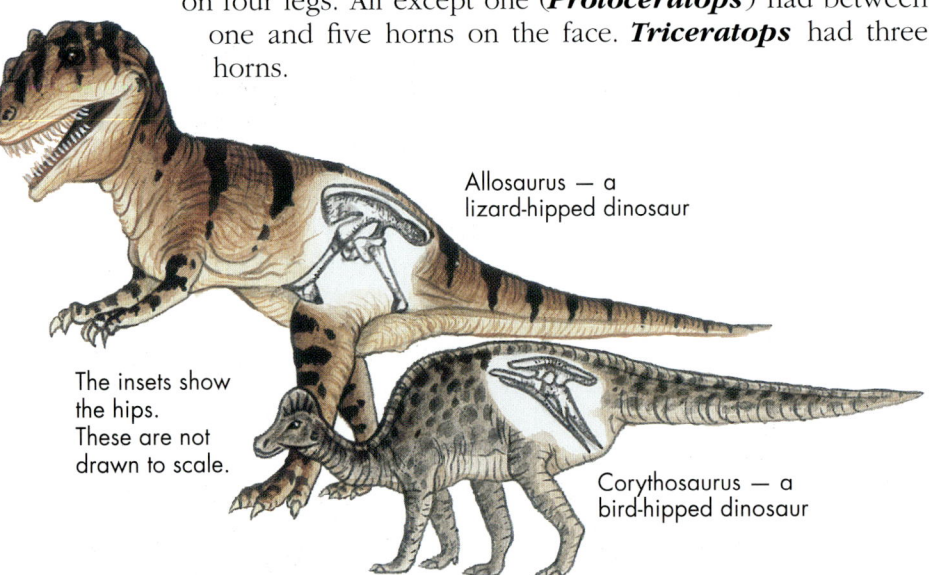

Allosaurus — a lizard-hipped dinosaur

The insets show the hips. These are not drawn to scale.

Corythosaurus — a bird-hipped dinosaur

Activities

Using data

Construct a table with the following headings: 'Dinosaur'; 'Movement (two legs or four legs)'; 'Feeding (meat or plants)'; and 'Hips (lizard-like or bird-like)'.

1. Fill in the table for the dinosaurs named on this page (names in **bold italic** type).
   (a) Which two features did the meat-eating dinosaurs have in common?
   (b) Can the way dinosaurs moved be used to separate bird-hipped dinosaurs from lizard-hipped dinosaurs?
   (c) What did the dinosaurs that were able to walk on two legs have in common?
2. Construct a key that can be used to classify the dinosaurs named on this page (names in **bold italic** type) into the seven groups (names in *italics*).

Imagine

If you could talk to a dinosaur, which one would it be, and what would you ask it? Try to find out the answers to your questions, and write up an article on dinosaurs.

Create

Use books from the library or from home to find or draw pictures of the following dinosaurs, which belong to the Mesozoic era (also known as the Age of Reptiles). Then make a mobile with the dinosaurs arranged in order within their time periods.

Triassic (225–200 million years ago): *Plateosaurus, Lesothosaurus*

Jurassic (200–140 million years ago): *Brachiosaurus, Stegosaurus, Allosaurus*

Cretaceous (140–64 million years ago): *Iguanodon, Ankylosaurus, Tyrannosaurus, Triceratops.*

Reflection

1. Sorting helps me to remember

Answer these questions in your workbook and compare your answers with the ideas you listed for the exercises on page 67 of this chapter.

(a) What have you learnt about classification?

(b) What makes classification 'easy' or 'hard' to understand?

(c) Why do scientists use classification?

2. Classification looks for similarities

(a) Give examples of different classification systems.

(b) Design a classification key for all living things. Discuss your answers with members of your group.

GROUP WORK (c) Take ONE classification system and design a fun way to teach it to a group of eight-year-olds. Demonstrate it to your class.

GROUP WORK (d) Classify the following items, giving reasons for your answers. If the illustrations do not give you enough information to do this, research further to get the details you require.

bat

funnel-web spider

blue-tongue lizard

wattle flowers

sundew

gingko tree showing cones and leaves

blue tiger butterfly

human embryo

cauliflower

3. Unpacking the past

GROUP WORK Design a presentation that shows what you know about life on prehistoric Earth.

4. Powerful words

(a) Review the list of new words you made while studying this chapter. Write down the meaning of each word. You will remember them if you use them often.

GROUP WORK (b) As a class, develop a timeline of the history of Earth. Add drawings to show the living things present in each time period.

GROUP WORK (c) A rare fossil find — a 220-million-year-old amphibian embedded in a piece of sandstone — is shown below. It is believed to be a brachiopod. The carnivorous (meat-eating) animal was about two metres long with small legs and possible gills.

(i) Draw a picture of what you think this animal might have looked like.

(ii) In what era and period did it live?

(iii) Why are scientists so excited about this find?

(iv) Find out how you can become a fossil expert.

CELLS

Cells are the basic units of all living things. The first cell appeared on Earth about 3.5 billion years ago. Today wide varieties of different cells abound. Although their size, shape and contents may vary, they are responsible for carrying out the functions that keep organisms alive. The differences in the cells of organisms are sometimes used to classify them into groups.

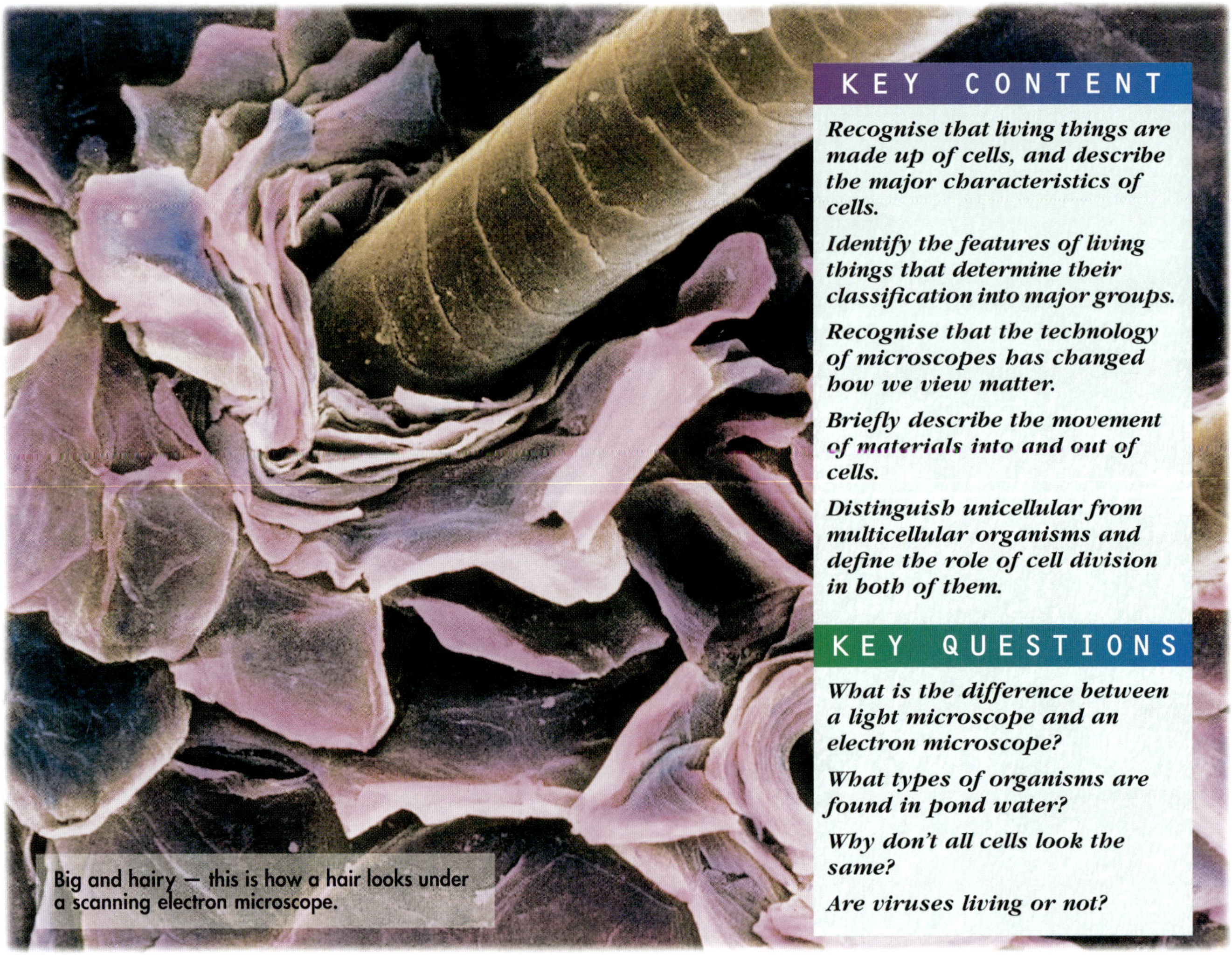

Big and hairy — this is how a hair looks under a scanning electron microscope.

KEY CONTENT

Recognise that living things are made up of cells, and describe the major characteristics of cells.

Identify the features of living things that determine their classification into major groups.

Recognise that the technology of microscopes has changed how we view matter.

Briefly describe the movement of materials into and out of cells.

Distinguish unicellular from multicellular organisms and define the role of cell division in both of them.

KEY QUESTIONS

What is the difference between a light microscope and an electron microscope?

What types of organisms are found in pond water?

Why don't all cells look the same?

Are viruses living or not?

Thinking about Cells

1. A short survey on cells

Answer the following survey questions in your workbook.

(a) When you see the word 'cell' what do you think about? What meaning does it have for you? (You may think of more than one meaning.)

(b) Write a few sentences using the word 'cell'.

(c) Write the meaning of each of the words below. If you don't know a word, write 'don't know'. But try to write a meaning even if you are unsure about it as it will help with your learning.

lens	membrane	microscope
magnify	micrometre	nucleus

(d) When referring to living things, the word 'cell' has a special meaning. Write down all you know about this type of cell.

(e) Give examples of any cells that you know about. Draw and label these examples.

2. Drawing and describing things

(a) A student pulled off a piece of onion skin and looked at it under the microscope. What do you think was the purpose of this?

(b) The diagram on the right is what the student saw. Describe what it is and try to explain what the structures in it might be.

(c) Below is another microscopic representation of a piece of onion. What is the difference between this diagram and the previous one?

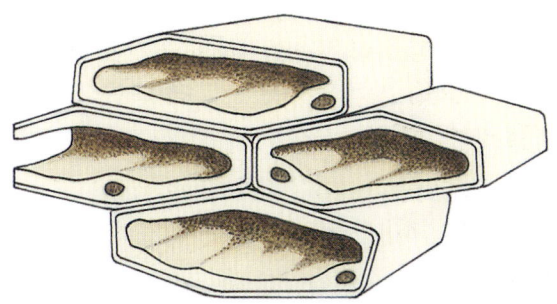

(d) Look at the diagrams below. Could these be diagrams of the same object? Give a reason for your answer. How might this relate to your study of cells?

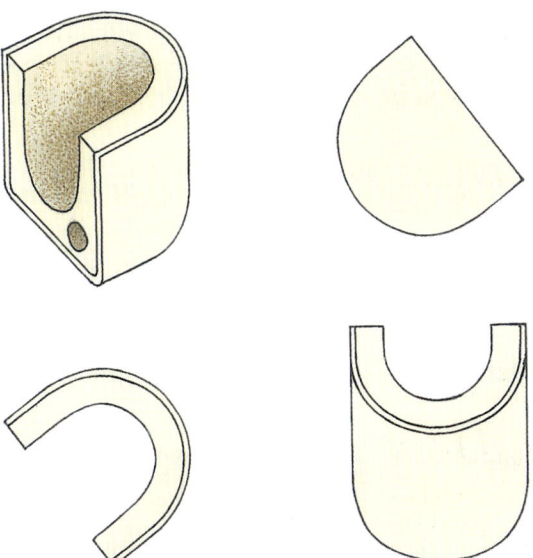

3. How living things are made

(a) Look at the body parts listed in the two diagrams below. In your workbook write the names of the body parts in a column. Then write a sentence next to each name, explaining something that you know about each body part.

(b) If you were classifying living things, would you group yourself and plants together? Give a reason for your decision.

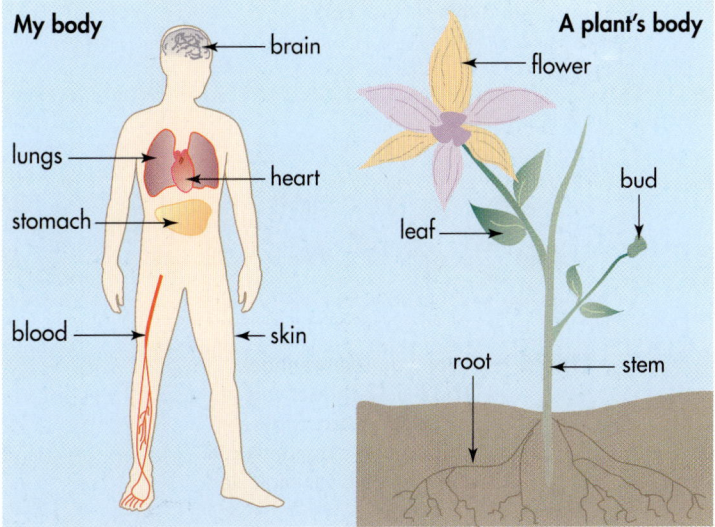

My body — brain, lungs, heart, stomach, blood, skin

A plant's body — flower, bud, leaf, root, stem

5.1
A whole new world

Over 300 years ago, an English inventor and scientist used magnifying lenses to observe the basic units of which all living things are made.

The *discovery* of *cells*

Robert Hooke looked at thin slices of cork under a **microscope** (= 'very small' + 'view') that he had made himself from lenses. He observed small box-like shapes inside the cork. He called the little boxes that he saw **cells**. Microscopes opened up a whole new world that had never been seen before.

Using microscopes to carefully observe different living things showed that they also were made of these tiny basic units. As the **magnification** provided by microscopes increased, it could be seen that although the basic structure of cells was similar, there were quite a few differences. Different groups of organisms often contained different types of cells. It was also discovered that different types of cells could be found within an individual organism.

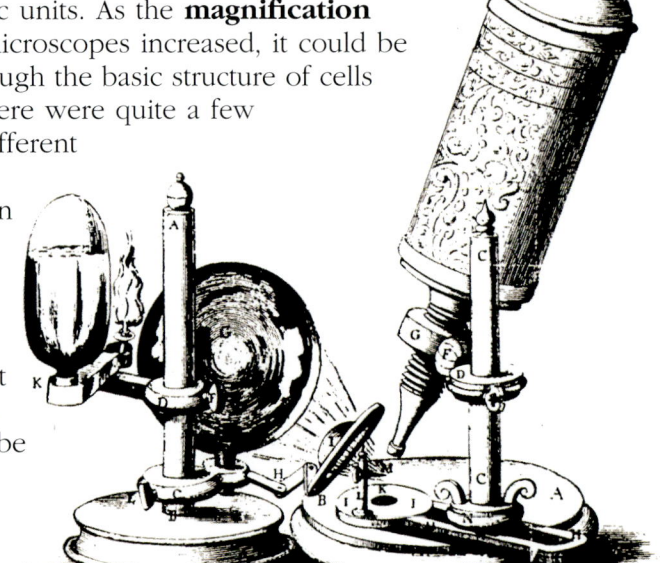
Hooke's microscope

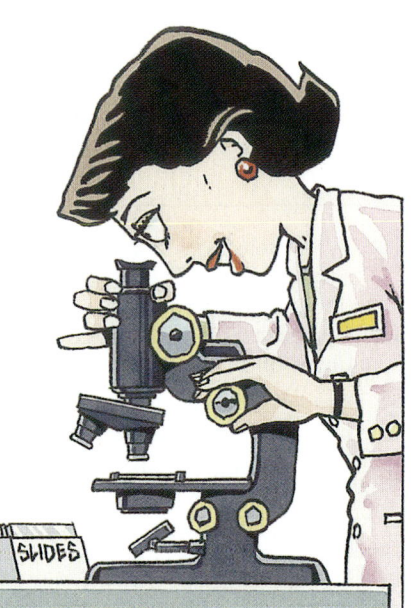

1665 — Robert Hooke uses the term 'cell' to describe the tiny box-like units in a thin slice of cork.

1683 — Leeuwenhoek discovers bacteria in saliva.

1824 — Rene Dutrochet (1776–1847) states that all plants and animals are made up of cells.

1839 — Theodor Schwann suggests that all animals are also made of one or more cells and that the cell is the basic unit of structure for all living things.

1600   **1700**   **1800**

1675 — Anton van Leeuwenhoek (1632–1723) discovers unicellular microscopic organisms in stagnant water which he calls 'animalcules'.

1831 — Robert Brown (1773–1858) reports on his observation of the nucleus in both plant and animal cells.

Timeline showing development of microscope and cell theory

Experiment 5.1 MAKING A MICROSCOPE

YOU WILL NEED

2 small, low-power magnifying
glasses (lenses)
a cardboard tube with the inside
painted matt black
other items as shown in the diagram

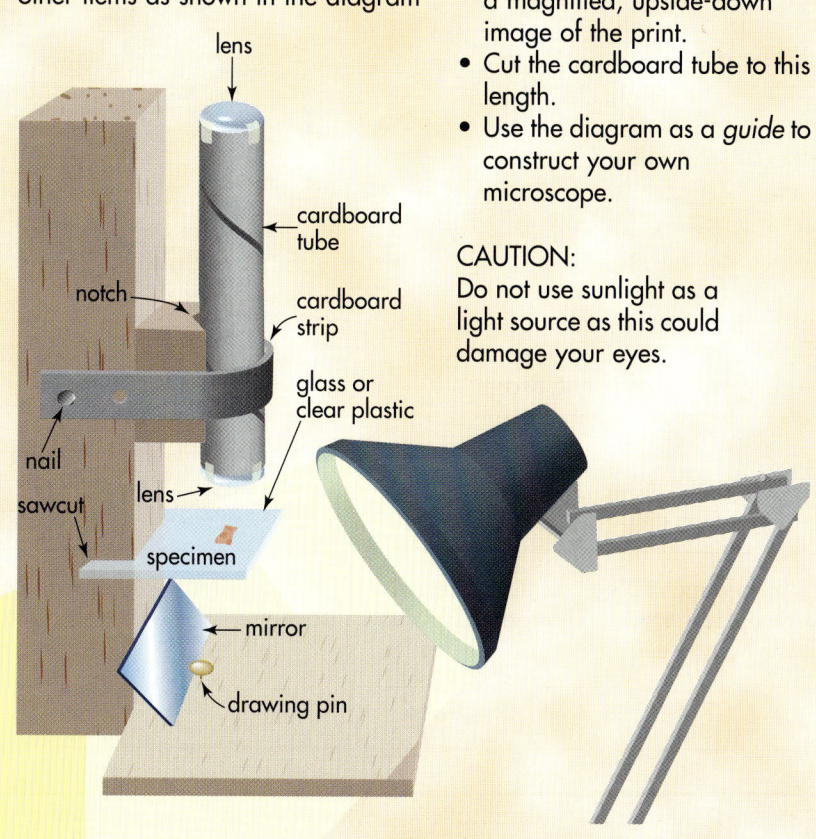

lens

cardboard
tube

notch

cardboard
strip

glass or
clear plastic

nail

lens

sawcut

specimen

mirror

drawing pin

- Hold the two lenses about
15 cm apart and look at
newspaper print or other
printed matter through them.
- Vary the distance until you see
a magnified, upside-down
image of the print.
- Cut the cardboard tube to this
length.
- Use the diagram as a *guide* to
construct your own
microscope.

CAUTION:
Do not use sunlight as a
light source as this could
damage your eyes.

20th century — Development
of the microscope
continues.

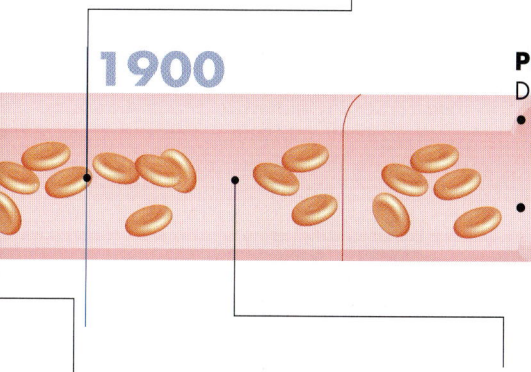

1900

PRESENT DAY —
Development of:
- transmission electron microscopes,
which show the internal structures
of cells
- scanning electron microscopes,
which show images of the surface
features (often involve coating of
the specimen with a every thin
layer of metal atoms).

58 — Rudolf Virchov suggests
that all cells arise from
cells that already exist.

1933 — Ernst Ruska builds
the first electron
microscope.

Activities

Using data: 'Micro-trivia'

Use the timeline below to answer
the following questions.
1. In which year did Hooke use
the term 'cells' to describe his
observations of cork slices?
2. What did Virchov suggest in
1858?
3. In which substance did
Leeuwenhoek discover
bacteria?
4. When did Ruska build the first
electron microscope?
5. State the differences between
cell observations made with a
scanning electron microscope
and those with a transmission
electron microscope.

Remember

1. Describe the appearance of
the cells that Hooke observed
in thin sections of cork.
2. What do all living things have
in common?
3. Do all cells look the same?
4. What do microbiologists
study?

Investigate

1. Why did Hooke use the term
'cells' for the little box-shaped
structures he observed in cork?
2. Gather information on how a
microscope works.
3. Research one of the scientists
in the timeline and present
your information in a poster.
4. Find out what people thought
living things consisted of
before Hooke's discovery of
cells. Write a story about your
findings.
5. Find out about a scientist called
Matthias Schleiden. Which of
the scientists on the timeline
was his work linked with?

Create

If you were living 300 years ago,
how might you react to being
told that you were made up of
cells? Is this different to the way
people would react today? What
might cause these reactions?
Construct a story, play or cartoon
that answers these questions.

It's a small world

Just because you can't see something, it doesn't mean that it's not there...

Types *of* microscopes

There are two types of microscopes that are often used. One type involves using light rays to see the image of the specimen. The other type involves the use of small particles called electrons.

You may have **light microscopes** in your school. When you use a **monocular** light microscope you use only one eye. A **stereo microscope** allows you to use both eyes. You need to use very thin specimens or objects when you use the monocular microscope. If you are looking at a living specimen you may see its cells. Stereo microscopes allow you to observe much larger specimens, like parts of plants, insects and other small animals. In many laboratories today an **electron microscope** is used. It gives greater magnification and a higher resolution than a light microscope.

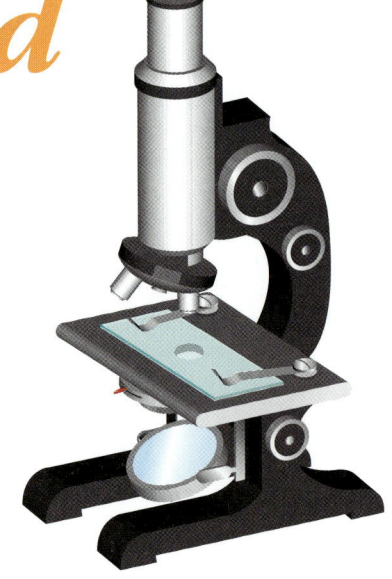

Monocular light microscope

Some comparisons between light microscopes and electron microscopes

Type of microscope	Magnification (how many times bigger)	Resolution (how much detail we can see)	Advantages	Disadvantages	Examples of detail that can be seen
light microscope	up to 1500×	up to about 500 times better than the human eye	samples prepared quickly; coloured stains can be used; living cells can be viewed	limited visible detail	see diagram of plant and animal cells
electron microscope	1 000 000×	up to about 5 million times better than the human eye	high magnification and resolution	only dead sections can be viewed	see diagram of plant and animal cells

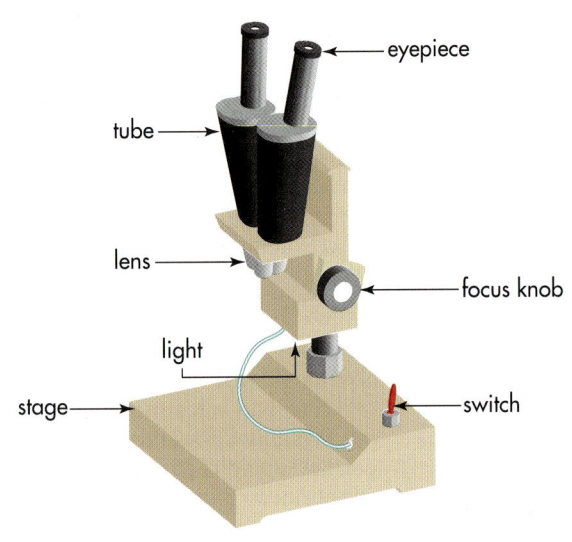

Stereo light microscope

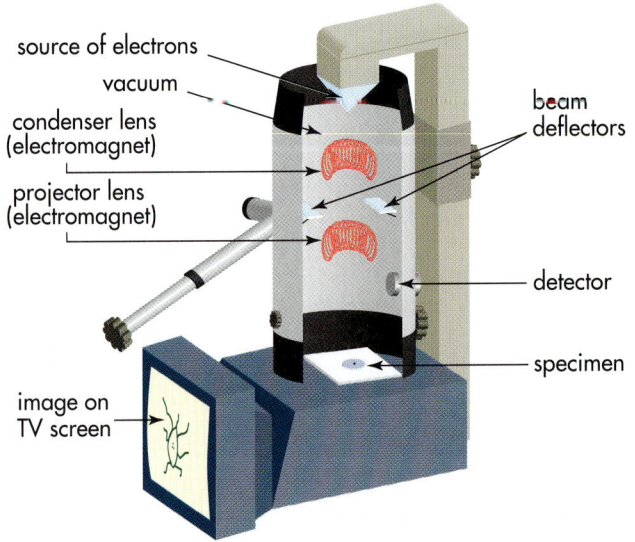

Scanning electron microscope

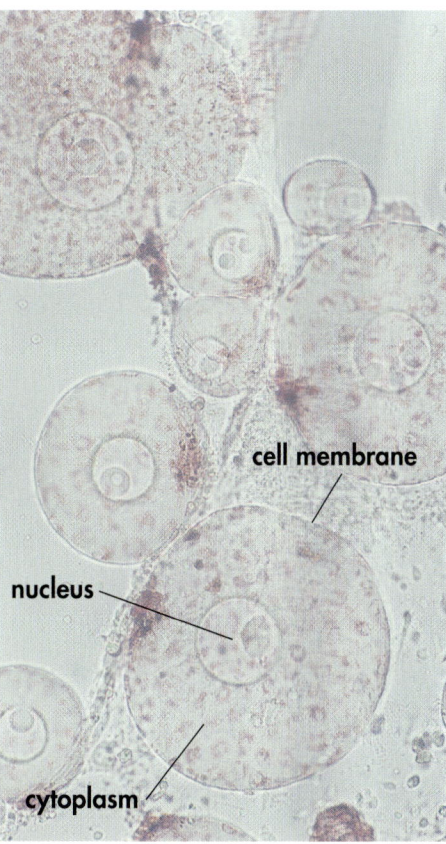

'Typical' plant (left) and animal cells (right) as observed using a light microscope. Several cells are shown in each case. You should be able to see this through your classroom microscope.

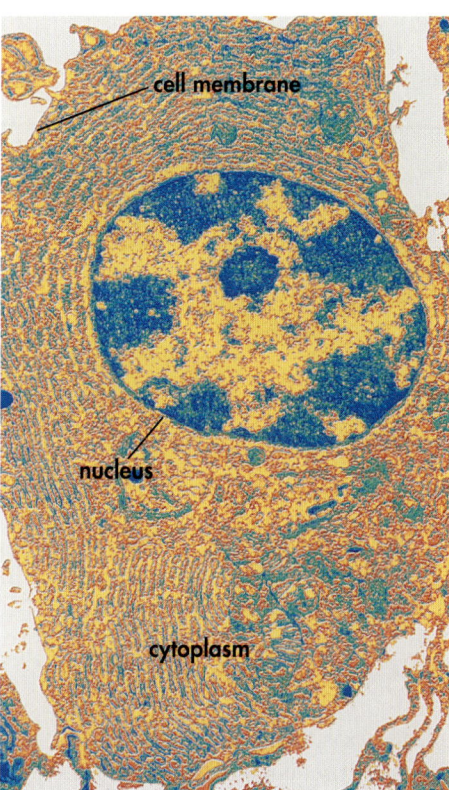

'Typical' plant (left) and animal cells (right) as viewed with a transmission electron microscope. For information on the parts of the cell, see pages 102–103.

Activities

Using data

Examine the pictures of the plant and animal cells as seen under the different types of microscopes. Construct a table that summarises differences in the pictures.

Remember

1. Describe the differences between:
   (a) a monocular light microscope and a stereo microscope
   (b) a light microscope and an electron microscope.
2. Draw a typical plant cell and a typical animal cell in the detail that could be seen using a light microscope.

Investigate

1. Observe ten different specimens (e.g. hair, fingers, pencil, insect, plant) under a stereo microscope. Sketch or describe what you see. Discuss the similarities and differences observed and any interesting findings.
2. Research how specimens are prepared for examination under an electron microscope.
3. Prepare a report on the activities of scientists involved in these studies on cells:
   (a) cytology, (b) biochemistry, (c) microbiology, (d) histology.
4. The electron micrographs on the left were made using a transmission electron microscope. The micrograph of skin and hair on page 92 was made using a scanning electron micrograph. Find and look at other electron micrographs made using the two types of electron microscopes. How are they different?

Create

Gather information on how the electron microscope was developed. Select the key points and design a poster showing the history of its development.

5.3

In focus

In order to zoom in on the units of life, you first need to be able to focus.

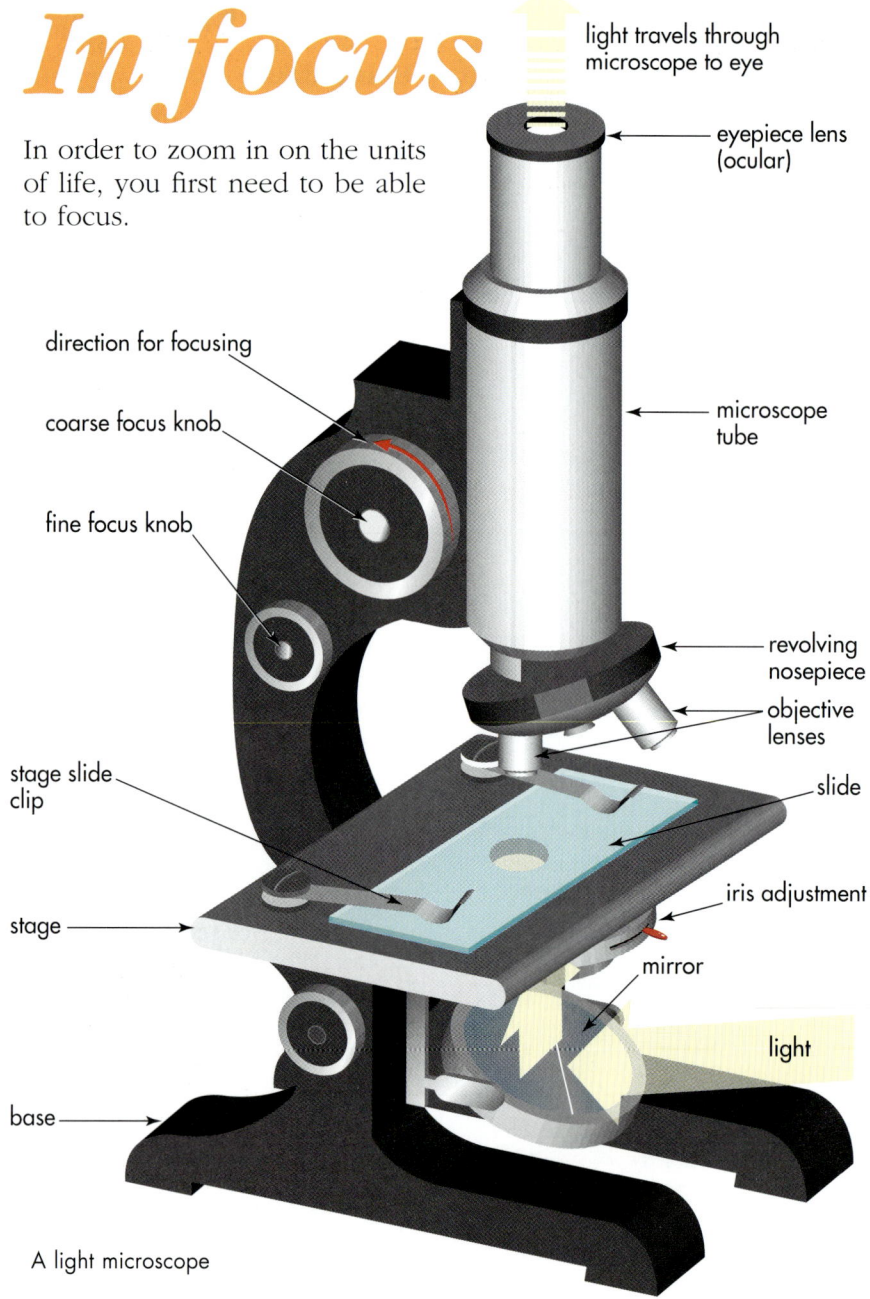

light travels through microscope to eye

eyepiece lens (ocular)

direction for focusing

coarse focus knob

fine focus knob

microscope tube

revolving nosepiece

objective lenses

stage slide clip

slide

stage

iris adjustment

mirror

base

light

A light microscope

Some *important points* to remember *when using* a *microscope*

1. When lifting the microscope, put one hand on the body of the microscope and one hand under its base.
2. The microscope should be used on a flat surface and not too close to the edge.
3. Take care that the light intensity is not too high, or it might damage your eye.
4. Return the shortest objective lens into position when finished.
5. Remove the slide and ensure that the stage is clean.
6. Make sure that when your microscope is not in use, it is always clean and carefully put away.

Using *a* microscope

1. Adjust your mirror so the proper amount of light passes through the hole in the stage.
2. Place the glass microscope slide (with a single hair specimen on top) onto the stage.
3. Ensure that you are using the objective lens with the lowest power (usually 10×).
4. While watching from the side, use the coarse adjustment to lower the objective lens until it is just above the stage. Pressing it down too far may shatter the slide.

How to focus your microscope — and how not to!

5. While looking through the eyepiece, carefully turn the coarse adjustment until the specimen is seen clearly.
6. Use the fine adjustment so that you can clearly see the details of your specimen.
7. Pencil a sketch of what you see.
8. Suggest how many times your specimen has been magnified.
9. You may now use an objective lens with a higher power.

Magnification

The two lenses that determine the magnification of your microscope are the eyepiece lens and the objective lens. Each lens will have a number on it that signifies its magnification. Multiplying the eyepiece number by the objective lens number will give you the magnification of the microscope. For example:

eyepiece: 10×
objective: 40×
magnification = 400×

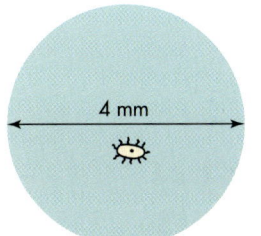

field of view 4 mm
magnification 40×

field of view 1.6 mm
magnification 100×

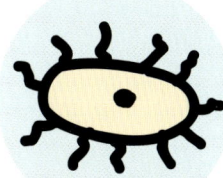

field of view 400 μm
magnification 400×

Field of view — your window to a tiny world: as the field of view gets smaller, the magnification gets larger.

Experiment 5.2 GETTING INTO FOCUS WITH AN 'E'

YOU WILL NEED
1 cm square piece of newspaper containing the letter 'e'
monocular light microscope
microscope slide
clear sticky tape

- Carefully stick the 1 cm square of newspaper onto a clean microscope slide using sticky tape.
- Using the microscope directions, get the paper into focus using the coarse adjustment and the lowest-power objective lens (smallest magnification).
- Carefully move the slide until you have an 'e' in focus.

1. In which direction did the paper under the microscope move when you moved the slide (a) towards you? (b) to the left?
2. Record the magnification that you are using.
3. Sketch and estimate how much of the viewed area is covered by the letter 'e' at this magnification.

- Change to a higher level of magnification by rotating to a higher power objective lens.

4. Sketch and estimate how much of the viewed area is covered by the letter 'e' at this magnification.
5. Summarise your results in a table, using diagrams.

Activities

Using data

Use the 'field of view' diagrams above to answer the following questions. (Note that 1000 μm = 1 mm.)
(a) Estimate the length of the specimen at 40×, 100× and 400× magnification.
(b) Describe the differences in your observations of the three different magnifications.

Think

1. When you are looking down the microscope, what happens when you move the microscope slide (a) to the left? (b) to the right? (c) towards you? (d) away from you?
2. If you are using an eyepiece with a magnification of 10× and an objective lens of 10×, how many times will the specimen viewed under the microscope be magnified?
3. If a specimen is 1 mm in length, how big will it appear if it is magnified 100×?

4. If a specimen takes up the entire field of view at 100×, how much of it will be seen at 400×?
5. (a) Sketch a line diagram of your microscope and label as many of its parts as you can, using the diagram on page 98 to help you.
   (b) How does your microscope differ from the one shown on page 98?
   (c) Discuss the advantages and disadvantages of the differences.
6. Copy and complete the table below.

Create

1. Make up a rhyme that helps you to remember how to use a microscope and includes the important points to remember.
2. Design and make a poster which shows either how a microscope should be used or what happens when you use it the wrong way.

Investigate

Construct a table that summarises the functions of the different parts of the microscope.

Ocular lens (eyepiece)	Objective lens	Magnification
5×	5×	25×
5×	10×	
10×		100×
	40×	400×

5.4
Zooming in on life

Now that you are in focus, let's zoom in on life.

How to *sketch* **what** *you see* under the *microscope*

Some points to remember

1. Use a sharp lead pencil.
2. Draw only the lines that you see and label only the structures that you can identify.
3. Your diagrams should take up about a third to half a page each.
4. Record the magnification next to each diagram.
5. State the name of the specimen and the date of observation.
6. A written description is also often of considerable value.
7. When you are viewing many cells at one time, it is often useful to select and draw only two or three representative cells for each observation.

20/5/2005

Nucleus
(stained dark
blue)

Cell
membrane

Cheek cells
100X

An example of a sketch from a microscope specimen

Preparing *a* specimen

Light microscopes function by allowing light to pass through the specimen to reach your eye. If the specimen is too thick, the object cannot be seen as clearly or may not be seen at all.

Careful peeling, scraping, slicing or squashing techniques can be used to obtain thin specimens of the object to be studied.

How to peel the skin off a spring onion

Preparing a wet mount slide

1. Place a drop of pond water on a clean glass slide.

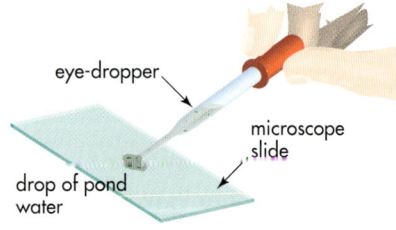

eye-dropper

microscope slide

drop of pond water

2. Gently place a cover slip (a very thin piece of glass which holds the specimen in place) on the pond water, by putting one edge down first.

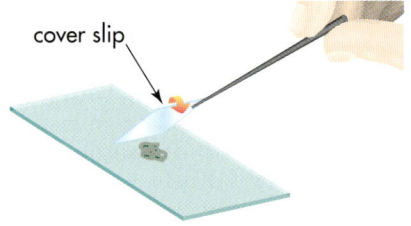

cover slip

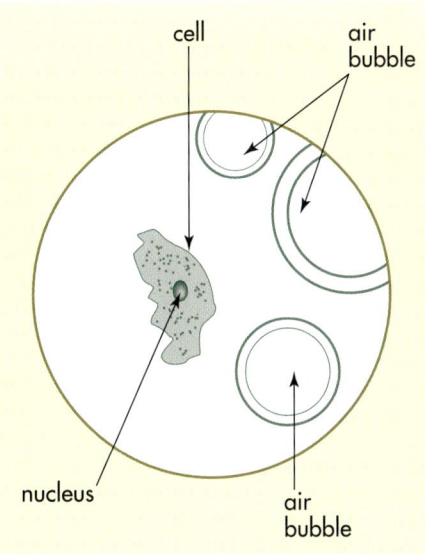

cell

air bubble

nucleus

air bubble

For example, iodine stains starch a blue-black colour. Take care when using these stains because they can stain you as well.

1. Add a few drops of iodine to a very small amount of squashed banana or a thin slice of potato on a microscope slide.
2. Gently place a cover slip on top as shown in the diagram on page 100. View the specimen.

3. Incorrect placing of the cover slip can result in air bubbles.

Staining a specimen

Many objects are colourless when viewed down the microscope, so specimens are often stained to make them easier to see. Methylene blue, iodine and eosin are some examples of stains often used. Each stain reacts with different chemicals in the specimen.

Experiment 5.3
MAKING SMALL HEADS BIGGER

YOU WILL NEED
light microscope
prepared slides of the heads of a variety of animals (e.g. tapeworm and insects)

• Use a light microscope to examine the prepared slides.
1. Draw sketches of what you see. Remember to include the magnification used.
2. How are they similar?
3. How do they differ?

Experiment 5.5
POND WATER

YOU WILL NEED
light microscope   pond water
microscope slides   pipette
cover slips

• Prepare a wet mount of the pond water on a microscope slide.
• Examine the pond water under the microscope.

Draw sketches and describe what you see.

Experiment 5.6
PEEL OR SQUASH AND STAIN

YOU WILL NEED
light microscope   cover slips
microscope slides   pipette

onion, banana or potato, water, methylene blue and iodine

• Peel some onion skin and carefully place on a slide with a drop of methylene blue.
• Cover carefully with a cover slip.
1. Record what you see under the microscope.
• Squash some banana or place a thin slice of potato on a slide and add a drop of iodine.
• Cover with a cover slip.
2. Record what you see under the microscope, and discuss the similarities and differences you observed between the specimens.

Experiment 5.4 KITCHEN AND WARDROBE DETECTIVE

YOU WILL NEED
light microscope and microscope slides
spatula
a selection of white powders (e.g. flour, salt, sugar, baking soda)
ground, instant and freeze-dried coffee
different brands or types of spices and leaf tea
fibres (e.g. cotton, linen, silk, wool, nylon and various combinations of these)
hairs (of members of your class or family, or of animals)

• Examine the listed substances and materials under the microscope.
1. Draw sketches of what you see and record comments or descriptions next to each.
2. Estimate the size of the specimens and summarise your results in a table.
3. Describe how your specimens differed.
• Try to determine the contents of an 'unknown mixture' that contains three or four of the substances and materials previously examined.

Activities

Create

Design a poster that shows others how to prepare a variety of specimens to be viewed under a microscope.

In the five kingdoms

No matter how different an organism looks on the outside, its cells have the same basic structure.

Cells of the five kingdoms

Although the basic cell structure is the same, variations in the design are used to classify organisms into five main groups or kingdoms. The five different kingdoms are **Animalia** (animals), **Fungi** (e.g. mushrooms), **Plantae** (plants), **Prokaryotae** (also called Monera) (e.g. bacteria and cyanobacteria) and **Protista** (a mixture of organisms that don't fit into the other groups) (e.g. algae and protozoans).

Some differences in the basic cell design in the five kingdoms

The brain of the cell

A large round structure called the **nucleus** is the control centre of the cell. It contains chromosomes that contain information to keep the cell alive and working properly. Organisms that consist of cells without a membrane around the nucleus are called **prokaryotes**. Those with cells that have a membrane around the nucleus are called **eukaryotes**. Prokaryotes such as bacteria were the first type of organisms to appear on Earth. Eukaryotes appeared about a billion years later. Plants, animals, fungi and protistans are examples of organisms containing eukaryotic cells.

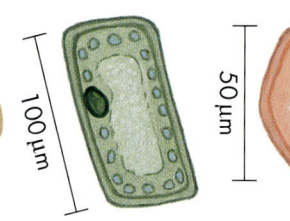

3 µm

Bacterium

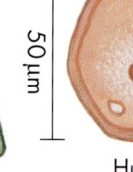

100 µm

Plant cell

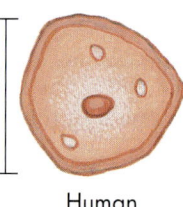

50 µm

Human cheek cell

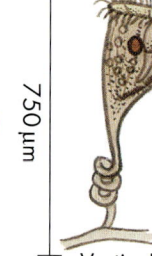

750 µm

Vorticella

Characteristic	Kingdom				
	Animalia (animals: e.g. lizards, fish, spiders, earthworms, sponges)	Fungi (e.g. yeasts, moulds, mushrooms, toadstools)	Plantae (plants: e.g. ferns, mosses, conifers, flowering plants)	Prokaryotae/ Monera (bacteria and cyanobacteria)	Protista ('leftovers': e.g. algae, protozoans)
number of cells	multicellular	usually multicellular but some unicellular	most multicellular	unicellular (single-celled)	most unicellular
nucleus	nucleus with membrane	nucleus with membrane; some fungi have several nuclei per cell	nucleus with membrane	no membrane-bound nucleus	nucleus with membrane
cell wall	absent	present	present	present	present in some
large vacuole	absent	absent	present	absent	present in some
chloroplasts	absent	absent	present	present in some	present in some

The original two kingdom system consisted of plants and animals. As scientists gained more knowledge, they introduced more kingdoms.

All *wrapped up*

Cells are wrapped in a **cell membrane**, which controls what goes into and comes out of the cell. Material made of small particles moves in and out of cells through pores in the cell membrane. Sometimes this movement requires energy. This movement is necessary to supply substances needed by the cell and to remove wastes.

Cytoplasm is the part of the cell inside the cell membrane but outside the nucleus. In the cytoplasm hundreds of chemical reactions take place, transferring energy, storing food and making new substances. This activity within the cell is called its **metabolism**.

Some cells have another boundary around the cell membrane, called the **cell wall**. This gives protection, support and shape to a cell.

Micro *factories* and *departments*

Structures called **organelles** are found in the cytoplasm of eukaryotes. They include mitochondria, chloroplasts, vacuoles and starch grains. The **mitochondrion** (plural: mitochondria) is the 'powerhouse' of the cell, because it supplies energy. **Chloroplasts** contain the green pigment **chlorophyll** which is used in **photosynthesis** (making food using sunlight). A **vacuole** is a large cavity in the cytoplasm which is filled with a watery fluid. Vacuoles store water and dissolved substances. In plants, this fluid is called **cell sap**. Vacuoles are partly responsible for the firmness of plants. Prokaryotes do not have organelles.

One cell *or* more?

Some organisms are made up of a single cell and are described as being **unicellular**. In this case the cell has to do all of the required jobs itself. Unicellular organisms reproduce by cell division; that is, one cell divides into two cells. **Multicellular** organisms are made up of many cells with different types of cells doing different jobs. Most plant and animal species, including humans, are multicellular organisms. Reproduction, growth and repair in multicellular organisms involve cell division.

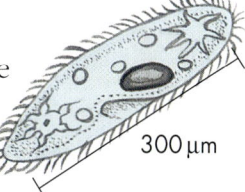
A *Paramecium* is a unicellular animal.

300 µm

How big *is* small?

The size of cells may also vary between organisms, and within a multicellular organism. Most cells are too small to be seen without a microscope. Special, very small units of measurement are used to describe their size. The most commonly used unit is a **micrometre** (µm) where 1 µm equals 1 millionth of a metre. Most cells are in the range of 1 µm (bacteria) to 100 µm (plant cells).

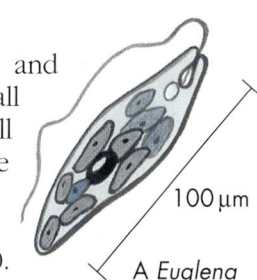
A *Euglena*

100 µm

Activities

Remember

1. What do all living things have in common?
2. Why is the nucleus important to the cell?
3. State the names of the five kingdoms and use the table to determine which kingdoms contain organisms that are eukaryotes.
4. What is the purpose of the cell membrane?
5. Why does cell division take place in:
    (a) a unicellular organism?
    (b) a multicellular organism?
6. State the differences between a mitochondrion, a chloroplast and a vacuole.

Think

Discuss the advantages, if any, of the five kingdom system.

Using data

Use the table on page 102 to answer the following questions.
1. In which kingdom(s) do the cells of an organism:
    (a) not have a cell wall, large vacuole or chloroplasts?
    (b) have a cell wall, large vacuole and chloroplasts?
    (c) have a cell wall, but no large vacuole or chloroplasts?
    (d) have a cell wall and a nucleus without a membrane around it?

Use the cell diagrams on pages 102 and 103 to answer questions 2–4.

2. Construct a table with the following headings: 'Name of organism', 'Type of cell', and 'Cell size (µm)'.
3. Present the sizes of the cells on a graph, with the horizontal axis representing the type of cell and the vertical axis representing the size of cell. Sketch each cell as accurately as you can, in the correct position on the graph. Which are the smallest and biggest?
4. Determine the average size for the cells shown on pages 102 and 103.

Create

Construct a labelled model of a cell from one of the kingdoms. Use materials available at home, such as egg cartons, cottonwool and plastic drink bottles.

5.6
The spice of life

Multicellular organisms such as humans are complicated. There are many tasks to be done to maintain the life of the organism. This is achieved by delegating tasks to different cells. Cells belong to different organs and systems, and life is maintained by cooperation between the systems.

In all *shapes* and *sizes*

Cells within an organism differ in their shape and size due to the particular jobs or functions that they carry out. The human body is made up of more than twenty different types of cells, with each type suited to a particular function.

Nerve cells develop thin, long fibres that quickly carry messages from one cell to another. Cells lining the trachea have hair-like cilia that move fluid and dust particles out of the lungs. Muscle cells contain fibres that contract and relax, and the human sperm cell has a tail or flagellum that helps it to swim to the egg cell.

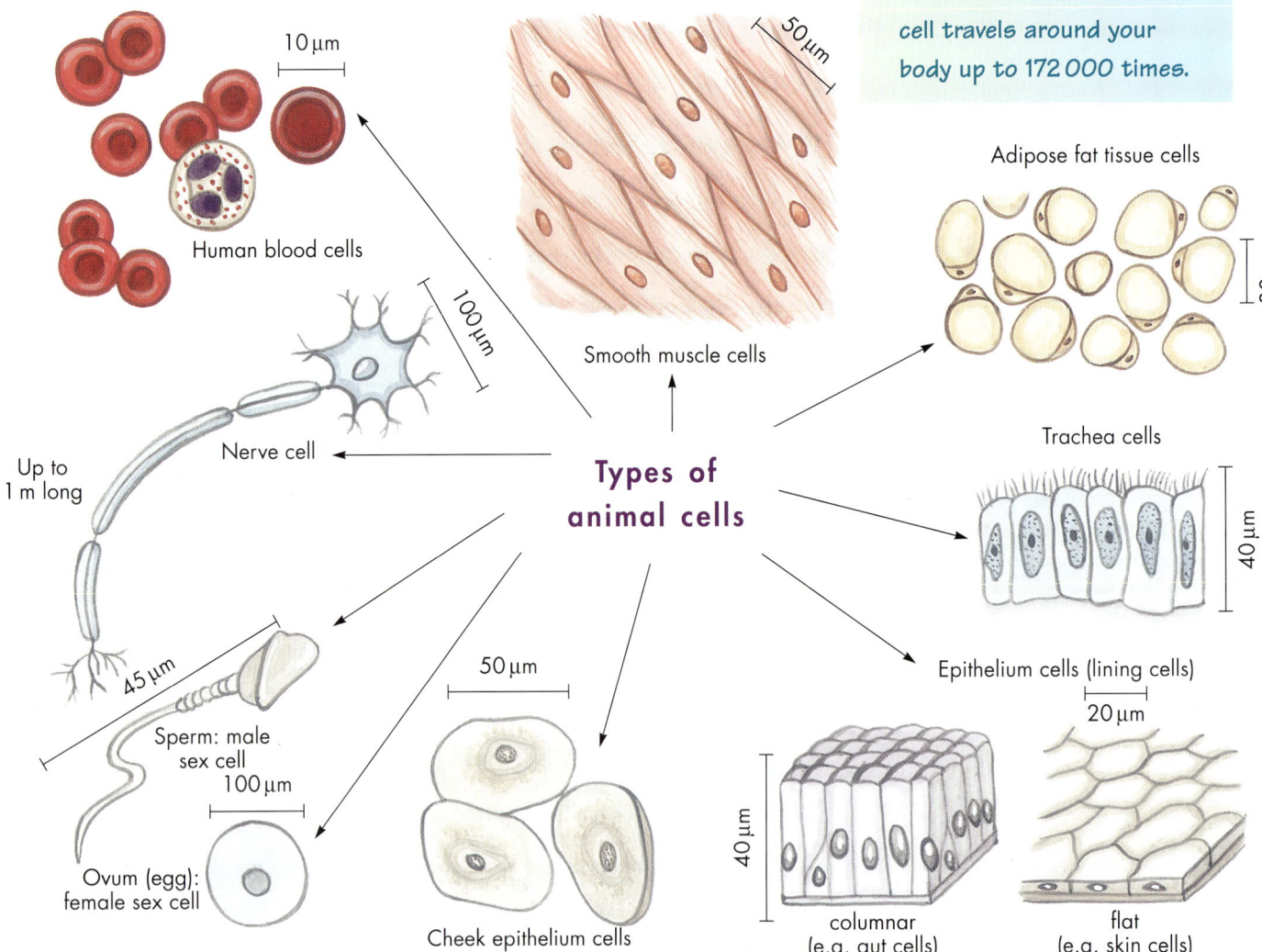

10 µm

Human blood cells

50 µm

Smooth muscle cells

100 µm

Nerve cell

Up to 1 m long

45 µm

Sperm: male sex cell

100 µm

Ovum (egg): female sex cell

50 µm

Cheek epithelium cells

Adipose fat tissue cells

30 µm

Trachea cells

40 µm

Epithelium cells (lining cells)

20 µm

40 µm

columnar (e.g. gut cells)

flat (e.g. skin cells)

Types of animal cells

All these animal cells have become differentiated from one type of cell, in the embryo before birth, to suit their different functions.

Experiment 5.7 ANIMAL CELLS — WHAT'S THE DIFFERENCE?

YOU WILL NEED
light microscope
prepared animal slides: blood cells, muscle cells, cheek cells, nerve cells

• Construct a table like the one below, making it large enough for all of your results.
• Use a microscope to observe the prepared slides, recording your observations in the table as you make them.
• Prepare a summary table that describes the similarities and differences observed between the different cells examined.

1. Which features did the animal cells have in common?
2. In which ways did the animal cells differ from each other?
3. Why are there some features that all cells possess?
4. Find out the functions of the different types of cells examined.
5. Propose (suggest) how the shape or size of the cells may assist the cell in doing its job.
6. Propose reasons for some of the differences observed between the cells.

Source of specimen	Type of specimen	Sketch of specimen	Description of specimen
animal	cheek cells	[Allow as much space as you can; draw and label only 2–3 cells, in pencil, and include magnification (and estimated size if possible).]	[Describe in words what the specimen looked like.]

Activities

Remember

1. Match the types of cells with their functions.

Type of cell	Function
1. muscle	(a) outside covering for protection
2. skin	(b) contracts and relaxes
3. red blood	(c) carries messages between cells
4. nerve	(d) carries oxygen from lungs to other parts

2. Which features do most cells have in common?
3. Describe some ways in which cells may differ.
4. Suggest why the cells in a multicellular organism are not all the same. Give examples in your answer.

Using data

(a) Using the illustrations on page 104, find the size (length or diameter) of the following different types of animal cells and arrange them in order of size: (i) adipose tissue cells, (ii) human blood cells, (iii) epithelium cells, (iv) smooth muscle, (v) cheek cells, (vi) sperm cells, (vii) nerve cells.

(b) Present your data in a table.
(c) Determine the average size of an animal cell.
(d) Use a bar graph to plot the sizes of the different types of cells.
(e) Comment on the differences between the cells.

Investigate, imagine and create

1. Research more about muscle, nerve, skin, or red or white blood cells. Using the information obtained, write a play, poem or story about a day in their life.
2. Construct a model of a nerve cell using food as your construction material.

Think

Copy and complete the table below.

Cell parts and functions in animal cells

Part	Function
cytoplasm	
nucleus	
cell membrane	

5.7
Focus on plants

Multicellular plants are also complicated and require groups of specialised cells, organs and tissues to maintain life. Because plants are in a different kingdom to animals, their specialised cells are different to those of animals.

Have *or* have not

Like animal cells, plant cells have cytoplasm, a membrane and a nucleus. Unlike animal cells, plant cells have a cellulose cell wall and a large central vacuole filled with cell sap. Plant cells also contain chloroplasts, which enable them to make their own food.

On the surfaces of leaves there are pairs of special cells called guard cells which surround tiny pores called stomata. The guard cells can change shape, opening or closing the stomata. Special cells on the roots extend into microscopic hairs that penetrate between soil particles. The hairs provide a large surface area through which water may be absorbed from the soil.

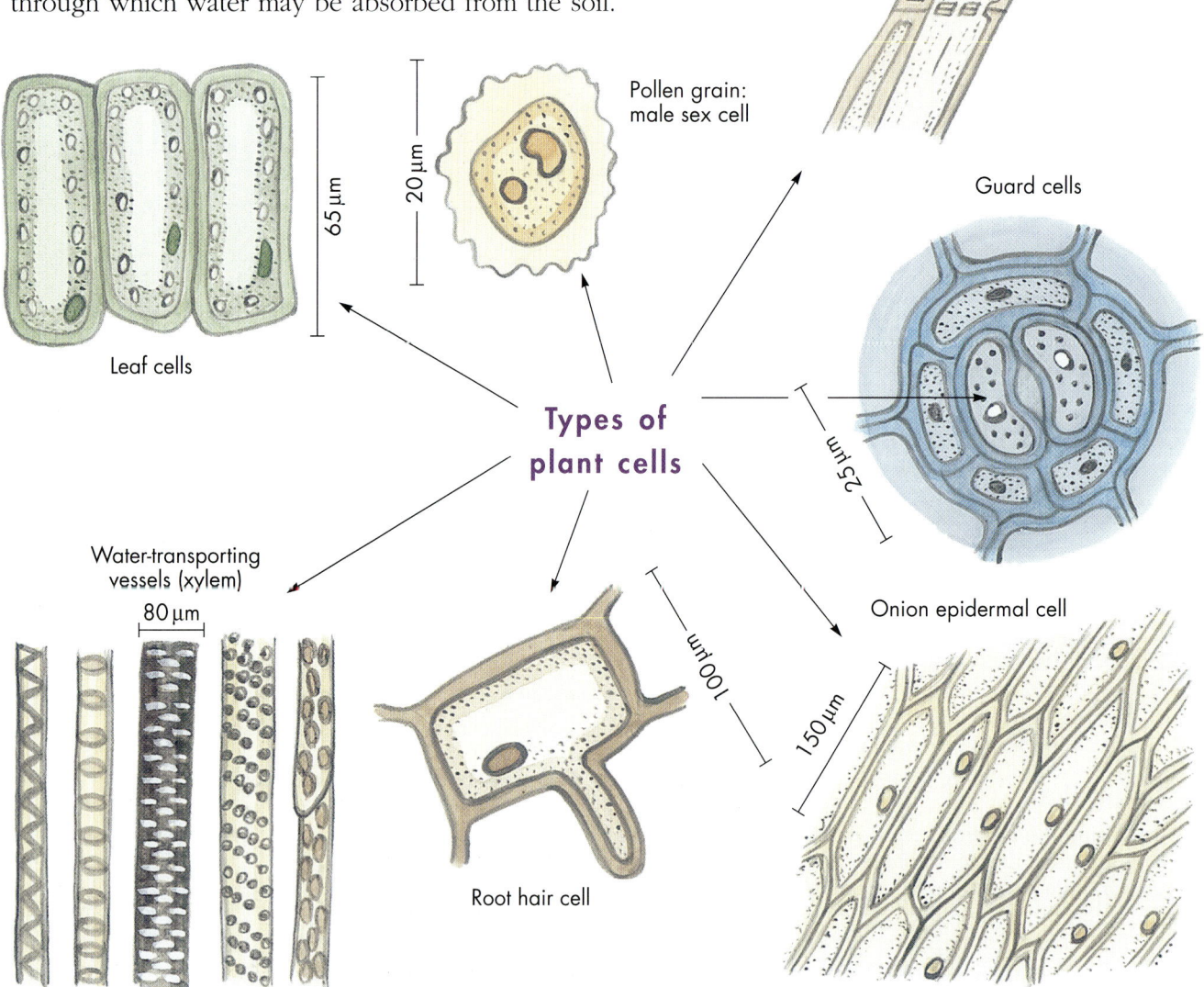

A plant cell with a purpose. (Sizes refer to the length for non-circular cells and the diameter for circular cells.)

Experiment 5.8 PLANT CELLS IN VIEW

YOU WILL NEED

light microscope
prepared plant slides: leaf epidermal cells, root hair cells, stomata/guard cells

- Construct a table like the one below, making it large enough for all of your results.
- Use a microscope to observe the prepared slides, recording your observations in the table as you make them.
- Prepare a summary table that describes the similarities and differences observed between the different cells examined.

1. Which features did the plant cells have in common?

2. In which ways did the plant cells differ from each other?

3. Why are there some features that all cells possess?

4. Find out the functions of the different types of cells examined.

5. Suggest how the shape or size of the cells may assist the cell in doing its job.

6. Suggest reasons for some of the differences observed between the cells.

Source of specimen	Type of specimen	Sketch of specimen	Description of specimen
plant	leaf epidermal cells	[Allow as much space as you can; draw and label only 2–3 cells, in pencil, and include magnification (and estimated size if possible).]	[Describe in words what the specimen looked like.]

Activities

Remember

1. Match the types of cells with their functions.

Type of cell	Function
1. root hair	(a) changes shape to open and close pores in the leaf
2. xylem	(b) increases surface area for efficient absorption
3. guard	(c) carries water and minerals up the plant

2. Which features do most cells have in common?
3. Describe some ways in which cells may differ.
4. Suggest why the cells in a multicellular organism are not all the same. Give examples in your answer.

Using data

(a) Use the illustrations on page 106 to find the size of the following different types of plant cells:
(i) leaf cells, (ii) onion epidermal cells and (iii) phloem cells. Arrange them in order of size.
(b) Present your data in a table.
(c) Determine the average size of a plant cell.
(d) Use a bar graph to plot the cell sizes of the different types of cells.
(e) Discuss the differences between the cells.

Think

Copy and complete the table below.

Cell structures and functions in plant cells

Structure	Function
cell wall	
cytoplasm	
chloroplast	
nucleus	
large vacuole	
cell membrane	

Investigate, imagine and create

1. Find out more about guard cells or leaf epidermal cells. Write a story or poem about what happens to them over 24 hours.
2. Construct a working model of a pair of guard cells, using sausage-shaped balloons.

SCIENCE *issues*

VIRUSES — LIVING OR NOT?

Viruses and micro-organisms are able to infect us. Viruses take over our cell machinery to make more of themselves; except by their effects on our bodies, we cannot detect their presence without complicated technology.

Cell-less

Bacteria are very small cells. Viruses are much smaller than bacteria. They do not have a membrane or cytoplasm. They do, however, contain substances found only in living cells. Viruses consist of a protein box, containing a tiny strand of a substance found in the cell nucleus of living cells. This substance is called nucleic acid. The nucleic acid holds the instructions for making new viruses.

Some of the shapes of viruses are shown below.

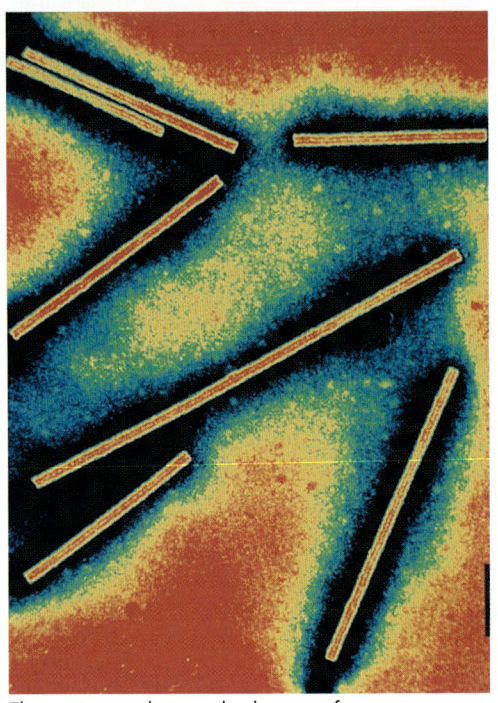

These viruses destroy the leaves of tobacco plants.

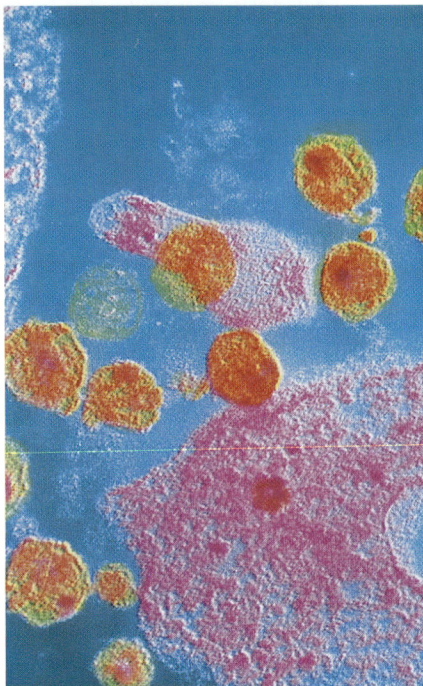

The red objects are the viruses that cause AIDS.

Influenza virus	Tobacco mosaic virus	Cold sore virus
100 nm	350 nm	150 nm
Polio virus	Adenovirus	Foot-and-mouth virus
12 nm	25 nm	10 nm

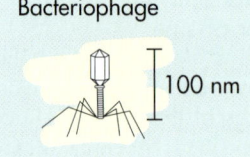

Bacteriophage

100 nm

Shapes of some common viruses. Did you know that a nanometer (nm) is equal to a millionth of a millimetre? Compare these sizes to the cells on the previous pages.

Using *others for their* needs

When they are inside living cells, viruses act as if they are alive. When they are outside living cells, they do not display the characteristics of living things. They can be isolated and crystallised in a similar way to chemical compounds. There are problems classifying viruses as living or non-living things. They contain substances found only in living things and they can reproduce. However they are not cells and can only reproduce inside a living cell. A virus may lie dormant for many years, until it comes in contact with a suitable living cell. It invades the cell and forces it to make hundreds of new virus particles. When the cell dies, it bursts open and releases the new particles, which may then infect other cells.

Smallest *infecting* smaller

Viruses that enter and destroy bacterial cells are known as bacteriophages ('bacteria eaters'). The diagram below shows how they infect the bacterial cell.

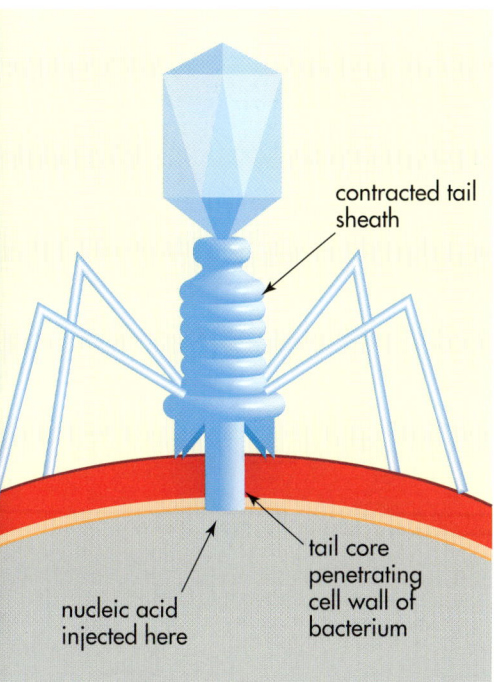

contracted tail sheath

tail core penetrating cell wall of bacterium

nucleic acid injected here

Bacteriophages are viruses that infect bacteria. The nucleic acid that is injected directs the bacterial cell to make more virus.

SCIFACTS

Viruses can be isolated and grown in tissue cultures for research; for example, to identify a disease or to make vaccines. Because they cannot grow on their own, they need to be grown in living cells. Fertilised hen eggs are sometimes used for this purpose.

Some *human diseases* caused by *viruses*

Chickenpox, smallpox, ebola, polio, influenza, measles, rubella (German measles), colds, severe acute respiratory syndrome (SARS) and acquired immune deficiency syndrome (AIDS) are all diseases caused by viruses.

Activities

Remember

1. How do viruses differ from animals, plants, fungi and bacteria?
2. What features do viruses have in common with animals, plants, fungi and bacteria?
3. Are all viruses the same shape and size?

Using data

(a) Use the information on page 108 to construct a bar graph that shows the names of the different types of viruses on the vertical axis and their size on the horizontal axis.
(b) Name the virus which is (i) the biggest and (ii) the smallest.
(c) Divide the viruses into groups on the basis of (i) their size and (ii) their shape.
(d) Construct an identification key (refer to chapter 4) for the viruses shown on these pages.

Think

1. (a) Identify the criteria used to determine whether something is living or non-living.
   (b) Suggest how many criteria need to be met before a decision can be made. Give a reason for your suggestion.
   (c) Are some criteria more important than others?
   (d) Which criteria do viruses meet?
2. Do you consider that viruses are living or non-living? Give reasons for your response.
3. When conditions are not suitable, seeds from plants may remain dormant rather than germinate. Lotus seeds which have been dormant for more than a century can germinate.
   (a) In their dormant state, were the seeds living, dead, or non-living? Explain.
   (b) How are these plant seeds similar to viruses?
4. Once you have picked a tomato from the plant, is it living, dead or non-living? Discuss.
5. Participate in a class debate on whether viruses are living or non-living.

Investigate

1. Find out more about some of the diseases that viruses cause. Display your information in a poster.
2. For a long time, fungi were not considered to be living things. Although they seemed to grow like plants, they did not have roots or leaves and did not produce seeds. List some characteristics that support describing fungi as living things.
3. Research how our knowledge of viruses has helped us to reduce disease. Present your results to the class.

Putting it all together

Summing up

Copy and complete the statements below to compile a summary of this unit.
The missing words can be found in the word list below.

1. All living things are made up of _____.

2. _____ are used in the observation and investigation of cells.

3. When you use a _____ light microscope you use only one eye, whereas you use two eyes with a _____ microscope.

4. _____ microscopes allow you to look at living specimens whereas _____ microscopes do not.

5. When you look down the microscope and move the slide to the right, what you see moves to the _____.

6. Both plant and animal cells usually contain a nucleus and _____.

7. Plant cells sometimes also contain a _____ and _____.

8. The _____ is the control centre of the cell; it keeps the cell alive and working properly.

9. Eukaryotic cells have a membrane around their nucleus, whereas _____ cells do not.

10. Of the five kingdoms _____, _____, Plantae and _____ have eukaryotic cells.

11. The _____ and _____ of cells may differ depending on their function.

12. Although viruses do not have true cells, they do contain _____.

Word list

nucleic acid	stereo	size
light	electron	Animalia
nucleus	cells	cytoplasm
prokaryotic	monocular	chloroplasts
Fungi	left	vacuole
microscopes	shape	Protista

Looking back

1. Copy and complete the table below:

Cell feature	Plant cells	Animal cells
cell wall	✓	✗
cytoplasm		
cell membrane		
chloroplasts		
nucleus		
large vacuole		

2. Draw and label a typical plant cell and a typical animal cell.

3. What's green and eats porridge? Identify the parts of the microscope on the right and use the code below to find out the answer to this riddle.

   Key list:
   O = revolving nose piece; U = objective lens;
   S = coarse focus; K = fine focus;
   D = microscope slide; L = stage slide clip;
   C = base; O = mirror; L = iris adjustment;
   I = stage; M = eyepiece lens.

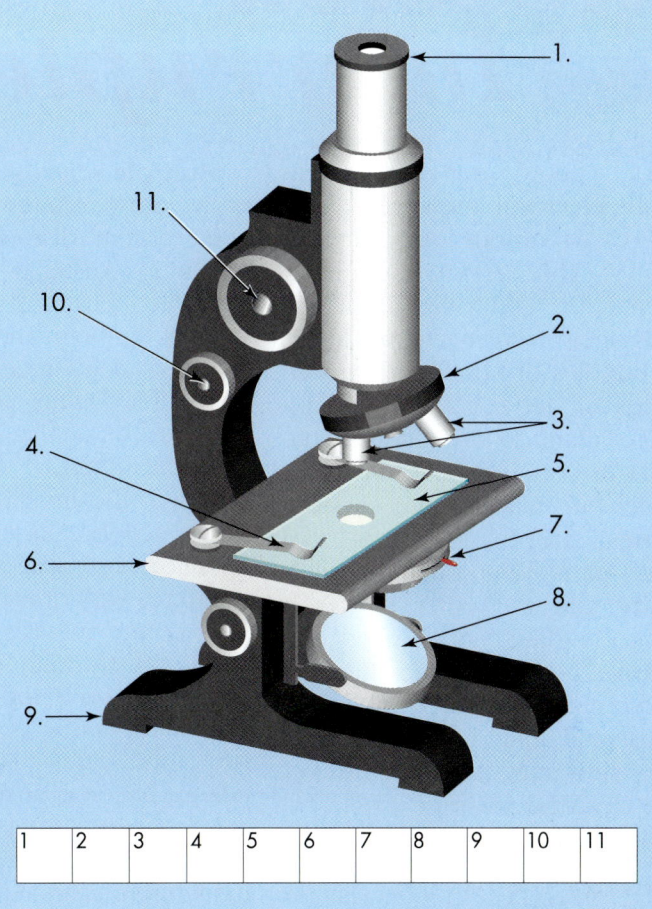

1	2	3	4	5	6	7	8	9	10	11

4. Unscramble the words using the clues provided.
   (a) Control centre of the cell   SEUNCLU
   (b) Surrounds the cell   ERAMMBNE
   (c) Contains cell sap   OCVAUEL
   (d) Part of the cell between the cell membrane and the nucleus   CATOPLMYS
   (e) Building blocks of all living things   LELSC
   (f) Living things   ASMOGNIRS

5. (a) Match the following cell names with the diagrams on the right.

   Euglena   (d)

   Paramecium

   onion epidermal cell

   nerve cell

   sperm cell

   guard cells

   root hair cell

   bacterium.

   (b) Identify the kingdom to which each of these cells belongs.

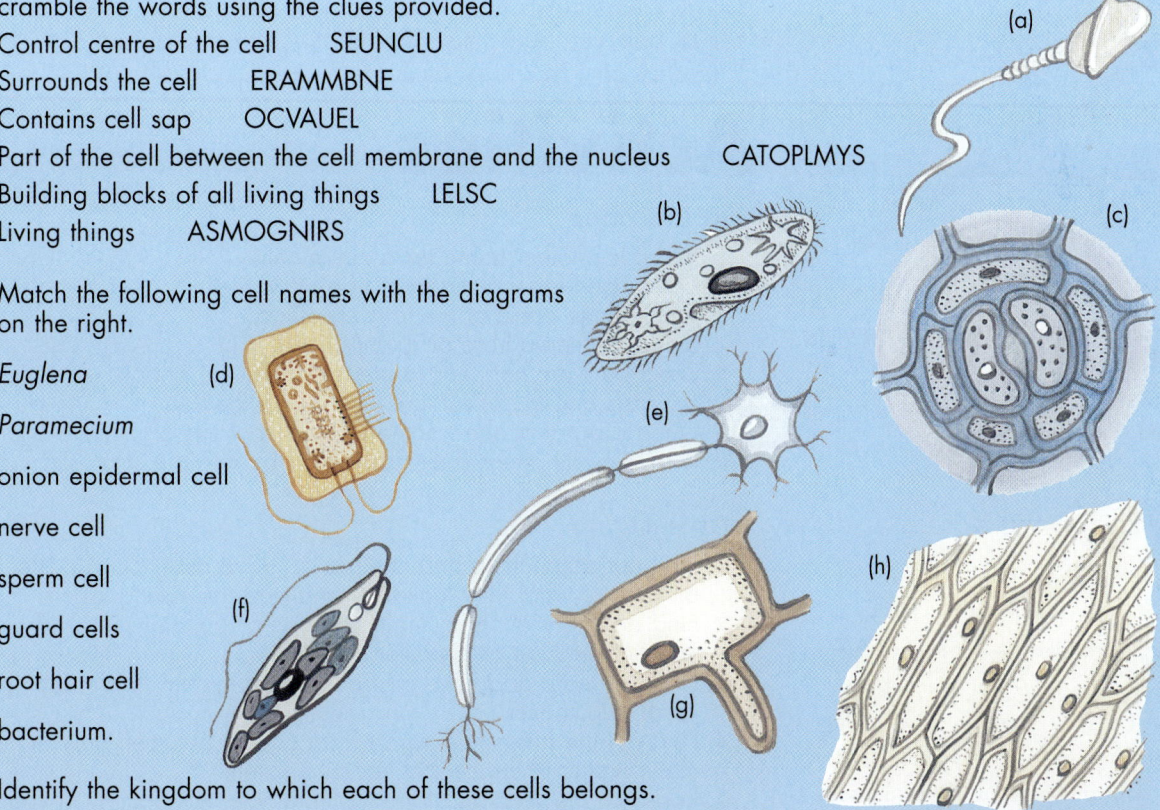

Your central nervous system sends electrical 'messages' along nerves to various parts of your body. Your everyday movements are controlled by these messages. Nerves are made up of bundles of hundreds or thousands of nerve cells. There are more than 2000 million nerve cells in your brain. Nerve cells, which are also known as **neurones**, are made up of two main parts. One part is the **cell body** and the other part is a long, tail-like fibre called the **axon**. The axon of most healthy nerve cells is covered by a fatty substance called **myelin**. This fatty substance helps the flow of the electrical message.

Multiple sclerosis (MS) is one of the most common central nervous system diseases in young adults in Australia. It is called 'multiple' because it affects many parts of the brain and spinal cord. 'Sclerosis' is a Greek word which means hardening, and describes hardened tissue that interrupts the electrical signals.

In MS, the myelin coat of the nerve cell breaks down and is replaced by scar tissue. This interferes with or even blocks the flow of the messages. Messages don't get through correctly, or sometimes go to the wrong area. The result is that body functions such as sight, walking and talking become uncontrolled.

MS is not a fatal disease and people who contract it live for many more years. Scientists don't know what causes it and no cure for it has yet been discovered. There is also no way to know exactly who might get it. Research has, however, shown a pattern in who is more likely to develop it.

Symptoms usually appear between the ages of 20 and 50 and slightly more women than men develop it. MS is also more common in populations in the temperate zones between 40° and 60° north and south of the equator.

Symptoms of MS vary greatly from person to person, and from time to time in the same person, but may include:
- loss of coordination
- extreme fatigue or unusual tired feeling
- numbness or pins-and-needles
- staggering or loss of balance
- dragging of feet
- shaking hands
- seeing double or uncontrolled eye movement
- speech difficulties.

Healthy nerve cell

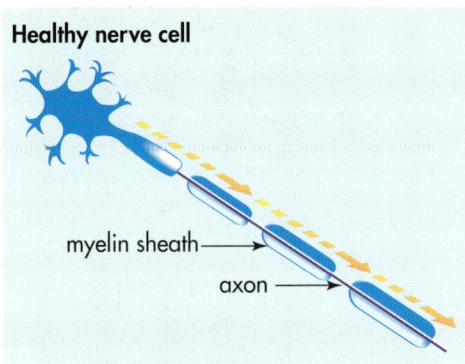

myelin sheath

axon

An electrical 'message' travelling along a healthy nerve cell

Damaged nerve cell

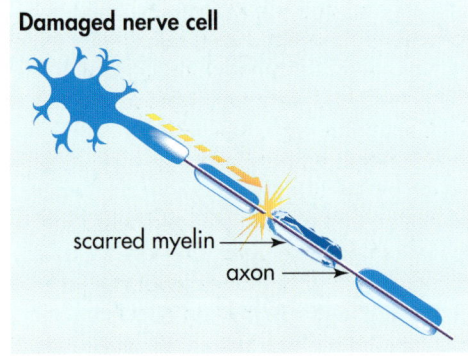

scarred myelin

axon

A damaged nerve, with the 'message' interrupted

Activities

Remember

1. What is another name for a nerve cell?
2. Sketch and label a diagram of a nerve cell.
3. What is the name of the fatty substance along the nerve fibre or axon?
4. Describe what happens to the nerve cells of people with multiple sclerosis and the effect that this has on them.
5. Using diagrams, show some of the symptoms of multiple sclerosis.
6. Is everybody affected the same way by multiple sclerosis? Explain.

Investigate

1. Find out about the different types of nerve cells. On a poster, draw pictures of what they look like, and add interesting labels.
2. Find out more about multiple sclerosis or poliomyelitis and present your information as a poster.
3. Find out more about the central nervous system (brain and spinal cord) in humans.
4. Find out the difference, apart from colour, between grey matter and white matter in the central nervous system.
5. Research the services of the Multiple Sclerosis Society in your state.

Reflection

1. Strategies for new words

This chapter contained many new names that may be difficult to remember. They are part of the language of biology and will become easier to remember as you use them more often.

(a) In your workbook, prepare a table with two columns. Without looking through this chapter, write down those words that you found easiest to remember in the first column. Now look through the chapter and in the second column write down the words that you found most difficult to remember.

GROUP WORK (b) Take part in a group discussion to see how common your 'easiest' and 'most difficult' words were with others in the group. The groups should then report back to the class.

(c) In what ways could you 'learn' to remember these 'most difficult' words better? Copy the following list into your workbook, and then tick the ways of learning that you most agree with or that you think work best for you. You may tick more than one box. Then have a class discussion about all these ways of learning with your teacher.

2. An analogy for the cell

When we make an analogy, we compare an object with something else so that we can better understand that object. For example, some people use the analogy of a room for a cell. They say 'the cell is like a room'.

(a) Why do you think a room is chosen as an analogy for a cell?

(b) Analogies are not always exactly like the objects to which they are compared. In your opinion, in what ways does a room differ from a cell?

(c) Can you think of another analogy for a cell?

3. Remembering about the cell

This exercise is best done in class without referring to the text.

(a) In your workbook, draw a rough copy of the cell shown on the right.

(b) Write in labels on the organelles at the end of each connecting line.

(c) Under your diagram, write the name of each organelle and what it does in the cell.

(d) Would you expect to find extra structures in a plant cell? If so, discuss with the class what they are and what they do. If you forget some of the names, you should write these down on a piece of paper or card and hang it somewhere so you will see the words and remember them.

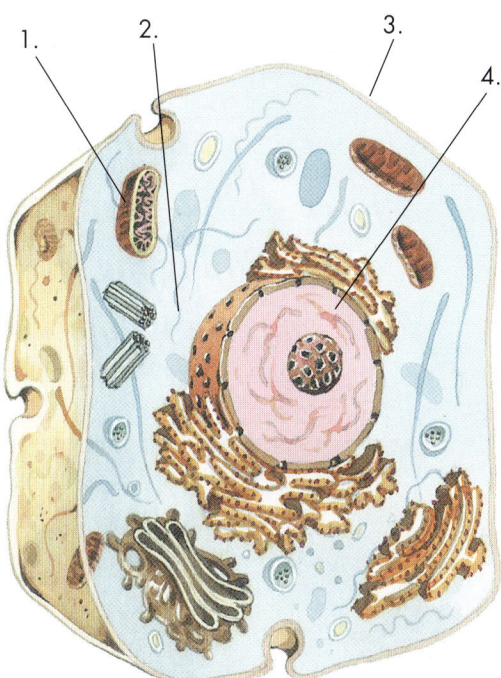

Inside an animal cell

4. Changing your ideas

(a) Write down the 'big ideas' that you have learned during this chapter.

(b) Write down all the skills that you have learned during this chapter.

(c) Did you change your mind about anything while studying this topic? Is there anything that you think differently about now? List all the ways you have changed your mind on particular topics.

(d) Look back at how you defined a cell in the exercises on page 93. How does it differ from how you would define a cell now?

(e) Do you still have questions about cells? List them now.

Draw a diagram that represents the word you are trying to remember.	❏
Do some rote learning (memorise).	❏
Complete a short quiz set by your teacher every second lesson. It would not be counted for marks, but would show your progress. Your teacher or another student would check your answers.	❏
Accept that you may not remember every new word straight away, but by reading the words in the future, you will become familiar with them.	❏
Have a mental picture or vision of what the word means and make a connection between the word and the picture in your head.	❏

FORCES IN ACTION

The way that all objects move depends on what forces are acting on them. A force is a push or a pull. While you are reading this, the muscles in your eyes are pulling the lens into the right shape so that the words are not blurry. Even objects that do not move have forces acting on them.

KEY CONTENT

Use everyday examples to explain how forces such as friction, electrostatic, gravity, magnetism, buoyancy and surface tension work.

Identify changes caused by forces and recognise that not all forces arise from direct contact.

Describe the force field for forces which act at a distance, and use examples to explain how these forces work.

Describe the effect of the Earth's magnetic field.

Recognise that all objects in the universe exert a force of gravity on all other objects in the universe.

KEY QUESTIONS

Why doesn't gravity make you fall through the floor?

How does a compass work?

Why is it so hard to walk on ice?

Why do male Olympic cyclists shave their legs?

Why are bicycle helmets necessary?

How does a car seatbelt protect you in a car accident?

What goes down . . . should come up. There are three forces acting on this bungee jumper. What are they?

Thinking about Forces

1. The language of force

alloys	magnetism
buoyancy	pull and push
electromagnetic	repel and attract
electrostatic	resistance
force	speed
friction	static
gravity	streamlined
grip	surface
impact	temporary
lubricants	surface tension
mass	terminal
magnets	variable
magnetic field	weight

 GROUP WORK

(a) Form a group of three or four people and assign roles to each group member. You will need:
- a recorder to draw up the table at the bottom of the page on a piece of butcher's paper. (Include three or four 'Meaning' columns depending on how many there are in the group.)
- a reader to read out the words from the box above
- a listener to respond by providing a meaning for each of the words.

(b) The reader slowly reads out the words one by one. The listener responds by stating a meaning for each word, or saying 'pass' if he or she doesn't know the meaning. When a meaning is given, the recorder fills in the 'Word' and 'Meaning 1' columns. (In a group of four, you could have two recorders taking turns at recording each meaning.) If the listener passes on a word, write in the word but leave the meaning space blank.

(c) Change over roles and repeat until everyone has had a turn at each role.

(d) In your group, talk about each word in your table and decide on an agreed meaning. Record this in the final column.

(e) Ask one member of your group to visit another group to check their views.

(f) Once you are satisfied with your agreed meanings, hang your table on the wall.

You are now ready to test your meanings by studying chapter 6. You can change or add to your meanings as you work through this chapter.

(g) What do you think the terms 'kinetic' and 'potential energy' mean?

2. The six forces

GROUP WORK The six words printed in green in the box above are the names of the forces you will learn about in this chapter.

(a) How might you come in contact with each force in your daily life? Share what you know in your group.

(b) Make a list of any forces that act on an athlete running a race.

Words	Meaning 1	Meaning 2	Meaning 3	Meaning 4	Agreed meaning

6.1

How fast?

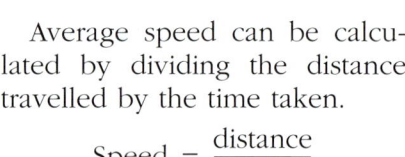

The fastest athletes in the world can run at speeds of about 37 kilometres per hour. The fastest swimmers in the world can swim at speeds of about 8 kilometres per hour.

Speed is a measure of how quickly distance is covered. To be more precise, it is a measure of the distance moved in one unit of time. The speedometer of a car measures the speed in kilometres per hour (km/h). It tells you how far the car would move in one hour.

How fast is Cathy Freeman?

Experiment 6.1 HOW FAST DO YOU WALK?

YOU WILL NEED
stopwatch
long measuring tape (at least 10 metres) or trundle wheel
calculator

- Measure out a distance of 50 metres.
- Use the stopwatch or the second hand of your own watch to measure the time in seconds that it takes you to walk the 50 metres.
- Work out your average speed in units of metres per second. Use your calculator to convert your speed in m/s to km/h. All you need to do is multiply the speed in m/s by 3.6.
- Gather the results for your class in a table like the one on the right.

Walking speeds of students

Speed (km/h)	Number of students
less than 4.0	
4.0–4.9	
5.0–5.9	
6.0–6.9	
7.0–7.9	
8.0 or more	

1. Draw a bar chart like the one below to display the results for your class.
2. What is the most common average walking speed of your class?

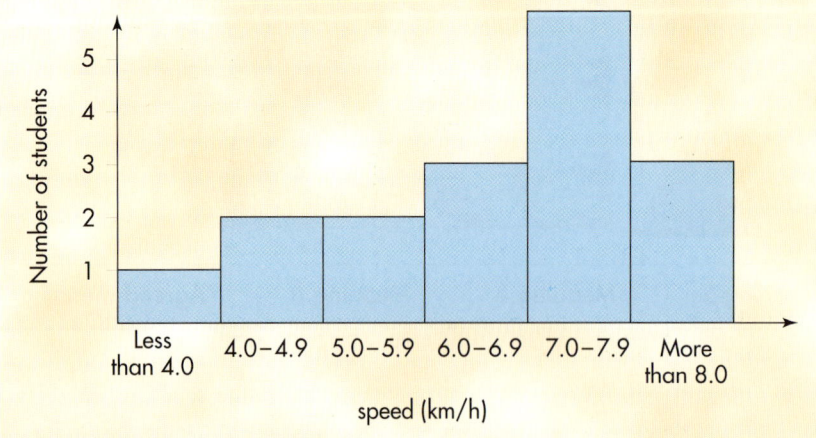

Average speed can be calculated by dividing the distance travelled by the time taken.

$$\text{Speed} = \frac{\text{distance}}{\text{time}}$$

For example, if you travel from Sydney to Melbourne, a distance of 900 km, in 10 hours, your average speed is given by:

$$\text{Speed} = \frac{900\,\text{km}}{10\,\text{h}} = 90\,\text{km/h}$$

Sometimes it is more sensible to measure speed in metres per second (m/s) than in kilometres per hour. For example, a mosquito flying through an open window to bite you on your arm while you sleep might fly a distance of 6 metres in 3 seconds. Its average speed would be given by:

$$\text{Speed} = \frac{6\,\text{m}}{3\,\text{s}} = 2\,\text{m/s}$$

Kinetic *or* potential?

Running a race as fast as Cathy Freeman requires a lot of energy. Energy is the ability to do work. But where does this energy come from? Cathy's body transforms the energy contained in the food she eats into muscle, and then into motion. Before she starts to run, Cathy has **potential energy** (energy stored in her body). But while she is running, this energy is changed into **kinetic energy** (moving energy).

A car at rest with fuel in its tank has potential energy. This potential energy is transformed into kinetic energy as the car starts to move. Its energy source is the fuel in the tank. It has no more energy once the fuel is used up.

An arrow held poised in a bow also has potential energy, which is then transformed into kinetic energy once it is released. Energy is transformed into movement that we can observe.

Activities

Think

1. Do you remember the fable of the hare and the tortoise? The giant tortoise can reach a speed of about 7.5 cm/s (13 seconds to travel 1 metre). The hare can run as fast as 20 m/s. If their race was 1 kilometre long, try to work out how long the hare slept if the result was a tie.
2. Give examples of measurements of speed that would use the following units:
   • cm/s • m/s • km/h • mm/day.
3. Draw a table like the one below and then add ten everyday situations involving potential or kinetic energy. Explain the reasons for your choices in the right-hand column.

Energy type	Situation or object	Explanation
potential	firewood	The firewood contains energy which will be released as heat when it is burnt.
kinetic	aeroplane in flight	The aeroplane is moving.

Using data

1. Use the speed formula and a calculator to work out the average speed of:
   (a) a two hour train trip from Sydney to Newcastle, a distance of 150 kilometres
   (b) a three hour flight from Perth to Albury, a distance of 3813 kilometres by air
   (c) a seven hour bicycle ride from Sydney to Wollongong, a distance of 92 kilometres.
2. Use your own average walking speed, determined in the experiment on page 116, to calculate how long it would take you to walk from Sydney to Melbourne, a distance of 900 kilometres:
   (a) without stopping
   (b) if you walked for only ten hours each day.
3. Use the speed formula and calculator to determine the average speed in m/s of each of the world record holders in the table below. Complete the table by converting the speed to km/h.

Investigate

Research to find out how a bicycle speedometer works, and compare this with the way a car speedometer works.

Record holder	Event	World record	Average speed (m/s)	Average speed (km/h)
Grant Hackett (M) (Australia), 2001	Swimming 1500 m freestyle	14 min 34.56 s		
Hicham El Guerrouj (M) (China), 1998	Athletics 1500 m	3 min 26.00 s		
Leisel Jones (F) (Australia), 2003	Swimming 100 m breaststroke	1 min 6.37 s		
Tim Montgomery (M) (USA), 2002	Athletics 100 m	9.78 s		
Matthew Welsh (M) (Australia), 2003	Swimming 50 m butterfly	23.43 s		
Michael Johnson (M) (USA), 1996	Athletics 200 m	19.32 s		
Haile Gebrselaisse (M) (Ethiopia), 1998	Athletics 10 000 m	26 min 22.75 s		
Thierry Toutain (M) (France), 1996	Athletics 50 km walk	3 h 41 min		

On the move

When a tennis ball is hit with a tennis racquet it is clear that a **force** is acting on the ball. Not only does the ball change its direction of movement, but while it is in contact with the racquet it changes its shape as well.

A force is a push or a pull. Forces are acting around you all the time and they can cause changes to occur. Sometimes the effects are obvious and sometimes they are not. At this moment, forces are acting inside your body to pump blood around. When you write, you use a force to push the pen or pencil.

Forces can start motion,

stop motion,

speed up or

slow down motion,

change the direction of motion,

change the shape of an object

or have no visible effect at all.

Experiment 6.2 WHAT CAN A FORCE DO?

YOU WILL NEED
rubber band   plasticine   tennis ball   coin

Copy the following table into your workbook. Then complete the activities and write down your observations. Take notice of any changes in the motion or shape of each object and what caused the change in the motion or shape.

What can a force do?

What to do	Observations	
	Changes in motion or shape	**What caused the change**
Stretch a rubber band.		
Squash a lump of plasticine.		
Push down on the floor with one foot.		
Drop a tennis ball. Observe what happens: (a) at the moment that you drop it (b) as it falls (c) as it hits the ground (d) as it goes up again.		
Flick a coin with one finger so that it slides along the surface of a table. Observe what happens after it is flicked.		

1. When you squash a lump of plasticine and stretch a rubber band, a change in shape is observed. What is different about the behaviour of these two materials?

2. Does the tennis ball change its shape at all when it hits the ground? What would happen to a falling lump of plasticine when it hits the ground? Will it bounce? Check your prediction.

Forces *at a* distance

When you drop a tennis ball it speeds up as it falls through the air. The force of **gravity** pulls it towards the Earth. Gravity is a non-contact force. An object does not have to be touching the Earth to be pulled towards it. **Magnetic** forces and **electrostatic** forces also work without touching. The area where these forces are observed is called the **field**.

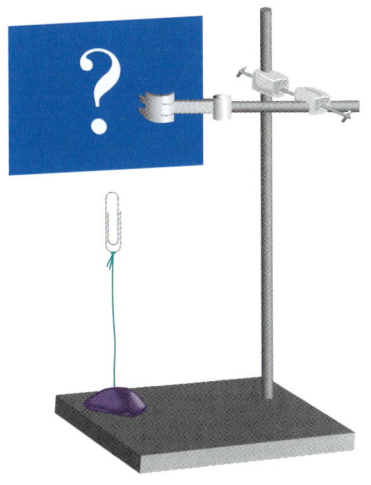

What is behind the card? (A force must be holding the paperclip in the air.)

More *than* one force

Almost never is there only one force acting on an object. You are probably sitting on a chair right now. What forces are acting on you and your chair? There must be at least one! The force of gravity is pulling you towards the centre of the Earth.

If gravity were the only force acting on you and your chair, what would happen to you?

Experiment 6.3 **ELECTROSTATIC FORCES AT A DISTANCE**

YOU WILL NEED
plastic ruler or rod
paper
nylon, wool and cotton cloths

- Charge a ruler by rubbing it with a nylon or wool cloth.
- Hold the charged plastic ruler close to a thin stream of tap water.
- Write as many observations as possible.
- Using the rest of your equipment, design your own experiment to find out more about electrostatic forces. Remember to make as many observations as possible.

1. Explain your observations using words like 'attract' and 'repel'.
2. Name all the forces acting in your experiment.
3. Use different materials to come up with other examples of electrostatic forces at work.
4. List some ways you encounter electrostatic forces in your daily life.
5. Ask your teacher to show you a Van de Graaf generator. Think about what you see, then write an explanation of what you think is happening.

Activities

Remember

1. Write a list of the things that a force can do.
2. Which of the following forces are non-contact forces? friction, electrostatic, magnetic, gravity
3. Why don't you fall through the floor?

Think

1. Copy the following table into your workbook. Complete it by thinking of two or three everyday examples of each of the effects of forces. You can complete your table with diagrams or words.

Everyday effects of forces

Effect	Examples in everyday life
starting motion	
stopping motion	
speeding up motion	
slowing down motion	
changing the direction of motion	
changing the shape of an object	
having no visible effect	

2. When you flick a coin so that it slides across a table, it slows down.
   (a) What is the name of the force that slows it down?
   (b) While your finger is still pushing the coin, there are four forces acting on the coin. Draw a diagram with arrows showing the direction in which each of the four forces pushes or pulls.
   (c) How many forces are acting on the coin after your finger stops pushing?
   (d) What would happen to the coin if there was no force acting on it?

What's the attraction?

Make a list of all the things that you come into contact with every day that use magnets. The pictures below will give you some clues. Share your ideas with others and compile a class list.

Magnets can attract certain materials without actually touching them. Magnetic forces can therefore be referred to as non-contact forces.

Magnets that retain their magnetism when removed from other magnets are called **permanent magnets**. Natural permanent magnets contain one or more of the elements iron, nickel and cobalt. The most common natural permanent magnetic substance is magnetite, also known as lodestone.

Magnets that might be found at home: fridge magnets, a cupboard door latch, magnetic knife holder and magnetic screwdriver

Experiment 6.5

MAGNETS, MAGNETS AND MORE MAGNETS

YOU WILL NEED
paperclips (many)
a magnet

- Pick up a single paperclip with a bar magnet. Use the attached paperclip to pick up a second paperclip. Make sure that the second paperclip does not touch the bar magnet.
- Continue adding paperclips until no more can be added.

1. Why do you think each of the paperclips is attracted to the one above it?

- Now gently separate the second paperclip from the first paperclip as shown below.

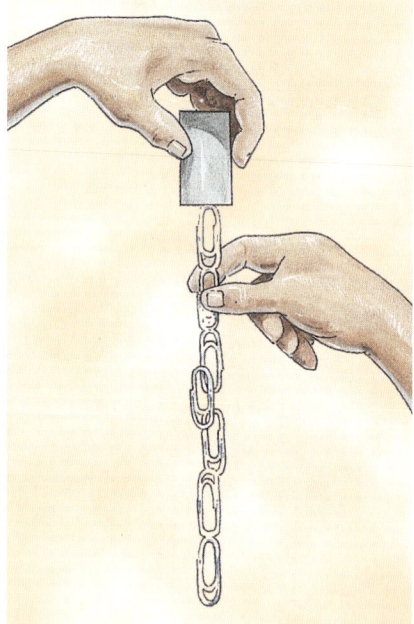

2. What happens when the second paperclip is separated from the first paperclip?
3. What happens to the other paperclips? Why?

Experiment 6.4   WHAT DOES A MAGNET ATTRACT?

YOU WILL NEED
a magnet
a selection of materials to be tested
(see the list below)

- Place a magnet close to a range of materials to find out which ones are attracted to it. Record your observations in a table like the one below.

Attracted	Not attracted

- Test as many items as possible including a pencil, paper straw, plastic straw, coin, iron nail, stainless steel spoon, aluminium foil, paperclip, copper wire.

1. Which materials were attracted to the magnet?
2. Are all metals attracted to magnets?
3. Of the materials that were attracted to the magnet, which one was attracted the most? Why do you think this was so?
4. Were any forces other than the magnetic force acting on the objects? If so, what were they?
5. Were there any unexpected observations? What were they?
6. What types of substances appear to be affected by the magnetic force?

- Do some materials 'block' the magnetic force? Design an experiment to find out.

Most permanent magnets are **alloys**, which are mixtures of iron, nickel or cobalt with other elements or each other. Items made of steel are attracted to magnets because steel is an alloy of iron, carbon and other substances.

Temporary magnets are those which lose their magnetism when removed from another magnet. The paperclips in the experiment on the left are temporary magnets while in contact with the permanent magnet. As soon as they are removed from the permanent magnet, they lose their magnetism.

All magnets, no matter what their shape, have a **north pole** at one end and a **south pole** at the other. If a bar magnet is suspended by string, it will always line itself up in the north–south direction. The north pole of the magnet is the end pointing towards the North Pole of the Earth. The south pole is the end pointing towards the South Pole of the Earth.

Experiment 6.7
MAKING YOUR OWN MAGNET

YOU WILL NEED
a large iron nail (about 75 mm long)
strong magnet
paperclips or small nails

- Take a large iron nail and stroke it with a strong permanent magnet. After each stroke, lift the magnet high above the nail before commencing the next one. Each stroke must be in the same direction and made with the same end of the magnet.
- After a total of 40 strokes, test your new magnet by trying to attract paperclips or small nails.
- Compare its strength with other magnets in your class.

1. Is your magnet a permanent or temporary magnet?
2. Which end of your magnet is the north pole? How do you know?

- Use your magnet to make a compass like the one shown below. You will need a container of water and a float. The bottom of a styrofoam cup will make a good float.
- Try this experiment using a sewing needle instead of an iron nail, and without using the float. Explain your observations.
- Try dropping your magnet on the ground. Test it to see the effect.

Make your own compass.

Experiment 6.6
POLES APART

YOU WILL NEED
2 bar magnets

- Take two bar magnets and identify the north and south pole of each. Position the magnets near each other as shown below. Take note of whether the magnets attract or repel each other in each case.

(a)	N	S
(b)	N	N
(c)	S	S
(d)	S	N

Attraction or repulsion?

- Complete the sentences to form your conclusion:
Like poles _____.
Unlike poles _____.

Activities

Remember
1. Which of the following statements is correct?
   (a) All substances are attracted to magnets.
   (b) All metals are strongly attracted to magnets.
   (c) Iron, steel and nickel are attracted to magnets.
   (d) Iron is the only substance attracted to magnets.
2. What is the difference between a permanent magnet and a temporary magnet?
3. How should two bar magnets be placed on a table so that they repel each other?

Think
Why does the north pole of a magnet point towards the North Pole of the Earth?

Create
1. Make a magnetic sculpture using a magnet, paperclips, nails, pins and other small materials containing iron.
2. Design and make a device using only paper or cardboard that will allow one magnet to be suspended in the air above another magnet.

Investigate
1. Design and complete an experiment to measure the strength of different magnets. Record your measurements in a table and display them using a bar graph.
2. The electromagnet combines electricity and magnetism. Find out how Michael Faraday's experiments in 1831 altered our technological development.

Invisible forces

Each of the iron filings in the photograph below is attracted to the magnet. The filings line up in the direction of the magnetic force around the magnet. The area where the magnetic force acts is called the **magnetic field**.

Iron filings sprinkled around a bar magnet

Magnetic *Earth*

The Earth, like the sun and some planets, has its own magnetic field. It is very much like the magnetic field of a bar magnet. Scientists are not sure why the Earth has a magnetic field.

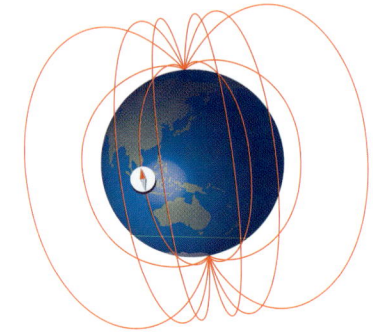

The Earth's magnetic field

A compass, like the iron filings in the experiment below, points in the direction of the magnetic field lines. In fact, any magnet free to turn will line itself up along the field lines. The north pole of the magnet is really the 'north seeking' pole of the magnet. Similarly, the south pole of a magnet 'seeks' the South Pole of the Earth.

Magnets *that can be* turned off

An electromagnet is a coil of wire wrapped around an iron core. When an electric current is passed through the coil, the iron is magnetised. When the current is turned off, the iron is no longer magnetised. Being able to turn a magnet on and off at will can be very useful. This photograph shows one such use. Electromagnets are also used in doorbells, buzzers, speakers, telephones, electric motors and generators.

An electromagnet is used to lift a huge load of scrap metal.

Experiment 6.8

MAPPING THE MAGNETIC FIELD

YOU WILL NEED
bar magnet in a plastic bag
sheet of A4 paper
overhead transparency
iron filings
small compass

• Place a bar magnet (in a plastic bag) in the centre of a sheet of white paper.
Cover the paper and magnet with an overhead transparency sheet.
• Carefully sprinkle iron filings over the transparency, gently tapping it to spread the filings out. Take care not to let iron filings touch the magnet.
• Draw a diagram of the pattern made by the iron filings. Label the north pole and south pole of your magnet on the diagram.

The pattern in your diagram is a map of the magnetic field around the bar magnet.

1. Where does the magnetic field appear to be strongest? How do you know this?
2. What happens to the strength of the magnetic field as you get further from the magnet?
3. Why are some iron filings standing up?
4. Place a compass at several positions around the magnet. The direction in which the compass needle points shows the direction of the magnetic field lines. Add arrows to your diagram to show the direction of the magnetic field.
5. Do the magnetic field lines run from north pole to south pole or from south pole to north pole?

Experiment 6.9 MAKING AN ELECTROMAGNET

YOU WILL NEED
1.5 m insulated copper wire
power supply
switch
paperclips (many)

- Set up the electric circuit as shown in the diagram below. Wind ten turns of wire around the nail. There will be a lot of wire left over but do not cut it.

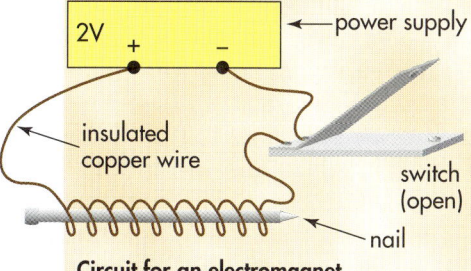

2V
+   −
power supply
insulated copper wire
switch (open)
nail

Circuit for an electromagnet

- Set the power supply to 2 volts and close the switch.

- Test your electromagnet by opening the switch and seeing how many paperclips it will pick up.

- Increase the number of times the wire is wound around the electromagnet and test again.

- Repeat this several times until you have wound almost all the copper wire around the nail. (Make sure all windings are in the same direction.) Predict your results each time.

- Draw up a table to record the number of windings, your predictions and your results.

- Predict what will happen if you increase the voltage to 4 volts. Test your prediction and add a column to your table to record these results.

1. What is the effect of increasing the number of turns around the nail?

2. What is the effect of increasing the voltage?

3. Test other materials to see if they are attracted to your electromagnet.

4. In your own words explain how your electromagnet works.

5. List as many possible uses for an electromagnet as you can.

Activities

Using data

Arianna made her own electromagnet to find out the effect of the number of windings around a nail on the number of paperclips that the nail could pick up. She used the circuit shown in the above experiment with the power supply set to 2 volts. Arianna then repeated her measurements with the power supply set to 4 volts and 6 volts. She recorded her observations in a table, then she constructed a graph (above).

1. How many paperclips did Arianna lift with 20 windings and the power supply set to 6 volts?
2. Arianna lifted twelve paperclips when the power supply was set to 4 volts. How many windings were there around the nail?
3. How many paperclips could Arianna expect to lift with 50 windings around the nail and the power supply set to 2 volts?
4. Can you suggest a way that Arianna would be able to make her results more reliable?

Remember

1. What is a magnetic field?
2. Copy the following diagram into your workbook. Draw an arrow at each of the positions A, B, C and D to show the direction in which a compass needle would point.

C
A
S   N   D
B

Think

1. Which way should a compass needle point if you hold it at the north magnetic pole? If you hold the compass horizontally, what will actually happen to the needle?
2. Is an electromagnet a permanent or temporary magnet?
3. Explain how the doorbell on the right works.

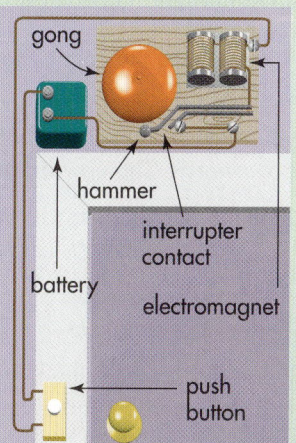

gong
hammer
interrupter contact
electromagnet
battery
push button

6.5

Walking on water?

The water strider is able to walk on water. Water striders are certainly light, but is that the only reason that they do not sink?

The water strider walks on water. Why can't you?

Experiment 6.10 WET FORCES

YOU WILL NEED
plastic ice-cream container or bucket
table tennis ball
coin
paperclip

- Push a table tennis ball to the bottom of a container of water and let it go.
- Repeat this with a coin.

1. How does the coin behave differently from the table tennis ball?

There are two forces acting on both the coin and the table tennis ball after you release them at the bottom of the container. Gravity pulls them both downwards. The upward push of the water is called buoyancy.

2. Is the buoyancy force on the table tennis ball greater or less than the pull of gravity? Which force is greater for the coin?

- Try to float a paperclip on the surface of the water. You will need to be gentle and patient.

If you did succeed, the force that kept up the paperclip is not buoyancy. It is surface tension. If the surface is not broken by the paperclip it can float. Once the surface is broken, the paperclip sinks.

The 500 g mass in the experiment opposite appears to weigh less because the spring balance does not have to pull as hard to balance the force of gravity. Its job is made easier by the buoyancy force. When you lift an object in water, it does not actually weigh less. It just seems to weigh less because of the buoyancy force.

Buoyancy is the upward push on an object which is floating on top of or submerged in a **fluid**. It acts in all liquids and gases.

Buoyancy is the force that keeps hot air balloons floating in the air. It is also the force that allows submarines to rise to the surface of the ocean.

The water appears to be held onto the coin in the experiment below by a skin. There is, in fact, no skin. The water is held in shape by **surface tension**. Surface tension is the pulling of particles in a liquid towards each other. Soaps and detergents reduce the surface tension of water.

Surface tension is what keeps the water strider from sinking and drowning. The small weight of the water strider is well spread out over the surface and is not large enough to push the water particles apart.

The buoyancy force of the water in the Dead Sea is so large you can lie back and read a book. The buoyancy is caused by the amount of salt in the water.

Experiment 6.11

ARE THINGS REALLY LIGHTER IN WATER?

YOU WILL NEED

stone length of string
spring balance bucket
500 gram mass

- Tie some string around a large stone. Suspend the stone in a bucket of water without letting it touch the bottom.

1. Does the stone feel any lighter?

- Use a spring balance to find the weight in newtons of a 500 g mass and record it. Without removing the mass from the spring balance, carefully lower it into the bucket so that it sits just under the surface of the water.
- Record the force measured by the spring balance. Use the diagram below to work out the size of the buoyancy force on the 500 g mass.

2. What is the size of the buoyancy force on the 500 g mass?
3. Is the 500 g mass really lighter?

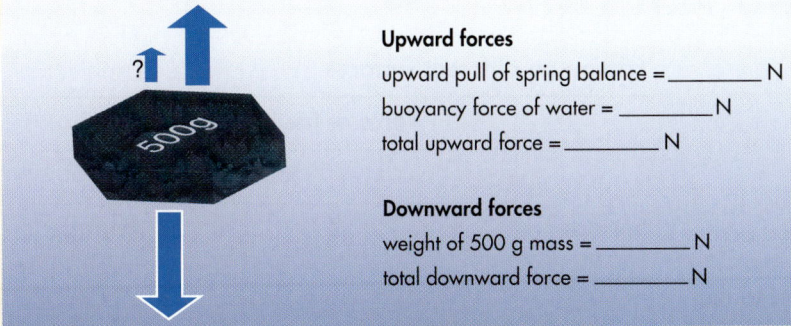

Upward forces

upward pull of spring balance = _____ N
buoyancy force of water = _____ N
total upward force = _____ N

Downward forces

weight of 500 g mass = _____ N
total downward force = _____ N

The total force on the mass is zero while it is sitting still under the surface. That means that the total upward force must be equal to the total downward force.

Experiment 6.12

HOLDING IT ALL TOGETHER

YOU WILL NEED

coin
eye-dropper
beaker
dishwashing detergent

- Estimate how many drops of water you could get onto a 5 cent coin without water spilling over the edge. With great care and from a very small height, test your prediction with an eye-dropper.

1. Were you surprised by your results?
2. What seems to keep the water on the coin?

- Repeat your test using water from a small beaker with a few drops of dishwashing detergent added to it.

3. What difference does the detergent make to your result?

Activities

Remember

1. Name two forces acting on you when you float on your back in a swimming pool.
2. What force keeps a water strider on the surface of water?
3. Explain the difference between buoyancy and surface tension.

Think

1. Which fluid produces the greater buoyancy force — air or water? How do you know?
2. Name the three forces acting on a water glider when it is standing on a still pond.
3. What happens to an object when you plunge it into a fluid and let go:
   (a) if the buoyancy force is the same as its weight?
   (b) if the buoyancy force is less than its weight?
4. Explain in terms of gravity, buoyancy and surface tension why humans can't walk on water.

Investigate

1. Different fluids produce different buoyancy forces. Drop a corn kernel or pea into a glass of water and another into a glass of soda water. Which liquid applies the larger buoyancy force? Try to explain why.
2. Design and carry out an experiment to compare the buoyancy and surface tension of water, olive oil and vinegar.
3. Find out what capillary action is and how it works.
4. Cut a slit in the end of a match and gently open it up a little. Float the match in a bowl of water. Carefully place a drop of dishwashing detergent in the split end of the match and watch what happens. Try to explain your observations.

6.6

Friction — Friend or foe?

Friction is the force applied to the surface of an object when it moves against the surface of another object. Both surfaces do not have to be moving. Friction acts where the surfaces touch. Friction can slow down an object or stop it from moving.

Friction limits how fast you can go. Rough surfaces produce more friction than smooth ones. To slow down quickly on rollerblades you need to use a stopper so that there is more friction. If there was no friction, you would not even be able to start moving forward. However, if there was too much friction, it would take too much effort to keep moving.

Experiment 6.13 MEASURING FRICTION

YOU WILL NEED
block of wood with hook attached
several identical blocks of wood
spring balance

- Copy the table on the right into your workbook.
- Use a spring balance to pull a block of wood across your desktop. As long as you pull steadily, the reading on the spring balance will be equal to the force of friction on the moving block.
- Record your reading in the table.

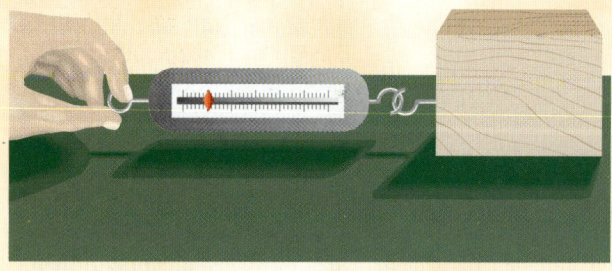

A spring balance is used to pull a block of wood across a surface.

- Repeat your measurement two more times on the desktop and calculate the average force of friction. Record all data in the table.
- Repeat this procedure on several other surfaces. Surfaces that you might test are: vinyl floor, carpet, doormat, concrete and bitumen.

Friction on different surfaces

Surface	Force of friction (newtons)			
	Trial			
	1	2	3	Average

- Summarise your results in a bar graph.

1. List the surfaces in order, from greatest friction force to least.
2. What feature of a surface seems to determine the amount of friction?
3. Why was it a good idea to repeat each measurement three times?

- Design and carry out an experiment to find out the effect of mass on the size of the friction force. Record your results in a table and display them on a line graph.

4. Do heavier objects experience more friction?

Getting *a grip on* things

You need friction to do many things. Even walking requires friction. Have you ever slipped on a banana peel?

When you walk you push your foot backwards against the ground so that the ground pushes you forward. Without friction your foot would slip backwards as it does on a banana peel.

Even holding objects in your hand requires friction. Have you ever dropped wet soap in the shower or bath?

Wet hands and wet soap provide no grip.

The force of friction is especially important to cars. Without friction, cars would not be able to turn corners or stop. The decrease in friction on wet or icy roads makes it very difficult to steer and stop a car.

Friction also causes problems in cars. In fact, it can cause a problem in any device where parts rub against each other. The rubbing together of parts in cars causes unwanted heat and also wears them down. Oil is used to reduce friction in car engines.

Activities

Remember

1. What is the force of friction?
2. What reduces friction?
3. What is the safest type of road surface for wet conditions?

Think

1. For each of the 'friendly friction' sketches, state:
   (a) how the friction force is being helpful
   (b) what would happen if the friction force was absent.
2. For each of the 'unfriendly friction' sketches, state:
   (a) how the friction force is being a nuisance
   (b) what could be done to reduce the effect of the force of friction
   (c) what could be done to reduce the force of friction.
3. Why are cars sometimes required to carry chains in and around ski resorts?
4. Does friction always oppose motion? Explain.

Investigate

Find out why car tyres have tread. Are wider tyres better than narrow ones? How does it affect your driving when the tread is worn away and the tyres become 'bald'? How does the tread make wet-weather driving safer?
You could also find out why sports shoes have different treads.

Friendly friction

Unfriendly friction

SCIENCE & technology

SMOOTH RUNNING

Objects can travel faster if they are smooth. Skis and surfboards are waxed and buffed to reduce friction and make them go through snow or water faster.

Olympic bobsled teams spend long hours smoothing and polishing the runners of their sleds.

Friction caused by a road surface is essential for the braking of cars, bicycles and other vehicles. However, friction also limits the speed of those vehicles. The smoother the surface, the faster a vehicle can go. Road surfaces need to be smooth so that vehicles do not waste fuel in overcoming too much friction. However, they need to be rough enough to allow vehicles to turn and brake safely in all types of weather.

Trains and trams run on steel tracks because they produce very little friction. That makes them cheaper to run than vehicles that move on rough surfaces. Imagine how powerful a bus would need to be to carry the same load as a long freight train!

Just rolling around

Ball-bearings are often used to reduce the friction on wheels as they spin around an axle. The picture below shows a cross-section through a rollerblade wheel and its bearing. Each wheel has a ball-bearing race on each side. The ball-bearings act as wheels, allowing the outside ring to 'ride' around the inside ring without sliding. (Rolling friction is much less than sliding friction. Try rolling and sliding an object.) The ball-bearings enable the wheels to turn faster, and reduce wear and tear as they lessen the amount of contact between the surfaces.

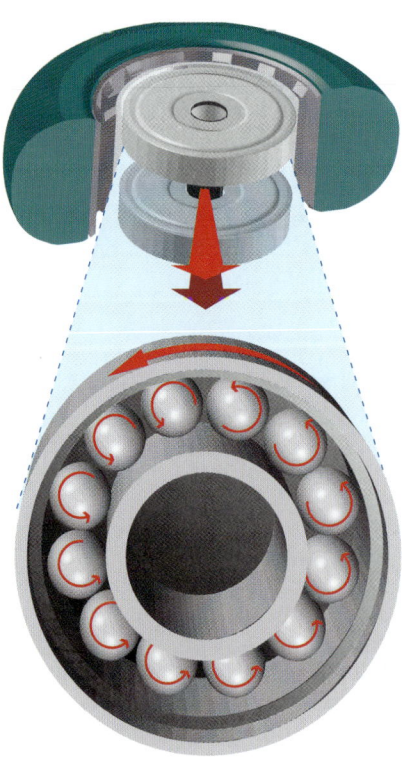

A rollerblade ball-bearing race

SCIFACTS

The solid surface producing the smallest amount of friction is made with a substance called PTFE (polytetrafluoroethene). It produces about the same amount of friction as wet ice. Its commercial name is teflon and it is used on non-stick cooking utensils.

• What is the advantage of low friction cooking utensils such as frypans?

Slippery stuff

What makes a door squeak? A squeaky door can be silenced with a few drops of oil. The oil reduces the friction within the hinge. Substances like oil, grease and petroleum are called **lubricants**. They reduce the force of friction produced by the rubbing of solid surfaces. Your joints contain a lubricant called synovial fluid to help stop bones from scraping against each other.

Lubricants are needed in machines where wear and tear, heat and noise result from surfaces rubbing against each other. Oil and grease are used to lubricate wheel bearings on skateboards, rollerblades and bicycles.

Friction *in* fluids

Any substance which is able to take up the shape of its container and can be poured is called a fluid.

Air and water are both fluids. Objects travelling through air and water experience fluid friction. Like rolling friction and sliding friction, fluid friction acts against the motion of objects. Fluid friction limits the speed of objects travelling through air and water. It increases the amount of fuel needed by cars, planes, motorised boats and submarines.

Cars, planes, water craft and bicycles are **streamlined** to reduce fluid friction. The faster a vehicle needs to travel, the more important streamlining becomes. Some athletes even shave their bodies to streamline them.

Brad McGee's helmet, clothing and bicycle are all designed to reduce fluid friction.

Friction *and* the space shuttle

One of the most dangerous stages of a space shuttle mission is the re-entry into the Earth's atmosphere. After travelling through space with almost no friction at all, it fires its engines to slow it down. The shuttle enters the atmosphere at a speed of about 26 000 km/h. Because it is travelling so fast, the force of fluid friction is large enough to slow it down to about 2000 km/h within minutes. The temperature on the surface of the wings reaches 1500°C. Over 25 000 special ceramic tiles on the surface of the shuttle prevent it from burning up. They protect the astronauts inside from the incredible heat. As it slows down, the size of the force of fluid friction on the shuttle decreases and it gradually cools down. It zigzags through the lower atmosphere, cooling down and getting into the correct landing path. About one hour after leaving its orbit, the shuttle lands at a speed of about 300 km/h.

The space shuttle re-entering the Earth's atmosphere. The tiles on the outside glow red hot.

Activities

Remember

1. List three ways in which friction can be reduced. Give an example of each method.
2. What is fluid friction? List some examples of fluid friction.
3. What is streamlining?

Think

1. Friction can cause objects to slow down. What else can it do?
2. Because trains run on steel tracks, the friction force opposing their motion is quite small. What major disadvantage does this have?
3. Motorists are advised that they will waste fuel if their tyres are under-inflated. Why is this so?
4. How is friction between the moving parts of a car engine reduced?
5. Olympic swimmers like Michael Klim wear smooth, tight-fitting suits, streamlining their bodies to reduce friction. Some of them even shave their heads.
   (a) Do you think that shaving heads or legs could give athletes an advantage? Why?
   (b) In which other sports do athletes shave parts of their bodies or wear clothing that reduces fluid friction?

Michael Klim

Imagine

Write and present as a play an account of a discussion between seven astronauts aboard the space shuttle as it leaves orbit, re-enters the atmosphere and lands. The re-entry is not as smooth as it should be and the temperature inside becomes dangerously hot. Be creative and dramatic but the play must end with a successful touchdown on Earth.

An attraction to Earth

What stops you and the Earth's atmosphere from floating off the surface of the Earth? The answer, of course, is the force of gravity. Gravity is the pulling force that attracts objects towards the centre of the Earth. The area where gravity acts is called the **gravitational force field**.

The force of gravity is not the same on all objects. The greater the **mass** of the object, the greater the force of gravity on it. Mass is related to the amount of material in an object or substance. All objects in the universe exert a force on all other objects in the universe because of their mass. Mass is a measure of how difficult it is to make an object move. The standard unit of mass is the **kilogram** (kg).

The force of gravity on an object or substance is called its **weight**. The standard unit of force is the **newton** (N). Because weight is a force it is measured in newtons.

Mass and weight — what's the difference?

At the Earth's surface, the force of gravity is about 10 newtons for every kilogram of mass. A 50 kg person therefore has a weight of about 500 newtons on Earth. On Mars, however, the force of gravity is only about 4 newtons for every kilogram. A 50 kg person would have a weight of only 200 newtons on Mars.

Measuring mass and weight

Mass is measured with a measuring scale or balance. The drawing on the right shows an old-fashioned measuring scale on which the mass being measured is compared with a known mass. A 2 kg pile of flour will balance the two standard kilogram masses no matter what the pull of gravity is.

A laboratory beam balance measures mass by balancing the object to be measured on one side with sliding masses on the other side.

Weight can be measured with a spring balance like the one shown on page 131. The weight of the object being measured pulls down on the spring and stretches it. The spring stretches evenly and has a pointer attached to it.

The 2 kg of flour will always balance the two standard kilogram weights.

Activities

Remember

1. Explain the difference between mass and weight.
2. The force of gravity is not the same on all objects. On what property of each object does it depend?
3. What is the weight on Earth of a person with a mass of 50 kg?

Think

1. Why will humans feel lighter on Mars? What will have changed — their mass or their weight?
2. If astronauts going to Mars have to take a device to measure out food, would you recommend that they take a beam balance or kitchen scales with a spring inside? Give a reason for your answer.

3. Belinda has a weight of 450 newtons on Earth. What is her mass?
4. Explain how you would use a spring balance to determine the mass of an apple.
5. Heath and Geoff are having an argument about basketball. Heath says that after the basketball leaves the shooter's hands on its way to the basket, there are no forces acting on it. Geoff insists that Heath is wrong and that once the basketball leaves the shooter's hands on its way to the basket, the force of gravity alone determines the path of the basketball through the air. Who is correct? You must, of course, assume that no other players touch the ball on its way to the basket!

Investigate

Would a rubber band be as effective as a spring in a force measurer? Design and conduct an experiment to find out. You will need to construct a table and a graph.

Imagine

Imagine that you are working in the first space laboratory on Mars. The pull of gravity is a little more than one third of what it is on Earth. Write a diary entry for your very first working day in the laboratory. Your diary entry should be an account of your day from 6 am when your alarm rings until 10 pm when you go to bed. Emphasise the effects of less gravity and don't forget that you need to keep physically fit.

Experiment 6.14 MEASURING WEIGHT

YOU WILL NEED
5.0 newton spring balance
set of slotted 50 gram masses
retort stand, bosshead and clamp

- Pull down on the hook of a 5.0 newton spring balance until it reads 1.0 newton. There are two forces acting on the hook. As long as the hook is not changing its motion, the upward force of tension is the same as the downward pull of your hand.

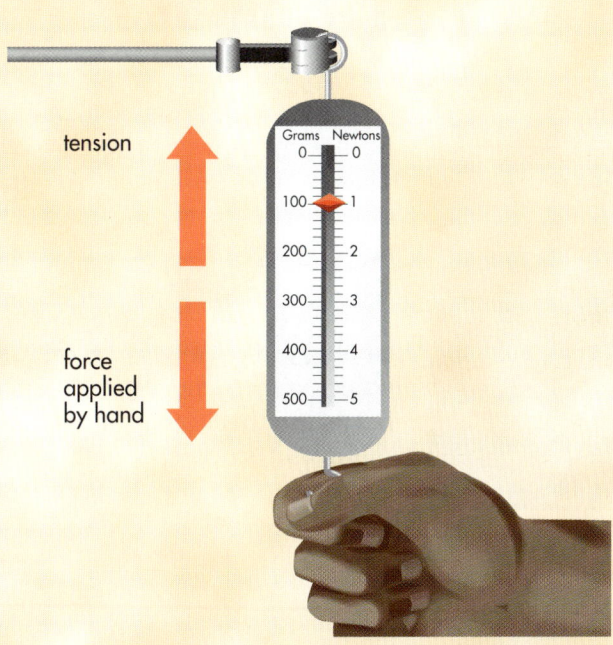

A spring balance. There are two forces acting on the hook.

- Pull the hook down until the spring balance reads 2.0 newtons. The downward pull has doubled.

1. What is the tension in the spring?
2. What has happened to the amount that the spring has stretched?

A spring is a good force measurer because if the pulling force on it doubles, the amount of stretch doubles. If the pulling force triples, the amount of stretch triples.

- Hang the spring balance from a rod fixed to a retort stand and adjust the pointer so that it reads zero.
- Attach a 50 g mass to the hook of the spring balance and record its weight in newtons in the table above right. Also calculate and record the mass in kilograms by dividing the mass in grams by 1000.
- Add 50 g at a time until you have a total mass of 400 g. In your workbook, record the mass in kilograms and weight in newtons as you go.

Measuring weight

Mass (g)	Mass (kg)	Weight (N)
50	0.05	
100	0.10	
150	0.15	

3. Why is it better to hang the spring balance from a rod rather than hold it in your hand?
4. Does the spring increase its stretch by the same amount each time 50 g is added?
5. How would your results be different if you conducted this activity on Mars?

- Use your results to complete a graph like the one below in your workbook.

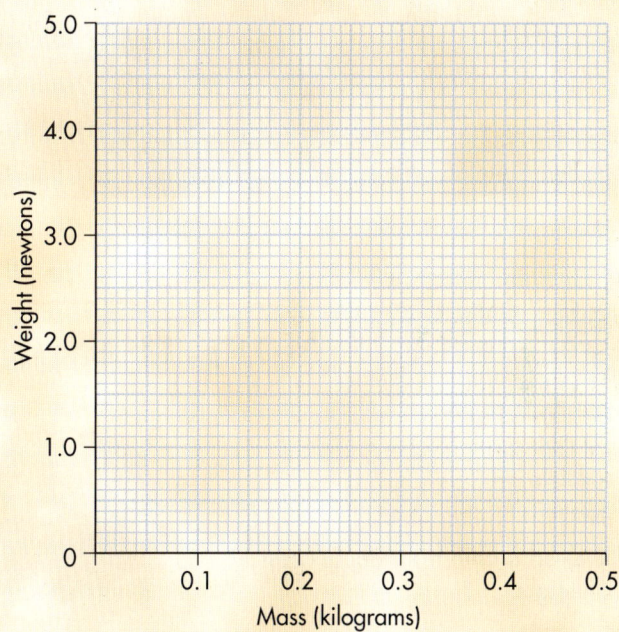

Graph of weight measured on a spring balance versus mass

- Draw a line through the points that you have plotted and continue your line to where you think it should be if you measured the weight of a mass of 500 g. This process is called **extrapolation**.

6. Is your line straight? Should it be straight?
7. What does your graph tell you should be the weight in newtons of a 500 g mass? Measure it and see how accurate your prediction is.
8. What is the relationship between weight in newtons and mass in grams at the Earth's surface?

Falling down

Imagine you are falling through the air with the skydivers in the photograph. What would you feel? You would quickly realise that gravity is not the only force acting on falling objects.

The way objects fall depends on the total force acting on them, not just the pull of gravity. Air in the atmosphere pushes back against all moving objects. This push is called **air resistance**. Air resistance is an example of fluid friction.

When the paper disc is dropped together with the coin in the second part of the experiment below, the coin shields it from the air that would normally push against it.

Speeding *up*

The air resistance on a moving object increases as the object moves faster. When cycling or running quickly, you feel the air pushing against your face. This happens even if there is no wind. When you slow down, you don't feel the same push of air against you.

Terminal *speed*

When an object starts to fall, it is moving slowly. There is not much air resistance. As the object speeds up, the air resistance gets larger. If the object travels fast enough, the air resistance can become as big as the force of gravity on the object. Once the air resistance balances the force of gravity, the object stops speeding up. It has reached its **terminal speed**.

There is more than one force acting on these skydivers.

Experiment 6.15 MORE THAN ONE FORCE?

YOU WILL NEED
20 cent coin
scissors
paper

- Drop a coin from about chest height.

The pull of gravity on the coin (its weight) pulls it down. It speeds up until it hits the floor.

1. How many forces are acting on the coin as it falls through the air?

- Cut out a disc of paper about the size of a 10 cent coin. Hold the paper disc in one hand and a 20 cent coin in the other, both at chest height.
- Drop them at the same time.

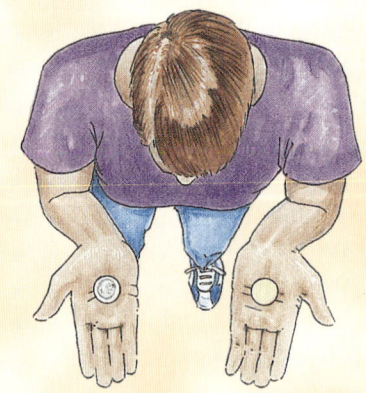
Drop the paper disc and coin from chest height at the same time.

2. Which object landed first?
3. What two forces were acting on the paper disc?
4. What is different about the forces acting on the coin?

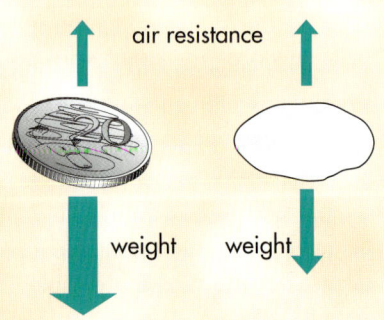
air resistance

weight   weight

The forces acting on a coin and a disc of paper as they fall separately

- Place the disc of paper on top of the coin and drop them together from waist height.

5. Which lands first?
6. How are the forces on the paper disc different from the way that they are drawn above?

Experiment 6.16   THE LANDING TIME OF A PARACHUTE

YOU WILL NEED

plastic from freezer bags
large paperclips or plasticine
cotton or nylon thread

scissors
stopwatch
metre ruler

Your task is to find out the effect of one of the following factors on the landing time of the parachute:
(a) mass of the skydiver
(b) size (area) of the canopy
(c) shape of the canopy.

Use plastic from freezer bags for the canopy. Cotton or nylon thread can be used to hold a model skydiver.

Your 'skydiver' could be represented by paperclips or plasticine.

Ensure that you do each of the following:
- Keep all things constant except the factor that you are deliberately changing, so that your tests are fair. This is called **controlling variables**.
- Repeat your measurements of time at least three times and work out an average.
- Draw up a table like the one below to record your results.

Area of canopy (square centimetres)	Time taken to fall (seconds)			
	Trial 1	Trial 2	Trial 3	Average
24 × 24 = 576				
21 × 21 = 441				
18 × 18 = 324				
15 × 15 = 225				
12 × 12 = 144				

Write a report of your investigation using the headings:
- Aim
- Hypothesis
- Materials
- Method
- Results and observations
- Discussion
- Conclusion.

Evaluate your results and make notes on how your design could be improved.

As an extra challenge after the investigation has been completed, see who can make the parachute that takes longest to reach the floor with a standard load of 5 paperclips from a height of two metres.

Activities

Remember

1. What two forces act on all falling objects in the Earth's atmosphere?
2. What happens to the air resistance acting on a falling skydiver if he or she speeds up?
3. Explain the meaning of terminal speed.

Think

1. When you drop a nail and a feather from the same height they reach the ground at different times. Explain, with the aid of a diagram, why this is the case.
2. When riding a roller-coaster on a still day, your hair blows around quite a bit. Why does this happen even though there is no wind?
3. A falling table tennis ball reaches its terminal speed quite quickly. A falling golf ball takes a long time to reach its terminal speed. Why?
4. Would a table tennis ball reach a terminal speed on the moon? Why?
5. What three forces are acting on the bungee jumper on page 114 just before reaching the water? Which force (hopefully!) is the largest?

SCIENCE issues

STAYING ALIVE

Every year in Australia, about 2000 people die as a result of road accidents. Many of the deaths and injuries can be avoided.

Safer cycling

Bicycle riders account for well over one third of the road accident injuries in the 10–14-year-old age group. The most serious injuries tend to be to the head and face. The wearing of bicycle helmets has greatly decreased the number of head injuries to cyclists.

A bicycle helmet is required by law.

A bicycle helmet contains a layer of polystyrene foam at least 1 cm thick inside a shell of hard plastic. The head of a cyclist falling to the road hits the ground at speeds of up to 20 kilometres per hour. Without a helmet, the cyclist's head suddenly stops when it hits the ground. The sudden impact can cause serious head injuries. With a helmet, the head stops more slowly as the plastic shell and polystyrene foam are crushed. The injuries are less severe.

The plastic shell and polystyrene foam of a helmet allow the head to stop more slowly as it hits the ground.

In cars, padded dashboards, collapsible steering wheels and airbags reduce injuries by allowing the upper body to slow down more gradually when a car crashes.

SCIFACTS

The rubber soles and 'air' pockets of some sports shoes are designed to soften the impact when the wearer lands on the ground. This decreases the amount of jarring to the knees, ankles and the rest of the leg. The pockets in these shoes contain a mixture of gases designed to slow your foot down more gradually as it hits the ground and help push it back up again.

In these shoes, air chambers in the sole offer cushioning and stability. Air flows back and forth between the chambers during the heel-to-toe walking action.

Experiment 6.17 EGGHEAD

YOU WILL NEED
hard-boiled egg
selection of packing materials, such as bubble wrap, foam rubber and newspaper
sticky tape
cardboard
wire

- Design, build and test a container which will hold a hard-boiled egg. Your aim is to create an egg container that will prevent the shell from cracking when it is dropped from a height of 1.5 metres onto a hard floor.

You are actually modelling a bicycle accident. The egg represents the head of a cyclist. Your container represents the helmet.

1. Draw a neat, labelled diagram of your egg container.

2. What features of your container were included to protect the shell from cracking?

3. If your egghead was 'injured', suggest how you could improve the effectiveness of your container.

Belt *up*

When a car collides head-on with an obstacle or another car, the occupants continue to move forwards after the car stops. They continue to move forwards until they are stopped by a force. Without seatbelts the occupants would fly forwards through the windscreen or their bodies would be stopped suddenly by the steering wheel, dashboard, roof or other parts of the inside of the car. Most deaths and injuries in car accidents are caused by a collision between the occupants and the inside of the car. With properly fitted seatbelts, car occupants stop as the car stops and are less likely to be killed or injured.

Your body is not the only thing that will keep moving once the car stops as a result of a collision. Any loose objects in the car will continue to move after the car stops. You should never leave any loose objects in the car. They are much safer in the boot! In one accident a driver was killed by a paperback novel that was sitting on the shelf behind the back seat. It continued to move after the car and driver (with properly fitted seatbelt) stopped. A corner of the book struck the driver in the back of the head, killing her instantly.

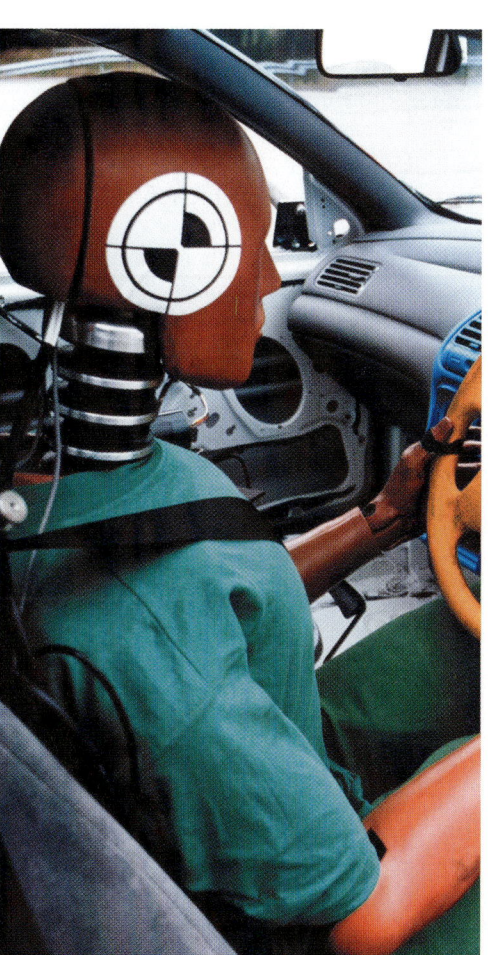

Crash test dummies are used to test the effectiveness of safety features in cars.

Experiment 6.18

CRASH TEST DUMMY

YOU WILL NEED

pencil sharpener or eraser
toy car   rubber band
block of wood   clamp
aluminium foil

- Clamp a wooden block to the end of a table.
- Place the pencil sharpener or eraser on the toy car to represent an occupant. Push the toy car towards the wooden block as fast as you can without your crash test dummy falling off. Observe the motion of the crash test dummy after the car collides with the wooden block.

1. Describe the motion of both the car and the crash test dummy after the collision.

- Modify this experiment to include seatbelts (using a rubber band) and/or a 'crumple zone' at the front of the car (using aluminium foil).

2. What difference does the rubber band and/or foil make to the motion of the crash test dummy after the collision?

Activities

Using data

Since 1972 it has been illegal not to wear a seatbelt when travelling in a car in Australia. The number of deaths due to accidents on Australian roads in 1970 was 3798. By 1986, the death toll on roads had decreased to 2883, even though there were almost twice as many cars on the road. Suggest at least three reasons for the decrease.

Remember

1. How do bicycle helmets protect your head in an accident?
2. Describe the likely motion of an unrestrained rear seat passenger in a car which collides with a tree at 60 kilometres per hour.

Think

1. Bicycle helmets were made compulsory in New South Wales in July 1991. Why do you think it was necessary to make a law to force people to wear them?
2. When a stationary car is hit from the rear by another vehicle, it is pushed forwards rapidly. Describe the likely motion of a front seat passenger:
   (a) with a head rest fitted to the seat
   (b) without a head rest fitted to the seat.

Investigate

1. Find out the meaning of the word 'inertia'.
2. Find out who Sir Isaac Newton was. What is Newton's First Law of Motion and how is it relevant to seatbelts in cars?

Create

Design a poster with the title 'Don't be an egghead. Wear a helmet.'

Putting it all together

Summing up

Copy and complete the statements below to compile a summary of this unit. The missing words can be found in the word list below.

1. Average speed can be calculated by dividing the _____ travelled by the _____ taken.

2. Energy that is stored is called _____ energy.

3. Forces can start motion, _____ motion, speed up or slow down motion, change the direction of motion, change the _____ of an object or have no visible effect at all.

4. _____ can attract some substances including iron.

5. Magnets have a _____ pole and a _____ pole.

6. Magnets have a magnetic _____ around them that can be detected with a compass.

7. _____ is an upward push on an object by a fluid.

8. Surface _____ is a force which acts at the surface of a liquid, making the surface behave like a skin.

9. _____ is a rubbing force applied to a surface by another surface.

10. Friction can be reduced by applying _____ between surfaces.

11. _____ is the force that pulls objects towards the centre of the Earth.

12. _____ is measured in kilograms while weight is a force measured in newtons.

13. Air resistance is an example of _____ friction which acts on objects moving through air.

14. Any changes to an object's motion are a result of the _____ forces acting on it.

15. Bicycle _____ reduce the likelihood of head injuries to cyclists by allowing the head to stop more slowly on impact.

16. _____ prevent car occupants from continuing their motion when a car stops suddenly in road accidents.

Word list

north	mass	field	stop
helmets	magnets	fluid	total
friction	buoyancy	distance	gravity
seatbelts	tension	lubricants	shape
south	time	potential	

Looking back

1. In your workbook complete a table listing the forces acting on the seven people in the illustration. You should be able to find at least 18 forces.

What the person is doing	Forces acting on the person (Use a diagram with labelled arrows to represent the forces.)
1.	
2.	
3.	
4.	
5.	
6.	
7.	

Bicycle track

2. Complete the crossword, using the clues below right.

Clues

Across

3. The unit of force
7. Measures how fast distance is covered
8. The unit of mass
9. Energy of a body while moving
11. A lubricant used to reduce friction in machines

Down

1. Must be worn in a car
2. Every magnet has two of these.
4. Part of compass which points north
5. An object in a fluid will do this if it does not float.
10. This metal is attracted to magnets.

Extension

Amazing magnets

Video and audio cassette tapes are plastic ribbons with a thin coating of iron particles. When the tape is recording, it moves past a small electromagnet called a recording head. The recording head sets up a magnetic pattern in the iron particles on the tape. When the tape is played back it moves past another electromagnet called the playback head. This head reads the magnetic pattern on the tape. The electronic components in your VCR or cassette player then convert the signals to picture and sound.

Computer disks also store information by forming magnetic patterns in iron-coated plastic. The disk drive uses an electromagnet to read the patterns on a disk and create new patterns.

Magnetic fields are used to allow specially designed trains to float above the track. These trains, called maglev (short for magnetic levitation) are quieter and are able to travel faster than conventional trains. Some maglev trains use magnetic repulsion to push the train up from the track. Others use magnetic attraction to pull the train up towards the bottom of the guideway. Maglev trains can travel as fast as 480 kilometres per hour.

It is believed that some animals use the magnetic field of the Earth to find their way when travelling long distances. Many animals use the position of the sun for navigation. However, homing pigeons are able to find their way home on cloudy days and even at night. Many migrating birds travel large distances over oceans without any landmarks to help them find their way. Some fish migrate across oceans without sighting land, the sun or stars. Magnetite and other magnetic substances have been found in the heads of these animals. There are, however, other possible explanations for the amazing navigation abilities of these animals.

Homing pigeons. Do they use the Earth's magnetic field?

Activities

Think

1. Why should videotapes be stored away from magnets and magnetic devices?
2. Give one reason why maglev trains might be able to travel faster than conventional trains.
3. Discuss with others how birds and fish might be able to find their way over large distances. Consider explanations other than the use of the Earth's magnetic field. Present a group report on your conclusions.

A maglev train

Drawing forces

Reflection

1. Floating bodies

Archimedes (287–212 BC) contributed many ideas to our understanding of the world. Find out about his Law of Buoyancy, some experiments he performed and inventions that he made.

2. Thinking about forces

Name the six forces you learnt about in this chapter.

(a) For each one give examples of how these forces affect your life.

(b) Design a way of explaining the importance of each of these forces to someone who has never heard of them. You might make a poster, a television or radio advertisement, a poem, a game or a demonstration.

3. Taking forces further

(a) Find out how an electroscope works. Build one as shown in the diagram below and conduct some experiments. Write a report to explain what you have observed.

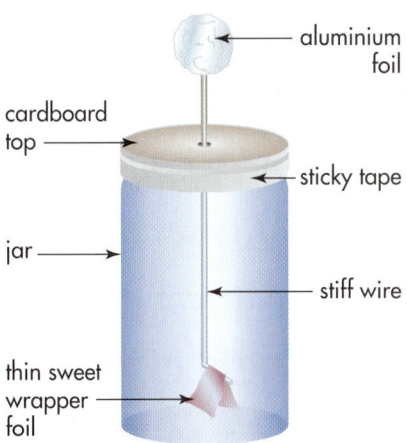

aluminium foil
cardboard top
sticky tape
jar
stiff wire
thin sweet wrapper foil

A simple electroscope

(b) What would happen to an object that was moving and had no forces acting on it? (Think about the coin you slid earlier for experiment 6.2 on page 118.)

(c) Electrostatic forces have many useful applications. For example, they are used in photocopiers and to reduce pollution by removing particles from chimneys. Find some other examples and choose one of these to research more thoroughly. Draw a simple diagram to show how this application works.

friction

gravity

surface tension

magnetism

electrostatic

buoyancy

Forces are all around us every day. Often we take them for granted.

PLANET EARTH

The Earth is one of nine planets that revolve around the sun. The solid outer crust of this planet is covered mostly with water and surrounded by a layer of gases that supports life. Beneath the crust are layers of rock and molten rock at temperatures of up to 7000°C.

The Earth as it is
seen from the moon.
Vital statistics of the Earth include:
• Age: about 4.5 billion years old
• Diameter at equator: 12 800 kilometres
• Mass: about 6 million billion billion kilograms.

KEY CONTENT

Describe features of the Earth's structure, its atmosphere and space.

Identify the gaseous composition of air.

Describe the causes, characteristics and effects of natural disasters involving movements in the Earth's crust.

Explain the method of formation and uses of igneous rocks.

Describe day and night as caused by the relative movements of the sun and Earth.

Explain erosion.

KEY QUESTIONS

Are you sure that the Earth is not flat?

What is inside the Earth?

What is the greenhouse effect?

Where is the ozone layer?

Why does the sun rise every day?

What causes the seasons?

Can a volcano suddenly appear from nowhere?

How are igneous rocks formed?

What makes the Earth shake?

Why are coastal sand dunes often fenced off?

Thinking about Planet Earth

You have already lived on planet Earth for more than 10 years. You will be amazed at how much you know about the Earth just through observing what's around you, asking questions and watching television.

1. Planet Earth mind map

GROUP WORK (a) In groups of 2–4, draw a mind map to show what you already know about planet Earth. An example of a mind map is provided below. In this mind map, questions have been included to suggest the different sorts of ideas and information that you could cover. Your mind map could look similar to this but, instead of questions, your mind map will show statements and facts from your group's combined knowledge.

Use a large sheet of paper, such as butcher's paper, and be as creative and colourful as possible. Start by drawing the Earth in the centre of the sheet and then add your own ideas in the form of words or pictures. As the example shows, it's possible to branch off from your initial ideas as one thought leads to another. Remember, it's important to use your own words and ideas.

An example of a mind map

(b) Once you have finished, share your mind map with another group. Take turns explaining your group's ideas and ask questions about the other group's mind map. Finally, add any new information you have gained to your own mind map.

2. Planet Earth words

(a) Write the list of words below into your workbook.

stratosphere	mesosphere
revolution	intrusive
batholith	extrusive
seismology	Richter scale
tsunamis	echolocation
submersible	troposphere
ionosphere	asthenosphere
lithosphere	hydrosphere

(b) Read through the list and tick the words that you know how to pronounce.

(c) Use the pronunciation guide at the back of the book to learn how to say the other words. Practise until you feel confident saying each word.

GROUP WORK (d) In a group, take turns pronouncing each word and stating what you think each word means (without referring to this chapter). It's okay if you don't know the exact meanings, but you can share what ideas or pictures the words bring to you.

You are now ready to start this chapter. As you work through, remember to correct, modify or add to your group's mind map. Use a different coloured pen to show the changed or added information. You will then have a record of your learning about the Earth.

Earth in the round

Over time, different cultures have had different ideas about the shape of our planet Earth. As far back as 1000 BC, the Greek poet Homer described Earth as a disc floating upon an ocean, with the sun being driven in a chariot across the sky each day by the sun god. The ancient Hindus believed the Earth was supported by four giant elephants standing on the back of a turtle, which itself floated in an ocean.

Around 600 BC, Thales of Miletus believed the Earth was a sphere. In 500 BC, Pythagoras, the famous mathematician, was the first person to suggest that the Earth revolved around the sun.

In 350 BC, Aristotle supported the view that the Earth was a sphere but he refused to believe it revolved around the sun. He preferred to believe the Earth was at the centre of eight concentric solid spheres. He believed these spheres were crystalline and transparent with each one carrying a heavenly body around the Earth. These bodies, in order from the Earth, were thought to be first the moon, then Mercury, Venus, the sun, Mars, Jupiter, Saturn and finally all the stars.

At the end of the third century BC, Eratosthenes made the first estimates of the Earth's diameter showing that, by that time, it was believed that the Earth was a sphere. Nearly 350 years later, in 151 AD, Ptolemy developed the theory that the planets were not in crystalline spheres but travelled in an orbit around the Earth. This view was held until Copernicus published his great work in 1543. This work explained in great detail why Pythagoras was in fact correct and the Earth did revolve around the sun, along with all the other planets in our solar system.

It can take a very long time for new ideas to be accepted as scientific truths. Today these ideas are well accepted as part of our basic scientific understandings about our universe.

We can confirm the shape of our planet, as space travel has allowed us to take photos of it from space. Our Earth is almost spherical in shape with slight flattening at both the north and south poles. The **equator** is an imaginary circle that divides the Earth into two halves, called the northern hemisphere and southern hemisphere.

Structure *of the* Earth

Crust

The outer layer or **crust** of the Earth is made mostly of solid rock. It is called the **lithosphere** and includes landforms, rocks and soil. It is a bit like a shell, varying in thickness from about 8 km below the oceans to about 40 km below the continents. Oceanic crust (underwater) is thinner than continental crust (above water).

Mantle

Below the crust is a region of partially molten rock. This **mantle** is about 2900 km thick and its temperature varies between about 500°C near the crust to about 2200°C at its deepest part. The hot, soft, semi-fluid upper part of the mantle is called the **asthenosphere**. It is just below the crust and is the source of magma that erupts onto the surface.

Outer core

About 2300 km thick, the **outer core** is so hot that the iron and nickel from which it is made is molten. The temperature varies from about 4000°C to about 6000°C.

At the surface

Only about 30 per cent of the surface of the Earth is dry land. The rest of the surface is water (the **hydrosphere**). About 97 per cent of the water at the surface is the salt water that makes up the oceans and seas. About 2 per cent of the water is stored as ice near the north and south poles. The rest is the fresh water that can be found in rivers, streams, lakes and ponds.

Above the surface

The region of gases above the surface of the Earth is called the **atmosphere**. It is a mixture of gases called **air**. The air in the atmosphere is essential for life on the planet. About 99 per cent of the air in the atmosphere is less than 80 km above the surface.

Inner core

Even though the temperature of the **inner core** may be as high as 7000°C, the iron and nickel in this part of the Earth is believed to be solid. This is because of all the weight pushing down on it. The inner core is about 1200 km thick.

North Pole northern hemisphere equator southern hemisphere South Pole

Activities

Using data

The centre of the Earth is about 6400 km from the surface. In 1864, the science fiction author Jules Verne wrote the novel *Journey to the Centre of the Earth*. It tells of an amazing journey through the inside of the Earth that begins with a descent into a volcano in Iceland. In fact, the deepest mines go down only 4 km into the Earth. The deepest drill hole into the Earth is about 14 km deep. The following table shows the temperature measured at different depths in a drill hole.

Temperature at different depths of a drill hole

Depth (km)	Temperature (°C)
0	15
1	44
2	73
3	102
4	130
5	158
6	187
7	215
8	242

1. Plot a graph to show how the temperature increases with depth. You will need to label the horizontal axis 'depth (km)' and the vertical axis 'temperature (°C)'.
2. Use your graph to predict the temperature at the following depths:
   (a) 2.5 km
   (b) 10 km.
3. About how many degrees does the temperature increase for each kilometre below the surface?
4. Use your answer to question 3 to predict the temperature at the centre of the Earth. Scientists estimate the temperature at the centre of the Earth to be about 7000°C. Explain why use of the data in question 3 gives a much higher prediction.

Remember

1. Describe the four major regions below the Earth's surface.
2. What are the terms used to describe:
   (a) the Earth's crust?
   (b) the part of the Earth's surface covered by water?
3. Who first proposed that the Earth was a sphere?

Think

1. Compare the ideas of Aristotle, Ptolemy and Copernicus about the shape of the Earth and its position in the solar system. Discuss why you think the views held by Pythagoras took so many centuries to be accepted.
2. Members of the Flat Earth Society believe that the Earth is flat and shaped like a dinner plate. They believe that photographs taken from space that show the Earth to be a sphere are part of a giant hoax. What do you think? Write down some observations that support your opinion.
3. Even though the inner core of the Earth is hotter than the molten outer core, it is believed to be solid. How could this be?
4. Investigate what Aboriginal and indigenous people's stories say about the structure of the Earth. Compare these ideas with our current ideas.

Create

Draw a scale diagram of the Earth using the following instructions. You will need a compass, a pencil and a sheet of plain A4 paper.

- Open up the compass so that the ends are 10 cm apart. Use it carefully to draw a circle with a radius of 10 cm.
- Using the same centre, draw two more circles, one of radius 5.5 cm and one of radius 1.9 cm.
- You have now shown three of the regions below the Earth's surface. Label the three regions.
- On your scale diagram, the crust would need to be represented by a pencil line on the surface. A thick pencil line would represent the thickest part of the crust while a thin pencil line would represent the thinnest part. On your scale diagram, the atmosphere would be about 2 mm thick. A thick blue line could be used to represent the atmosphere.
- Complete the labelling of your diagram and then colour it.

The air up there

Surrounding the Earth is a region of gases called the atmosphere. The mixture of gases in the atmosphere is called air. The atmosphere can be divided into several layers, as shown below. About three-quarters of the air in the atmosphere is within the first layer, called the **troposphere**. Weather conditions are mostly caused by changes in the troposphere.

The higher you go in the troposphere, the lower the temperature becomes. Above the troposphere the temperature begins to increase again. The higher you go, the less air there is. Even though the **ionosphere** is by far the largest part of the atmosphere, it contains only 1 per cent of the air. The atmosphere does not have a definite end. It gradually becomes thinner as you go higher. Some very light particles of air can be found as high as 1500 km above the Earth's surface. Once you leave the Earth's atmosphere you enter space, the part of the universe where the density of matter is very low.

What's in the air?

Dry air near the surface is mostly **nitrogen** and **oxygen**. Water vapour is also present in the air. The amount of water vapour varies from almost zero up to about four per cent.

Other gases in the air include **carbon dioxide** and **ozone** (present in minute quantities — in larger quantities ozone is poisonous for humans to breathe).

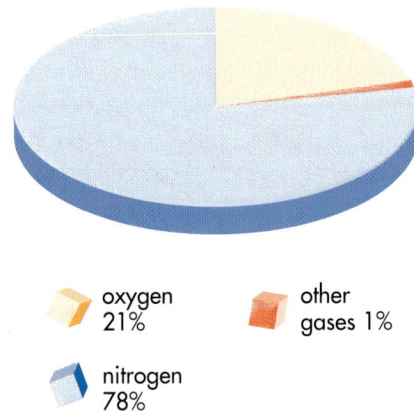

oxygen 21%

other gases 1%

nitrogen 78%

Dry air near the surface consists mostly of nitrogen and oxygen.

Keeping the atmosphere in balance

The air in the atmosphere is needed by plants and animals, which need oxygen to live. In breathing, animals replace oxygen with carbon dioxide. During the day, plants use carbon dioxide to help them make their own food. In doing so, they produce and release oxygen.

Fuels that are made of the remains of dead animals and plants are called **fossil fuels**. Coal, oil, gas and petrol are fossil fuels. When fossil fuels are burnt by power stations, cars, factories and in homes, oxygen is used up and carbon dioxide is released.

Together, plants and animals help to keep the amounts of oxygen and carbon dioxide in the atmosphere in balance. The amounts should not change much at all. The atmosphere should be in balance.

However, the balance is under threat. The amount of carbon dioxide in the air is increasing. There are two main reasons for this:

1. The burning of fossil fuels. The people of Earth are using more fossil fuels every year. Australians add about 70 million tonnes of carbon dioxide to the atmosphere each year by burning fossil fuels.

2. The clearing of forests. Trees absorb carbon dioxide from the air and produce oxygen. As they are cleared, another means of keeping the atmosphere balanced is removed. In Australia, two-thirds of all forests that existed 200 years ago have been cleared.

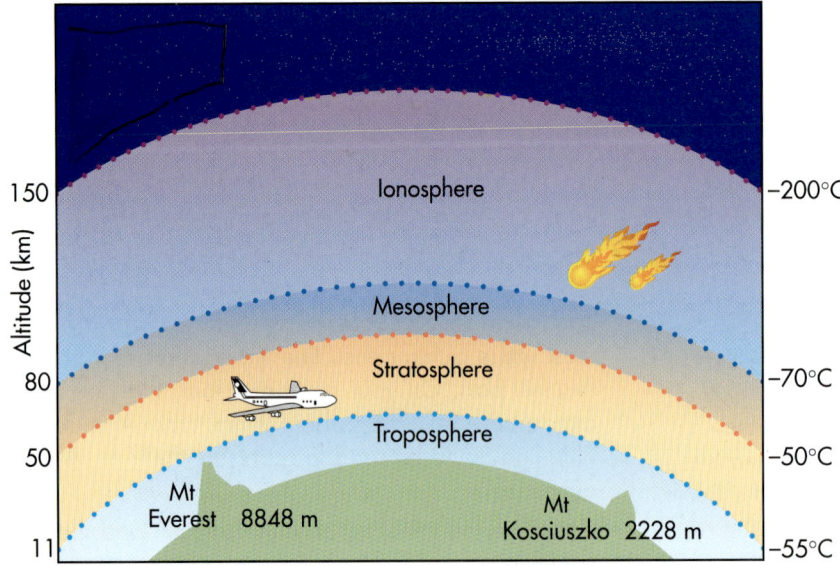

Layers in the Earth's atmosphere

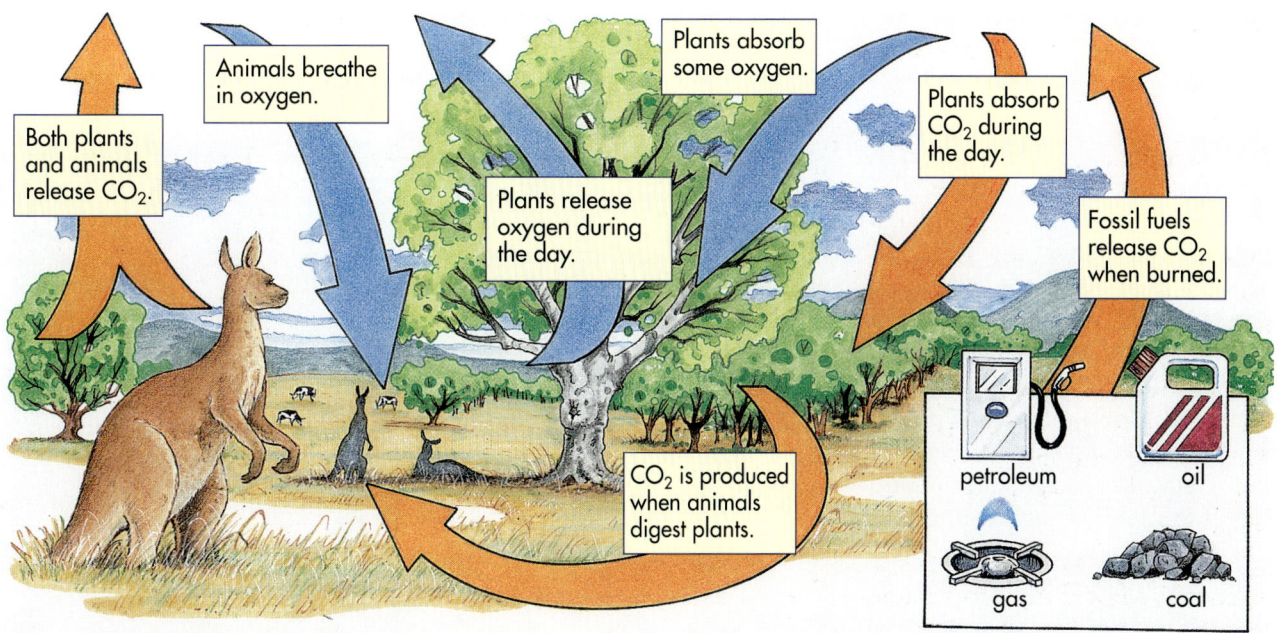

The movement of oxygen and carbon dioxide between living things and the atmosphere

Labels in the diagram:
- Both plants and animals release CO₂.
- Animals breathe in oxygen.
- Plants absorb some oxygen.
- Plants release oxygen during the day.
- Plants absorb CO₂ during the day.
- Fossil fuels release CO₂ when burned.
- CO₂ is produced when animals digest plants.
- petroleum
- oil
- gas
- coal

Greenhouse *effect*

Heat from the sun enters the atmosphere and warms up the Earth's surface. At night, this heat escapes through the atmosphere. Without the atmosphere, too much heat would escape and the Earth would be bitterly cold at night. The gases in the atmosphere trap some of the heat. This trapping of heat is called the **greenhouse effect**.

Carbon dioxide traps more heat than most of the other gases in the atmosphere. Many people are concerned that the increasing amount of carbon dioxide in the atmosphere will cause the Earth to heat up enough to change the climate and sea levels.

Ozone *layer*

While there is some ozone in the air we breathe, most of the ozone in the atmosphere is in the upper **stratosphere**. Even though ozone makes up only a small part of the stratosphere, it is often referred to as the ozone layer. Ozone is especially important to life on Earth because it blocks out more than 95 per cent of the sun's **ultraviolet (UV) rays**. Any decrease in the amount of ozone in the stratosphere is damaging to all living things because more UV rays reach the surface. For humans, this means a greater risk of sunburn and skin cancer which are caused by UV rays.

Some chemicals used by humans drift up into the stratosphere, causing chemical reactions that reduce the amount of ozone. These chemicals include CFCs (chlorofluorocarbons), which were used in aerosol spray cans and older air-conditioners and refrigerators.

Activities

Remember

1. What is air?
2. What are the two most abundant gases in the Earth's atmosphere?
3. Why is the amount of carbon dioxide in the Earth's atmosphere increasing?

Think

1. Why is most of the air in the atmosphere close to the surface?
2. Why isn't the oxygen in the Earth's atmosphere used up by the breathing of humans and other animals?
3. What is the difference between space and the Earth's atmosphere?

Investigate

1. The gases that trap heat in the Earth's atmosphere are referred to as greenhouse gases. What gases other than carbon dioxide are greenhouse gases? In Kyoto in 1997, 150 nations agreed to cut their greenhouse gas emissions. Use your library and the Internet to find out more about the Kyoto Protocol, its targets for cutting emissions and Australia's position on it.
2. Find out how scientists test for carbon dioxide and oxygen.

Sunrise, sunset

Each day the sun rises in the east, moves across the sky and sets in the west. The ancient Egyptians believed that the sun god, Re, sailed a boat across the sky each day. The ancient Greeks explained the movement of the sun as the daily journey of the sun god, Helios, across the sky in a chariot. It is not surprising that early astronomers explained day and night by suggesting that the sun moved around the Earth.

In 1543, Nicolaus Copernicus proposed that the Earth, along with the other known planets, revolved around the sun. Over 60 years later, after the invention of the telescope, Galileo Galilei made observations that supported the idea that the sun, rather than the Earth, was the centre of the solar system. But he was threatened with execution by the Catholic Church in 1633 for his support of the idea and was forced to publicly deny his belief. He spent the rest of his life under house arrest.

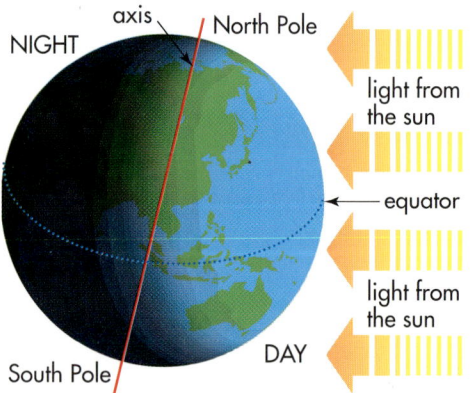

Only one half of the Earth can face the sun at any one time. This diagram shows Australia in daylight.

Sir Isaac Newton, born in 1642, the same year that Galileo died, showed clearly that the sun was, in fact, the centre of the solar system.

Even though the Earth moves around the sun, there are reasons for the apparent motion of the sun and why day and night occur. The Earth rotates on its own axis, as do all the other planets. The Earth's axis is an imaginary straight line between the South Pole and the North Pole. The axis is tilted at an angle of 23.5° from vertical, as shown on the right. It takes 24 hours to complete each rotation. As the Earth rotates from west to east, the sun appears to move from east to west.

Explaining *the* seasons

As the Earth moves around the sun, its axis remains tilted. This movement of the Earth around the sun is called **revolution** and its path is called an **orbit**. One complete orbit takes $365\frac{1}{4}$ days. The time taken for the Earth, or any other planet, to revolve around the sun is called a year. The diagram below shows that during a complete orbit the axis is sometimes tilted towards the sun, while at other times it is tilted away from the sun.

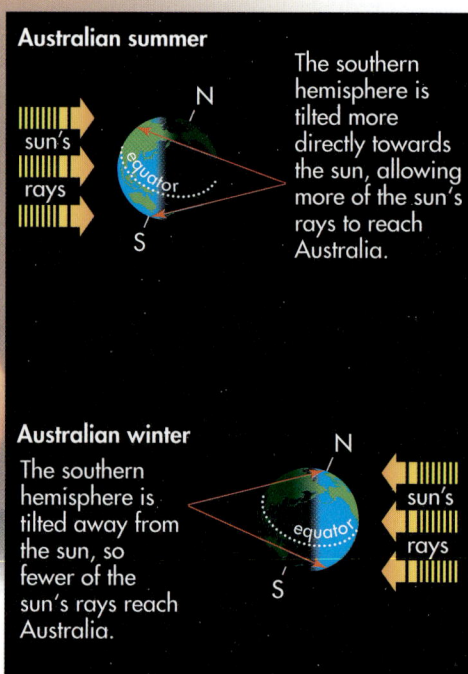

The tilt of the Earth's axis and its path around the sun help explain the seasons.

While the southern hemisphere experiences summer, the northern hemisphere is experiencing its winter. During this time the South Pole is in constant daylight while the North Pole is in darkness. The diagram on the right shows why summer is warmer than winter.

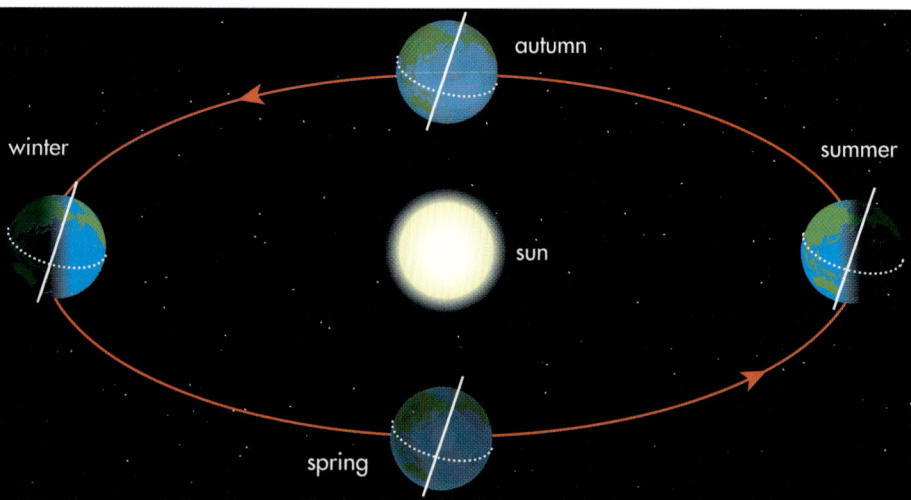

As the Earth orbits the sun, the seasons change. This diagram shows the seasons as they are in the southern hemisphere.

Activities

Remember

1. Explain the difference between the revolution and rotation of the Earth.
2. How long does it take the Earth to complete one rotation and one revolution?
3. Use some well-labelled diagrams to explain how the seasons occur.

Think

1. Explain, with the aid of a diagram, why the South Pole is in darkness during the southern hemisphere's winter.
2. Use the drawing on the right to answer the following questions.
   (a) Which of the locations A, B, C, D and E are:
      (i) in daylight?
      (ii) experiencing summer?
   (b) Of the locations that are in daylight, where will the sun set first?
   (c) Which locations will experience the longest day and the shortest day?

3. Calculate how many rotations the Earth has completed since you were born.

Investigate

1. What is daylight saving? Debate its advantages and disadvantages.
2. Find out what makes the sky red at sunrise and sunset.
3. Why was the Catholic Church opposed to Copernicus' ideas?

Imagine

Imagine that you are living in Antarctica near the South Pole. How would the seasons compare with those in Australia? Explain how the changes would affect your lifestyle and daily routine.

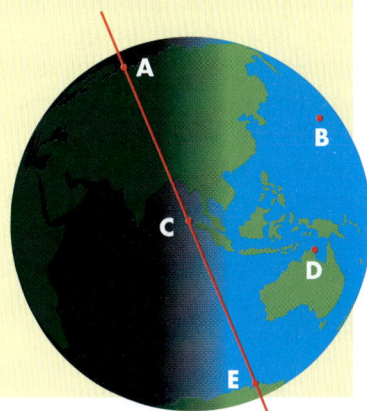

Experiment 7.1 DAY AND NIGHT

YOU WILL NEED

geographical globe or polystyrene ball about 7 cm in diameter

knitting needle or skewer
marking pen
projector

- If you do not have a geographical globe, carefully push a knitting needle through the centre of a polystyrene ball. The knitting needle represents the axis of the Earth.
- Label the north and south poles on your model Earth. Draw the equator and an outline of Australia on it and label the directions north, south, east and west as shown. Mark the city or town where you are now with a small cross on your model.

- Turn on the projector and hold the model Earth in the light so that the axis is tilted as shown. Observe the ball from the side. The light from the projector represents the light coming from the sun.
- Position the ball so that your location is on the boundary between light and dark. Slowly turn the ball so that the 'sun' rises and sets in the correct directions from your location.

1. Does the Earth rotate from west to east or east to west? Explain how you know this.
2. Explain why sunset occurs in Perth about two hours later than it does in Sydney.
3. This experiment shows how a model can be used to explain day and night. With the axis tilted as shown in the diagram on the left, does the model represent summer or winter in Australia?
4. What do you notice about the days and nights at the north and south poles of your model?

- Repeat your observations with the axis tilted away from the 'sun' instead of towards it.

5. How have the days and nights at the north and south poles changed?
6. Does the model represent summer or winter in Australia when it is tilted this way?
7. Use your model to decide whether the daylight hours are longer in summer or winter.

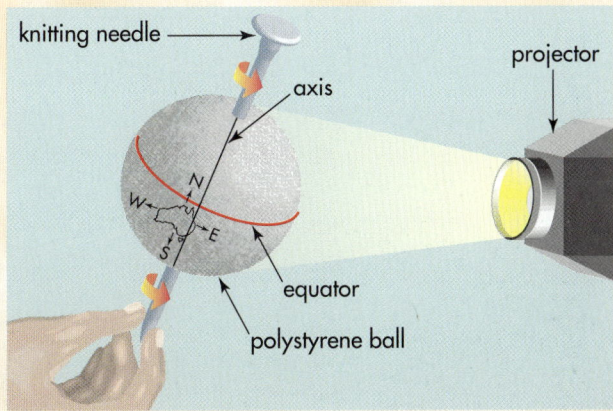

In which direction does the Earth rotate?

SCIENCE issues

SOIL ON THE MOVE

Physical **erosion** is the movement of soil and rock from one place to another. This type of erosion is a natural process, caused by the wind and water. In alpine areas, erosion is also caused as glaciers push boulders, rocks and smaller particles down mountains.

Some of the most spectacular land and coastal features of planet Earth are caused by erosion. The Grand Canyon in the United States of America, the Twelve Apostles near Port Campbell, Victoria, and Wave Rock in Western Australia have been formed by erosion.

Erosion is responsible for many of the Earth's most spectacular features. The Grand Canyon has been carved out over millions of years by the Colorado River.

Soil *erosion*

Good soil is a valuable resource. It contains nutrients needed for the growth of plants. It is, therefore, vital in feeding the Earth's population. Wind and water have always gradually moved soil from one place to another. Although erosion is a natural process, human activity often causes it to occur more quickly.

As a result of the removal of forests and native grasses and the overgrazing of cattle and sheep, Australia's topsoil is rapidly being blown and washed away. In fact, in the 200 years since Europeans came to Australia, over two-thirds of all forest trees have been removed.

The wind lifts soil particles that are not protected by plants. Plants shelter soil from the wind. Their roots help hold the soil together and prevent it from being blown away.

The photograph on the right shows the result of soil erosion that was made worse by drought.

Soil can be washed away by running water in rivers and streams. When rain strikes soil which is not held together by plants, the soil can be scattered in all directions. If the land is not perfectly flat, small streams will start flowing downhill, taking some of the soil with them. The small streams continue downhill, merging into each other, forming larger streams and eventually rivers.

The removal of vegetation and overgrazing of animals are not the only ways that humans have been speeding up the process of erosion. The introduction of just twenty-four rabbits to mainland Australia in 1859 has made a major and unfortunate contribution to erosion. The rabbits bred quickly and, by 1890, there were 600 million rabbits in New South Wales alone. They ate their way through huge amounts of vegetation, removing roots that protected the soil from erosion. Their burrows broke up soil, allowing it to be washed away in heavy rain.

The use of trailbikes, four-wheel drive vehicles and bushwalking can speed up erosion. Such activities remove vegetation and need to be restricted to areas that are not as sensitive to erosion. Coastal sand dunes are badly affected by these activities and are often fenced off.

Winds blew precious topsoil from drought-affected farms over Griffith, New South Wales, in November 2002.

Experiment 7.2

MODELLING SOIL EROSION

YOU WILL NEED

a stream tray or other metal or wooden tray
sand
wooden block
rubber tubing to fit a water tap
small plastic lid (from an orange juice container)
twigs, matches or cotton buds to act as trees

- Pack slightly damp sand into the tray so that it is fairly level.
- Use a small block of wood to raise one end of the tray slightly. Place the other end of the tray on the edge of a sink or over an empty bucket.
- With one finger, make a slightly winding groove in the sand as shown in the diagram below.

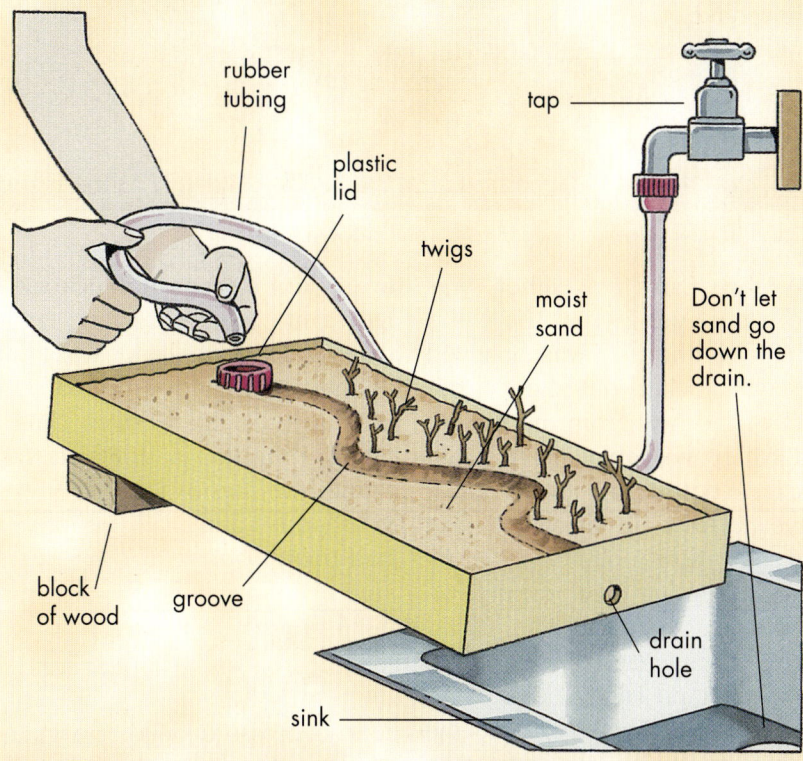

Using a stream tray to model the erosion of soil by a winding river

- Plant 'trees' along one edge of your model river using twigs, matches or cotton buds.
- Place the plastic lid in the sand at the top of the groove and aim the rubber tubing from the tap over it.
- Turn on the tap so that water flows slowly but steadily into the plastic lid, overflowing into the groove. Don't let the sand go down the drain.

1. Describe what happens as the water flows down your model river. Take particular notice of the difference between the two sides of the river.
2. Is there any particular part of the river where erosion is more apparent? Which part?
3. Where is the eroded sand deposited?
4. The main aim of this experiment is to examine the effect of plants on the amount of erosion. State your conclusion.

S C I F A C T S

About 43 per cent of the Earth's dry land is desert or desert-like. In Australia, the situation is much worse. About 90 per cent of Australia's soil is not suitable for growing crops. That makes what is left extremely valuable.

Activities

Remember

1. What is physical erosion?
2. What are the two main causes of physical erosion on planet Earth?
3. List at least two ways that soil erosion can be reduced.

Think

1. Is soil erosion likely to be a problem on the moon or Mars? Why? If so, will there be more or less erosion than on Earth? Why?
2. Why has the amount of soil erosion increased in Australia rapidly since Europeans came 200 years ago?
3. Is there any soil erosion evident in your local area? If so, how could it be prevented or reduced?

Create

Design a poster that will encourage people not to use an area sensitive to erosion for recreational activities.

Investigate

1. Find out what contour ploughing is and how it reduces erosion on farms.
2. Find out how some deserts are being used to grow crops.

Mountains of fire

Volcanoes are formed when molten rock, or **magma**, bursts through a weakness in the Earth's crust. Many of the world's active volcanoes are found close to where the continental crust meets the oceanic crust. Magma on the surface of the Earth is called **lava**. The eruption of a volcano is usually spectacular, releasing red-hot molten rock (lava), ash, dust and gases. The word 'volcano' is derived from the name of the ancient Roman god of fire, Vulcan. A scientist who studies volcanoes is called a 'vulcanologist'.

Birth *of a* volcano

On a cool winter's day in 1943, a small crack opened up in a field of corn in Mexico. When red-hot cinders shot out of the crack, the shocked farmer tried to fill it with dirt. The next day, the crack had opened up into a hole over two metres wide. A week later, the dust, ash and rocks erupting from the hole had formed a cone 150 metres high! Molten lava began spewing from the crater, destroying the village of Paricutin. Within a year, the new mountain, named Paricutin, was 300 metres high. When the eruptions stopped in 1952, Paricutin was 410 metres high.

Dead *or* alive?

Volcanoes which are erupting or which have recently erupted are called **active volcanoes**. Mt Pinatubo in the Philippines, which erupted in June 1991 killing 300 people, is an active volcano. There was so much smoke and ash coming from Mt Pinatubo that scientists believe

Paricutin, a new volcano. It began as a small crack in a field of corn.

that the Earth's weather was cooler for over a year. The cloud of smoke and ash was believed to have blocked out about 4 per cent of the heat from the sun.

Extinct volcanoes are those that have not erupted for thousands of years. They are effectively dead and are most unlikely to erupt again. There are many extinct volcanoes in Australia. The Glasshouse Mountains in Queensland and the Grand High Tops in Warrumbungle National Park are the remains of cooled lava trapped in the central vents of volcanoes. Belougery Spire is a fine example of a 1060-metre-high volcanic plug. Other evidence of past volcanic activity can be found in the Border Ranges and Lamington National Parks. Mount Gambier in South Australia is an extinct volcano whose collapsed craters have filled with water to form beautiful clear lakes.

Volcanoes that have not erupted for over 20 years and are not considered to be extinct

are called **dormant volcanoes**. Dormant means 'asleep' and these volcanoes could 'wake up' at any time and erupt. Mount St Helens in the western United States erupted in 1980, devastating the surrounding countryside and killing 57 people. It had been dormant for 123 years.

What *comes* out?

As the pressure builds up in the magma chamber, ash and steam emerge from the vents of a volcano. The lava is a mixture of molten rock, called magma, and gases including steam, carbon monoxide and hydrogen sulfide ('rotten egg' gas). When the volcano erupts, lava flows from the vents and red-hot fragments of rock, dust and ash, steam and other gases shoot out of the crater. Exploding gases often destroy part of the volcano. The larger fragments of rock blown out of the crater are called **volcanic bombs**.

The lava flowing from a volcano can be runny or pasty like toothpaste. If it is runny it can flood large areas, forming **shield volcanoes**. Volcanoes that are tall and cone-shaped are called **composite volcanoes** and are made from layers of ash, pasty lava and mud.

Thick, pasty lava builds up on the sides of volcanoes and can also block the vents as it cools. When this happens, gases build up in the magma below. As the pressure increases, the volcano can bulge and 'blow its top', thrusting rocks, gases and hot lava high into the air. When Krakatoa in Indonesia blew its top in 1883, the explosion could be heard over 4000 kilometres away. The tidal wave caused by the sudden explosion drowned about 36 000 people.

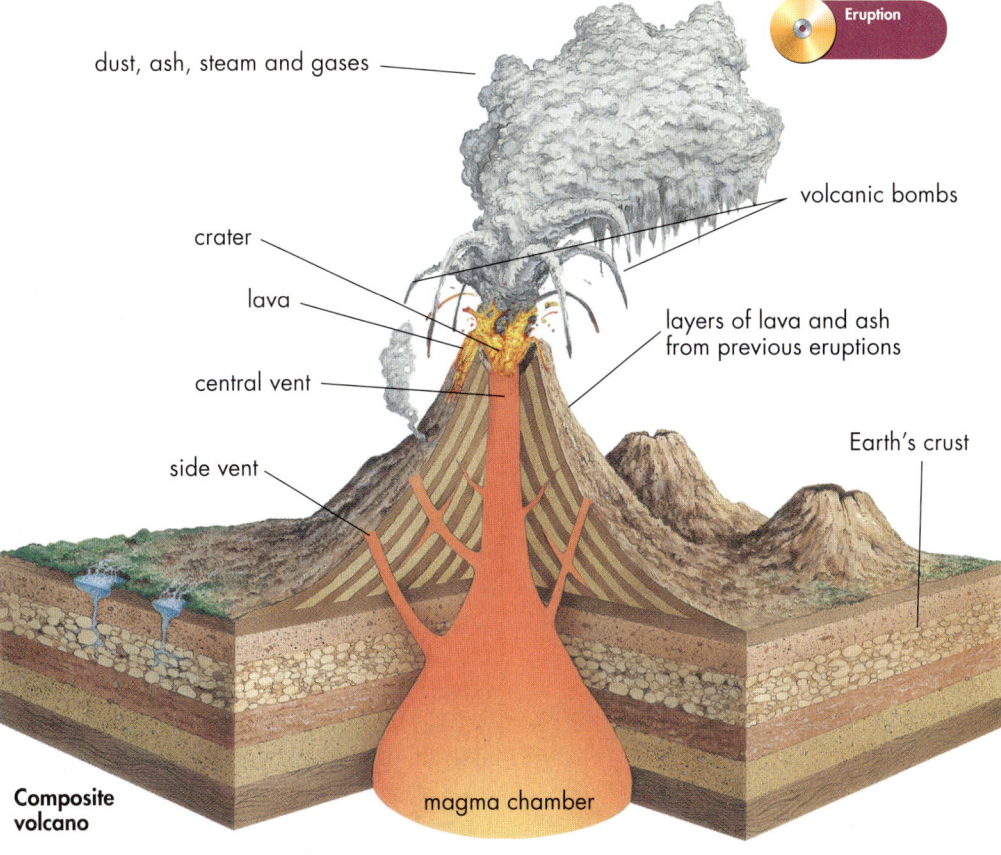

Eruption

dust, ash, steam and gases

crater

lava

central vent

side vent

volcanic bombs

layers of lava and ash from previous eruptions

Earth's crust

Composite volcano

magma chamber

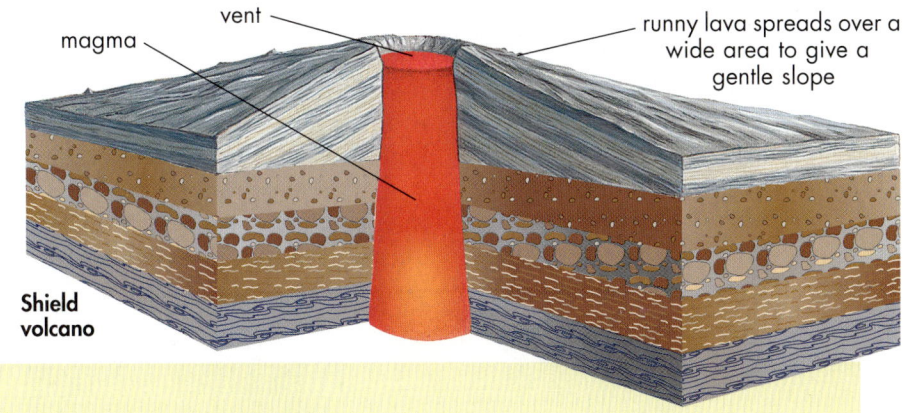

vent

magma

runny lava spreads over a wide area to give a gentle slope

Shield volcano

Activities

Remember

1. What materials emerge from a volcano crater during an eruption?
2. What is the difference between a dormant and an extinct volcano?
3. What can cause a volcano to 'blow its top'?

Think

1. Explain how a volcano can affect the world's weather.
2. What is the difference between magma and lava?
3. Locate active volcanoes on a map of the world. Investigate any patterns or reasons for their location.

Imagine

Imagine that you are the Mexican farmer who found the crack that gave birth to the volcano Paricutin. Write an account of what you saw and how you felt during the week after you first found the crack.

Create

Make a model volcano. You could make a papier-mâché model by shaping some chicken wire into a cone with a small crater at the top. Soak small pieces of newspaper in a pasty mixture of flour and water and attach the sticky newspaper to your wire cone. You will need to apply several layers of newspaper. Use colour to brighten up your model.

Investigate

1. Write an account of a recent volcanic eruption. Some that you might choose from are:
   • Rabaul, Papua New Guinea 2003
   • Kilauea, Hawaii 2003
   • Mount Etna, Sicily 2002.
2. Two of the most famous volcanoes in the world are Mt Vesuvius and Mt Krakatoa. Find out where they are, when they erupted and what damage they caused. Why do people still choose to live close by?

Hot rocks

Igneous rocks are those that have formed as a result of the cooling of magma from beneath the Earth's crust. The word 'igneous' is derived from *ignis*, the Latin word for fire. The words 'ignite' and 'ignition' come from the same Latin word.

Classifying *igneous* rocks

Igneous rocks can form above or below the surface of the Earth. Those that have formed from magma that cooled below the surface are called **intrusive rocks**. They cool slowly and become visible only when the rocks and soil above them erode. Large bodies of intrusive rock are called **batholiths**. They can stretch over distances of up to 1000 kilometres.

Igneous rocks that are formed from lava cooling above the surface are called **extrusive rocks**. They generally cool very quickly. Igneous rocks that form from lava spilling from underwater volcanoes are also classified as extrusive rocks.

The appearance of igneous rock depends on two major factors:
* which minerals it contains
* how quickly it cooled.

The minerals in an igneous rock determine its colour and hardness. When lava or magma cools, crystals are formed. The size of the crystals in an igneous rock depends on how quickly it cooled.

Intrusive rocks (sometimes called plutonic rocks) have larger crystals than extrusive rocks because the crystals have more time to grow. When lava emerges from a volcano, contact with the cool air or cold water makes it cool very quickly, not allowing large crystals time to grow.

Some *common* igneous rocks

Basalt

A dark-coloured rock with small crystals, **basalt** is formed when volcanic lava cools quickly on the ground or under the ocean. The ocean floor is covered with basalt that has formed from the lava of underwater volcanoes. Basalt covers much of northern New South Wales and is also found in places closer to Sydney such as Mt Wilson and Bondi Beach.

The Organ Pipes in Keilor, Victoria, are columns of basalt. As the lava cooled it cracked, forming these remarkable hexagonal columns.

Granite

Granite is a white, pink or grey rock with flecks of black and glassy minerals. Granite crystals are large. Granite is often used in buildings, monuments and gravestones. It is durable and can be polished smooth to produce a glassy appearance.

Extrusive rock forms from lava that cooled quickly above the surface.

Earth's surface

Intrusive rock forms from magma that cooled slowly below the surface.

Igneous rocks can form below or above the Earth's surface.

Pumice

Pumice is a pale, very light rock with a 'frothy' appearance. It is formed when lava erupts violently into the air, cooling while gases are still escaping from it. Pumice is used in rock or powder form for scrubbing, scouring and polishing.

Experiment 7.3 DOES FAST COOLING MAKE A DIFFERENCE?

YOU WILL NEED

freshly made saturated solution of potassium nitrate
potassium nitrate
spatula
250 mL beaker
3 test tubes and test tube rack

test tube holder
Bunsen burner, heatproof mat and matches
crushed ice
safety glasses
hand lens

CAUTION: Safety glasses must be worn during this experiment.

- Half fill a beaker with crushed ice.
- Quarter fill a clean test tube with saturated potassium nitrate solution. Add a spatula of potassium nitrate to the solution.
- Gently heat the solution over a Bunsen burner flame until the added potassium nitrate has dissolved or until the solution starts to boil.
- Pour half the warm solution into each of two clean test tubes.
- Place one test tube in the beaker of crushed ice and the other test tube in the rack to cool.

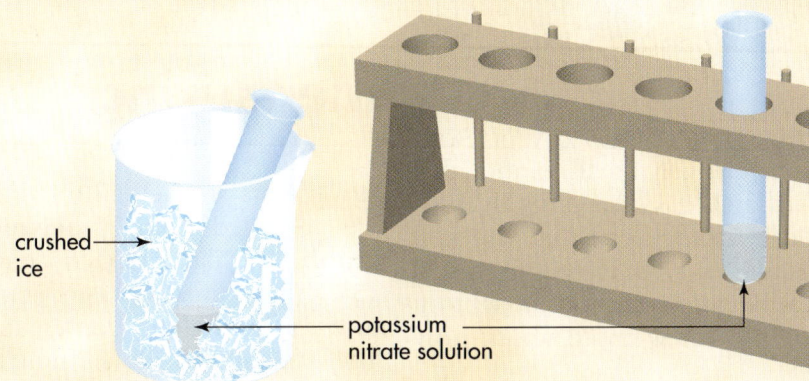

crushed ice

potassium nitrate solution

Cool one solution quickly and the other one slowly.

- When crystals have formed in each test tube, examine them with a hand lens.

1. Draw a labelled diagram of some crystals in each test tube, concentrating on their shape and size.
2. Which test tube contained the largest crystals — the one that cooled quickly or the one that cooled slowly?
3. Which type of igneous rock would you expect to have the largest crystals, those that cool slowly beneath the surface or those that cool quickly above the surface or underwater?
4. Why do safety glasses need to be worn in this experiment?

Scoria

Like pumice, **scoria** is a very light rock. It is formed when chunks of lava cool as they fall around the crater of a volcano. Scoria is used in gardens for underground drainage. Water soaks down through the dirt and fills up the spaces between the lumps of scoria. Scoria also soaks up some of the water.

Obsidian

Obsidian is a smooth, glassy rock with no visible crystals, and is usually black. It is formed when lava cools too quickly for visible crystals to form.

Activities

Remember

1. What are two differences between intrusive and extrusive rocks?
2. What is a batholith?
3. Complete the sentence: Large crystals form when magma cools _____, while small crystals form when lava cools _____.
4. Summarise the differences between granite and basalt.
5. Why is granite used in many buildings?
6. Why are basalt crystals so small?

Think

1. What do the words igneous, ignite and ignition have in common?
2. How would you decide if an igneous rock came from a volcano?
3. Rhyolite is an extrusive rock that contains the same minerals as granite. In what way would you expect it to be different from granite?
4. Why is pumice so light?

Shake, rattle and roll

It was 10.27 in the morning and Claire **was on school holidays.** The house was quiet. Her parents were at work and Tim, her older brother, had gone out to buy some milk. Claire walked to the kitchen and poured herself some orange juice. Just as she was about to pick up the glass, the orange juice rippled as if somebody had dropped a stone in it. The silence was broken as the cups, plates and glasses in the cupboards started rattling. The floor was vibrating. Claire was terrified. Small cracks appeared in the plaster walls and dust fell from the ceiling where larger cracks were appearing.

Through the window Claire could see the electricity wires swinging in the air. There was a wide crack in the road and the footpath in front of the house had collapsed. She struggled to keep her balance but all she could think of was her brother Tim. Was he safe? The rattling and shaking continued for what seemed ages, then suddenly stopped. All was still. Claire sat down, pale with shock. She jumped with fright as the front door burst open. It was Tim, smiling and holding two cartons of milk.

This earthquake took place in the New South Wales city of New-castle on 28 December 1989. It was a relatively small earthquake, but because it occurred in a built-up area it claimed 13 lives. It registered 5.6 on the Richter scale, less than the one that wrecked the Western Australian town of Meckering in 1968, which registered 6.8. Claire had not realised that an earthquake could occur right on her own doorstep. She now wished she knew more about how earthquakes are produced.

Claire and Tim were both very frightened. They were able to contact their parents by mobile phone but there was no electricity. The house became very hot without airconditioning but they were too frightened to go outside.

Power was restored after an hour and the radio reports indicated that the earthquake had lasted for less than a minute. Nobody in their family had been injured. Claire and Tim's parents arrived home from work early and the family spent a quiet few hours listening to more radio reports and talking about the earthquake. They did not want to leave the house for fear of the predicted aftershock.

Why earthquakes happen

Earthquakes are caused by movements in the Earth's crust up to 700 kilometres below the surface. Rocks below the surface, under great pressure, sometimes move against each other — sliding, pushing and sometimes moving apart. This movement causes vibrations or **tremors** on the Earth's surface. These tremors occur when the continental and oceanic crusts meet. When the tremors are sudden and strong they are called earthquakes.

The **epicentre** of an earthquake is directly above the point below the surface where the movement in the crust began. The epicentre of the Newcastle earthquake was 5 kilometres west of the town.

Measuring earthquakes

Movements in the Earth's crust are recorded with a **seismograph**. The illustration on page 155 shows what a seismograph records during an earthquake. The strength of an earthquake can be measured in a number of ways, the most well-known being the **Richter scale**.

The Richter scale does not always give a true indication of the destructive power of an earthquake. In a crowded city, small earthquakes can cause many deaths, injuries and much damage, cutting off water, gas and electricity supplies, while larger earthquakes in remote areas cause little injury and damage.

Three earthquakes hit the town of Tennant Creek in January 1988. The largest of the three was at 12.30 pm and registered 7.0 on the Richter scale. The epicentre of the earthquake was 40 kilometres north of the town. Had it been closer to the town, damage would have been far greater and serious injuries and deaths could have resulted.

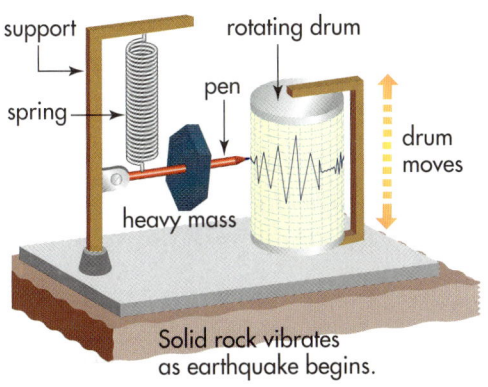

support
rotating drum
pen
spring
drum moves
heavy mass
Solid rock vibrates as earthquake begins.

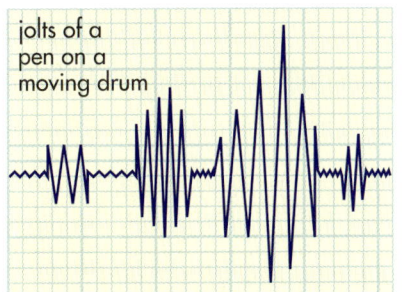

jolts of a pen on a moving drum

An earthquake recorded on a seismograph. A strip of paper moves past a stationary pen. When the seismograph is jolted by the earthquake it jumps up and down. However, the pen is attached to the heavy mass which does not move. As the paper turns on the drum, the pen leaves a record of the vibrations.

Giant *waves*

Earthquakes occurring under the water or near the coast can cause giant waves called **tsunamis**. They travel through the ocean at speeds of up to 800 kilometres per hour. When they approach land, tsunamis slow down as the water becomes shallower. As they slow down, the waves build up to heights of up to 30 metres. Tsunamis are responsible for many deaths and injuries following earthquakes many kilometres away.

Experiment 7.4 MAKING A SEISMOGRAPH

YOU WILL NEED

a retort stand, bosshead and rod
spring
cardboard
A4 paper
sticky tape
felt pen
500 g or 1 kg weight (or a can full of sand)

- Set up the equipment as shown in the diagram on the right.
- Have your partner move the cardboard past the pen while you thump the surface on which your seismograph sits.

1. Does the model work?
2. How could you improve the model?

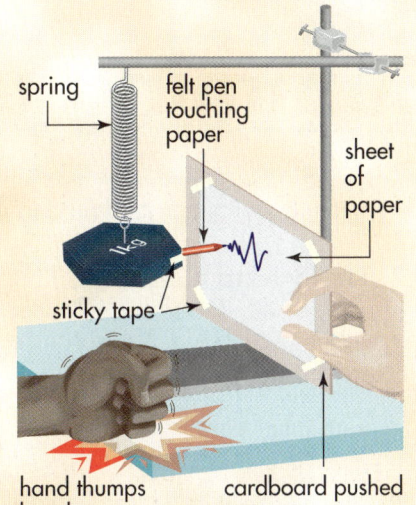

spring
felt pen touching paper
sheet of paper
sticky tape
hand thumps bench
cardboard pushed past pen

A model seismograph

Activities

Using data

The table below shows the number of people killed in some of the major earthquakes in recent years.

Year	Location	Number of deaths	Richter scale measurement
1997	Jahalpur, India	38	5.8
1998	Papua New Guinea	2 183	7.0
1999	Chi-Chi, Taiwan	2 400	7.7
2000	Napa, USA	0	5.0
2001	El Salvador	844	7.7
2001	Coastal Peru	75	8.4
2001	Gujarat, India	20 085	7.7
2003	Bam, Iran	40 000	6.6

1. Which two earthquakes best show that the Richter scale measurement does not indicate the loss of life in earthquakes?
2. What factors, apart from the Richter scale measurement, affect the likelihood of deaths in an earthquake?
3. Draw or use spreadsheet software to produce a bar graph to display the Richter scale measurement of the earthquakes listed in the table.

Remember

1. Describe some of the effects of earthquakes.
2. What causes an earthquake?
3. Explain the difference between an earthquake and a tremor.
4. What is the epicentre of an earthquake?

Investigate

Research to find out why earthquakes are more likely to occur in some areas than others.

Putting it all together

Summing up

Copy and complete the statements below to compile a summary of this unit.
The missing words can be found in the word list below.

1. The Earth has a _____ shape.

2. The Earth can be divided into distinct layers — atmosphere, _____, mantle, outer core and inner core.

3. The temperature inside the Earth gets _____ as you move towards the centre.

4. The atmosphere consists of many gases but is mostly nitrogen and _____.

5. The balance of gases in the Earth's atmosphere is under threat as a result of _____ activity.

6. The Earth _____ about its own axis, completing one full rotation in 24 hours.

7. The Earth orbits the sun, making a complete _____ in about 365 days.

8. Day and night and the seasons can be explained by the relative movement of the Earth to the _____.

9. _____ are formed by the release of molten rock, ash and other particles from beneath the Earth's surface.

10. Igneous rocks are those that are formed from _____ rock.

11. _____ rocks can form above or below the Earth's surface.

12. The size of crystals in igneous rocks is determined by the _____ at which they cooled.

13. _____ are caused by movements of rocks below the Earth's surface.

14. A _____ is an instrument used to measure the strength of earthquakes.

15. _____ is the movement of soil and rock from one place to another.

16. _____ is a vital resource as it contains nutrients essential for plant growth.

17. The rate of erosion is more rapid than it should be as a result of human activity, especially the removal of _____ and other vegetation.

Word list

oxygen	seismograph	crust	volcanoes
trees	erosion	rotates	sun
igneous	spherical	higher	human
earthquakes	molten	soil	rate
revolution			

Looking back

1. Unjumble the words below to reveal some of the layers of the Earth and its atmosphere. For each of the layers that you find, state:
   (a) what is in the layer
   (b) where it lies.

   NOOZE YEARL   THEERPSOORP
   TALEMN   SPOTTEESHRAR
   NERNI CROE   STRUC

2. Complete this word puzzle, using the clues below.

   (a) _____ _____ _____ _____ _____ P _____ _____ _____ _____
   (b) _____ _____ _____ _____ L _____
   (c) A _____ _____ _____
   (d) _____ _____ _____ _____ N _____ _____ _____
   (e) _____ _____ _____ E _____ _____
   (f) _____ _____ _____ _____ T

   (g) _____ _____ _____ _____ E _____ _____ _____ _____
   (h) _____ A _____ _____
   (i) _____ _____ _____ _____ R _____ _____ _____
   (j) _____ _____ _____ T
   (k) _____ _____ _____ _____ H _____ _____ _____

   Clues
   (a) The region of gases surrounding the Earth
   (b) A type of igneous rock formed when volcanic lava cools
   (c) An imaginary line that runs from north to south through the centre of the Earth
   (d) Describes volcanoes that have not erupted for thousands of years
   (e) Type of rock that forms as a result of the cooling of molten material
   (f) The path of the Earth around the sun
   (g) The point on the surface below which an earthquake begins
   (h) Molten rock that flows from a volcano
   (i) The most abundant gas in the atmosphere
   (j) The Earth is not this — although some still believe it is.
   (k) A scale used to measure earthquakes

3. The length of a day on the planet Venus is 243 Earth days. The length of a year on Venus is only 225 Earth days. Explain how it is possible for a day to be longer than a year.
4. Give at least two reasons why people are concerned about the removal of trees from forests.
5. Imagine that you are given the task of describing your planet to an alien from a distant galaxy. You are, however, limited to a maximum of 200 words. Write your description. You are not able to use diagrams and must write more than 100 words.

Extension
Deep quest

Our knowledge of the ocean floor is relatively new. Until about 60 years ago, most people thought that the bottom of the ocean was quite flat. Exploration of the ocean floor was not possible until **echolocation** was used. Although humans could not actually venture deep in the ocean, it was possible to send sound waves down from ships. The use of **sonar** (**so**und **n**avigation **a**nd **r**anging) to determine the depth of the ocean floor is similar to the use of echolocation by bats and some other animals to find their prey.

The depth can be calculated using the measurement of the time taken for sound to return to the ship and the speed of sound in water. Sonar can also be used to detect schools of fish and large objects, such as submarines.

More detailed information about what is on the ocean bottom has come from exploration in **submersibles**. In 1960, two scientists descended to a depth of almost 11 kilometres in a submersible.

What's *down* there?

The surface of the ocean floor consists of mountains, valleys and plains, very much like the land.

The **continental shelf** is the gently sloping edge of a continent and is only about 200 metres under the water.

Ocean ridges are long ranges of volcanic mountains. They rise up to about 1000 metres above

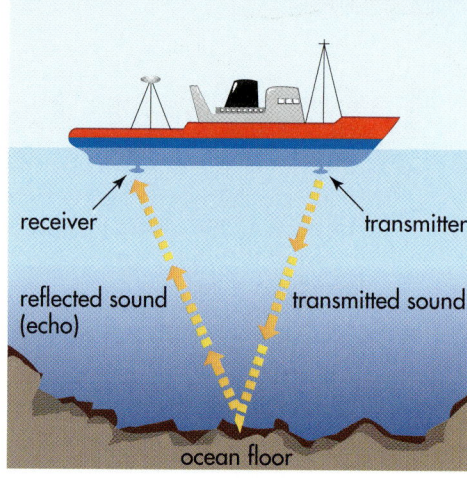

Sonar can be used to map the ocean floor.

the ocean plains. The mountains are continually pushed aside by magma seeping from the centre of the ocean ridges. The magma cools, becoming new rock. The ocean ridges are the largest features of planet Earth, covering about one fifth of the surface.

Activities

Remember
1. Where are the deepest parts of the ocean?
2. What is sonar and how is it used in ocean exploration?

Think
1. Why was exploration of the ocean floor not possible before the invention of sonar?
2. Ocean ridges can be described as the birthplace of new rock. Why?
3. What is a submarine volcano?

Investigate
Research and report on the living things that survive in the deep, dark depths of the ocean.

Imagine
Imagine that you had to design a submersible that could carry two humans down to a depth of 10 000 metres. Remember that all observations need to be made from inside the vehicle. Draw a diagram of the submersible and write a list of the features that it would need.

The deepest parts of the oceans are in **ocean trenches**. The deepest point of all is about 11 000 metres below sea level in the Mariana Trench in the Pacific Ocean, about 2000 kilometres directly north of Cape York, the northern tip of the Australian continent.

Volcanic eruptions are common on the ocean floor. **Submarine volcanoes** are often large enough to break the surface of the ocean, becoming volcanic islands.

The largest submarine volcano is Mauna Kea in Hawaii which, although only 4205 metres above sea level, rises over 10 000 metres from the ocean floor. (Mount Everest rises about 8900 metres above the continent of Asia.)

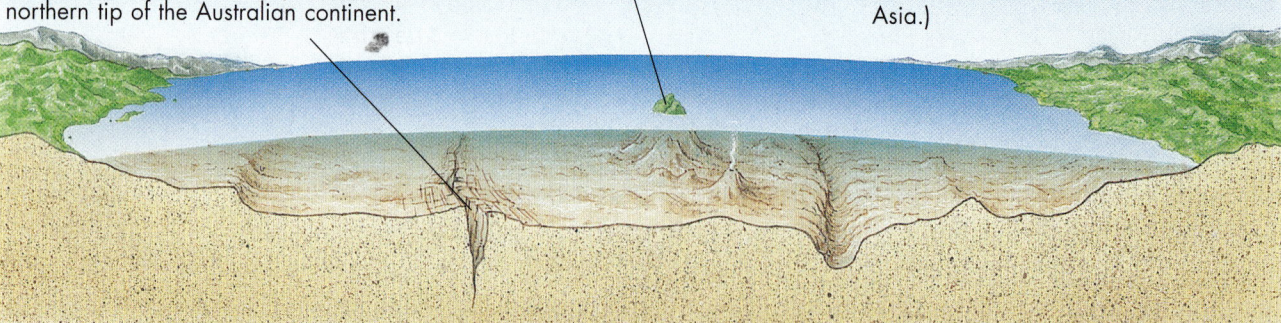

Reflection

What have I learnt?

(a) Look carefully at your group's original mind map. Identify all the information you have changed or added since the start of this topic. Make your own personal mind map using this new knowledge. Now study your own mind map and identify the new knowledge that you found most interesting. Invent a way to teach this to a primary school student. You might create a quiz, puzzle, poem, rap, drama or poster — whatever you think would be most suitable.

(b) Write three questions you would like answered to extend your learning about the topics covered in this chapter. Over the next few weeks, do your own research to find these answers. Check the library, ask people you meet or write letters to people or companies that might be able to help you.

(c) What were the names of the igneous rocks studied in this chapter? Research some other igneous rocks and create a model or poster to describe them.

Granite boulders rounded by wave action

GROUP WORK (d) Batholith, boss, dyke, laccolith, lopolith, phacolith, sill and stock are all names for land features formed by movements in the Earth's surface. Divide this list of features between members of your group. Draw diagrams or make models to explain the features allocated to you. Take turns explaining each feature to the others in your group.

(e) Find a map of the world that shows the location of volcanic activity and earthquakes. Compare them and write an explanation of your observations. Why do you think people still choose to live in zones where earthquakes or volcanic activity occur?

GROUP WORK (f) The greenhouse effect and soil erosion are often quoted as having drastic effects on humankind's survival in the future. As a group, research both of these and list some ways to reduce their effect.

(g) Research the landforms and rocks that are found in your local area and make a collection of local rocks. You may be lucky enough to find some rock cuttings made by road works. If you look carefully at these, you will be able to see a record of what happened to the ground in that area in the past.

Have you added the new information (in red) on this mind map to your own?

THE SOLAR SYSTEM

The Earth is just one of nine planets that revolve around the sun. The sun, together with the planets and the many other objects that move around it, make up the solar system. This chapter will take you on a journey to the sun, the planets and other heavenly bodies.

NASA's *Cassini* probe to arrive at Saturn in 2004

KEY CONTENT

Describe the features of the solar system.

Use scales to demonstrate relative sizes, distances and orbits of planets and moons.

Recognise the force of gravity and centripetal force in the solar system.

Compare the geology of the planets to illustrate their similarities and differences.

Identify excessive ultraviolet radiation as potentially harmful to living things.

Discuss modern technologies involved in space probes.

KEY QUESTIONS

How big is the sun compared to the planets?

Why is the sun hot?

What are the other planets like?

Why is the planet closest to the sun not the hottest one?

Which planets have moons?

What are the rings around the larger planets made of?

Can an asteroid have a moon?

What killed the dinosaurs?

How do we know so much about the planets without going there?

Thinking about The solar system

1. Make a model of your ideas about the solar system

(a) This is not a test, but it will help you to identify your own ideas about the solar system, which are really the starting point for this topic. You require no reference material as this activity is about what you think now, not what you can read in books.

This is what you need to do.
- On a large piece of paper, draw a diagram of the solar system, in order from the sun to the outer planets.
- Name each planet and name the largest and the smallest planet.
- Beside each planet write any information you know about it.

GROUP WORK (b) Now share your ideas in a group. This will allow you to compare your initial ideas with other students' views. This discussion of initial ideas will also prepare you for the following activity and this chapter's first experiment, 'The scale of the solar system'.

2. What 'big ideas' have you gained already?

What has impressed you most about the solar system? What trends have you noticed? Write these ideas in your workbook.

Think! Reflect!

3. Words from the solar system

(a) Some of the words specific to a study of the solar system are shown below. Write down your meanings for these words as you understand them at present. If there are any other words that you think should be included, add them to the list.

GROUP WORK (b) Share your meanings with the class or with your group. Note that these are a collection of ideas with no 'right' and 'wrong' answers at this stage. They may lead to an interesting discussion and some questions.

vacuum   rotation   satellite   space   moon   solar   orbit   revolution   asteroid   planet

4. What happens when . . .

(a) Read the following questions and write down your answers in your workbook.

(i) Why doesn't an astronaut fall through space when he or she comes out of a spacecraft? Why doesn't a heavy planet fall through space?

(ii) The Earth has more water than any other planet in the solar system. Why doesn't the water flow off the Earth?

(iii) Did people always think the Earth was round and the sun was in the middle of the solar system?

(iv) Why do we have leap years?

(b) Now write your own questions about the solar system.

GROUP WORK (c) Discuss your answers to both sets of questions with your group.

A family of nine

The sun is the centre of the system of heavenly bodies that is called the solar system. Our sun is found within a larger group of stars called the Milky Way **Galaxy**.

The Earth is one of nine **planets** that revolve around the sun. These nine planets travel around the sun in an almost circular path called an **orbit**. The orbits are in the shape of an ellipse but some are more circular than others. An ellipse is a slightly flattened circular shape.

The orbit of Pluto is tilted and less circular than the orbits of the other planets. At most times, Pluto is the furthest planet from the sun. However, because of the more flattened shape of its orbit, Pluto was closer to the sun than Neptune between 1979 and 1999.

Light from the sun is reflected off the planets allowing us to see

The nine planets of the solar system. This diagram is not drawn to scale. The planets are really much further apart.

Experiment 8.1   THE SCALE OF THE SOLAR SYSTEM

YOU WILL NEED
cardboard
marking pens
long measuring tape or trundle
    wheel
basketball
2 golf balls (or table tennis balls)
2 marbles
2 peas
3 silver cachous (the small shiny
    spheres used to decorate cakes)

- Make 10 large cardboard labels for your class: one for the sun and one for each planet.
- Collect a basketball to represent the sun, and each of the items listed in the table on the right to represent the planets, and move to a large outdoor area.
- One student should be selected to hold the 'sun' and its label. Nine groups of students should also be selected to carry the 'planets' and their labels to the correct distances from the 'sun'.

(The model created here is not quite to scale. The distances from the 'sun' to the 'planets' listed in the table below are one-tenth of what they need to be to produce a scale model.)

A model of the solar system

Planet	Item representing planet	Distance from the 'sun' (metres)
Mercury	silver cachou	1.5
Venus	pea	2.7
Earth	pea	3.7
Mars	silver cachou	5.7
Jupiter	golf ball	20
Saturn	golf ball	36
Uranus	marble	72
Neptune	marble	110
Pluto	silver cachou	150

1. Describe your model in words. Does it surprise you in any way?
2. Explain how you could make this a working model.

them. The planets Mercury, Venus, Mars, Jupiter and Saturn can all be seen from Earth without using a telescope and were discovered in ancient times. They were noticed among the many stars in the sky because they moved in regular patterns against the background of stars. In fact, the word 'planet' comes from the Greek word 'wanderer'.

The most distant planets, however, cannot be seen without telescopes and were discovered more recently. Uranus was discovered accidentally by William and Caroline Herschel with a telescope in 1781. Neptune was discovered in 1846 by Le Verrier and Pluto was first photographed in 1930.

A closer *look at* the planets

Eight of the planets fall into two distinct groups:

- The **terrestrial planets** are those that are similar to Earth. They are small and solid. Mercury, Venus, Earth and Mars are terrestrial planets.
- The larger, outer planets are referred to as the **gas giants**. Jupiter, Saturn, Uranus and Neptune fall into this group. These huge planets do not have a solid surface.

Pluto is in neither group. It is not similar to Earth. In fact it is smaller than our own moon. Unlike the gas giants, its surface is frozen solid.

All of the planets spin, or **rotate**, on their axes as they orbit the sun. The Earth rotates once every 24 hours. This period is called one day. Jupiter takes only about 10 hours to rotate. That means that a day on Jupiter would be only 10 hours long. The planet Venus takes 243 Earth days to complete one full rotation.

Activities

Using data

The table below shows how the size and distance from the sun of other planets compare with Earth.

How the other planets compare with Earth

Planet	Diameter at equator (Earth = 1 unit)	Average distance from the sun (Earth = 1 unit)
Mercury	0.38	0.39
Venus	0.95	0.72
Earth	1.00	1.00
Mars	0.53	1.52
Jupiter	11.2	5.19
Saturn	9.41	9.43
Uranus	3.98	19.1
Neptune	3.81	29.9
Pluto	0.24	39.3

1. Follow the instructions below to produce two scale drawings of the solar system. The first drawing will show how the sizes of the planets compare with each other. The second drawing will show how far the planets are from the sun.
   (a) On a sheet of A3 paper, draw a circle to represent the size of each of the nine planets. Use the diameter in Earth units from the table above and a scale of 1 cm = 1 Earth unit. Colour and label each planet.
   (b) Turn the sheet over and rule a 40 cm line. At the left end of the line, draw a large dot and label it as the sun. Use the distances in Earth units from the table to draw a dot representing each planet on your line. Again, use a scale of 1 cm = 1 Earth unit. Label each planet.
2. Which planet is closest in size to the Earth?
3. Do the planets appear to fall into groupings, either in size or in distance from the sun?
4. Discuss why it is not possible to represent both the size and the distance from the sun on the same diagram.

Remember

How long does it take the Earth to complete one full rotation? How does this compare with Jupiter and Venus?

Think

Why were Uranus, Neptune and Pluto discovered much later than the other planets?

Investigate

Johannes Kepler (1571–1630) studied the motion of the planets known during his lifetime. He discovered two laws about how planets moved. Research these laws and how his discoveries were received by the community in Graz, Austria, where he lived at the time. Are his ideas accepted today?

8.2

Star performer

The sun is 149.5 million kilometres from Earth and is the centre of the solar system. It is one of billions of stars in the universe. The planets, asteroids, meteoroids and comets all revolve around the sun, trapped by its huge gravitational pull. The sun is vital to life on Earth, providing the planet with heat and light.

CAUTION: Never look directly at the sun! Serious eye damage can be caused.

helium. There are small traces of other materials such as carbon and iron. Like all of the planets, the sun rotates about its own **axis**. It therefore has two poles and an equator. Because it is not solid, different parts of the sun rotate at different speeds. At its equator, the sun rotates once every 25 days. At the poles, it takes 34 days for a full rotation.

The huge pull of gravity within the sun produces great amounts of heat and pressure. There is

enough heat and pressure to allow nuclear reactions to take place in the sun's core. The hydrogen is changed to helium in an explosive nuclear reaction that releases huge amounts of energy. It is this nuclear reaction that keeps the sun and all other stars shining.

The temperature at the surface of the sun is about 6000°C. The temperature at its centre, where the nuclear reactions take place, is believed to be about 15 000 000°C.

Profile *of the* sun

The sun makes up 99.8 per cent of the total mass of the solar system. The diagram below shows how it compares in size with the planets (the sun is the largest circle).

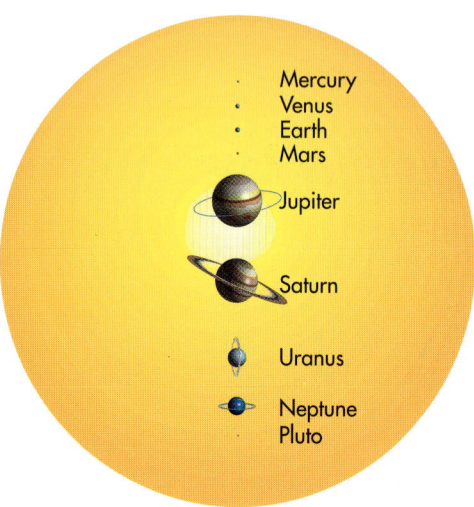

- Mercury
- Venus
- Earth
- Mars

Jupiter

Saturn

Uranus

Neptune
Pluto

The sun is very much larger than the planets.

The sun's diameter is 1.4 million kilometres, 110 times that of Earth. In fact, it would be possible to fit 1.3 million Earths into the space occupied by the sun. About 75 per cent of the sun is hydrogen. Most of the rest is

Experiment 8.2

WHAT KEEPS THE PLANETS IN THE SOLAR SYSTEM?

YOU WILL NEED
styrofoam ball or table tennis ball
one metre of strong thread or string
sticky tape
large metal nut or similar weight
hollow plastic tube or empty biro
case

- Tape a piece of thread to a styrofoam ball or table tennis ball and pass it through a hollow plastic tube. Tie the other end to a large metal nut or similar weight. The ball represents a planet and the plastic tube represents the sun.
- Move to a distance of at least one metre from all other people. Hold the plastic tube in your hand and whirl the ball in a circle as shown in the diagram on the right.

1. What force prevents the ball from flying off into the distance?
2. The planets are obviously not tied to the sun with a string. What is the name of the force that keeps the planets from escaping from the sun and the solar system?

3. Predict what would happen to the ball if the thread was cut.

- Cut the thread just below the plastic tube while the ball is being whirled and observe the motion of the ball.

4. What would happen to the planets if the sun suddenly disappeared from the solar system?

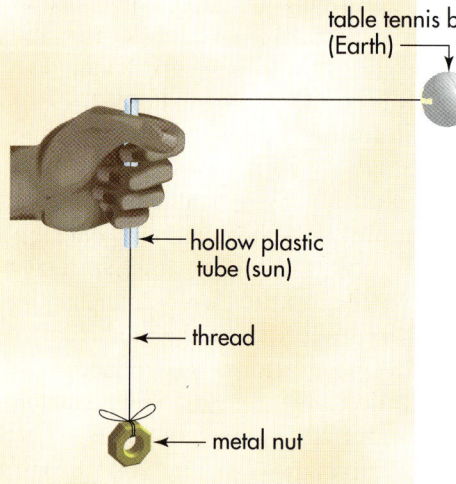

table tennis ball
(Earth)

hollow plastic
tube (sun)

thread

metal nut

There must be a force to keep the ball moving in a circle. What force keeps the planets in orbit around the sun?

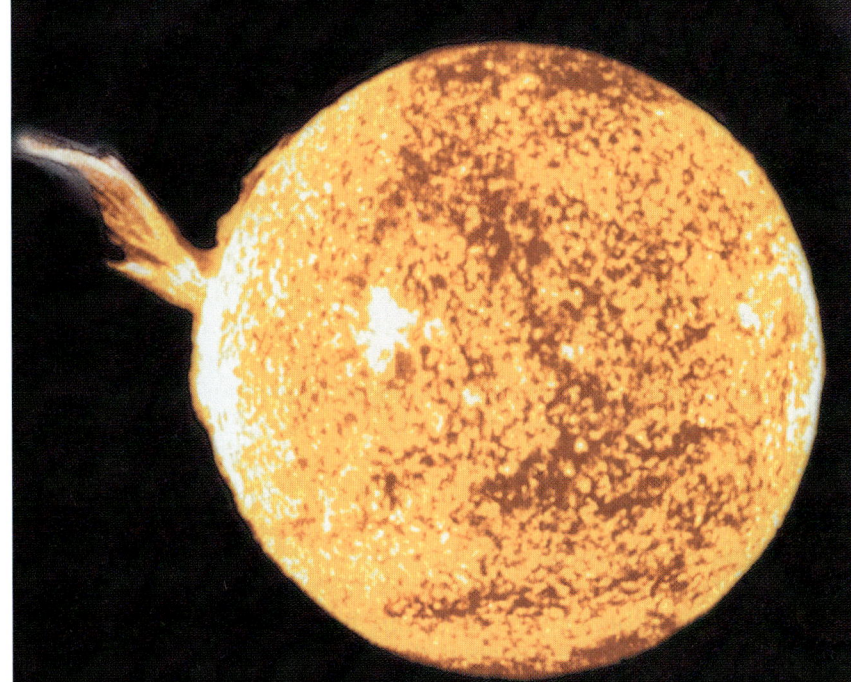

The surface of the sun. The disturbance visible at the left is a solar flare. Solar flares are believed to be caused by electrical storms on the sun and can last up to half an hour.

Energy *from the* sun

The sun provides the planets with heat, light and other forms of energy. The energy released from the sun is called **solar energy**. Solar energy reaches all of the planets.

Life exists on Earth because the atmosphere allows the right amounts of each type of solar energy to reach the surface. Solar energy provides:

- the light needed by plants so that they can grow and make their own food. Animals rely on plants as a source of food. Even animals that do not eat plants eat other animals that do eat plants. Animals also need light to be able to see.
- heat which keeps the atmosphere, the Earth's surface and bodies of water warm enough to support life. The sun controls our climate. Heat is released from the sun in the form of **infra-red radiation**. Infra-red radiation is not visible to the human eye. Some gases in the Earth's atmosphere absorb infra-red radiation from the sun. This makes the atmosphere heat up. The same gases also stop infra-red radiation from leaving the Earth. This process is called the **greenhouse effect**. The atmosphere of Venus is mostly carbon dioxide which absorbs a lot of infra-red radiation. The greenhouse effect is responsible for the extremely high temperatures on Venus.

- **ultraviolet radiation**, which is needed by humans to help the body make vitamin D. The amount required can be obtained by being outdoors for just a few minutes. However, the ultraviolet radiation emitted from the sun is the cause of sunburn and can lead to skin cancer. The ozone high in the Earth's atmosphere absorbs much of the ultraviolet radiation reaching the Earth from the sun. If humans were living and working in sunlight on the moon or Mars, they would need a lot more protection from the ultraviolet radiation than on Earth because there is no ozone on the moon or Mars. Ultraviolet radiation, like infra-red radiation, is not visible to the human eye.

- other forms of radiation including radio waves, microwaves, X-rays and gamma rays.

Together, all of the different forms of energy coming from the sun are referred to as the **electromagnetic spectrum**.

Activities

Remember

1. What is the sun?
2. What force keeps the planets, asteroids, meteoroids and comets in orbit around the sun?
3. What happens inside the sun to provide the huge amount of energy that it releases?
4. Use the clues below to reveal some of the forms of energy released by the sun.
   (a) This type of radiation causes sunburn and skin cancer.
   (b) Without this, plants are unable to make their own food.
   (c) This type of radiation heats the atmospheres of Earth and Venus.

Think

1. Without the sun, life on Earth would not be possible. Why?
2. Why is there no greenhouse effect on Mars?
3. Why would you need protection from the sunlight on Mars even though it is very cold?
4. Discuss why all of the Earth's fossil fuels, including coal, petroleum and natural gas could be described as stored solar energy. (Think about how they are formed.)

Investigate

Find out what sunspots are and how they are believed to affect the Earth.

Terrestrial neighbours

The four small and solid planets nearest to the sun — Mercury, Mars, Earth and Venus — are called the terrestrial planets. Terrestrial means 'like Earth'. Our knowledge of Mercury, Venus and Mars has increased rapidly since 1962. In that year, the first visit to another planet by a space probe took place when *Mariner 2* flew above the clouds of Venus. Since then, space probes have landed on Venus and Mars, sending back data and pictures of their atmospheres and surfaces. Before the space probe visits, our knowledge of these planets was based on observations with telescopes from Earth.

Mercury

PROFILE
Named after Mercury, Roman messenger of the gods.
Average distance from the sun: 58 million kilometres.
Diameter at equator: 4900 kilometres.
Period of rotation (length of day): 59 Earth days.
Period of orbit around sun (length of year): 88 Earth days.
Surface gravity: 0.38 times that of Earth.
Surface temperature: believed to range from −180°C to 420°C.
Satellites: none.

Mercury is the closest planet to the sun and quite small compared to Earth. The surface of Mercury is very much like that of the moon. It is very heavily cratered and has mountains, valleys and flat plains just like the 'seas' on the moon. Until 1974, when the space probe *Mariner 10* flew close to Mercury, the planet was believed to have no atmosphere. *Mariner 10* found traces of the gases helium and hydrogen and even smaller amounts of several other gases. Because the pull of gravity on Mercury is quite small compared to the Earth, gases tend to escape into space.

The temperatures on Mercury are extreme, generally ranging from −180°C to 420°C. The very thin atmosphere allows heat to escape quickly, so the part of Mercury not facing the sun gets very cold. There is recent evidence to suggest that temperatures on the part of Mercury facing the sun could get as high as 700°C at times.

There is very much more to learn about the planet Mercury. Because it is so close to the sun, it is very difficult to observe, even with telescopes. Astronomers on Earth use radar, a device using radio waves to measure the distance of objects, to observe its surface. While this work continues, and as more space probes fly near the planet, we will find out more.

Venus

PROFILE
Named after Venus, Roman goddess of love and beauty.
Average distance from the sun: 108 million kilometres.
Diameter at equator: 12 100 km.
Period of rotation (length of day): 243 Earth days.
Period of orbit around sun (length of year): 225 Earth days.
Surface gravity: 0.91 times that of Earth.
Surface temperature: average about 450°C.
Satellites: none.

Venus is the closest planet to the Earth and the second-closest planet to the sun. Venus is about the same size as Earth. It is the brightest object in the night sky apart from the moon. The thick clouds above the planet made the surface of Venus a mystery until space probes were able to take photographs in 1974 and 1975. Even though space probes first flew past Venus in 1962, very little knowledge was gained. The atmosphere of Venus was so heavy and hot that early spacecraft and their instruments were crushed or melted.

The atmosphere of Venus is almost entirely carbon dioxide. This means that heat does not escape easily. As a result, the range of temperatures is small and the average temperature is much higher than that of Mercury even though Venus is almost twice as far from the sun.

The surface of Venus is mostly flat and rocky with two large areas of mountains. It is not very hospitable because of the high temperature, heavy atmosphere and the presence of sulfuric acid in the atmosphere.

Mars

PROFILE
Named after Mars, Roman god of war.
Average distance from the sun: 228 million kilometres.
Diameter at equator: 6800 kilometres.
Period of rotation (length of day): 24.5 hours.
Period of orbit around sun (length of year): 687 Earth days.
Surface gravity: 0.38 times that of Earth.
Surface temperature: usually ranges from about −120°C to about −30°C.
Satellites: 2.

Mars has about half the diameter of Earth. After Earth, its orbit is next-furthest from the sun. Like Mercury, it has a small pull of gravity and a thin atmosphere. The atmosphere on Mars consists almost entirely of carbon dioxide. The thin atmosphere and lack of clouds made it possible to observe the surface, from Earth using telescopes. In fact, in 1877, one astronomer observed what appeared to be canals on the surface, leading to speculation that there was life on Mars. In 2001 the spacecraft *Mars Odyssey* detected sub-surface ice on Mars. This ice could provide a source of water to support a manned mission to Mars.

In early 2004, NASA landed two identical robots on Mars: *Spirit Rover* and *Opportunity Rover*. Within a short time of landing, *Spirit Rover*, which was located in the Gustav crater, started sending photographs back to Earth. The surface showed a long deep valley that appears to be a dried lake. *Opportunity Rover* also quickly started examining bedrock and has excited scientists by showing that the area was once covered by water. This is evidence that there may once have been life as we know it on Mars. To see what these probes discover, go to www.jaconline.com.au/corescience2e and click on the NASA link for *Core Science 1*.

The most prominent feature of Mars is the red dust and the carbon dioxide ice poles and large volcanoes. The largest volcano is the 25 km high Olympus Mons. Its height is well over double the height of Mt Everest.

Mars has two small natural satellites, or moons, Phobos and Deimos. Phobos, the larger of the two, has a diameter of about 20 km and orbits Mars once every 7.5 hours. Deimos, with a diameter of only 10 km, travels around the planet once every 30 hours.

Activities

Remember

1. Why has our knowledge of the terrestrial planets increased so rapidly during the past 30 years?
2. Which of the terrestrial planets, Mercury, Venus and Mars, is:
   (a) closest to the sun?   (b) furthest from the sun?
   (c) smallest?   (d) largest?
3. Which gas makes up most of the atmosphere on the planet Venus?
4. Why has it been widely believed that life existed on Mars?

Think

1. Compile a list of similar features of the planets Mercury, Venus and Mars.
2. What are the major differences between the features of Venus and of Earth?
3. What are the major differences between the features of Mars and of Earth?

4. Evaluate the planets Venus and Mars and recommend the planet that would be more suitable for a space laboratory in which humans could live and work. Give reasons for your choice of planet.
5. The atmospheres of Mercury and Mars are very thin. What effect does the thin atmosphere have on the temperature on the surface of these planets?

Create

Use the Internet to find out more about Mars, then create a tourist brochure to entice people to visit the planet. Include information about:
- the trip to and from Mars
- accommodation
- weather conditions
- the atmosphere and surface
- sights to see
- how to get around while on the planet
- leisure activities
- excursions to the two moons.

8.4
Gas giants

The four largest planets, Jupiter, Saturn, Uranus and Neptune, lie well beyond the planet Mars. These planets are called the gas giants because they are like huge balls of gas. The gas giants do not have a solid surface like the terrestrial planets Mercury, Venus, Earth and Mars. They gradually change from gases in their deep atmospheres to liquids and solids closer to the centre. The gas giants are composed mainly of hydrogen, helium and methane. The space probes *Voyager 1* and *Voyager 2* flew past the gas giants between 1979 and 1989, discovering many new moons and showing that all of the gas giants had ring systems around them. In 2004, *Voyager 1* was more than 13.5 billion kilometres from Earth.

The space probe *Galileo* orbited Jupiter for 8 years, until it was de-orbited and sent crashing onto the planet's surface. *Galileo* provided information about the moons of Jupiter.

Jupiter

PROFILE
Named after Jupiter, king of the Roman gods.
Average distance from the sun: 778 million kilometres.
Diameter at equator: 142 700 kilometres.
Period of rotation (length of day): 10 hours.
Period of orbit around sun (length of year): about 12 Earth years.
Pull of gravity: 2.9 times that of Earth.
Temperature: average about –140°C.
Satellites: 17.

Saturn

PROFILE
Named after Saturn, Roman god of agriculture.
Average distance from the sun: 1425 million kilometres.
Diameter at equator: 120 000 km.
Period of rotation (length of day): 10.7 hours.
Period of orbit around sun (length of year): 29.5 Earth years.
Pull of gravity: 1.3 times that of Earth.
Temperature: average about –170°C.
Satellites: 28.

Jupiter can be seen from Earth without the aid of a telescope. Its largest four moons can be seen with a small pair of binoculars. Jupiter is heavier than all of the other planets put together. A giant hurricane, called the Great Red Spot, is over twice the size of the Earth. This hurricane was first observed over 300 years ago! Jupiter rotates so quickly that it bulges at its equator. A thin ring of fine dust was detected around Jupiter by both of the *Voyager* space probes in 1979.

Like Jupiter, **Saturn** bulges at its equator because of its rapid rotation. The system of rings around Saturn's equator is several kilometres thick. There are seven rings, which consist of thousands of smaller ringlets. The ringlets appear to be made up of small particles of ice-coated rock revolving around the planet like tiny moons. Saturn would be able to float on water. In 2004 the Cassini space probe will reach Saturn to examine its rings.

Activities

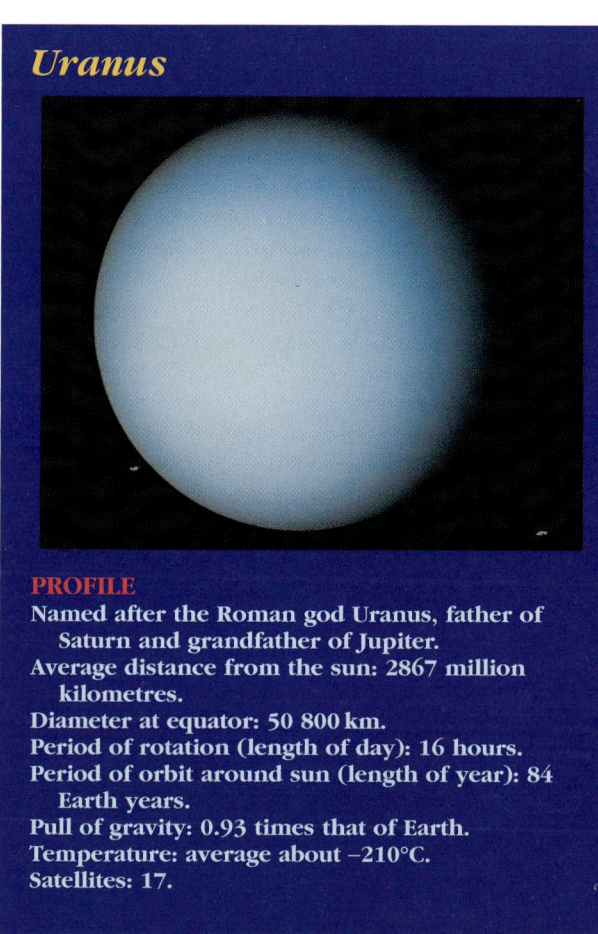

Uranus

PROFILE
Named after the Roman god Uranus, father of Saturn and grandfather of Jupiter.
Average distance from the sun: 2867 million kilometres.
Diameter at equator: 50 800 km.
Period of rotation (length of day): 16 hours.
Period of orbit around sun (length of year): 84 Earth years.
Pull of gravity: 0.93 times that of Earth.
Temperature: average about −210°C.
Satellites: 17.

Neptune

PROFILE
Named after Neptune, Roman god of the sea and navigators.
Average distance from the sun: 4486 million kilometres.
Diameter at equator: 48 600 km.
Period of rotation (length of day): 16 hours.
Period of orbit around sun (length of year): 165 Earth years.
Pull of gravity: 1.2 times that of Earth.
Temperature: average about −220°C.
Satellites: 8.

Uranus appears blue from the Earth due to methane in its atmosphere. The axis of rotation of Uranus is almost in line with the sun. This means that Uranus spins almost horizontally, causing light from the sun to fall on one pole for a very long time. Like Jupiter and Saturn, Uranus bulges at the equator because of its rapid rotation. This rapid rotation also creates very strong winds in its atmosphere. Uranus has a system of about 11 rings which are smaller and fainter than those of Saturn.

Neptune, like Uranus, appears blue from the Earth due to the methane in its atmosphere. Neptune has a system of five faint rings which appear to consist of dust particles. It has a large dark spot similar to Jupiter's Great Red Spot. This dark blue spot, which is larger than Earth, is believed to be a giant storm. It was discovered in 1989 by the space probe *Voyager 2*, which also discovered six of the planet's eight moons. One of Neptune's moons, Triton, is the coldest known body in the solar system.

Rocks in space

The solar system contains many objects other than the sun and the planets. Most of the planets have large bodies called **satellites** revolving around them. Natural satellites are called **moons**. Many of these moons were discovered by space probes such as *Pioneer* and *Voyager*. *Pioneer 10* was the first space probe to leave our solar system. After 30 years, it is still sending data back to scientists.

Asteroids

Thousands of small, irregular objects called **asteroids**, or minor planets, revolve around the sun just like the major planets. Most of them are between the orbits of Mars and Jupiter. This region is sometimes referred to as the **asteroid belt**. The largest asteroid, Ceres, is about 970 km in diameter. The smallest known asteroids are only about 1 km across.

The orbits of asteroids are more oval in shape than the orbits of the planets. This brings them quite close to the sun and to the orbit of Earth. In 1991, a small asteroid passed within 170 000 km of Earth. That is less than half the distance from the Earth to the moon and dangerously close. It passed Earth at a speed of about 72 000 kilometres per hour.

In 1993, the space probe *Galileo*, on its way to Jupiter, discovered the first known moon of an asteroid. A body of rock about 1 km across was photographed orbiting a potato-shaped asteroid called Ida. It is likely that many asteroids have moons.

Most asteroids have irregular shapes.

Jupiter and four of its moons

The moons vary greatly in size. Deimos, the smaller of the two moons of Mars, is only about 10 kilometres in diameter. The largest known moon in the solar system is Ganymede, one of the 16 moons of Jupiter. It is larger than the planet Mercury.

Comets

Comets are balls of rocky and metallic particles amidst ice and frozen gases. Most of the mass of a comet is in its nucleus. A bright glowing tail of dust and gases becomes larger as the comet moves closer to the sun. Up to millions of kilometres long, the tail is blown away from the sun by the solar wind.

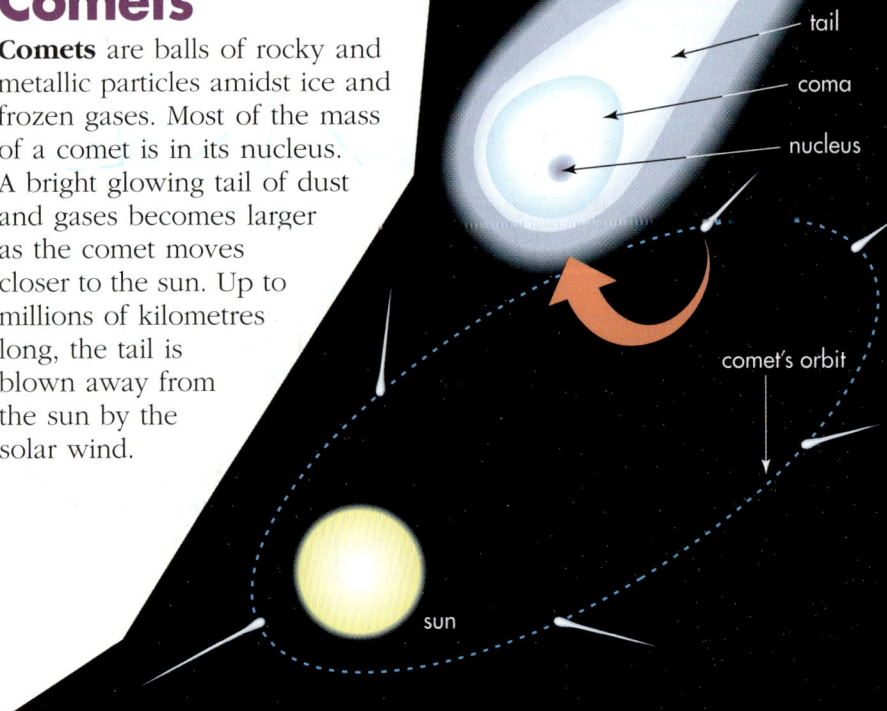

tail
coma
nucleus
comet's orbit
sun

The orbit of a comet is long and narrow. The tail gets longer as the comet approaches the sun and points away from the sun due to solar winds.

The orbits of comets are longer and narrower than the orbits of the planets. It is believed that comets are formed from dust and ice in the cold, outer regions of the solar system.

The most famous comet is Halley's comet. It was named after Sir Edmond Halley, who correctly predicted that it would return every 76 years. The orbit of Halley's comet extends beyond the orbit of Neptune. We see it as it passes near Earth on its path to and from the sun. This last happened in 1986.

Meteoroids

Occasionally people observe bright streaks of light called 'shooting stars' in the night sky. The streaks of light are called **meteors**. They are created when a lump of rock or metal burns up as it passes through the Earth's atmosphere. These lumps of rock or metal that travel around the solar system orbiting the sun are called **meteoroids**. Most of those that cross the path of the Earth's orbit are so small that they burn up completely before they reach the ground. Those that are large enough to reach the ground are called **meteorites**. Meteorites hit the ground with speeds of up to 70 km per second, or 252 000 km per hour. They are very hot and explode on impact, leaving craters much bigger than themselves. The Wolf Creek crater in Western Australia, pictured above right, has a diameter of 850 metres. The crater's rim rises about 25 metres above the surrounding plains and the crater's floor is about 50 metres below the rim.

Some scientists believe that a meteorite caused the extinction of the dinosaurs about 65 million years ago. They believe that the impact of the meteorite lifted tonnes of dust into the atmosphere, blocking out sunlight from the surface for several months. This would have killed all plants and changed the climate, making it impossible for larger animals like dinosaurs to survive.

The Wolf Creek meteorite crater in Western Australia

Activities

Remember
1. What name is given to natural satellites of planets?
2. What is the asteroid belt?
3. What are comets made of?
4. What is a meteorite?
5. What is the difference between a meteor and a meteoroid?

Think
1. Distinguish between a planet and a moon.
2. How are asteroids different from moons?
3. In which year is Halley's comet next likely to be visible from Earth?
4. Why is the tail of a comet blown away from the sun?

Imagine
Write a story about a meteorite crashing into the Earth about 65 million years ago. Dinosaurs roamed the land at that time. Begin your story with the sentence: 'The fireball sped through the sky in front of the midday sun and there was a huge explosion'.

SCIENCE & technology

PROBING THE SOLAR SYSTEM

Ever since ancient times, humans have gazed at the planets and wondered what they were really like. The invention of the first telescope in 1608 allowed astronomers to find out more about the nearer planets. However, there were still many mysteries. The surface of the planet Venus could not be viewed because it was always covered in thick clouds. Telescopes were not powerful enough to reveal details of the surface of Mars. The question of whether there was life on Mars was left unanswered.

Since the launch of the first artificial satellite *Sputnik 1* in 1957, our knowledge of the solar system has grown rapidly.

Space probes carry cameras and other instruments with which to gather data on the atmospheres and surfaces of the planets. They can send back information about temperature and chemical composition of the atmosphere and surface. Those space probes that land have mechanical arms that collect soil samples. They have equipment on board to analyse samples and send the results back to Earth. Probes can also send samples back to Earth for analysis.

Exploring the solar system — a brief history of space probes

Year of launch	Mission	Achievements
1957	*Sputnik 1* (USSR)	first artificial satellite in space
1959	*Explorer 6* (USA)	first TV pictures from space
1961	*Vostok 1* (USSR)	first human (Yuri Gagarin) in space
1962	*Mariner 2* (USA)	first successful Venus fly-by
1965	*Mariner 4* (USA)	first successful fly-by and close-up pictures of Mars
1969	*Apollo 11* (USA)	first human landing on moon
1970	*Venera 7* (USSR)	first soft landing on Venus
1971	*Mars 2* (USSR)	first impact of spacecraft on Mars
1971	*Mars 3* (USSR)	first soft landing on Mars and first TV pictures from surface
1972	*Pioneer 10* (USA)	first fly-by and close-up pictures of Jupiter
1973	*Pioneer-Saturn* (USA)	first fly-by and close-up pictures of Saturn
1973	*Mariner 10* (USA)	first fly-by and close-up pictures of Mercury
1977	*Voyagers 1 and 2* (USA)	first fly-by and close up pictures of Uranus and Neptune; *Voyager 1* left the solar system in 2003
1989	*Magellan* (USA)	mapped entire surface of Venus
1989	*Galileo* (USA)	orbited Jupiter until 2003 when it was crashed into Jupiter's surface
1996	Hubble telescope (USA)	collected data on near and far objects in the universe
1996	Mars Global Surveyor (USA)	gathered information about the atmosphere, magnetic properties and surface of Mars
1997	*Cassini* (USA)	provided details of Saturn's rings and satellites
1999	*Stardust* (USA)	collected interstellar and comet dust particles to be returned to Earth in 2006
2001	*Genesis* (USA)	collected samples of solar wind for analysis on Earth in 2004
2002	RHESS1	studying energy released from the sun
2003	Mars Express Orbiter	mapping minerals on the surface of Mars
2003	Mars Exploration Rovers	*Spirit* and *Opportunity Rovers* gathering and analysing rocks on the surface of Mars

Opportunity Rover on the surface of Mars. Mechanical arms are used to collect samples of rock for analysis.

1957–2003.

The information gathered by the space probes is sent back to Earth using radio waves. Their signals are picked up by **radio telescopes**, which have huge dishes to collect the radio waves. The tracking station at Tidbinbilla, near Canberra, shown in the photograph below, receives radio waves from space probes. As well as receiving data from space probes, the Tidbinbilla Space Tracking Station sends commands to the computers on board the space probes and provides a two-way radio link between space shuttles and the Earth.

scientists to calculate the distance to the target object. This technique is called **radar ranging**. Radar ranging was first used in 1961 to measure the distance to the planet Venus.

The technique of radar ranging is especially useful in showing the shape of the surface of the planet Venus, which cannot be seen with optical telescopes and cannot be photographed with normal cameras. The *Magellan* spacecraft used radar ranging to map the entire surface of Venus. The radar images sent back to Earth reveal a spectacular surface.

This radar image of the surface of Venus was sent back to Earth by the *Magellan* space probe.

The radio telescope at Tidbinbilla, near Canberra. The dish, 70 metres in diameter, collects radio waves and reflects them back to the antenna, which is positioned above the dish.

Probing *from a* distance

Radio waves can be sent from Earth to the planets or even further. The radio waves reflected back from a target object can then be detected by radio telescopes. The photo of the Tidbinbilla Tracking Station shows that radio telescopes look very different from optical telescopes, which gather light to allow us to see distant objects. The time taken for the radio waves to return can then be used by astronomers and other

Activities

Remember

1. What information about planets can space probes gather that cannot be obtained by telescopes?
2. How do space probes get the data that they gather back to Earth?
3. Write down two differences between an optical telescope and a radio telescope.
4. What is radar ranging and what can it be used for?
5. How can knowledge of the planets of the solar system be obtained without space probes?

Think

1. Complete the word puzzle on the right. In this puzzle you will find the names of eleven missions that were important in the history of exploration of the solar system. The mission names may be spelt across, down, diagonally or even backwards. No name appears more than once!
2. Propose why it is so difficult to be certain about the future of space exploration.

Investigate

Two space probes were named *Magellan* and *Galileo*. Find out who Magellan and Galileo were, when they lived and what they achieved.

R	E	G	A	Y	O	V	K	V
M	E	L	T	O	F	E	O	E
A	G	E	B	L	X	S	M	N
G	I	R	N	L	T	N	A	E
E	X	P	L	O	R	E	R	R
L	A	F	K	P	I	D	I	A
L	V	C	P	A	Z	P	N	Q
A	S	G	A	L	I	L	E	O
N	H	M	S	U	M	A	R	S
S	P	U	T	N	I	K	Y	J

Putting it all together

Summing up

Copy and complete the statements below to compile a summary of this unit. The missing words can be found in the word list below.

1. The _____ _____ consists of the sun and all of the heavenly bodies that revolve around it.

2. The Earth is one of _____ planets revolving around the sun.

3. The planets, apart from Pluto, can be divided into two groups — the _____ (Earth-like) planets and the _____ giants.

4. The _____ makes up 99.8 per cent of the total mass of the solar system.

5. The pull of _____ towards the sun keeps the planets in orbit around it.

6. The sun's radiation provides the planets with _____ and light.

7. _____ is the closest planet to the sun.

8. The atmosphere of the planet _____ was heavy and hot enough to crush and melt early spacecraft.

9. Jupiter, Saturn, Uranus and Neptune all have _____ systems.

10. The planet _____ is usually the furthest planet from the sun.

11. The features of planets are greatly influenced by their _____.

12. Natural satellites that revolve around planets are called _____.

13. As well as the planets, smaller objects called _____ and comets, orbit the sun.

14. Comets are balls of rocky and metallic particles amidst ice and _____ gases.

15. Streaks of light in the night sky called 'shooting stars', or _____ are made by lumps of rock or metal burning up in the atmosphere.

16. Our knowledge of the solar system has grown rapidly as a result of information sent back from _____ _____.

17. _____ telescopes are used to receive data from distant space probes.

Word list

meteors	heat	terrestrial	Mercury
gas	ring	moons	probes
gravity	radio	frozen	system
nine	asteroids	space	atmospheres
Venus	sun	solar	Pluto

Looking back

1. You will find fifteen heavenly bodies of the solar system in the word puzzle below. They may be spelt across, down, diagonally or even backwards. The heavenly bodies include all of the planets and three natural satellites. The leftover letters spell out an occasional visitor to the Earth's night sky. Complete the puzzle to identify the visitor.

S	U	N	H	V	E	N	U	S
M	E	R	C	U	R	Y	A	N
L	E	U	A	L	E	R	D	E
P	M	T	Y	N	E	S	E	P
L	O	A	E	T	U	C	I	T
U	O	S	I	O	O	S	M	U
T	N	P	M	A	R	S	O	N
O	U	P	H	O	B	O	S	E
J	E	A	R	T	H	M	I	E
T	A	S	T	E	R	O	I	D

2. Write a list of the planets of the solar system in order of their usual distance from the sun. Use different-sized letters for each planet — the largest letters for the largest planet and the smallest letters for the smallest planet.

3. (a) What are we?
    We are smaller than the planets.
    There are at least 60 of us in the solar system but there could be more.
    At least one of us orbits an asteroid but we generally orbit planets.
    Apparently, none of us go near Mercury or Venus, but you can never be sure.
    One of us orbits the Earth every 29.5 days.
   (b) What am I?
    I am one of many heavenly bodies that orbits the sun.
    I am usually very cold but get warmer when I come close to the sun.
    I was near the Earth when the author Mark Twain was born and next time I came back, he died.
    I visit the outer regions of the solar system.
    I have a tail.

4. Make up your own 'What am I' or 'What are we' questions for objects in the solar system. Write 5 clues for each object, starting with difficult clues and ending with easier ones. Test your questions by reading them in order to a partner. Choose at least 3 objects and write questions for each.

5. Light is not the only form of energy emitted by the sun. What other forms of energy come from the sun?

6. How would you expect the space probes that land on the surfaces of planets to be different from those that fly past or orbit planets?

7. Imagine that it is the year 2120 and the Olympic Games are being held on Mars for the first time.
   (a) Write an account of how the small pull of gravity and other features of the planet would affect your favourite Olympic event.
   (b) Would any events need to be scrapped for an Olympic Games on Mars? Why?

Extension
Rendezvous with Venus

On 15 December 1970, the space probe *Venera 7* entered the atmosphere of the planet Venus. A parachute slowed its descent. The heat was intense as the probe fell through an atmosphere made up almost entirely of carbon dioxide.

As the space probe approached the yellow cloud below, it began to creak. *Venera 7* rocked violently as it crashed through the yellow cloud. The noise would have been incredible! However, there was nobody to hear it. No human could survive the conditions on this craft.

The space probe *Venera 7* falling through the unfriendly atmosphere of Venus

The outer shell of the probe buckled in slightly. The pressure of the atmosphere was huge — about 90 times that of the Earth's atmosphere. Lightning from the yellow clouds of sulfuric acid droplets jolted the probe. Then there was a huge thud as the battered and scorched space probe hit the surface. There were no cameras to take photos. However, there were measuring instruments and a radio transmitter to send data back to Earth. *Venera 7* was able to transmit data for 23 minutes before its communication system failed.

At the surface of Venus, the atmosphere pushes on each square centimetre of the space probe's shell with a force equal to the weight of a 90 kilogram mass on Earth. Earlier probes had been crushed by the pressure as they attempted to land. *Venera 7* was stronger than the earlier probes and was also designed to withstand temperatures of up to 530°C.

The first black-and-white photographs of the surface were sent back to Earth in 1975 by the space probes *Venera 9* and *Venera 10*. It was another 7 years before *Venera 13* and *Venera 14* sent back clear colour photographs.

The *Venera* space probes, launched by the USSR, gathered a lot of data on the atmosphere of Venus and a little about the surface. Space probes from the USA added to the knowledge gained. However, detailed information about the surface was not obtained until more recently. The NASA space probe *Magellan* flew just above the surface in 1991, taking pictures of the surface using radar (radio waves). *Magellan* found craters that seem to be the result of volcanic activity. Lava flows were also found. The photograph on page 173 shows a radar image sent back to Earth by *Magellan*.

SCIFACTS

On Venus you could have an Earth birthday at least once every day! A day on Venus is 243 Earth days long. That is how long it takes the planet to complete a rotation around its own axis. However, because Venus takes 225 Earth days to orbit the sun, a year is only 225 days long. A year on Venus is shorter than a day on Venus!

Activities

Remember

1. What is the most abundant gas in the atmosphere of Venus?
2. What is in the yellow clouds blanketing the planet Venus?
3. Compare the atmospheric pressure on Venus with that on Earth.
4. What caused earlier Venus space probes to be crushed?

Think

1. Why did it take so long for space probes to land successfully on Venus?
2. Why do you think there is no water on the surface of Venus?
3. List some factors that would make it difficult for space probes to land on the planets Mars and Jupiter.

Imagine

1. Draw a picture of your impression of the surface of Venus.
2. Write a story about the first human landing on the planet Venus.

Reflection

Now that you have studied the solar system, it's worthwhile to look back and think about what you have learned. The following activities will help you to do this.

1. What impressed you most about the solar system?

Write a short essay outlining the things that most impressed you during your study of the solar system. They may be visual aspects, such as photographs, or some information that you had never thought about before. Share your views with other students and your teacher.

2. Modelling the planets' rotations

Make a working model of the sun and one other planet using some common objects (see examples below) and demonstrate it to your class. Remember to show the spinning planet moving around the sun. Why is this a better representation than a drawing? What keeps your planet from falling into the sun? What force could pull your planet into the sun?

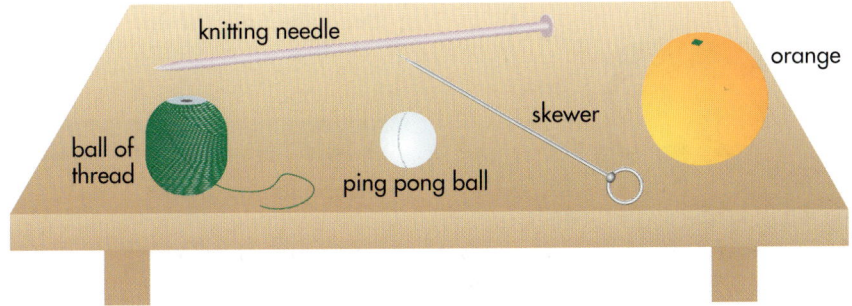

3. Profiles of the Earth and Pluto

Profiles of all the planets in the solar system, except the Earth and Pluto, can be found on pages 166–9. They each include a photograph and important information. Construct a profile for the Earth and Pluto in the same format.

You may have to research the information using multimedia resources, books or the Internet (remember to acknowledge your sources of information). And you may want to substitute drawings of the planets (as seen from space) for the photographs. You may easily find a photograph of the Earth, but it may be difficult to find one of Pluto. Why? When you have completed the profiles, share your information with other students.

4. A survey about space

Survey your neighbours

You do not remember the first moon landing and all the excitement as pictures of the astronauts bouncing along the moon's surface were first shown. You have a good excuse for this — you were not born then! But how well do your parents and other people remember this event? Find out by designing and carrying out a survey in your neighbourhood.

5. What did you notice?

(a) Which planets go around the sun the fastest?
(b) Are these planets closer or further away from the sun?
(c) Does this affect the length of their year or the length of their day? Is there any pattern? Write your conclusions in your workbook.
(d) Make a table to show the similarities and differences between all the planets in the solar system.

6. Space stations

Assess the difficulties that humans could have in setting up and living in a space station. Compare your responses with others.

SEEING AND HEARING

Most of the animal kingdom relies on the senses of seeing and hearing to gather information about the environment. In fact, the very survival of most animals depends on seeing and hearing. Light and sound are the forms of energy to which eyes and ears respond.

KEY CONTENT

Describe and build instruments that produce and control light and sound and describe their operation.

Describe the characteristics and applications of the transmission and reflection of light and sound.

Describe the relationship between the characteristics of sound, the vibration properties of the source and the sound wave.

Explain how animals use their senses to detect and respond to their environments.

Describe how the ear works.

KEY QUESTIONS

How do you hear?

How can you make a loud sound with a string?

How is a didgeridoo played?

Why can't you stop a sneeze when pepper gets in your nose?

Why do your ears pop?

Why do elephants have such big ears?

Are you the same as your mirror image?

How can bats see in the dark?

Thinking about Seeing and hearing

1. Eyes and ears

GROUP WORK You use your eyes and ears all the time. They help you to make sense of your world. Before you start this chapter, think about what you already know about your eyes and ears by completing the following exercises.

(a) With your group or partner, brainstorm a list of all the words you know that are related to your eyes and ears.

(b) Draw a mind map using all the words in your list. You can include additional words if new ideas arise while you are linking and connecting words. (See pages 232–4 if you need to refresh your memory about mind maps.)

(c) Once you have finished your mind map, take time to consider the following questions.
  (i) Which words do you feel really confident about?
  (ii) Which words do you feel less confident about? (That is, which words do you feel you need more information about to understand the concept well?)

(d) Compare your mind map with another group's, and then keep yours for reference as you learn more about your eyes and ears.

(e) Finish by listing all the questions that you would like to find answers for by the time you reach the end of this chapter.

By the time you have worked through this chapter, you should be able to answer the questions and write meanings for the words on your list.

2. Making sense of the world

List all of your senses. Choose one and write a report about how this sense works to help you survive.

3. Great inventions

GROUP WORK Scientists have made many new discoveries because new technologies have allowed them to see objects that are either very small or very distant.

(a) Name some technologies that have helped us to see, hear and understand more.

(b) Pick one example of a new technology and write a story reporting the discovery of this exciting new technology for a newspaper or journal. Make sure you include how you think it will help humankind. You can use your imagination in doing so, but make sure you include some facts about the technology.

(c) Find out something about the discoverer(s) of this new technology and how it was first received in the community.

4. Reflection on light

Many times each day we see our reflection in mirrors or shining surfaces. Work in pairs to answer the following questions:

(a) Think about how your reflection appears in a mirror then explain your thoughts about how this occurs to your partner.

(b) With your partner, make a list of everything that has to be present for your reflection to appear.

(c) Periscopes are used in submarines to see what is happening on the surface of the water. Explain how you think a periscope works.

5. Common sense

Keeping your eyes and ears in top condition is very important. What common dangers to eyes and ears do you come across every day? What can you do to protect these valuable sensory organs? Design a table to present your answers.

6. Energy transformations

(a) What do you think is meant by the term 'energy transformation'?

(b) Describe some forms of energy you already know about.

(c) Ask your friends or family what they think about when they use the word 'energy'.

(d) Explain how one form of energy may be transformed into another form of energy.

Out of the darkness

Without light from the sun, the world would be in darkness. Plants would not grow and all other life on Earth would not exist. Light is one of the forms of energy that come to us from the sun. It is a form of energy not needing a medium as it is able to travel through space (which is a vacuum) at about 300 000 km per second.

Objects or substances that give off their own light are said to be **luminous**. Examples of light sources are shown below.

Most of the light sources shown are **incandescent**. They emit light because they are hot. The sun, all other stars, light globes and flames are incandescent. Other sources, such as fluorescent tubes, the paint on the hands and numerals of clocks and watches, fireflies, glow-worms and some deep-sea fish, emit light without getting hot — they are not incandescent. Living things that emit light without heat are referred to as **bioluminescent**. An example is the angler fish.

Most things that you see are not luminous. They do not emit their own light. Light from luminous objects, such as the sun, light globes or fluorescent tubes, strikes them and is reflected into your eyes. The moon is not a luminous object. Its surface reflects light from the sun.

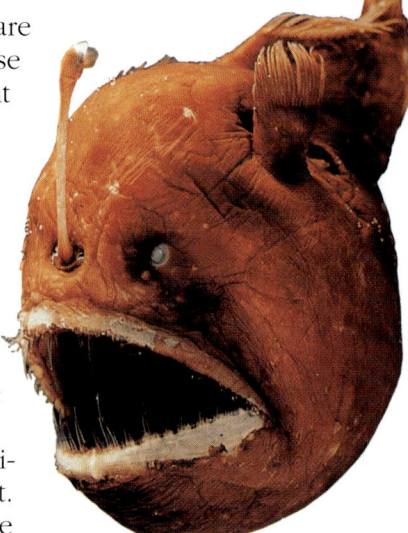

The angler fish, living in darkness about 4000 metres below the ocean surface, uses a luminous lure to attract its prey.

Each of the light sources shown here is luminous.

Experiment 9.1 SEEING THE LIGHT

YOU WILL NEED
moderately dark room
torch or projector
well used chalk duster

- Shine the torch or projector onto a nearby wall.

1. What do you see on the wall?
2. Can you see the light beam between the light source and the wall?

- Now hit the chalk duster with your hand so that chalk dust falls between the light source and the wall.

3. Can you now see the light beam between the light source and the wall?
4. What happens to the light from the source to make it visible?

Experiment 9.2 SEEING THINGS

YOU WILL NEED
a room that can be darkened

- Darken the room as much as you can.

- Concentrate on the darkest wall you can find and look carefully at the features that you can see.

1. Does the wall appear to be giving off light of its own?

- Now turn on the lights, open the curtains or blinds and look at the features of the wall again.

2. Can you see more or less detail when the room is well lit?
3. Where does the light that allows you to see the features of the wall come from?

Light beams are only visible when there are particles in the air to scatter the light into your eyes. The light beam from a street light can be seen if there is smoke or fog in the air.

How *light* travels

Although light cannot normally be seen as it passes through the air, conclusions can be formed about how it travels. For example, light travels in straight lines.

If light did not travel in straight lines, shadows would not be the same shape as the objects that make them. The experiment on the right shows that shadows can be fuzzy or sharp.

The darkest part of a shadow is called the **umbra**. The lighter part on the outside of the shadow is called the **penumbra**. In a dark room, the umbra gets no light from the light source. The penumbra does get some light from the source. As the light source gets smaller or further away, the penumbra gets smaller and the shadow gets sharper.

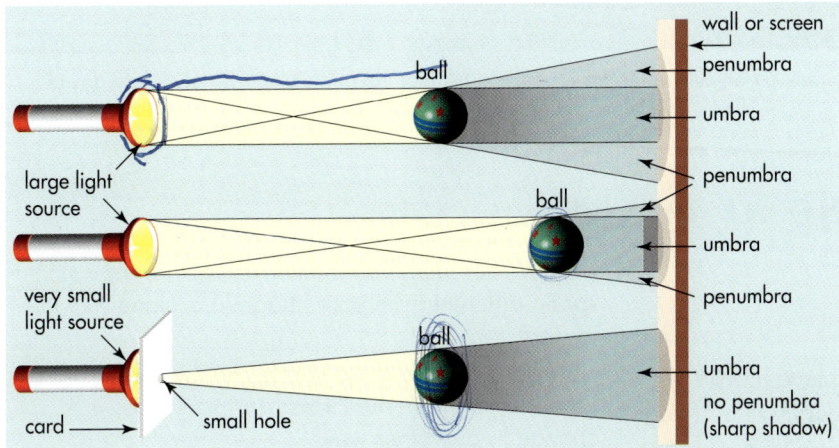

Shadows can be fuzzy. They often have two parts — the umbra and penumbra.

Experiment 9.3
CASTING SHADOWS

YOU WILL NEED
moderately dark room
candle and matches or torch
white card for screen

- Hold your screen vertically about 60 cm from your light source. Place your hand about midway between the light source and screen so that it makes a shadow on the screen.
- Observe the shadow as you move your hand closer to the light source.

1. How does the size of the shadow change?
2. Describe any other changes in the shadow.
3. Draw a simple diagram to explain why the shadow changes.

Experiment 9.4 JUST CHECKING

YOU WILL NEED
small length of rubber tubing or hose
candle and matches or a torch

- Look at the small light source through a straight piece of rubber tubing. Now bend the tubing slightly.

1. Can you still see the light source?
2. Does this observation support the idea that light travels in straight lines?
3. Draw a diagram to show why you are unable to see the light source through the bent tubing.

Activities

Remember

1. What is light and how fast does it travel through space?
2. (a) What does 'incandescent' mean?
   (b) List two examples of light sources that are incandescent.
   (c) List two examples of light sources that are not incandescent.
3. Why do you see the beam of light from a torch if it is foggy?
4. Outline some evidence that supports the conclusion that light travels in straight lines.

Think

1. Which of the following objects are luminous?
   (a) the sun
   (b) the moon
   (c) the stars
   (d) a burning candle
   (e) this page
2. Which of the following objects are incandescent?
   (a) the sun
   (b) a firefly
   (c) a burning match
   (d) a glowing fluorescent tube
3. Explain how it is that you can see this page even though it does not emit light of its own.
4. Explain, with the aid of diagrams, why shadows are sometimes fuzzy and sometimes sharp.
5. The speed of light is 300 000 kilometres per second. How long does it take light to travel from the sun to the distant planet Pluto when it is 6000 million kilometres from the sun?

Investigate

Find out more about animals that are bioluminescent.

Reflections

When you look in a mirror you see an **image** of yourself. If the mirror is a plane, or flat mirror, the image will be very much like the real you. If the mirror is curved, the image might be quite strange, like the one in the photograph on the left.

The images in mirrors are formed when light is reflected from a very smooth, shiny metal surface behind a sheet of glass. Images can also be formed when light is reflected from other smooth surfaces, such as a lake.

What does this person really look like?

An image on still water. How can you tell that the photograph is not upside down?

Experiment 9.5 LOOKING AT IMAGES

YOU WILL NEED
plane mirror
shiny tablespoon or soup spoon

- Look at the image of your face in a plane mirror. Wink your right eye.

1. Which eye in your image appears to wink?

- Write the word 'IMAGE' on a piece of paper and place it in front of the mirror so that the word faces the mirror.

2. Which letters in the image look different? Which letters look the same?

- Write down how you think an image of the word 'REFLECTION' will look in the mirror. Test your hypothesis.

3. Was your hypothesis correct?

- Look at your image on the back of a spoon. This surface is convex. Convex means 'curved outward'. Move the spoon closer to you and then further away.

4. How is your image on the convex side of the spoon different from your image in a plane mirror?

5. How does the size of the image change as you move further away from the curved surface? Does it change in any other way?

- Look at your image on the front of the spoon. This surface is concave. It is curved inward. Move the spoon as close to your eyes as you can, then further away.

6. How is your image on the concave side of the spoon different from your image in a plane mirror and on the other side of the spoon?

7. How does the image change as you move further away from the curved surface?

8. List some places where you have seen curved mirrors. State whether the mirrors are convex or concave and explain why they are used.

Activities

Experiment 9.6   A-MAZE-ING MIRRORS

YOU WILL NEED
plane mirror
copy of the maze below

- Place the maze flat in front of a mirror. Look at the image of the maze and use a pencil to follow the maze without crossing the lines. Do not look at the maze itself — only at its image in the mirror! If you don't trust yourself, have a friend hold a piece of card so that you can see only the image.

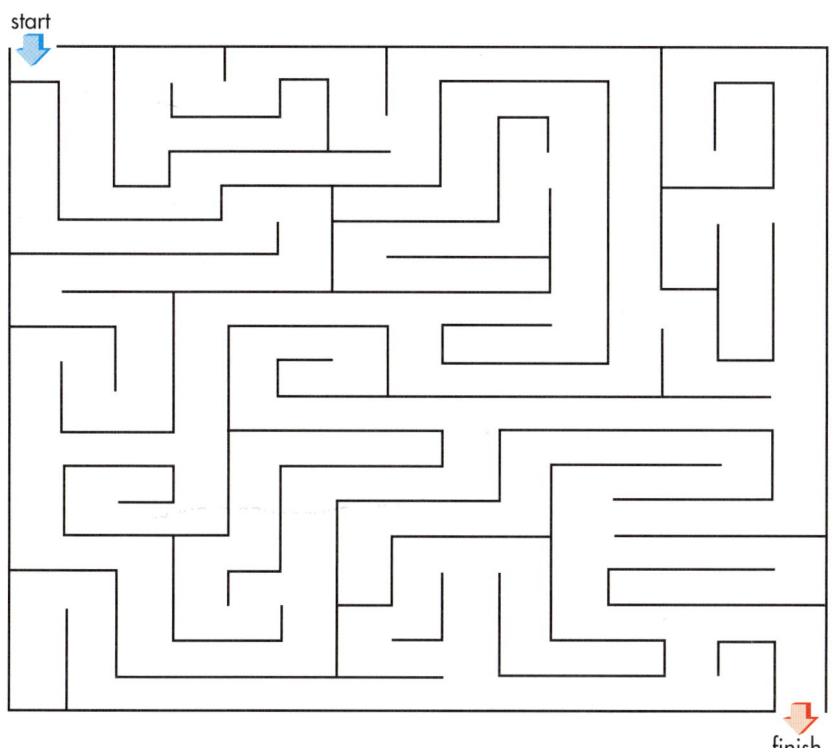

start

finish

Can you complete the maze without crossing the lines, using its mirror image?

Lateral *inversion*

The sideways reversal of images that you see when you look at yourself in a mirror is called **lateral inversion**. The sign on the ambulance in the photograph is printed so that drivers in front of it can read the word 'AMBULANCE' easily in their rear-view mirrors.

Why is the word 'AMBULANCE' printed in reverse?

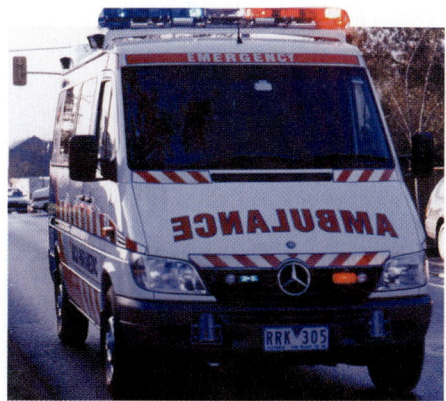

Remember

1. What does a mirror do to light in order to form an image?
2. In which type of mirror can your image be upside down?
3. How is your image in a plane mirror different from the real you?

Think

1. Why do dentists use concave mirrors to examine teeth?
2. Which type of mirror is used to help you see around corners?
3. How will the word 'TOYOTA' on the ambulance look in the rear-view mirror of the driver in front of it?

Investigate

Look up the laws of reflection. Design and carry out some simple experiments that demonstrate these laws.

Create

Design and build a simple periscope like the one shown below. You will need stiff card, scissors, two small mirrors, sticky tape or glue, a pencil and a ruler. Write an explanation of how it works using diagrams and real examples.

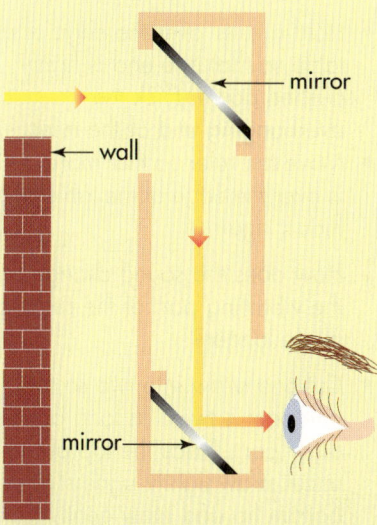

mirror

wall

mirror

A periscope uses mirrors to enable you to see around corners or over objects.

9.3 Making sounds

Humans and other animals rely heavily on sound to communicate with each other. You can use your voice, whistle or tap something to make a sound. How else can you make a sound?

Good vibrations

All sounds are caused by **vibrations**. When you speak or sing, the vocal cords in your throat vibrate. You can feel the vibrations if you put your hand over the front of your throat. These vibrations cause the air in your throat and mouth to vibrate. The air around you then vibrates. The sound is heard by you or someone else when air surrounding you vibrates, in turn causing your eardrum to vibrate. The travelling vibration is called a **sound wave**. This sound wave is a form of energy that must have a medium in which to travel.

The highness or lowness of a sound is called its **pitch**. The more quickly an object vibrates, the higher the pitch of the sound it makes. A short string vibrates more quickly than a long one. It therefore has a higher pitch. When you blow across the top of a straw, the air inside it vibrates. If the straw is shorter, the air inside vibrates faster, producing a higher pitched sound.

Making it louder

If you pluck a stretched guitar string while it is not attached to a guitar, it vibrates but makes very little sound. If you strike a stretched drum skin while it is not attached to the drum, it makes very little noise. Even your own vocal cords make very little noise while they are vibrating. In each of these cases a vibration is needed to create the sound but an enclosed region of air is needed to make the sound louder.

Experiment 9.7   VIBRATIONS AND PITCH

YOU WILL NEED
ruler
2 straws
scissors
small beaker and large beaker
spatula

- Hold a ruler over the edge of a table so that one end is firmly pushed down. Flick the overhanging end of the ruler.
- Move the ruler so that more of it is over the edge of the table and flick it again.

1. How does the sound change as the vibrating part of the ruler is made longer?

- Cut one straw into two so that one part is twice as long as the other part. Place the top of the uncut straw lightly against your bottom lip and blow gently across the opening. Listen to the sound made.

- Blow across the two shorter pieces of straw in the same way and listen to the sounds.

2. How does the sound change as the straws get shorter?

- Tap the side of a small beaker gently with a spatula and listen to the sound. Do the same with a larger beaker.

3. How do the sounds compare?
4. How would you change each of the following to make a higher pitched sound?
   (a) the length of a vibrating strip of wood
   (b) the length of a tube of air
   (c) the size of a cymbal

Experiment 9.8

MAKING IT LOUDER

YOU WILL NEED
guitar
guitar string
tuning fork

- Pluck a stretched guitar string. Listen to the sound it makes.
- Pluck a similar string attached to a guitar.

1. How does the sound of a plucked string change when it is attached to a guitar?

- Strike a tuning fork on the sole of your shoe and listen to the sound it makes. While it is still vibrating, place its base on a solid table surface.

2. How does the sound change when the tuning fork is placed on the table?
3. Explain why the sound changes.

The air inside the body of an acoustic guitar is set vibrating by the strings. The air inside a drum vibrates when the drum skin is struck. The vibrating air inside your throat and mouth makes the sound created by your vocal cords loud enough to be heard.

The *sounds* of *music*

With an acoustic guitar, the vibrations are made by plucking the strings. The air around the sound hole vibrates, causing the air inside the body of the guitar to vibrate. In an electric guitar, a microphone or pick-up detects the vibrating air and converts it to electrical energy. An amplifier is then used to make the sound louder. The pitch of the sound made by a guitar is increased by shortening the strings using your fingers, tightening the strings or using lighter strings.

A saxophone's vibrations are first made by a thin wooden reed. The air inside the saxophone then vibrates, making a loud sound. The pitch can be changed by using keys to open or close holes. When all the holes are closed, the saxophone contains a long column of air, producing a low pitched sound. As holes are opened, the length of the air column becomes shorter and the pitch increases.

The didgeridoo has no holes to change the length of the column of vibrating air. The player blows into the instrument using loosely vibrating lips to control how quickly the air inside vibrates.

Activities

Remember

1. Explain how all sounds are made.
2. If you blow across the top of a straw, a sound is made. How could you increase the pitch of the sound?
3. Which vibrates more quickly — a long string or a short string made of the same material?
4. A plucked guitar string makes very little noise on its own. Why does it sound much louder when it is attached to a guitar?

Think

1. Explain how different notes are played on:
   (a) a single string of a guitar   (b) a recorder   (c) a xylophone.
2. How is the higher pitched note obtained on each of the three instruments in question 1?
3. Complete the gaps in the following table.

Musical instrument	What vibrates first?	What makes the sound louder?
guitar	plucked string	air inside guitar
trumpet	player's lips	
drum		air inside drum
saxophone		air inside saxophone
	string hit by hammers	air inside instrument

Create

Make a string telephone. You will need about 5 metres of string and two open and empty cans. Punch a small hole in the bottom of each can. Thread the string through each hole and tie a knot to keep the string in place. Hold the cans far enough apart so that the string is tight. Talk into the can at one end while your partner listens at the other end.

1. How does the sound travel from one can to the other?
2. Does the sound change if you make the string tighter or looser?
3. Would a string telephone work without the cans? Why are the cans used?

Getting the message

You remain aware of your environment and the changes that occur around you by using your senses. Your sense organs contain special cells called **receptors** that respond to stimuli. A **stimulus** is a feature of the environment that your body can detect. The table below shows how your senses respond to your environment.

Spreading *the message* around

The senses are just part of your body's communication system. The system:

- receives messages (stimuli) from the environment
- sends the messages to the brain (or sometimes directly to other parts of the body) through nerves
- interprets the messages and decides how to respond to them
- sends messages through nerves to other parts of the body, telling them how to respond.

All this happens very quickly. Your brain is capable of receiving, interpreting and sending out millions of messages each second. The messages travel through the nerves at speeds of about 100 metres per second.

Responses to messages that follow this entire pathway (shown below) are called **conscious responses**. They involve the brain and require some thinking. Packing up when you hear the school bell or siren at the end of a lesson is an example of a conscious response. The stimulus is the sound of the bell or siren.

Reflex *actions*

Sometimes a message bypasses the brain and goes from the receptors in the sense organ to the spinal cord and back to the muscles. The muscles respond very quickly because no thought is required. Responses that do not involve the brain are called **reflex actions**. Some examples of reflex actions are:

- sneezing when pepper gets in your nose
- pulling your hand back when you touch a hot object.

Can you think of some other examples?

Your senses

Sense	Sense organ	Receptors	Stimulus
sight	eye	special cells called cones and rods at the back of the eye	light
hearing	ear	hairs in the cochlea inside the ear	sound
touch	skin	separate receptors for each type of stimulus	heat, cold, light contact, pain, pressure, movement
taste	tongue	tastebuds	sweet, salty, bitter and sour substances
smell	nose	olfactory nerves inside nose	odours

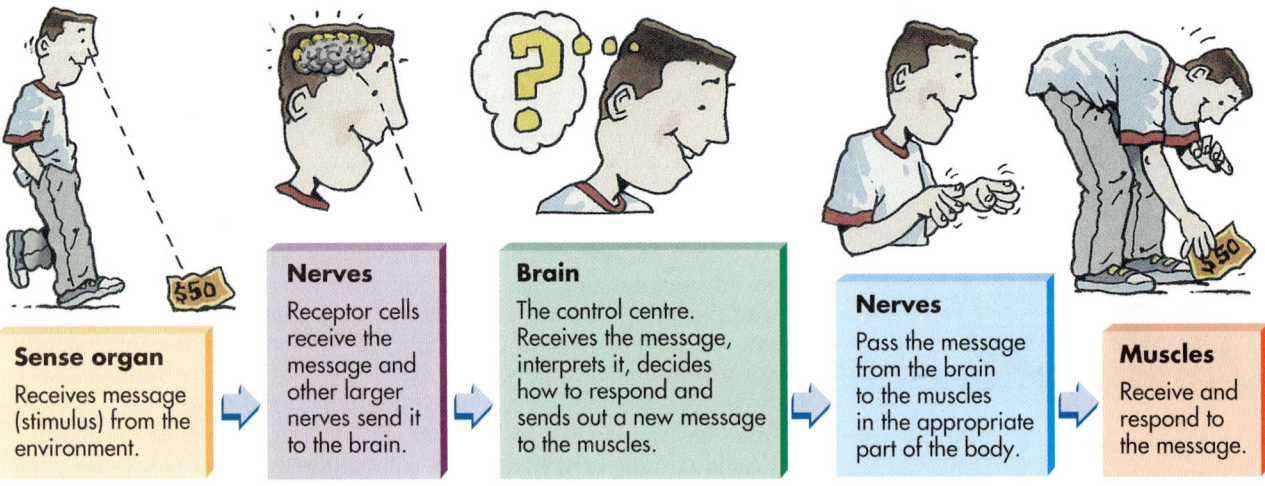

Sense organ
Receives message (stimulus) from the environment.

Nerves
Receptor cells receive the message and other larger nerves send it to the brain.

Brain
The control centre. Receives the message, interprets it, decides how to respond and sends out a new message to the muscles.

Nerves
Pass the message from the brain to the muscles in the appropriate part of the body.

Muscles
Receive and respond to the message.

Your body's communication system

Experiment 9.9

HOW QUICKLY CAN YOU RESPOND TO A STIMULUS?

YOU WILL NEED
metre ruler

- Hold out the hand that you normally write with while your partner holds the metre ruler between your thumb and fingers without touching. Make sure that the top of your hand is at the 'zero' on the ruler and that your thumb and index finger are about 2 cm apart.
- When you are ready, ask your partner to drop the ruler soon. Your task is to catch the ruler as soon as you see your partner drop it.

reaction distance

Measuring reaction distance

- Record the reaction distance to the nearest centimetre in the table below.
- Repeat this procedure twice more, recording the reaction distance in the table.
- Calculate the average reaction distance.

1. What do you think would happen if you repeated the reaction distance test with your other hand? Will the average reaction distance be greater, the same or less? Write down your hypothesis, then test it.
2. Was your hypothesis supported by your results? If not, suggest why.

Reaction distance

	Reaction distance (cm)			
	Trial 1	Trial 2	Trial 3	Average
writing hand				
other hand				

3. Which sense was used to detect the stimulus in this experiment?
4. Was catching the ruler a conscious response or a reflex action? Give a reason for your answer.
5. Why was it necessary to repeat the measurements three times for each hand?
6. If a friend suggested that it would have been better to repeat each test ten times to obtain a more accurate result, would you agree? Give a reason for your answer.

Activities

Remember

1. What is a receptor?
2. What is a stimulus?
3. Name the sense organ corresponding with each of the following stimuli: sourness; cold; perfume; light; sound.
4. What is the difference between a conscious response and a reflex action? Give one example of each.

Think

1. Complete the table below by indicating whether each event is a stimulus or a response.

Event	Stimulus or response
you pull your hand away from a hot cup	
the phone rings	
a dog barks at an intruder	
a traffic light turns green	
you shiver after getting out of a swimming pool	

2. Write down whether each of the following is a conscious response or a reflex action:
   (a) stopping at a red traffic light
   (b) blinking when a bright light flashes unexpectedly in front of you
   (c) a dog's mouth watering when it sees food
   (d) answering the doorbell.
3. Suggest where the term 'knee-jerk reaction' might come from.

Investigate

Design your own investigation to find out if it is possible, with practice, to decrease the time taken between receiving and responding to a stimulus. You could use the technique for measuring reaction time described in the experiment on the left or devise your own method.

9.5
In the wink of an eye

Most of the information that you gather about the world around you is obtained through the sense of sight. The eye allows you to receive the light that comes from luminous objects like the sun, electric lights and fire. If you could detect only objects that gave off their own light, you would not see very much! Your eyes also receive light which is reflected from non-luminous objects and substances. The walls of the classroom, for example, can be seen only because light from the sun or fluorescent tubes bounces off the walls. Some of that reflected light enters your eyes.

The **cornea** is the clear outer 'skin' of your eye. It is curved so that the light approaching your eye is bent towards the pupil. The clear, jelly-like **lens** bends or focuses light onto the **retina**. The lens is connected to muscles which can make it thick or thin. This allows your retina to receive a sharp image of distant or nearby objects.

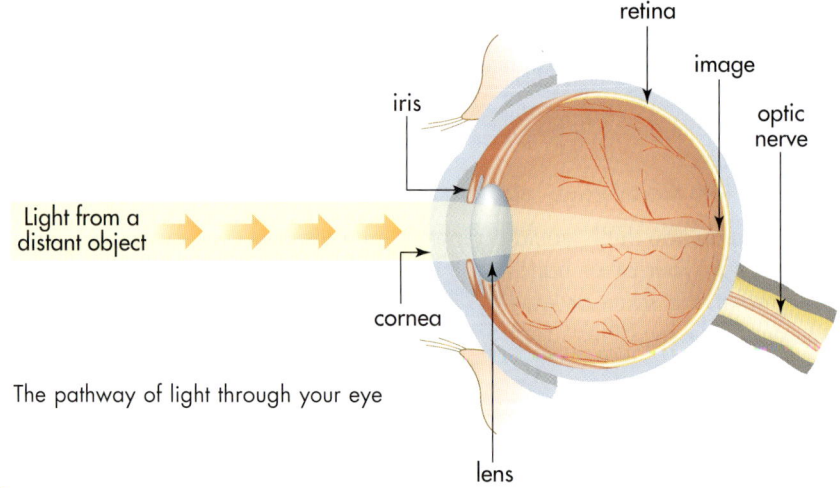

Side view of a human eye

Although your eye receives the light and produces an image of what you see, it is your brain that interprets and makes sense of the image. The receptors on the retina respond to the amount and colour of light by sending signals to the **optic nerve** which, in turn, sends signals to your brain.

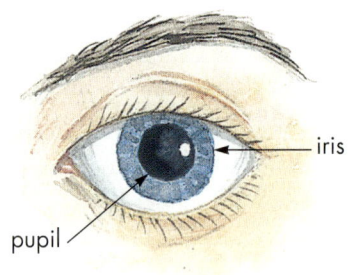

Close-up of a human eye

Some of the light that is reflected from the page you are now reading enters your eye through your **pupil**. The pupil is simply a hole in the **iris**. The iris is the colourful part of your eye. It is a ring of muscles that opens and closes to make the pupil large or small. If you are in a dark room, the pupil needs to be large so that as much light as possible can enter your eye. Outside on a sunny day, your pupil needs to be small so that not too much light gets in. The opening and closing of your iris is a reflex action, that is, you don't have to think about it.

The pathway of light through your eye

Experiment 9.10

IN THE DARK

- Cup your hands loosely over both eyes so that you cannot see anything but your hands. Keep your eyes open. Look at the insides of your hands.
- After about one minute, have your partner look carefully at your pupils and tell you what they observe.

1. What happens to the iris as the hand is removed?
2. Explain these observations.

Looking *after* your eyes

Your eyes are very important for detecting and responding to your environment so they must be treated with care. Your eyes have several natural protection devices. The cornea is kept clean by tears that are released every time you close your eyes. They keep the cornea clear of dust and other small particles that could damage it. Your eyebrows and eyelashes protect your eye from damage by water and small particles. Blinking is a reflex action that closes your eyes when they are threatened by a rapidly approaching object. When dust or other small particles get into your eye, it responds by releasing tears to wash them away.

You should not rub your eyes if foreign particles get into them. That could move the particles further in, making them more difficult to remove and increasing the damage to your eye. In the laboratory, if a substance does get into your eye, your teacher should be notified immediately.

There are many instances when extra protection is needed in the form of safety glasses. Your teacher will inform you when they need to be used in the science laboratory.

Experiment 9.11

ARE TWO EYES BETTER THAN ONE?

- Stretch one arm out in front of you with your thumb up. Have your partner step back one arm's length from your thumb, close his or her right eye and try to touch the top of your thumb with one finger.
- Try it again with both eyes open.
- Try it again with the left eye closed instead.

1. Did your partner succeed with the left eye, right eye, neither or both?

- Now swap roles and try this yourself.
- Design a table of results for the whole class.
- Complete the table and use it to construct a bar graph to display the class results. The graph should help you reach a conclusion.

2. Is it easier to estimate distances with two eyes open?

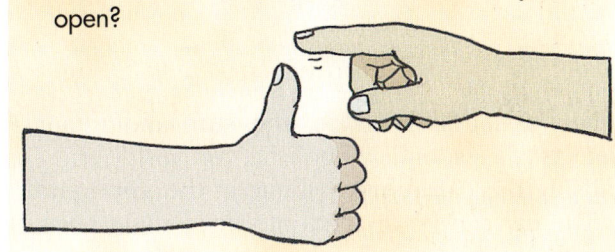

Activities

Remember

1. Complete the table to describe and state the purpose of each of the main parts of the eye.

Parts of the eye

Part	Description	Purpose
cornea		
pupil		
		changes the size of the pupil
lens		
	'screen' at the back of the eye	

2. How does the information received by the eye get to your brain?
3. How does your eye naturally protect itself from damage by small particles?

Think

1. When you walk into a dark room at night you cannot see anything. A minute later, without any additional light, you can see. What behaviour of the eye allows this to happen?
2. Explain fully why it is necessary to wear safety glasses when performing heating experiments in the science laboratory. What should you do if a substance does get into your eye? What should you not do?

Imagine

Imagine that you are a beam of light coming from a torch. Describe your journey as you travel through the eye to the optic nerve and on to the brain.

Investigate

1. Find out why people blink. Do some people blink more than others? Why do you think this is so?
2. What is night blindness? What causes it? How can it be avoided?

What did you say?

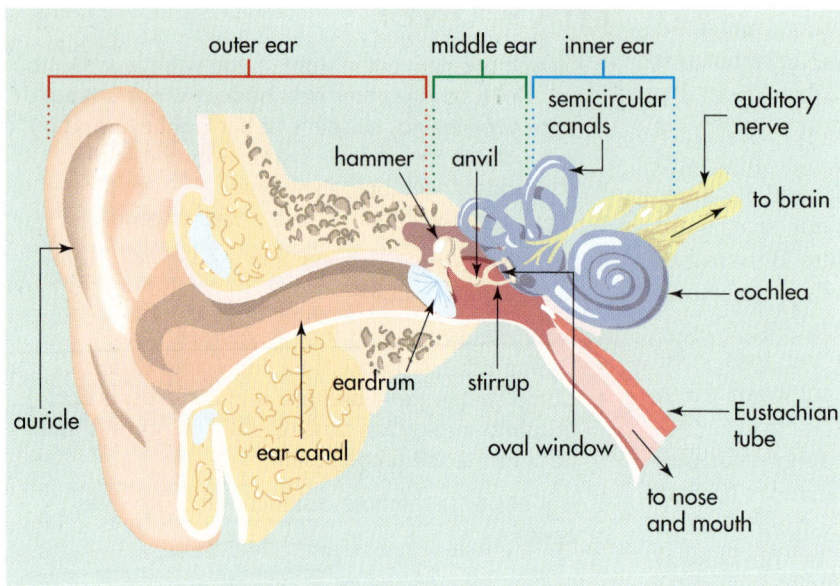

When a sound is made, the surrounding air vibrates. Your ear detects the sound when the air inside the ear canal vibrates, causing the eardrum to vibrate at the same rate.

The ear can be divided into three main parts. They are the outer ear, the middle ear and the inner ear.

Outer *ear*

The outer ear funnels the air vibrations through the **ear canal** to the eardrum. The **eardrum** is a thin flap of skin, or **membrane**, that vibrates in response to the vibrating air particles. The fleshy, outer part of the ear is called the **auricle**.

Middle *ear*

The middle ear contains three small bones called the hammer, the anvil and the stirrup. These three tiny bones (known as the **ossicles**) pass on the vibrations to the inner ear through the **oval window**.

Inner *ear*

The inner ear contains the **cochlea** and the **semicircular canals**. The cochlea is a snail-shaped system of tubes full of fluid. When vibrations are passed through the oval window by the stirrup, the fluid moves tiny hairs inside the cochlea. These hairs are attached to the receptor nerve cells that send messages on their way to your brain through the **auditory nerve**. The semicircular canals also contain a fluid. However, they are not involved in hearing sound. When you move your head, the fluid in the semicircular canals moves hairs that send signals to the brain. The signals provide your brain with information to help you keep your balance.

SCIFACTS

When you are landing or taking off in a plane, your ears 'pop'.

If you climb steeply, the air pressure inside your middle ear remains the same while the air pressure outside drops. The air inside pushes on the eardrum causing an uncomfortable feeling.

The 'popping' is caused as the Eustachian tube, which is normally closed, opens. This allows air to rush out of your middle ear to your nose and mouth. The pressure is then the same on both sides of the eardrum.

When you descend quickly the 'popping' occurs as the air rushes into your middle ear to balance the increasing pressure outside. If you swallow hard you can make the 'popping' happen sooner.

Looking *after your* ears

Your ears are very sensitive and need to be looked after. Your eardrum is very easily damaged. For this reason, you should never put anything in your ears.

The ear canal contains wax and tiny hairs which, together, trap dust and other small particles that could damage your eardrum. Sometimes the wax builds up and hardens, blocking up your ear canal. Never try to remove this wax yourself! Your doctor can remove it for you.

Loud noises can also damage your ears. This is especially a problem if you are exposed to loud noise for a long time.

The eardrum is easily damaged. Ear protection is needed when working with noisy machinery, such as racing cars.

Activities

Remember

1. Complete the table about the parts of the ear.

Part	Description	Purpose
eardrum		
	three small bones in the middle ear	
	an opening into the inner ear	to allow vibrations to pass into the cochlea
cochlea		contains receptor cells for hearing
		allows air to move between the middle ear and the mouth and nose

2. How does the information received by the ear get to your brain?
3. The semicircular canals in your ear are not involved in hearing. What is their purpose and how do they work?
4. How is the eardrum protected from damage through dust and other small particles?

Think

1. When you clap your hands a sound is heard. Explain how the sound gets from your hands, through the air and through your ear.

2. Two astronauts in space working outside the space shuttle are unable to hear each other, no matter how loudly they speak or even yell. Yet when they are inside the space shuttle with helmets on they can hear each other easily. Why is there a difference?

3. Why should you never try to remove ear wax yourself?

Investigate

Design an experiment to find out how well you can predict the direction from which the sound of a hand clap comes. You could extend your experiment to investigate:

- the effect of different types of sounds

- whether your ability to locate sounds is better inside or outside

- whether background noise makes it harder to locate sounds.

Perhaps you can suggest some other variables that you could investigate.

ENERGY TRANSFORMATIONS

Once scientists learnt how to transform sound, light and heat energy from one to another, it opened up the development of new technologies that improve our quality of life and allow us to explore our universe.

The planets Uranus, Neptune and Pluto could never have been discovered until the **telescope** was invented. The **organisms** that cause disease cannot be seen without the aid of a **microscope**. Telescopes and microscopes are just two devices that are used to extend the sense of sight.

The sense of hearing can be extended too. Doctors use stethoscopes to listen to your heartbeat. Hearing aids make sounds louder to assist people with some types of hearing impairment.

Extending *the* sense *of* sight

Lenses are used in microscopes, telescopes and binoculars to extend your sense of sight when objects are too small or too far away to see with your eyes. They are also used in spectacles to correct sight problems caused when images are not focused properly on the retina.

A magnifying glass can be used to make print on a page appear larger. It can also be used to focus sunlight into a point on a sheet of paper, which transforms light energy from the sun into heat energy. After a few moments, the point on the paper becomes hot and soon scorches the paper, which eventually bursts into flames. A glass bottle discarded in the bush can act like a magnifying glass, turning the sun's light energy into heat that can start a bushfire.

Binoculars act as magnifying glasses to bring the action closer.

Exploring *space*

Space probes and satellites extend our ability to gather information from deep space. The information they collect is beamed back to Earth in radio waves, which are collected by antennas and radio telescopes. A radio telescope is often called a 'dish', because it has a large curved dish to collect these signals. The signals are sent to a focus point above the dish, rather like a magnifying glass focusing the sun's light. After the radio signals have been concentrated, they are picked up by an antenna which turns them into electrical signals. These electrical signals are then fed into a computer which turns them into a picture.

The power of a radio telescope is limited by the size of its dish. To allow a radio telescope to gather finer detail and better quality data, astronomers combine dishes into an array. An array can be two or more dishes placed side by side or located on different parts of the Earth's surface. An array can gather radio waves as if it were one enormous dish, which increases greatly the amount and quality of information received.

Experiment 9.12
MAKING IT SEEM LARGER

YOU WILL NEED
hand lens or magnifying glass
small objects, such as leaves, shells, small insects in a jar, tissue paper, granite
sharp lead pencil

- Use the hand lens to look closely at the print on this page and the tip of your finger.
1. Describe the difference that the hand lens makes to what you see.
2. Draw and label a diagram of a letter 'e' and the tip of your finger as seen through the hand lens.
- Use the hand lens to look closely at a selection of small objects.
3. Draw and label each object as seen through the hand lens.

The Hubble, which is both an optical telescope and a satellite, is in orbit about 600 kilometres from the Earth's surface. Its orbit is adjusted each time the space shuttle visits it to repair or upgrade equipment. Hubble has a pair of solar panels to transform the sun's light energy into electrical energy, which then powers all the equipment on board.

The Hubble telescope collects the sun's rays to provide power for its equipment.

Embryonic clouds, forming from clouds of gas, photographed by Hubble telescope

The telescope tube is 13 metres long and 4.3 metres across; an opening at one end of the tube allows light from stars and galaxies to enter. The incoming light is reflected onto a 2.4 metre diameter, curved mirror which reflects the light back towards a smaller secondary mirror. This second mirror focuses the incoming light more and directs it towards a light detector which transforms the light energy into electrical energy. Finally, the energy is transformed into a television signal. A radio dish on the outside of Hubble then transmits this signal back to Earth where it is received and converted into a picture.

Focus point of a radio telescope

Making *light*

Lasers extend our ability to communicate and are used in digital recordings and fibre optics. They produce powerful beams of light. High-energy lasers can cut accurately through metal. In a **laser** (**l**ight **a**mplification by **s**timulated **e**mission of **r**adiation), electrical energy is transformed into light energy. Energy is pumped into one substance called a medium, which can be a solid, liquid or gas. The atoms in the medium get excited by the energy and eventually release light, which is then focused into a laser beam.

The Australian Telescope Compact Array near Narrabri, NSW

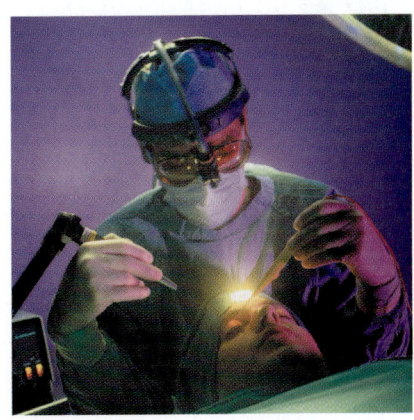

Doctor using laser in surgery

An electric light bulb also transforms electrical energy into light energy. The filament in a light bulb is made of tungsten, which is a metal with a very high melting point. When the light bulb is turned on, electricity flows through the tungsten filament. The filament becomes red-hot and emits light. The filament would burn out very quickly if it were allowed to combine with oxygen; to prevent this the bulb is filled with a gas called argon.

Extending *the sense of* hearing

The earliest hearing aids were cone shaped. Modern hearing aids are battery powered and, like the earlier devices, amplify vibrations so that they can reach the cochlea. However, modern hearing aids do this by transforming sound energy into electrical energy. The hearing aid amplifies, or increases, the sound and feeds it into the ear where it is interpreted and sent to the brain via the auditory nerve.

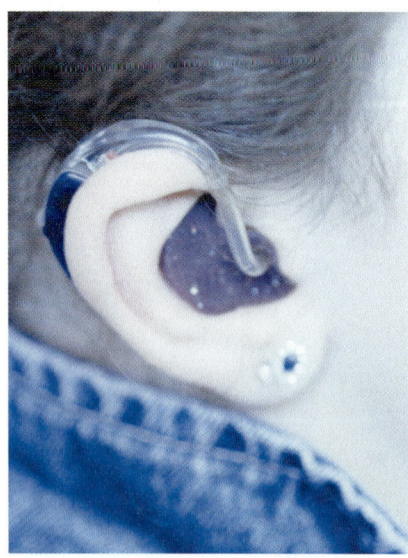

A modern hearing aid

Many people who have severely or profoundly impaired hearing are unable to benefit from hearing aids. Profoundly hearing-impaired people hear no sounds at all.

Australian scientists have developed a device that has allowed some people who are profoundly hearing impaired to detect sound for the first time in their lives. The **cochlear implant**, or **bionic ear**, shown below, is surgically placed inside the ear.

A receiver is attached to the mastoid bone of the skull via a small hole drilled by the surgeon. The surgeon also places electrodes in the cochlea in the inner ear. This amazing invention allows sound energy to be transformed several times before it is finally fed through to the brain via the auditory nerve.

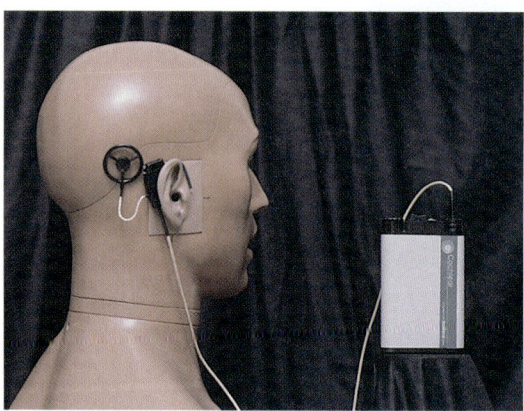

Bionic ear headset and speech processor

Sound waves are first amplified by a microphone in a headset worn outside the ear. They are then sent to the speech processor (a small computer worn in the pocket or on a belt) where they are converted into electrical signals. These electrical signals are sent to the transmitter which converts them into radio waves. The receiver picks up the radio waves and converts them back into electrical signals that are sent to the electrodes within the cochlea. These electrodes stimulate the auditory nerve sending the electrical or nerve impulse to the brain.

Storing *sound*

A compact disc or CD allows us to listen to our favourite sounds whenever we like. Sounds are stored digitally on a compact disc. To do this, sound is first transformed by a microphone into an electrical signal. This signal is then transformed into a digital code called a binary code, which is made up of ones and zeros to represent the same sound heard by the microphone. On a compact disc, the zeros become little pits and the ones are the smooth bits on the surface. All codes produced by the sound are laid down on the compact disc in a huge spiral several kilometres long.

To retrieve the information on the CD, an optical reader decodes the tracks, turning them back into voltages and then into sounds. The optical reader uses a system of mirrors and lenses to direct a laser beam at the tracks. When the laser beam hits a smooth surface, it is reflected onto a photodiode, which converts the light to an electrical signal. When the laser beam hits a pit, there is no reflection and so no signal. This produces a series of on-off electrical pulses like the ones that were created when the sound was originally recorded on the CD.

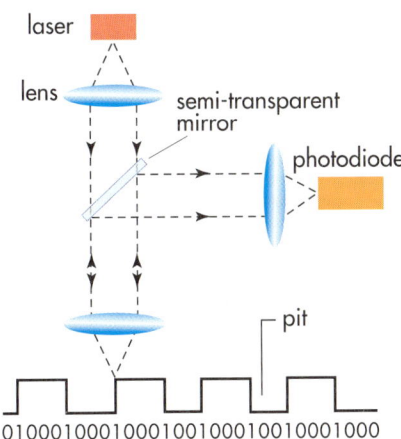

0100010001000100100010010001000

When the laser beam detects a pit edge, it is reflected back to the photodiode to produce a '1'.

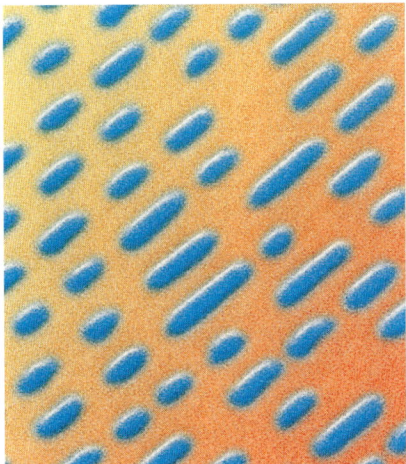

The surface of a CD is a very long spiral of pits.

Television uses sound and light energy together.

Sound *and light* together

Television uses sound and light technologies together. A television station is assigned a specific channel or radio frequency on which to send its programs out to its audience. Both sound and light energy are transmitted on radio waves. At your home, an antenna or receiving dish picks up the radio waves. It sends them to other equipment in your television which transforms the radio waves back into the sound and vision that was recorded in the studio. Lots of energy transformations allow this to happen smoothly.

Experiment 9.13

MAKING IT SEEM LOUDER

YOU WILL NEED

a ticking watch   sheet of paper, about A4 size
metre ruler   blindfold

- Have your blindfolded partner sit on a chair. Hold a ticking watch close to your partner's right ear. The left ear should be covered with an open palm.
- Move slowly away until your partner indicates that the sound of the ticking watch can no longer be heard.
- Measure and record the approximate distance from the watch to your partner's right ear.
- Make a funnel with a sheet of paper. Place the narrow end of the funnel close to, but not touching, your partner's right ear. Your partner should be able to hold it in place.

CAUTION: Take care not to put the cone into the ear canal.

- Again, move the ticking watch slowly away from your partner, starting near the end of the funnel, until it can no longer be heard. Measure and record the approximate distance between the watch and your partner's right ear.

1. What difference does the funnel make?
2. How does the funnel work?
3. Look at your own ears. Why do you think they are that shape?

Activities

Remember

1. In what devices are lenses used to extend the sense of sight?
2. Explain what the bionic ear is and how it works.
3. Explain how either light or sound can be transformed into different forms of energy.

Think

1. Telescopes and microscopes both use lenses to extend the sense of sight. They are, however, used for different purposes. What is each of these devices used for?
2. A compact disc stores our favourite music. Explain how this is achieved.

Investigate

1. Find out who Helen Keller was and why she became famous.
2. Why was the work of Edwin Hubble so important?
3. Find out about the positive and negative impacts of the invention of the cochlear implant.

9.8
Ears, eyes and more

There is an amazing variety of ears and eyes in the animal kingdom. An animal's ears and eyes must be suited to where it lives, how it finds its food and how it protects itself from predators.

Hey, *big ears!*

Animal ears generally serve two purposes. They detect sounds and keep balance. Animals that live in hot climates often have ears that help keep them cool. Large ears expose a lot of skin to the air. This allows heat to escape from the animal's body into the air. The desert fox shown below does not sweat. If it did, it would lose too much water. It keeps cool with its large ears. The polar bear also shown below, on the other hand, has very small ears. It needs to keep its body warm and would lose too much heat from big ears.

A polar bear

A desert fox

The size of its ears can be important to an animal's survival in hot and cold climates.

The African elephant's ears enable it to hear low-pitched sounds from other elephants over four kilometres away. They also use their giant ears to release heat, sometimes flapping them to cool down more quickly.

Mammals are the only animals with auricles. Auricles are the fleshy flaps on the outside of the ear.

The African elephant's big ears are not just for hearing.

Eyes *in the* dark

Animals that sleep during the day and are active at night are called **nocturnal** animals. The possum and tarsier are examples of nocturnal animals, as is the owl. Each of these animals searches for food in the dark. Their eyes need to be able to detect the limited amount of light that is available. Many of these animals have big eyes with very large pupils. The pupils are the holes that allow light to pass through the eye to the retina.

Not all nocturnal animals have large eyes. Many have very well developed senses of hearing, smell or touch to make up for the lack of light. They often have large ears or whiskers. The bilby, also known as the rabbit-eared bandicoot, has poor eyesight but survives well at night due to its keen senses of hearing and smell.

A tarsier

Nocturnal animals often have big eyes with large pupils.

An owl

Looking *for an* echo

Animals such as bats, whales, dolphins, porpoises and some cave-dwelling birds survive well in the dark without large eyes by using **echolocation**. These animals make high-pitched sounds and listen to the echoes of the sounds as they bounce off objects. Bats living in caves emit short bursts of high-pitched clicks as they fly in the dark, searching for their insect prey. Their large ears move as they fly and detect echoes caused when the sounds bounce off insects or obstacles, such as cave walls.

Bats use echolocation to find their food.

Eyes *and* ears *in the* deep

Whales, dolphins and porpoises benefit from using echolocation because of the lack of light under the water. They are able to use the echo from their high-pitched clicking sound to detect schools of fish. They can even tell the size of each fish using the echo. Fish that live more than 100 metres below the surface of the water are in almost total darkness. Many of them have large eyes. Others have a well developed sense of smell. Some, like the angler fish, shown on page 180, take advantage of the darkness by emitting light to attract their prey.

The marine hatchetfish emits a greenish-blue light from organs on the lower parts of its body. The light does not help the hatchetfish to see because it is capable of looking only upwards. It makes it invisible to its predators swimming below. The greenish-blue light is just like the dim light coming from the ocean surface.

Insect eyes *and* ears

Insects have **compound eyes**, made of up to 10 000 tiny lenses. Each lens gives the insect a view of only one direction. All the views together give the insect a total image. While insects do not see the amount of detail in objects that we do, their compound eyes allow them to detect movement easily.

Some insects have ears but they are not on their heads. The ears are membranes like eardrums on the surface of their bodies. A cricket has an ear just below the knee of each of its front legs. A grasshopper has an ear on each side of its body just below the wing. Most insects, however, do not have ears but detect vibrations with sensitive hairs on their antennae or other parts of their bodies.

Activities

Remember

1. Why does the desert fox have such large ears?
2. What are auricles?
3. Why do many nocturnal animals have very large eyes?
4. Explain how bats that live in dark caves find their food and avoid flying into the rock walls.

Think

1. Possums have large whiskers. Why are these important to the possum at night?
2. The tarsier, a small mammal that lives in the tropical rainforests of South-east Asia, has very large pupils. Photographs of the tarsier taken at night often show smaller pupils (see photograph opposite). Why?
3. Rabbits have eyes on the sides of their heads rather than in front. What advantage does that give them?

Investigate

1. Find out how snakes detect sound.
2. Find two examples of technologies that use echolocation. Explain the benefits the technologies have on our lifestyle.

Enlarged view of the head of a dragonfly

Putting it all together

Summing up

Copy and complete the statements below to compile a summary of this unit.
The missing words can be found in the word list below.

1. Objects that emit light are said to be
luminous

2. Most things that you see are not luminous but
reflect light into your eyes.

3. Images form in _mirrors_ because light is
reflected from their smooth surface.

4. _curved_ mirrors produce different
images from flat mirrors.

5. All sounds are caused by _vibrations_.

6. Sound is a form of _energy vibration_ which needs
a medium to travel through.

7. The rate at which vibrations occur determines the
pitch of the sound that they cause.

8. Sense organs contain _receptors_ that
respond to a stimulus.

9. Messages are mostly sent from sense organs to
other parts of the body through the
brain.

10. The receptors in the eye respond to
light.

11. The eye produces an image of what you look at
by focusing light on the _retina_.

12. Vibrations of air are transferred by the eardrum
to the _middle_ and inner ear.

13. Eyes and ears are very sensitive and need to be
treated with great _care_.

14. The sense of sight can be extended with
telescopes and _microscopes_

15. An impaired sense of hearing can often be
extended with hearing aids or cochlea
implants

16. The power of a radio telescope is limited by the
size of its _dish_.

17. Modern technology is able to _transform_
different types of energy from one to another in
equipment we use every day.

Word list

reflect	curved	receptors	pitch
light	care	mirrors	middle
luminous	microscopes	brain	transform
implants	vibrations	retina	energy
dish			

Looking back

1. Complete this crossword, using the clues provided.

Clues

Across

1. The taste of sugar
4. The thin flap of skin at the entrance to the ear
5. The taste of vinegar
8. Used to view organisms too small to see with the eye
10. This is the pathway from the eye to the brain (two words).
15. Images are formed on this surface at the back of your eye.
16. These receptors share their name with a crunchy food item in which ice-creams are sold.
17. The sense organ for smelling
18. This is received on the retina but can also be seen on a TV screen.

Down

2. An organ for hearing
3. These keep the eye free of dust and also appear when you peel onions.
6. The curved outer part of your eye
7. Used to view distant objects
9. The ring of muscle that gives your eye colour
11. You are one of these and have two of these.
12. A clear, jelly-like object in the eye that brings light to a focus
13. A stimulus that is not quite hot
14. You are unable to do this with both eyes closed.

2. Copy the table below into your workbook, and add the missing information.

Sense	Sense organ	Receptors	Stimulus
		special cells called cones and rods	
	ear		
touch		separate receptors for each type of stimulus	
	tongue		sweet, salty, bitter and sour substances
smell		olfactory nerves	odours

3. Explain how hitting the skin on a drum makes a loud sound. Make sure that your explanation includes the words *vibrate*, *air* and *louder*.
4. Copy the diagram of the ear into your workbook and fill in the missing labels.
5. Why is a hearing aid of no use at all to some hearing-impaired people?
6. Why do elephants have such big ears?
7. Use the diagram to explain how the cochlear implant would be inserted into the ear. Explain how it can transform sounds and transmit them so that the person can hear.

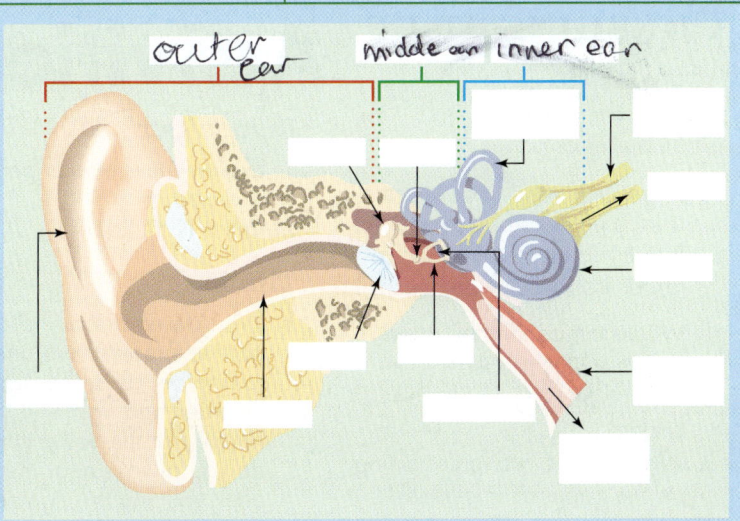

Extension
Flash, crash, boom!

During a storm you see flashes of lightning and later you hear thunder. Lightning is a giant electric spark moving between clouds and the ground or other clouds.

In the experiment below, rubbing the ruler causes it to become 'charged', so that the number of 'positively' charged particles in the ruler is different from the number of 'negatively' charged particles. Opposite charges are attracted to each other. The charged particles in the ruler attract the oppositely charged particles in the paper using an electrostatic force often called static electricity. Removing a synthetic jumper quickly causes a build-up of either positive or negative charges. In the dark, you see sparks which are the energy released when the charges move to neutralise each other.

Similarly, fast-moving clouds in a storm become polarised; the top part of the cloud becomes positively charged and the bottom becomes negatively charged. The negatively charged particles are attracted to the positively charged particles in other clouds or the ground. In an electrical storm, so much negative charge is built up that it moves as a giant spark through the air.

The flash of lightning heats up the air around it to temperatures of up to 30 000°C. The hot air expands, its particles crashing into the surrounding cold air particles. Thunder is the noise created by the crashing particles.

Unbalanced charge moves from cloud to cloud or from a cloud to the ground.

Experiment 9.14

CHARGING IT UP

YOU WILL NEED
plastic pen
small pieces of paper

- Rub a pen vigorously on your shirt, jumper or blazer and use it to try to lift a small piece of paper from your workbench.

1. Would the pen lift the paper before it was rubbed?
2. What type of force lifts the paper?
3. What are the two forces acting on the paper as it is lifted?

Activities

Remember

1. Explain how clouds become charged.
2. What is thunder?

Think

1. Why do electrically charged particles move from one cloud to another or to the ground?
2. Thunder and lightning actually happen at the same time. Why do you always hear the thunder after you see the lightning?

3. Explain why you should avoid sheltering under a tree during an electrical storm.
4. Why is there no spark when you place a charged plastic pen near a small piece of paper?

Create

Design a poster to warn people how to avoid being struck by lightning in an electrical storm.

Reflection

1. Mind map revisited

GROUP WORK (a) Revisit the list of words and mind map that you made with your group or partner about your eyes and ears. Write meanings for the words on your list. Update the mind map by correcting any errors and adding your new understandings.

(b) Redraw your mind map on your own to see how much you remember. When you run out of ideas, look at your original mind map to get started again. Practise until you can redraw it from memory.

(c) Now try and draw a mind map to cover everything you have learnt while studying this chapter. You will need a large sheet of paper!

2. Music

Listen to your favourite piece of music. Try to identify all the different sounds you can hear. For each individual sound, describe what is vibrating to make the sound and how the pitch is changed.

3. Surveying

Conduct a survey to see what people know about their senses.

(a) Write a short explanation about conscious responses and reflex actions (describing how each one works). Then make a list of mixed examples of both conscious responses and reflex actions.

(b) Read the explanation and the list to the people you are surveying, and ask them to decide if each example is a conscious response or reflex action.

(c) Collate your responses and make a conclusion about what your survey results told you.

(d) How could you improve the way you present your survey so that all respondents understand the differences between reflex responses and conscious actions?

4. Making models

GROUP WORK Make a model of an eye or an ear and label all the parts. Present your model to the class and explain how it works.

5. Avoid losing your senses

Sometimes, we lose the power of our eyes or ears because we do not take simple precautions. Make a poster reminding people about possible dangers to eyes or ears, including hints on how to prevent them from being damaged.

Experiment 9.15
MEASURING THE SPEED OF SOUND

YOU WILL NEED

2 garbage lids   earmuffs
trundle wheel   stopwatch
a partner

- Have one person (the noise maker) put on the earmuffs and hold the lids.
- Move to a position about 350 m (measured with the trundle wheel) from the noise maker.
- Signal to the noise maker to bang the lids hard over his or her head.
- Start the stopwatch once you see the lids come together and stop it once you hear the noise. Write down the time shown on the stopwatch.
- Repeat your experiment several times and average your results. Use the formula

$$\text{speed} = \frac{\text{distance}}{\text{time}}$$ to work out the speed of sound.

- Prepare a report outlining your experiment and comment on how your results compare with the real value.

How would you work out the speed of sound in water? Would you expect it to be higher or lower than the speed of sound in air?

CORE SCIENCE SKILLS

Solving problems, making new discoveries, critically examining situations to prove cause and effect and seeking out facts to improve our understanding or discover the truth are all part of the world of the scientist. Making discoveries is very rewarding. As a scientist, you need to be patient, persistent, logical, a keen observer and critical of your own results. An effective scientist develops many skills over a lifetime.

KEY CONTENT

Use drawings, tables, keys, flow charts, surveys, graphs data loggers and databases to collect, organise and present results.

Make careful measurements and understand the limitations of techniques and instruments.

KEY QUESTIONS

What approach does a scientist take to solving problems?

What makes learning easy or difficult?

What skills do scientists need to get results?

A scientist studying paper chromatographs

Introducing Core skills

Science is about looking at the world around you and applying highly developed investigative skills to understand your surroundings. This section will help you to develop these skills to become a super scientist! The skills we will be covering could be grouped under two headings:

• science skills   • learning skills.

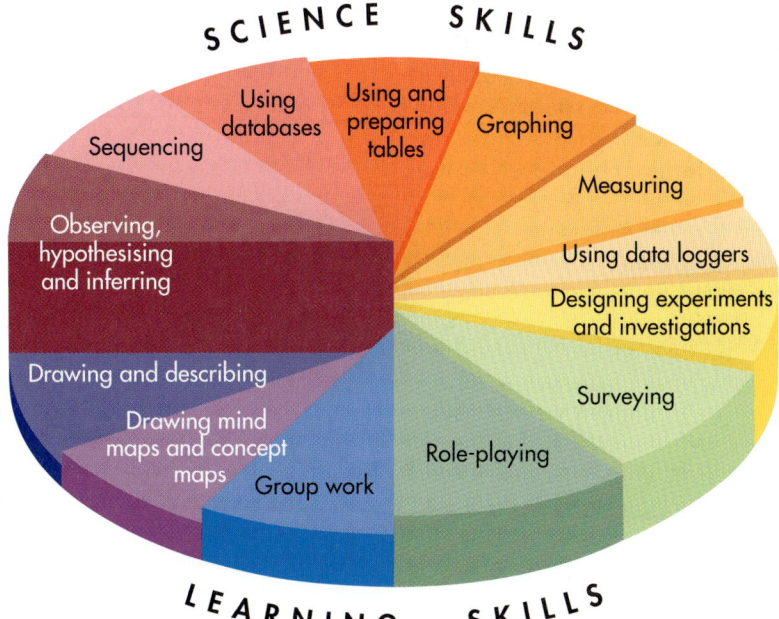

SCIENCE SKILLS

- Using databases
- Sequencing
- Using and preparing tables
- Graphing
- Observing, hypothesising and inferring
- Measuring
- Using data loggers
- Designing experiments and investigations
- Surveying
- Drawing and describing
- Drawing mind maps and concept maps
- Role-playing
- Group work

LEARNING SKILLS

Science skills

Science skills help you to be a more effective scientist. As a scientist you will ask questions about what you see around you. Designing experiments, recording your observations, analysing your results, looking for trends and drawing conclusions will help you to find answers that improve your understanding. Managing your results and recording your observations will be easier if you develop and use the following skills:

- **observing, hypothesising** and **inferring** to obtain information and make it meaningful (see pages 10–11)

- **sequencing** to organise ideas into a logical order
- **using** and **preparing tables** to record results in a form that is easy to interpret
- **graphing** to show information visually
- **measuring** to get accurate results
- using dataloggers to collect results automatically
- using databases to store and sort information
- **designing experiments** and **investigations** to test hypotheses (see pages 10–11, 22–3 and 240–2).
- **surveying** to collect data.

All of these skills can also be useful in other areas of your life.

Learning skills

Learning skills help you to remember and think about what you learn. Learning is a process during which you take in new information. You may change your existing views because you keep on learning as you progress through life.

Learning can be one of the most exciting and rewarding activities. Think of something you really enjoy doing (it doesn't have to be at school!). Perhaps it's playing sport or a computer game. How do you feel when you improve your performance or find a new way to solve a problem? When you are interested and motivated, learning is both easier and exciting.

Learning skills are useful tools in all subjects, not just science. Like any tool, the idea is to use the ones that work best for you in a particular situation. The following learning skills will help you to understand new or difficult concepts:

- **drawing** and **describing** to express ideas and views
- drawing **mind maps** and **concept maps** to make connections between ideas or words
- **group work**, which gives you the opportunity to discuss and share ideas
- **role-playing** to get a clear understanding of difficult ideas.

I know this now, but how do I make sure I remember it?

Try talking about it or writing it down.

Sequencing

What is sequencing?

Sequencing is organising information or data into a particular order, such as the order that steps are performed in an experiment, which is called a time sequence. Material that is suitable for sequencing has dates or words that indicate time (such as 'after' and 'then'), and these are useful in working out the order.

Why sequence?

Sequencing is usually carried out to:

- make the order of steps in a process clear, so that the process can be followed correctly
- make a piece of text more understandable
- highlight the order of events so that the time scale can be seen more clearly.

When do we sequence?

Sequencing should be used whenever material is difficult to read or interpret, and when the material is suitable for sequencing (such as steps in a process, cause and effect situations and historical trends). Sequencing is most commonly used to put into order objects or ideas that are out of order.

How do we sequence?

The simplest types of sequencing are flow charts that make a process clear, flow charts that simplify text and timelines.

Flow charts that clarify processes

To make the steps in a process clear, a flow chart or flow diagram can be used. A flow chart is a set of statements, in order, joined by arrows. To read a flow chart, start at the statement before the first arrow and then follow the direction of the arrows. An example of a flow chart is shown on the right. The symbols used in this example have specific meanings, borrowed from computer programming. They are shown below:

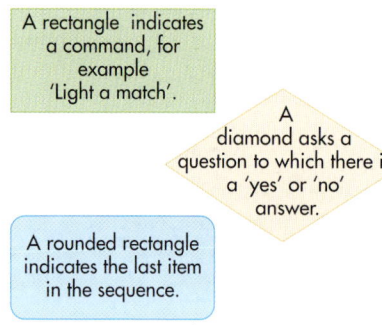

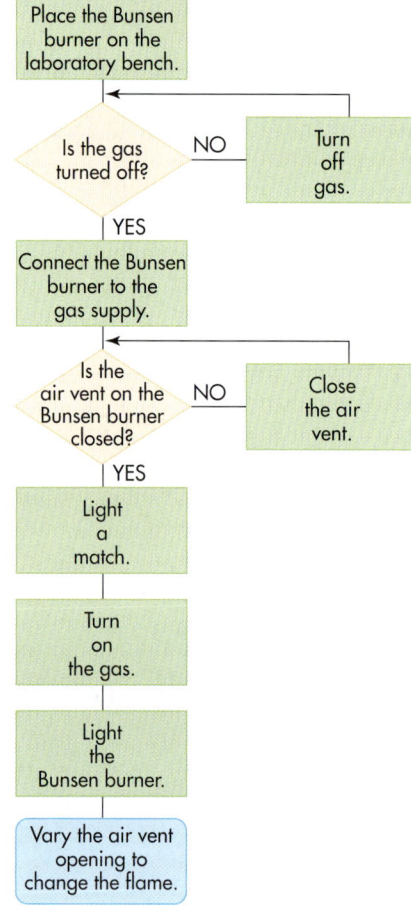

How to use a Bunsen burner

A flow chart using computer programming symbols

The flow chart above right can also be written in a form that does not use computer conventions, such as the following chart.

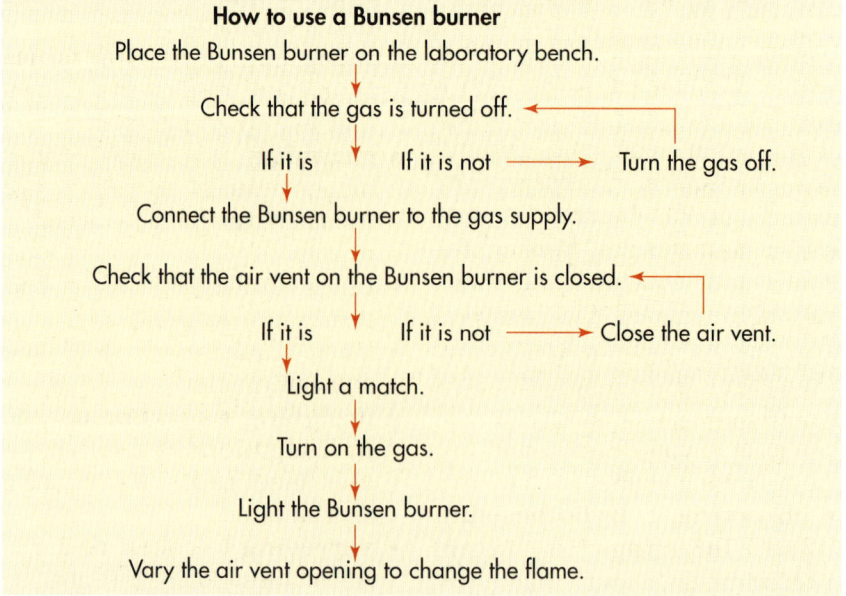

Another type of flow chart

Flow charts that simplify text

To make a piece of text more understandable, a less formal flow chart diagram may also be used. Consider the following information about concrete.

Concrete — a very important mixture

Concrete is an artificial stone that is used in buildings, bridges, dams and pavements. Have you ever been curious about how concrete is made and what chemicals it contains?

Concrete in our world

While many people think that concrete is a modern invention, concrete made from crushed volcanic rock and brick was used by the Romans about 2000 years ago. After the fall of the Roman Empire, the use of concrete died out and was not revived until the development of modern commercial concretes in Britain in the 19th century.

So what makes up concrete?

Concrete is made by mixing cement, water and coarse and fine **aggregates** (rock particles or sand). The proportion of each material affects the properties of hardened concrete. The aim is to mix these materials in measured amounts to make concrete that is easy to transport, easy to put in place and strong and durable when set.

Cement

Chemically, cement powder is a mixture of four minerals that come from crushed rocks such as limestone and shale. These are:
* tricalcium silicate — a mixture of calcium oxide and silicon dioxide
* dicalcium silicate — the same as tricalcium silicate but with less calcium oxide
* tricalcium aluminate — a mixture of calcium oxide and aluminium oxide
* tetracalcium aluminoferrite — a mixture of calcium oxide, aluminium oxide and iron oxide.

When mixed with water, the cement powder forms a paste. This paste acts like a glue and holds or bonds the aggregates together. The most common type of cement sold in Australia is Type A Portland cement. When set, this cement resembles a type of stone that is quarried on the Isle of Portland, a peninsula on the English Channel coast.

Water

Water must be clean, fresh and free from unwanted chemicals. Sea water cannot be used as the salts it contains may rust the steel reinforcement in concrete.

Aggregates

Aggregates may be coarse (crushed rock and gravel) or fine (fine and coarse sand). They should be:
* **strong** and **hard** to give a stronger final concrete
* **durable** to stand up to wear and tear and weathering
* **chemically inactive** so they do not react with the cement paste
* **graded** so they fit together well. A range of grain sizes gives a stronger, denser concrete.

Reinforced concrete

Around 1865, experimenters set concrete around steel wire mesh. This combines the compression, hardness and fire-resisting properties of concrete with the strength of steel. Steel and cement expand and contract in a similar way. Such a combination of steel and concrete can resist bending, shear (cutting forces) and torsion (twisting forces). So reinforced concrete has become very popular in modern buildings and skyscrapers. The steel used may be in the form of mesh, rods or bars.

The information in the text box above can be split up into four different flow charts, as shown on page 204. Drawings can be included to make the subject matter clearer, as shown in flow charts C and D.

The use of concrete began with the Romans 2000 years ago.

↓

After the Roman Empire collapsed, concrete's use died out.

↓

Concrete was revived in the 19th century in Britain.

↓

At the end of the 19th century reinforced concrete was developed.

↓

The development of reinforced concrete enabled modern skyscrapers to be built.

Flow chart A — The history of the development of concrete

Concrete is made of

Cement — A mixture of four chemicals

Water — It must be pure

Coarse and fine aggregates — They may be coarse or fine

↓

They should be:
• strong and hard
• durable and clean
• chemically inactive
• graded

Flow chart B — The structure of concrete

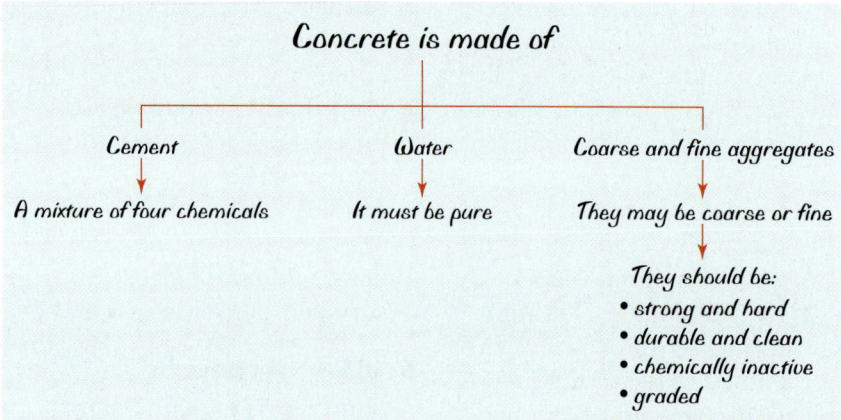

Cement, water and aggregates are mixed.
Step 1: Water is added to cement to make a paste.
Step 2: Coarse or fine aggregates are added to cement paste to form concrete.

Concrete is made from...

Flow chart C — How to make concrete

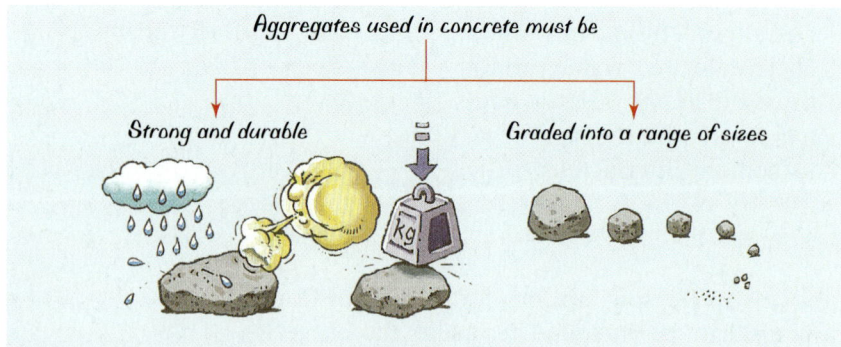

Aggregates used in concrete must be

Strong and durable   Graded into a range of sizes

Flow chart D — The characteristics of aggregates

Timelines

To highlight the order of events, a timeline may be used. Timelines are often used to show sequences in history and therefore can be applied to historical sequences in science. The timeline below was constructed to show the sequence and time spans between the following events.

1. The universe began 10 billion years ago.
2. Galaxies were formed 5 billion years ago.
3. The Earth was formed 4.5 billion years ago.
4. Life forms originated on Earth 3.8 billion years ago.
5. Plants and animals evolved 2.5 billion years ago.
6. Humans evolved 2 million years ago.

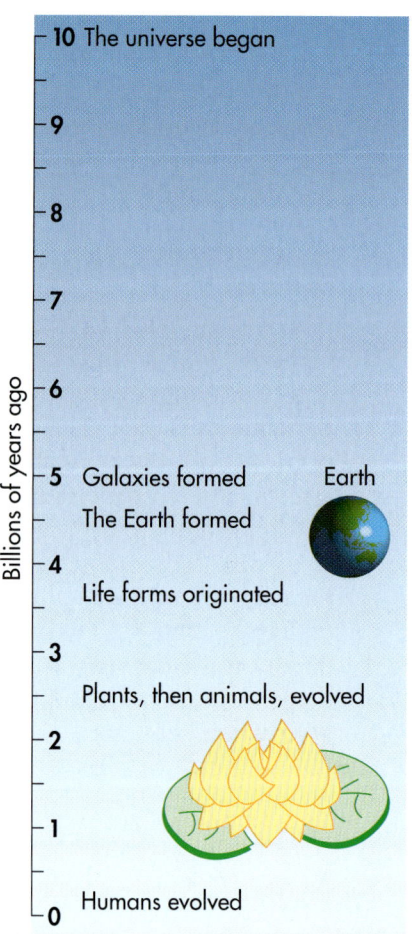

A timeline

Activities

1. (a) Create your own flow charts or timelines to make the following pieces of information easier to understand. Choose the most appropriate sequencing technique for each piece of information.

How to filter a mixture

Prepare a fluted filter paper by folding the circle of paper into half and then into quarters. Then open one of the segments and place the paper in the funnel. Moisten the paper with a small amount of water. This helps the paper to adhere to the funnel rather than flattening out. Hold the beaker containing the mixture to be filtered at an angle above the funnel. Pour the mixture down a glass rod and into the filter paper lining the funnel. Care must be taken to ensure that the liquid is not poured above the edge of the filter paper. If the solid from the mixture is required, extra liquid may need to be added to the beaker to wash out all the solid.

Why do earthquakes happen?

The centre of the Earth is thought to be composed of a hot metallic core. Outside the core is a layer called the mantle. Heat from the core is transferred to the mantle, causing rocks from the mantle to move slowly towards the surface of the Earth. This may take thousands of years. When these rocks reach the crust (the Earth's outer layer), they cause the plates of the crust to move past each other. This causes shock waves in the rock which travel through the crust and can cause great damage to buildings.

(b) Compare your methods with other students and discuss the following questions.
   (i) Did you leave any sentences out of your sequencing? Why?
   (ii) Did the sequencing help to make the material clearer for you?
   (iii) What other methods could be used with sequencing to make information clearer?

2. (a) Read the sequenced flow chart on the right and convert it to a piece of writing. You must write full sentences, don't just copy the sequence. Try to make it an interesting piece of writing.

(b) Here is a more difficult sequence. Change it into a piece of writing.

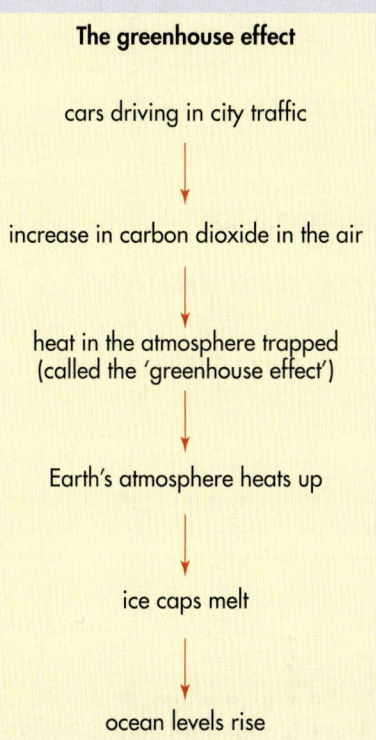

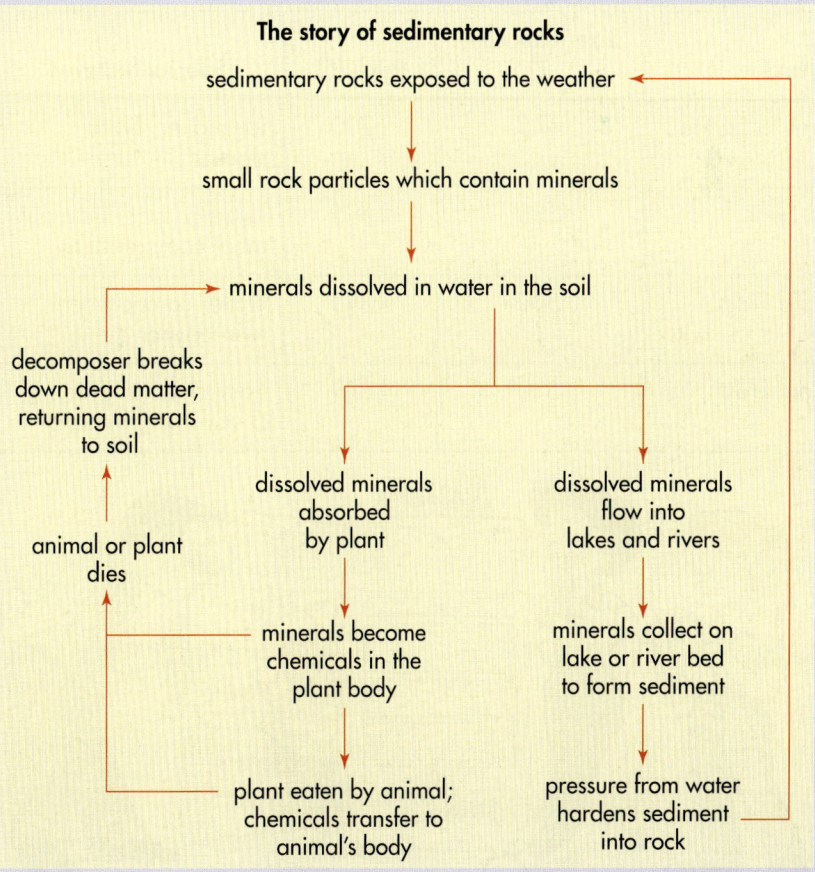

Preparing tables

What is a table?

A table is a grid of rows and columns into which data (information) is placed.

Why use tables?

It is often easier to read information when it is organised in a table, rather than described in lines of text. This is because the data have been reduced to their simplest form and have no distractions, such as extra words, surrounding them.

Tables make it is easier to:

- study relationships between pieces of data
- make conclusions
- use the data for other activities, such as graphing.

When do we use tables?

You can use tables whenever at least two sets of data are collected. A table is suitable for data that involve both words and numbers. For example, your family wants to buy a new refrigerator and does some research on the various brands. This data collection could be inserted in a table such as the one below. This would help your family decide which refrigerator is the best value for money.

Do you think that all families would choose the same refrigerator if they used the table below? Explain your answer.

How do we prepare a table?

A table should have:

- a clear and simple title
- a set of rows and columns
- headings for the columns, which should include units if the data have been measured in units. (In some tables, the rows also have headings.)

There are many examples of tables in everyday life, such as train timetables and tide tables. The table below shows the predicted times and heights of high and low tide at Fort Denison for the first half of March 2004.

Details of current models of refrigerator

Brand	Size (capacity) (L)	Price ($)	Special features
Freeza Fridge	475	1200	ice-maker, bottle stocker
Hi Spot	588	1895	large crisper, slide-out meat compartment
Cold Frost	500	1395	chiller compartment, twin crisper
Cool Frost	510	1549	easy clean shelves, 5 star energy rating

Times and heights (metres) of high and low waters

	Time	m		Time	m
MON 1	0347	1.4	MON 8	0250	0.3
	1055	0.6		0908	1.8
	1653	1.1		1530	0.2
	2214	0.7		2136	1.6
TUE 2	0453	1.5	TUE 9	0336	0.3
	1154	0.6		0949	1.7
	1753	1.1		1604	0.2
	2315	0.7		2217	1.6
WED 3	0545	1.5	WED 10	0424	0.3
	1238	0.5		1033	1.6
	1836	1.2		1642	0.3
				2300	1.6
THU 4	0003	0.6	THU 11	0517	0.4
	0630	1.6		1121	1.5
	1315	0.4		1721	0.4
	1913	1.3		2348	1.6
FRI 5	0046	0.5	FRI 12	0615	0.4
	0711	1.7		1215	1.3
	1349	0.3		1806	0.5
	1947	1.3			
SAT 6	0127	0.4	SAT 13	0042	1.6
	0749	1.7		0724	0.5
	1422	0.3		1320	1.2
	2021	1.4		1900	0.6
SUN 7	0207	0.4	SUN 14	0145	1.6
	0828	1.8		0845	0.5
	1455	0.2		1441	1.1
	2058	1.5		2012	0.7

Part of the tide table for Fort Denison, March 2004.

An example of how to prepare a table

While on a biology excursion, the teacher and students tested two methods of counting small animals in the leaf litter (dead leaf cover on the ground) from different environments.

They counted beetles, earwigs and ants found in samples of leaf litter. The samples were collected from a woodland, a forest and a shrubland. They used two methods to do this (methods 1 and 2).

A student from the group studying beetles wrote down the data below:

Using method 1 we found 10 beetles in the forest, 5 in the woodland and none in the shrubland. Using method 2 we found 12 beetles in the forest, 8 in the woodland and 2 in the shrubland.

Another student from the group who had been studying earwigs wrote the following.

18 earwigs in the forest, 15 in the shrubland and 35 in the woodland using method 1.

20 earwigs in the forest, 20 in the shrubland and 38 in the woodland using method 2.

A student from the group who had been studying ants wrote down the following information.

In the forest we found 12 ants using method 1 and 14 using method 2.

Then in the shrubland there were 9 ants (method 1) and 11 (method 2).

In woodland there were 10 ants (method 1) and 16 ants (method 2).

The teacher told them that their data were very difficult to read and interpret. She asked the students to share their data and design a table that would present the data clearly. The students went away, tried a few designs and settled for the design shown below.

Distribution of beetles, earwigs and ants in different environments

| | Number of animals | | | | | |
| | Beetles | | Earwigs | | Ants | |
Environment	Method 1	Method 2	Method 1	Method 2	Method 1	Method 2
Forest	10	12	18	20	12	14
Shrubland	0	2	15	20	9	11
Woodland	5	8	35	38	10	16

Activities

Answer the following questions, referring to the example on page 209.

1. Explain your opinions on the difference between the students' written reports and the table.
2. (a) How would you interpret the table? Extract the main ideas and make a few conclusions.
   (b) How could you improve the reliability of your conclusions?
3. Use the data from the table on page 209 to answer the following questions.
   (a) Which animal was most common in the forest?
   (b) Which animal was least common in shrubland?
   (c) Which animal was most common over all three environments?
4. Why is it easier to understand the data in the table than the original data collected by the students? Give a detailed reason for your answer.
5. A chemistry student boiled red cabbage leaves in water to obtain an indicator solution. (An indicator is a substance that changes colour in acid and base.) She also made an indicator from nasturtium leaves. She tested both indicators using:
   • acid
   • base (the opposite of an acid)
   • a neutral solution (distilled water
   • three samples of water (tap water, sea water and river water).

   Her results are shown in the copy of her workbook above right:

   (a) Design a table for the results collected by the student.
   (b) Decide whether each sample of water was basic, neutral or acidic.

The colour of the red cabbage indicator when first made was pink.

The colour of the nasturtium indicator when first made was yellow.

The colour of the red cabbage indicator in acid was red, and in base it was blue. It was pale purple in a neutral solution.

The nasturtium indicator was yellow in base, red in acid and orange in distilled water.

The results with the water samples were:
• tap water was red in both indicators
• sea water was purple in the red cabbage indicator and orange in the nasturtium indicator
• river water was slightly blue in the red cabbage indicator and pale yellow in the nasturtium indicator.

6. There are two forms of plastic polyethene which are commonly used. They are LDPE (low density polyethene) and HDPE (high density polyethene). Read the following information about them and then convert the information into a table using three columns.

Low density polyethene has a density of 0.93 g/cm^3 and a tensile strength of 11.0 N/mm^2 (newtons per square millimetre). It is transparent and very flexible, and is used to make transparent bags and 'squeezy' plastic bottles.

High density polyethene has a different appearance to low density plastic. It is opaque, tough and not very flexible. Its density is 0.96 g/cm^3 and its tensile strength is 31.0 N/mm^2. It is the material from which supermarket bags and rigid plastic bottles are made.

(a) Did you succeed in putting the information into three columns? Explain how you did it.
(b) Would you have preferred to set up your table differently? Explain your views.
(c) What do the words density, opaque, flexible and rigid mean? Share your ideas with others.
(d) Which plastic would you use if you wanted to make food containers for the freezer? Explain your choice.
(e) Collect all the wrapping material stored in your kitchen, such as plastic food wrap. Find out what chemical each one is made of and prepare another table with this information.

Graphing — the basics

Why use graphs?

Values or measurements obtained from an investigation are called data. Having collected the data, it is important to present them clearly so that another person reading or studying them can understand them. Organising data as a graph is a widely recognised way of making a clear presentation. It makes the information easier to read, interpret, show trends and make conclusions.

A graph, especially a line graph, can also be used to find values other than those used in the investigation. This can be done by interpolation or extrapolation (see page 216).

What is a graph?

A graph is a diagram that shows the connection between two or more things using dots, lines or bars. There are four different types of graph: a pie chart or sector graph, a bar chart or column graph, a histogram and a line graph.

Pie chart (or sector graph)

A **pie chart** (also known as a **sector graph**) is a circle divided into sections that represent parts of the whole. This type of graph can be used when the data can be added as parts of a whole. The example below shows the food types, vitamins and minerals that make up the nutrients in a breakfast cereal.

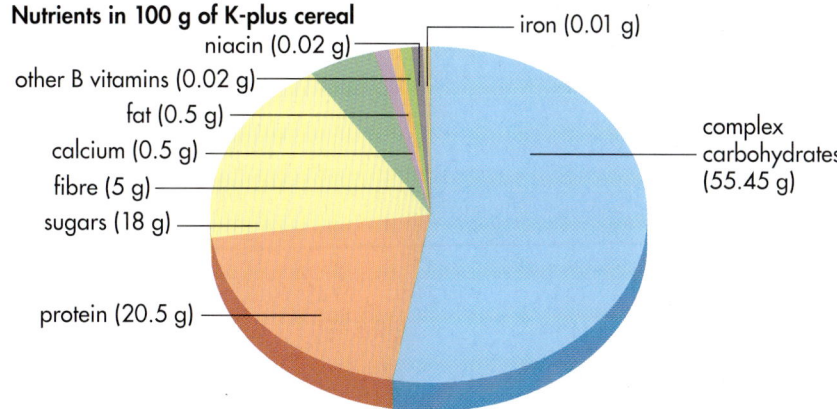

A pie chart

Column graph (or bar chart)

A **column graph** (also known as a **bar chart**) has two axes and uses rectangles (bars or columns) to represent each piece of data. The height or length of the bars represent the values in the data. The width of the bars is kept constant. This type of graph can be used when the data cannot be connected together and are therefore not continuous.

The example below on the left shows data on the average height to which different balls bounced during an experiment. Each bar represents a different type of ball. The example on the right shows the lengths of different metal bars when heated. Each bar represents a different metal bar.

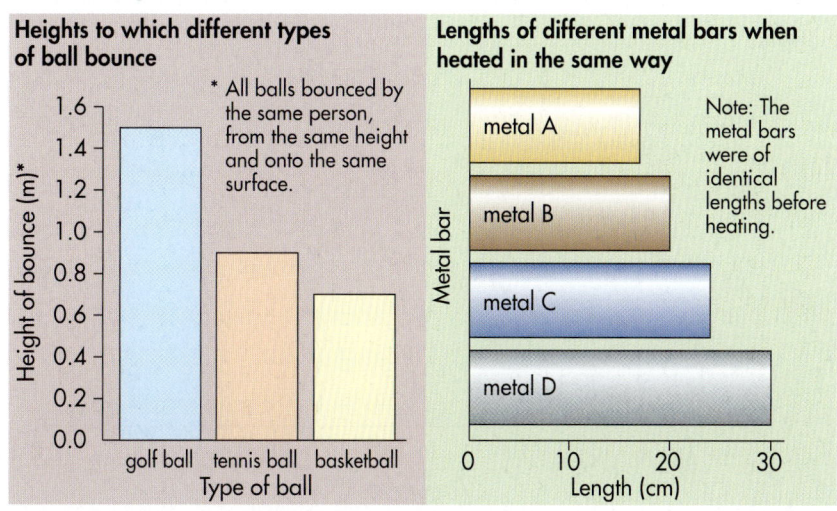

Two column graphs (also known as bar charts)

Histogram

Histograms are similar to column graphs except that the columns touch each other because the data are continuous. They are often used to present the results of surveys. In the histogram below, each column represents the number of students that reach a particular height.

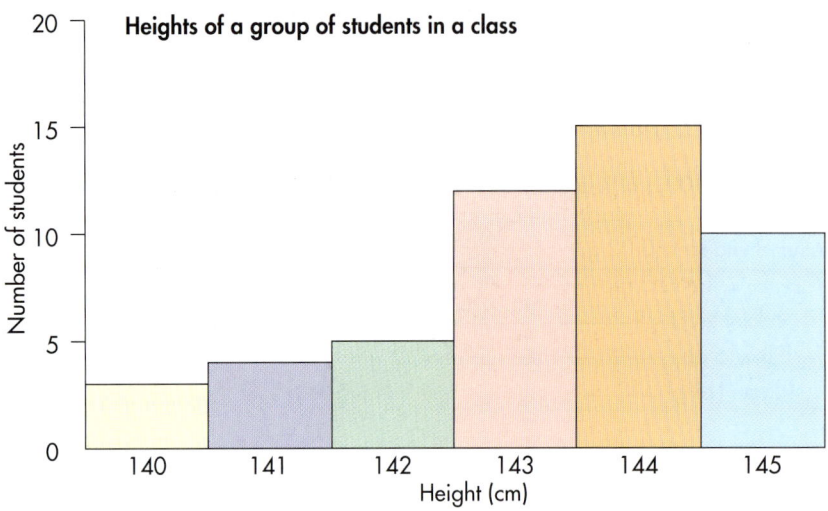

A histogram

Line graph

A **line graph** has two axes — a horizontal axis and a vertical axis. The horizontal axis is known as the **x-axis**, and the vertical axis is known as the **y-axis**. The line graph is formed by joining together a series of points or drawing a line of 'best fit' through the points. Each point represents a set of data for two variables, such as height and time. Two or more lines may be drawn on the same graph.

Line graphs are probably the most common type of graph used in school science. They are used to show continuous data, that is, data in which the values follow on from each other. For example, the line graph below shows the change in the solubility of a salt in water as the temperature of the water increases.

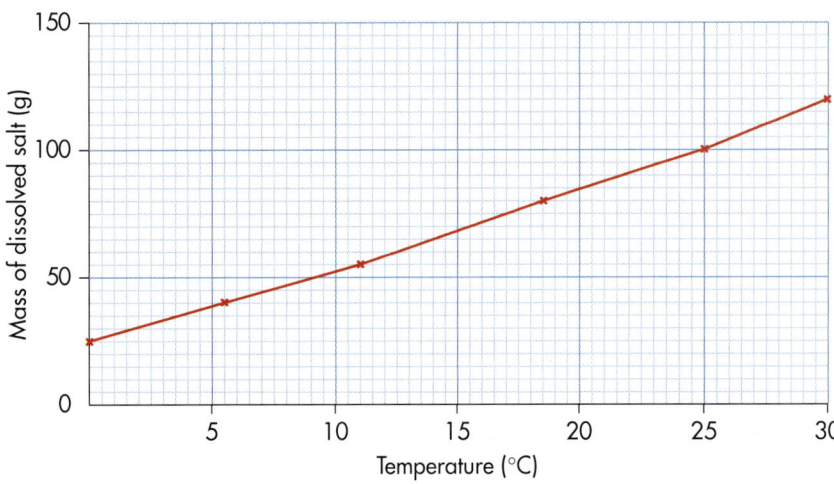

A line graph

Activities

1. Prepare a column graph using the following information on the nutrients present in a serving of ice-cream.

Nutrients in 30 g serving of ice-cream

Nutrient	Amount (g)
protein	2.00
fat	6.00
carbohydrate — polysaccharide	11.00
carbohydrate — sugars	10.00
cholesterol	0.02
calcium	0.10
potassium	0.80
sodium	0.05

2. The table below gives the energy contained in various types of food.
   (a) Assess why these data are not suitable for graphing.
   (b) Specify what you would need to do to make them suitable.

Energy content of foods

Food	Energy (calories)
apple (medium)	75 000
bread (1 slice)	100 000
butter (1 tbs)	100 000
chocolate cake (medium slice)	250 000
cornflakes (1 serving)	75 000
milk (large glass)	150 000
orange (medium)	50 000
sugar (1 tbs)	50 000

3. The following table shows the percentage composition of salts present in sea water.
   (a) Prepare a sector graph from this table.

Salt composition of sea water

Salt	Percentage
calcium carbonate	0.34
calcium sulfate	3.60
magnesium bromide	0.22
magnesium chloride	10.90
magnesium sulfate	4.70
potassium sulfate	2.50
sodium chloride	77.24
all others	0.50

   (b) Apart from sodium chloride, the salts of what metal are the most abundant in sea water?
4. The following table shows the uses of plastics in Australia.
   (a) Select a suitable graph type and prepare a graph from this table

Uses of plastics in Australia

Use	Percentage
agriculture	4.0
building	24.0
electrical/electronic	8.0
furniture and bedding	8.0
housewares	4.0
marine, toys and leisure	2.0
packaging and materials handling	31.0
transport	5.0
others	14.0

   (b) Choose two uses of plastic from your graph. For each use, state a particular item that is made of plastic.
   (c) There has been recent controversy about the waste products that humans create.
      (i) Can you suggest any uses of plastics that would contribute to waste products? List them and explain your choices.
      (ii) Can you suggest alternatives to reduce the amount of plastic waste products?
5. Prepare a column graph using the information in the table below on the amount of energy required by males and females for various activities.

   (a) Why do you think males use more energy per hour than females for the same activity?
   (b) The following list shows the activities for an average female for one day. How many kilojoules would this female need to consume to provide the energy for the day's activities?

Activity	Number of hours
sleeping	8
light activity	4
sitting, reading and desk work	10
gardening	1
basketball	1

   (c) If an average male spent a similar day, how much energy would he need?

Amount of energy required for various activities

Activity	Energy used per hour by average female — 58 kg (kJ)	Energy used per hour by average male — 70 kg (kJ)
sleeping	240	300
sitting, reading, desk work and studying	360	450
light activity, such as driving, playing piano and standing with only arms moving	480	600
walking slowly and gardening; working as a shop assistant or machinist	720	900
physical work, such as factory or farm labouring; sports, such as cycling, tennis and cricket	960	1200
heavy physical work, such as loading, stacking and carrying; vigorous sports, such as jogging, basketball, hockey and football. (Activity that leads to sweating.)	1440	1800
very heavy physical work and vigorous sports, such as football, hockey, running and swimming. (Activity that causes free sweating, requiring short bursts of extreme energy.)	2400–4800	3000–7200

Drawing a line graph

There are a number of things you need to remember when drawing a line graph to make the graph easier for a reader to understand, such as a clear title and correct labels on the axes. The diagram below outlines the parts of a typical line graph.

1. Grid. Graphs should always be drawn on grid paper to ensure that the values are accurately placed. Drawing freehand on lined or plain paper is not accurate enough for most graphs.

2. Title. Tell the reader what the graph is about! The title should describe the results of the investigation or the relationship between variables.

3. Setting up and labelling the axes. Graphs represent a relationship between two variables. When choosing which variable to put on each axis, remember that there is usually an independent variable (which the investigator chooses) and a dependent variable. For example, if students wished to find out how far a runner could run in 15 seconds, they may choose to measure the distance covered every five seconds. The time of each measurement has been chosen by the students, and is the independent variable. The distance that is measured is therefore the dependent variable. Usually the independent variable is plotted on the horizontal x-axis and the dependent variable on the vertical y-axis.

After deciding on the variable for each axis, you must clearly label the axes with the variable and the units in which the variables are measured. These units are written in brackets after the name of the variable.

4. Setting up the scales. Each axis should be marked off into units which cover the entire range of the measurement. For example, if the distance ranged from 0 m to 96 m, then 0 m and 100 m could be the lowest and highest values on the vertical scale. The distance between top and bottom values is then broken up into equal divisions and marked. The horizontal axis must also have its own range of values and uniform scale (which does not have to be the same scale as the vertical axis).

The most important points about the scales are:
• they must show the entire range of measurements
• they must be uniform, that is, show equal divisions for equal increases in value.

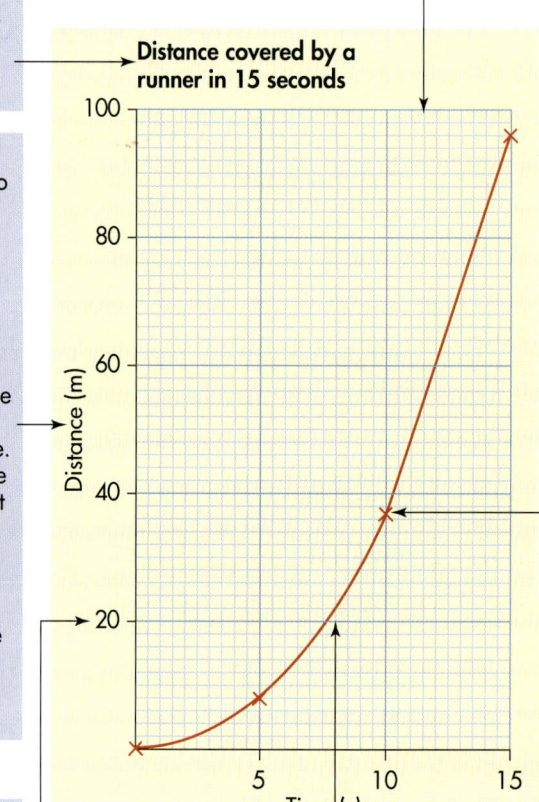

Distance covered by a runner in 15 seconds

5. Putting in the values. A point is made for each pair of values (the meeting point of two imaginary lines from each axis). The points should be clearly visible. Include a point for (0, 0) only if you have the data for this point.

Data table

Distance (m)	Time (s)
0	0
8	5
37	10
96	15

6. Drawing the line. A line is then drawn through the points. A line that follows the general direction of the points is called a 'line of best fit' because it best fits the data. It should be on or as close to as many points as possible. Some points follow the shape of a curve, rather than a straight line. A curved line that touches all the points can then be used.

The type of data you are graphing may lead you to expect either a straight line or a curve. For example, you might expect the temperature increase of water being boiled to be presented as a straight line because the temperature increases at a steady rate. The growth rate of a red panda (see page 217) would be curved because the panda will have growth spurts. Inspection of the data will help you to decide whether your line should be a straight line or a smooth, curved line.

The parts of a line graph

Try this DRAWING A LINE GRAPH

A student conducted an experiment to see how temperature affected the amount of sugar that would dissolve in a cup of tea. Each cup contained the same volume of tea, and the sugar was stirred in at an equal rate for each cup. The following results were obtained:

Amount of sugar dissolved in one cup of tea

Mass of sugar dissolved (g)	Temperature (°C)
4	0
30	20
60	40
98	60
120	80
160	100

Graph the data in the table above using the steps and diagrams below.

1. Set up the grid.

2. Give the graph a title.

Effect of temperature on the amount of sugar dissolved in tea

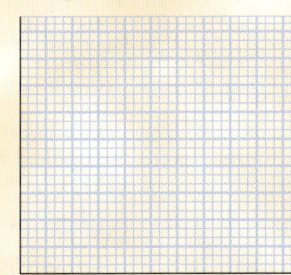

3. Set up the axes and label them.
4. Place the scales on the axes.

Effect of temperature on the amount of sugar dissolved in tea

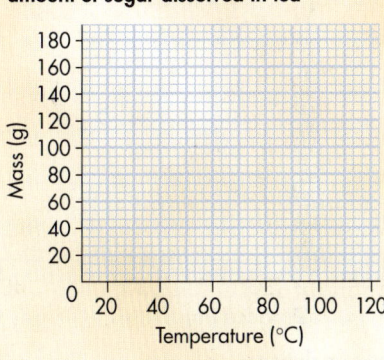

5. Plot each pair of values as a point marked with an **x**. Make sure each part is clearly visible. Don't forget to plot (0, 4) because you have the data for this point.

Effect of temperature on the amount of sugar dissolved in tea

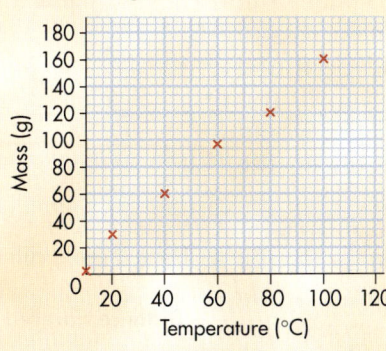

6. Draw a line of best fit, that is, a line drawn in between the points so that some points are on the line, some are below it and some are above.

Effect of temperature on the amount of sugar dissolved in tea

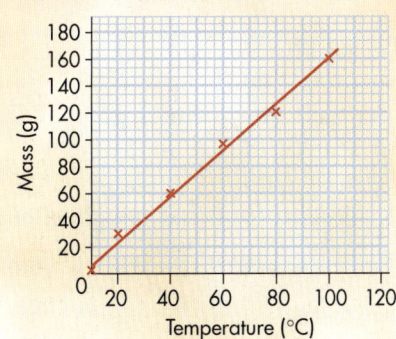

Activities

1. The data in the following table relate the speed of a car to its stopping distance (the distance the car travels after the brakes are applied).

Relationship between the speed of a car and its stopping distance

Speed of car (m/s)	Stopping distance (m)
0	0
10	12
20	36
30	72
40	120

(a) Graph the data.
(b) Make a conclusion about the information in the graph.
(c) How could this information be applied to your everyday life?

2. The boiling point of water changes with air pressure. For example, water may not boil at 100°C at the top of Mount Everest, where the air pressure is less than the pressure at sea level. The following data show the boiling point of water at various air pressure values.

Boiling point of water at different air pressures

Boiling point of water (°C)	Air pressure in kilopascals (kPa)
0	0
20	1
40	7
60	21
80	45
100	101
120	200

(a) Graph the data.
(b) Describe the shape of your graph.
(c) What is the pressure of the atmosphere at sea level?
(d) Would it take a longer or shorter time to boil water at the top of Mount Everest, compared to the time it would take at sea level? Explain your answer.

Using line graphs

Consider the experiment on page 215 on dissolving sugar in tea. In what ways could you interpret this graph? What can you say about it? You could say that as the temperature rises, more sugar will dissolve, but this could just as easily be read from the data table. Line graphs, however, do not always have a straight line. Graphs may have curved lines, lines that climb steeply and then level off or lines that form peaks or troughs. Data that form such line graphs may not be easy to understand in table form.

S C I F A C T S

The word 'graph' means something drawn or written and is widely used in many different subject areas. 'Graphics' means drawings and diagrams which may be done by hand, instrument or computer. Graphic art is art using lines and strokes.

Interpolation

By studying the graph in the previous example, you can also work out the amount of sugar that would dissolve for temperatures other than those actually measured in the experiment. This is called **interpolation**, that is, finding the value of one variable using any value from the other variable range. For example, if you wanted to find out the amount of sugar that dissolves when the tea is heated to 50°C, you could draw a vertical line up from 50°C on the x-axis to meet the graphed line, and then a horizontal line across to the (vertical) y-axis. The value would be found at the point where this line meets the y-axis. You could say that at 50°C, 80 grams of sugar would dissolve (see dotted line 1 in the graph on the right).

Similarly, if you wanted to know what temperature is required to dissolve 130 grams of sugar, you could use the same method. You would find that 130 grams of sugar would dissolve when the temperature is 80°C (see dotted line 2 in the graph on the right).

Extrapolation

In many cases it is also possible to assume that the two variables will hold the same relationship beyond the values that have been plotted. This is called **extrapolation**. Consider the graph on the right. It shows the amount of force that needs to be applied to pull a block a certain distance. Values have been plotted up to a force of 1.3 newtons and a distance of 32 cm. If you wanted to predict the amount of force needed to make the block move 40 cm, the line on the graph can be projected onwards (as the dotted lines show). This extrapolation shows that a force of 1.6 newtons will move the block 40 cm.

Effect of temperature on the amount of sugar dissolved in tea

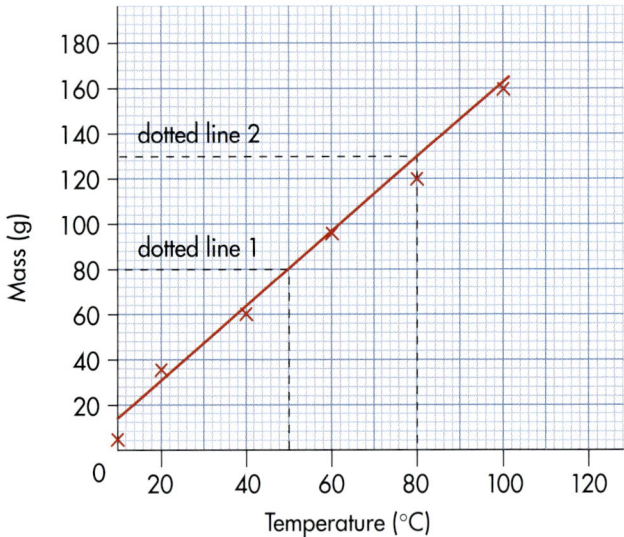

Using a line graph for interpolation

Distance travelled when different forces are applied to a block

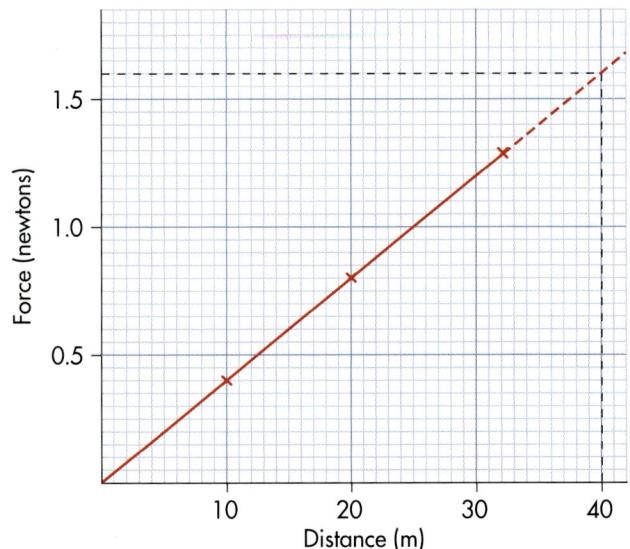

Using a line graph for extrapolation

Activities

1. The following graph shows the increase in mass of a growing plant.

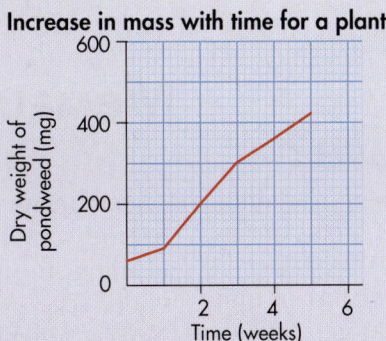

Increase in mass with time for a plant

(a) What was the mass of the plant after $3\frac{1}{2}$ weeks of growth?
(b) How long did it take for the plant to grow to 250 grams?
(c) Predict the mass of the plant after 6 weeks of growth.
(d) Can you be sure that your extrapolation for question (c) is accurate? Suggest reasons why it may not be accurate.
(e) Would the interpolations from questions (a) and (b) be more accurate than your extrapolation? Discuss your ideas in class.

2. Singalia and Sallyana are two red panda cubs born at Sydney's Taronga Zoo. The table below shows their masses during their first 22 weeks. The photograph above right shows one of the cubs being weighed.

Red panda cubs' masses (grams)

Week	Singalia	Sallyana
1	213	219
2	285	290
3	330	349
4	365	377
5	403	408
6	465	452
7	536	514
8	564	576
9	594	610
10	650	637
11	703	680
12	714	740
13	814	796
14	872	812
15	956	806
16	1111	786
17	1043	890
18	1130	1000
19	1163	1083
20	1182	1162
21	1225	1218
22	1335	1270

(a) Graph both sets of data onto a grid. Use different symbols for the points for each panda and label each line with the panda's name. You may have to extend the vertical axis to fit in the scale for the pandas' masses (or else convert the masses to kilograms and plot in kilograms).
(b) Describe the growth of each of the panda cubs. How do they compare with each other?
(c) How long did it take the cubs to double their mass measured in week 1?
(d) Did the pandas grow at the same rate during the 22 weeks?
(e) Which were the fastest and slowest growth periods for each panda?
(f) What age were each of the cubs when they reached 1 kg?
(g) At what age would you predict each cub to reach 1.5 kg? Explain how you made your prediction. What assumption did you make to answer the question?

3. Jane and Greg decided to test how quickly water would boil when using either the yellow flame or blue flame of the Bunsen burner. They set up identical experiments, except that Jane used a blue flame and Greg used a yellow flame. Their results are graphed below.

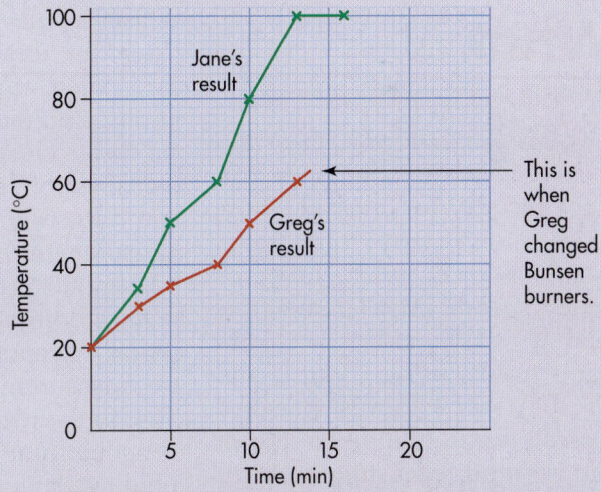

(a) How long did it take for Jane's water to boil?
(b) What was the temperature of Greg's water when Jane's water boiled?
(c) In your own words, explain how you worked out the answers for these two questions.
(d) Jane removed her beaker and Greg quickly placed his beaker over Jane's Bunsen burner. Assuming that the temperature of Greg's beaker did not drop while swapping Bunsen burners, predict the time at which his water would boil. Using your own words, explain how you predicted this.

Measurement—the basics

The mass is equal but what about the volume?

Measurement — it's a skill!

What *is measurement?*

If you do it accurately, measurement gives you a number you can record to answer how much, how many, how long, what distance, what mass or what speed. Measurement is vital to a scientist, who compares results using controls and variables. It removes personal biases because the measurement can be repeated using the same measuring instrument.

Why *measure?*

Measurements allow you to describe your observations using units and numbers. This allows you and others to repeat experiments and accurately compare results.

When *do we measure?*

You will be surprised how often you use measurements during each day. Your school day is measured out in periods of time and at work people get paid by a measure of the hours or days that they have worked. How many other examples of measurements can you think of?

In science, measurements are commonly used in experiments and are very important when drawing conclusions.

How *do we measure?*

You first need to make a decision about the accuracy required for your measurements. In science you usually require accurate measurements so that others can repeat the experiment and compare their results with your results. You then need to choose the best measuring instrument available for the task and learn how to use it correctly to avoid measurement errors.

Scientific measurements need to have both **accuracy** and **precision**. Accurate measurements are measurements that are as close to the real value as possible using the best measuring instrument available. If your measurement has precision, then you will be able to get the same result several times. Accuracy has to do with the quality of the measuring device, while precision depends on your measurement skills.

The golden rule for measuring is to be thorough. Record all results and repeat your measurements so that you are confident of your results.

Measurement *standards*

Measurement standards ensure that measurements have the same meaning in different parts of the world. The Australian standards of mass, length, time, voltage and other quantities in the metric system are kept at the National Measurement Laboratory in Lindfield, New South Wales. Australia's copy of the standard kilogram, Copy Number 44, is an exact duplicate of the International Prototype Kilogram kept in Paris. Number 44 is sent back to Paris about once every 20 years to check that it is still accurate.

The laboratory's standards are used to set the values of high accuracy measuring equipment. This equipment is then used by other calibration laboratories across Australia to set the values of measuring equipment used in trade and industry. This means that any measurements made in Australia, using traceable reference standards, are comparable with those in other countries which have a similar measurement system.

Australia's Copy Number 44 of the standard kilogram is made of a platinum-iridium alloy.

Base *units of* measurement

For a measurement to be useful, everyone must understand and agree on the units used. An international system which has seven base units was adopted by international agreement in 1960. This system is called SI after the French name, Le Système Internationale d'Unités. This system of measurement units is used by scientists throughout the world.

Base unit	Symbol	Quantity
kilogram	kg	mass
metre	m	length
second	s	time
kelvin	K	temperature
mole	mol	amount of substance
ampere	A	electric current
candela	cd	luminous intensity

All measurements must contain both a number and a unit. Prefixes are used to express smaller or larger multiples of the base unit. So a *centi*metre equals 100th of a metre and a gram equals 1000th of a *kilo*gram. List some other measurement units that you know or commonly use, and see if you can relate them to a base unit.

Kelvin

Kelvin is the standard base unit for temperature, but Celsius is most often used in school experiments, weather reports and other everyday activities involving the measurement of temperatures. Celsius is easily converted to kelvin by adding the figure 273. So 25°C equals 298 K.

Activities

1. List all the measurements you have made in the past week. Separate your list into two groups:
   (a) measurements that needed to be accurate
   (b) measurements that were just general and required little accuracy.
2. This section is about making accurate measurements. For all the accurate measurements you have made in the past week, list the equipment you used to make the measurements.
3. For the following activities, explain some possible consequences if the measurements involved were not made accurately. Present your answers in a table.
   (a) a cake divided into eight pieces
   (b) a blood sugar reading made by a diabetic person
   (c) ingredients for a stir-fry recipe
   (d) time spent in the sun with sunscreen on
   (e) number of pills given to a patient
   (f) time film is exposed to light
   (g) distance for a 400 m sprint.
4. What does Australia use as standards for time, length and mass?
5. The following organisations make up Australia's national measurement system:
   • the National Measurement Institute
   • the National Association of Testing Authorities (Australia)
   • Standards Australia.
   Find out about each of these organisations. What is their role? Where are they located?
6. Make a list of the names of measuring equipment used at school and outside school. Include the units used by each piece of equipment.
7. Find the meaning of the following prefixes used with base units.
tera	hecto	milli
giga	deca	micro
mega	deci	nano
kilo	centi	pico
8. Convert the following to kelvin.
   (a) 0°C   (b) 40°C
   (c) 15°C   (d) −10°C
9. What would 0 K (zero kelvin) read in degrees Celsius?

Measuring skills

Successful measurements are a result of your measuring skills and your ability to correctly use the measuring instrument. The following skills will make your measurements more accurate and precise. Keep these in mind whenever you are measuring.

Measuring skills
1. Choosing the best instrument for the job
2. Using the instrument correctly
3. Identifying and avoiding measurement errors
4. Knowing the outside factors that might influence your result
5. Recording your results accurately

Choosing the best instrument for the job

Knowing the accuracy of your measuring instrument allows you to pick the best instrument for your purpose. Accuracy relates to how well an instrument measures or compares to the standard. A 30 cm plastic ruler for everyday use does not require a high degree of accuracy, unlike a measuring device used in business or trade.

This one is best. I only want to measure 5 mL

Using the instrument correctly

Measuring instruments are designed to give the best results possible when used correctly. They are often delicate and require careful handling.

How to use an electronic balance.

Identifying and avoiding measurement errors

Measurement errors happen either when the wrong instrument is used or when the operator has been careless. A scientist makes many measurements each day. It is important to understand how to avoid making measurement errors. Even if you recognise that you have made an error, you should still record the measurement and then explain why the result is incorrect and should not be included in your results.

Experiment S.1 UNDERSTANDING MEASUREMENT ERRORS

YOU WILL NEED
30 cm ruler and metre ruler
tape measure and trundle wheel
paper and chalk
beam balance and electronic balance
10 mL, 25 mL, 50 mL and 100 mL measuring cylinders
salt

Cumulative error
- Draw two lines 20 cm long. For the first line, measure and draw it in one step. For the second line, draw it in sections by joining up 20 × 1 cm lines.
- Use three different instruments to measure 2 metres.

Parallax error
- Mark a dot on a page.
- Place the zero mark of a ruler at the dot, then place your head on the table at the zero mark. Look along the ruler and place a dot at 20 cm.
- Now sit up and look directly down at the ruler and mark off at 20 cm.

Operator error
- Find three different ways to measure the same 5 g of salt.
- Transfer 10 mL of water four times using different measuring cylinders and ending with the water in the original cylinder.

Meniscus
- Using a 5 or 10 mL measuring cylinder and an eye-dropper, count how many drops of water there are in 2 mL of water.
  Compare your results with other members of the class.

1. Explain why you had different measurements in each of these four experiments.
2. What can you do to avoid measurement errors?

Knowing the outside factors that might influence the result

Now that you know how to use measuring instruments correctly and how to avoid errors, let's think about other factors that could affect your results.

1. Temperature can have a big effect on the measurement of volume. The amount of space a substance takes up is different depending on the temperature. To make the measurement information complete, you need to include the temperature of the substance being measured. For example, when a block of dry ice is taken from the freezer and placed inside a rubber glove at room temperature, the rubber glove will expand as the dry ice warms up and turns into a gas.

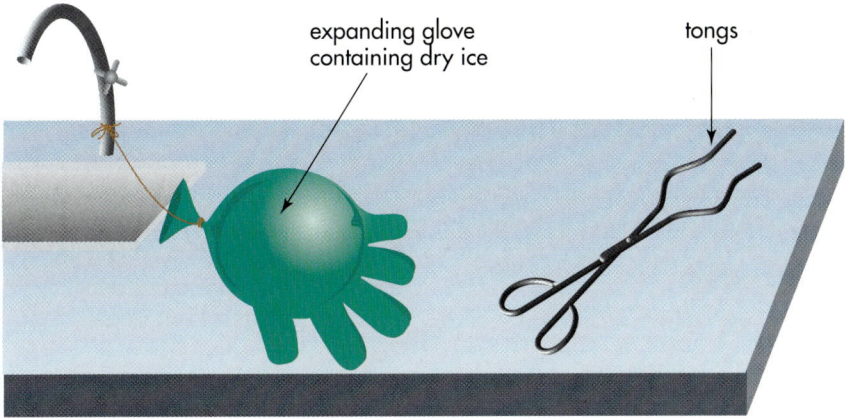

expanding glove containing dry ice

tongs

When dry ice warms up, it expands.

2. Humidity could affect a measurement. If the substance you are measuring combines with water from the air, it may increase in mass and you will no longer be measuring only what you intended to measure. For example, if sodium hydroxide (caustic soda) is left exposed to the air for long enough, it will absorb enough water from the air to look like a puddle. You would need to complete your measurement quickly to ensure the least possible exposure to air.

3. Dust or any other contamination in a weighing container could be a factor when measuring a powder. It can change the mass of the substance you are measuring.

4. Vibrations will affect the efficiency of balances, so they are usually placed on firm counters such as concrete benches.

Science laboratories are designed to take all of these factors into account. They control temperature and humidity and are kept very clean. Measurement instruments are kept in specially designed areas to ensure that they give the most accurate result when used correctly.

Recording your results accurately

It is useful to decide how you will record your measurement before you start to measure. A table format usually works well. It is recommended that you draw up an appropriate table before you begin to measure, and then record your results directly into the table. This avoids any errors in copying figures from one piece of paper to another. Remember to include units for each measurement and record your measurements in significant figures.

Significant figures

Significant figures consist of the numbers you are sure of in your measurement, plus one last number that you estimate. For example, when weighing objects on a balance that has one gram intervals, the needle may show a measurement between the intervals. Look at the balance indication shown in the diagram below. As the measurement is somewhere between 50 grams and 51 grams, you could estimate the result. In this example, your result is more accurate if it is reported as 50.8 grams, rather than just 50 grams.

What measurement is shown?

Similarly, the thermometer shown in the diagram below is calibrated to measure in one degree intervals. You could estimate to get the result 48.8°C.

What temperature is shown?

It is important to remember that your measuring instrument must be capable of measuring at the accuracy you require. For example, a student completing a student research project was measuring the amount of caffeine in different drinks. Initially, he found that he could not measure any differences using the equipment in his school laboratory. He realised it was his equipment rather than his technique that was the problem. He then approached an analytical laboratory to ask if he could use their more accurate equipment. His results then became quite significant and allowed him to draw an excellent conclusion to his project.

Activities

1. Try measuring 5 mL of any liquid using 10 mL, 50 mL and 100 mL measuring cylinders.
   (a) Which one is most accurate? Explain your answer.
   (b) What rules would you apply in future for this sort of measurement?
2. (a) Complete the activity for each measuring instrument in the table to the right. Your teacher will first show you how to use each one correctly, and explain how to avoid errors.
   (b) In your workbook, draw each instrument and write some hints for correct use next to each drawing.
3. Find out what a micrometer and vernier calliper are used for. What units do they measure?
4. How do you measure speed and density? What are the correct units for each?
5. What unit is used to measure force?
6. A group of students measured the outside of their textbook using a ruler and obtained the following results.

	Length (mm)	Width (mm)
Student 1	280	215
Student 2	276	215
Student 3	275	210
Student 4	280	220
Student 5	280	210
Student 6	280	215
Mean	278.5	214.1

They worked out the mean for their results and thought this might be a good answer for the correct dimensions of the textbook.
   (a) Can you list some reasons for the different results?
   (b) What would you do to find the correct dimensions of this textbook?
   (c) How could you ensure the greatest accuracy for this measurement?
7. Examine a range of measuring instruments and find out the uncertainty of each. Put your results into a table.

Instrument	Activity
A thermometer	• Measure the temperature of water as it boils. • Measure the temperature in: (a) your room or classroom (b) the refrigerator (c) the freezer.
A measuring cylinder	• Measure 5 mL, 50 mL and 100 mL of water. • Explain 'meniscus' to a friend.
A multi-arm beam balance	• Carry out experiment 1.7 'How well can you measure mass and volume?' on page 21.
A stopwatch	• Measure time for a friend as the friend counts his or her pulse for one minute. • Measure the time taken to run a certain distance.
A tape measure, ruler and trundle wheel	• Use all three instruments to measure the width of your classroom. • Compare your results with others. Which instrument would give the most accurate result?
A burette, volumetric (or conical) flask and pipette	• Your teacher may wish to demonstrate these instruments.

Using data loggers

What is a data logger?

A data logger is a type of scientific recording instrument. It collects and stores measurements. These measurements are called **data** because they are numbers. A data logger has to be attached to a measuring instrument called a **sensor**. The sensor does the measuring and sends the measurements to the data logger.

The real advantage of working with a data logger is that it can store thousands of individual measurements. The measurements can be taken in quick succession or over a long period of time, and the data logger can be programmed to do this automatically. This is why scientists often use data loggers in their work. Of course, to be at all useful, the stored measurements must be easily accessed. That is why the data logger is also attached to either a computer or an instrument called a graphics calculator. The computer or calculator takes the data and, using special software that comes with the data logger, it shows the data as a table, a graph or both.

Using data loggers to measure temperature

You might remember an experiment in chapter 1 (experiment 1.6, page 16) that involved heating water in a beaker. The measuring instrument you used was a thermometer (see page 17). You looked at the thermometer every minute and observed the temperature, which you wrote down in a table. You then made a line graph of temperature against time. If you used a data logger with a temperature sensor instead of the thermometer, then it could have taken the temperature every second and sent it to a computer which would have automatically tabulated the temperature data and graphed it as well.

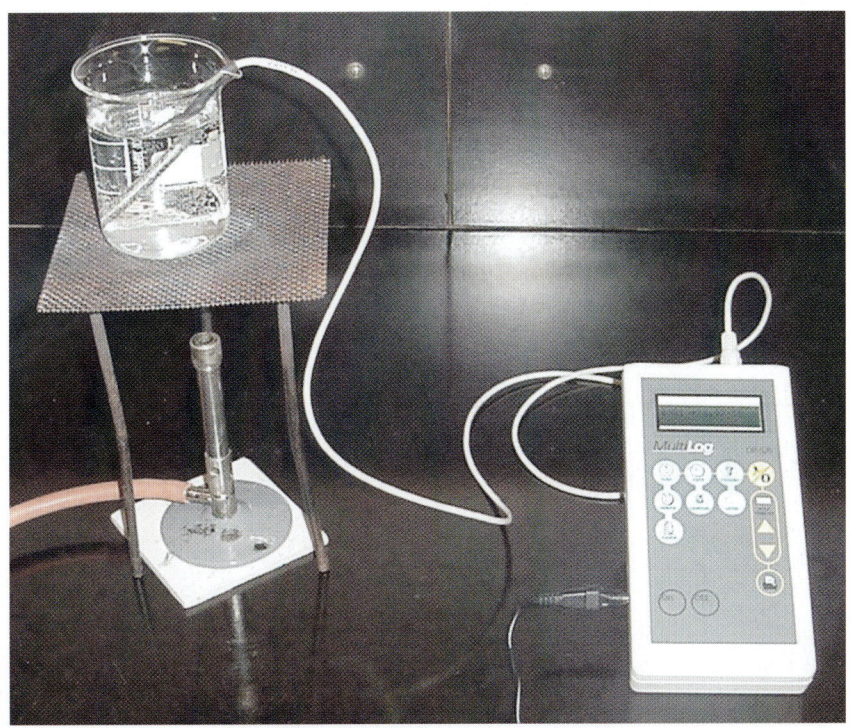

A data logger and temperature sensor being used to record the temperature rise of water in a beaker being heated to boiling point

Data loggers are attached to sensors that take the measurements, and to computers that can show the data in tables and graphs.

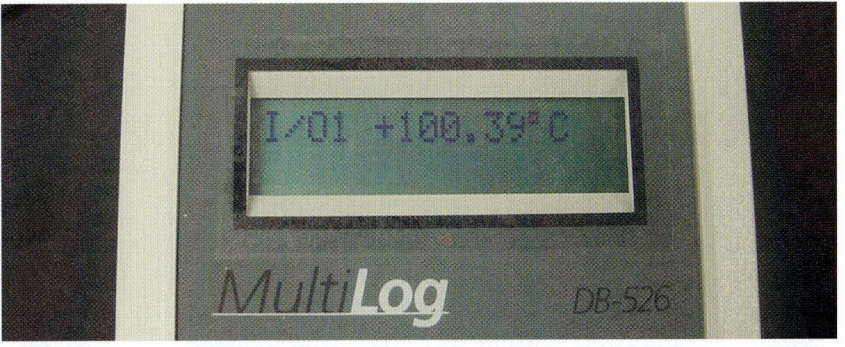

The screen on the data logger shows the current temperature of the water.

Other *uses for data* loggers

Data loggers can be used for just about any experiment where measurements are taken. All that is needed is the appropriate sensor to be plugged in. It is even possible to plug in several sensors to take different measurements at the same time.

Some of the many different sensors that are available include:
- temperature sensors capable of measuring several hundred degrees
- light intensity sensors
- sound wave sensors (microphones)
- motion sensors
- magnetic field sensors
- acceleration sensors
- force sensors
- electric current and voltage sensors
- humidity sensors
- blood pressure sensors
- heart rate sensors.

One type of sensor that isn't necessary is a time sensor (stopwatch) because the data logger has its own inbuilt clock which is very accurate. In fact, one of the most useful things about data loggers is their ability to collect measurements at very small and precise time intervals, even as many as a thousand measurements in one second!

Activities

Using data

The computer screen below shows data collected by a data logger for the experiment in which water is heated to boiling point in a beaker. A temperature sensor was used to take the measurements.

If you were at this computer, you could scroll through every temperature measurement in the table. The computer has graphed all these data. Now let's see how much you've learnt about interpreting line graphs.

1. How often did the data logger collect temperature readings?
2. How long did the whole experiment go for?
3. How many individual temperature readings has the data logger stored?
4. About when did the heating of the water begin?
5. What was the temperature of the water when heating began?

6. What was the temperature of the water when heating finished?
7. About when did the water begin to boil?
8. Between 100 and 400 seconds, at what rate (in degrees per second) did the water temperature rise during heating?

Think

1. The water continued to be heated even when its temperature reached boiling point, yet its temperature did not rise beyond 100°C. What has happened to all the energy that was being put into the water if it isn't causing the water temperature to rise? (*Hint*: Remember the particle model of matter.)
2. If you are at home boiling water for an egg, is there any point in leaving the hot plate on high once the water has reached boiling point? Will the egg cook any quicker? Explain.

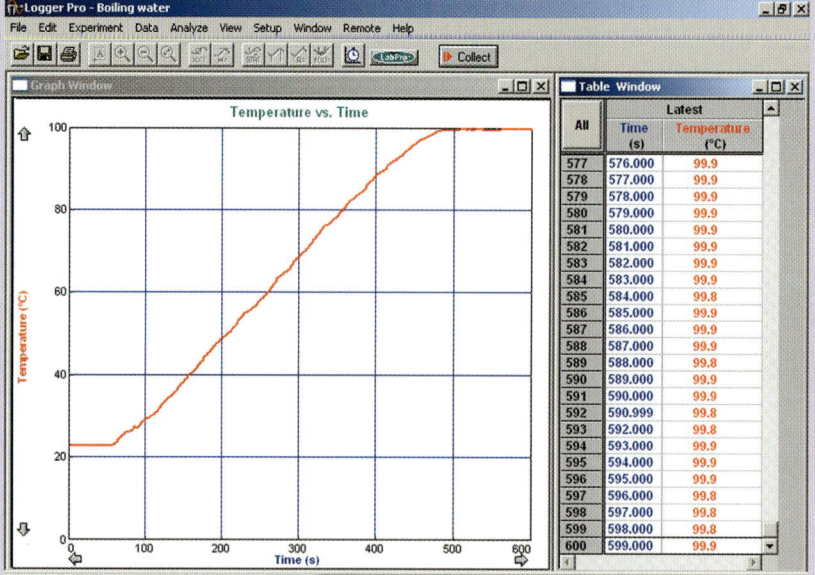

Using databases

What *is a* database?

You use **databases** all the time without even thinking about them. When you look up a phone number in the White Pages, you are using a database of people in your city or town who have telephones. When you look up a book's table of contents, you are looking at a database of the chapter names and the page numbers where you can find them. The index at the back of books and your train or bus timetables are also databases.

The phone book is a huge database of people with telephones in your city or town.

Another way of thinking of a database is to describe it as a 'table of data'. Of course, you have been making tables of data yourself all year. (Maybe you have worked through some of the activities in *Preparing tables* on pages 208–10.) A telephone book is a huge table with three columns of data — names, addresses and telephone numbers. The contents of a book is a table with just two columns — chapter titles and page numbers.

A database can also be called a 'catalogue'. A complete list and description of a company's goods for sale is called a catalogue; so is the list of the books, magazines and other material in your school or local library.

Electronic *databases*

A database on paper has limitations. You can cross-reference only two things and then usually only in a specific order. For example, you can look up a person's telephone number easily only if you first look up their name and address. You can't do the reverse — that is, you can't look up a phone number and find out the name of the person who has that number (unless, of course, you have a lot of time and patience).

For this reason, most databases are now stored electronically. To find a library book we can go to a computer — it doesn't even have to be physically in the library — and click on the library's catalogue. We can perform a **search** for topics, authors, date of publication and more. We can **refine** our search and perhaps look for just magazine articles or videos. We can even read a short summary (synopsis) of each article. This is all possible because computers are very good at storing lots and lots of data and retrieving it very quickly.

Unlike a database on paper, a computer can store data (such as the topic and author of a book) in a table with as many columns as we like and it can search any one of the columns rather than just the first one. And it does all this very quickly. The only problem is that a computer can't actually think, so it is up to the person who designs the database to do so very thoughtfully so that it will be easy to search.

HMM, let's do a search of your favourite food.

Computers can't think for themselves, so database designers need to make sure that the database is easy to search.

Why use an electronic database in science?

Scientists often have huge amounts of data that they need to organise and search (or allow others to search). For example, the scientists who help the police to solve crimes are called forensic scientists. They know that a substance called DNA, which is found in every one of our cells, is unique to each human being; that is, no two people on the planet have the same DNA unless they are identical twins. Forensic scientists are setting up a database of DNA from convicted criminals which helps police to crack unsolved crimes. Police can compare any DNA in tissue found at crime scenes with the DNA database.

As each person on the planet has a unique set of DNA, police can solve crimes by matching DNA samples from crime scenes to DNA information stored on a database.

Astronomers are scientists who study some of the millions of stars and galaxies in our universe. The huge amount of information they gather is organised in computer databases so that they, or other astronomers around the world, can search the data to use in their research projects.

Designing *databases*

Just as a table is made up of columns and rows, so too is a database — except that we call the columns **fields** and the rows **records**. If we made the telephone directory into a computer database then it would have three fields: name, address and telephone number. Each person's details would then be a record. It would look something like screen A below.

Activities

Using data

Making a database of the planets

If you remember back to when you studied the planets of our solar system in chapter 8, you will recall that we know quite a bit about each one. Much of this information has been summarised in pages 166 to 169 and might be quite easy to put in a table. Before you begin designing any table or database, you must plan your fields (columns).

Let's set up the following fields:
- order from the sun
- planet
- type of planet
- distance to sun
- diameter
- period of rotation
- period of orbit
- surface gravity
- surface temperature
- satellites.

The database called Microsoft Access® is used by many companies and scientists. If it is installed, you will probably find it on your computer's desktop by clicking *Start* then *Programs*. The icon for Access is shown below. Ask your teacher if you need help locating the program.

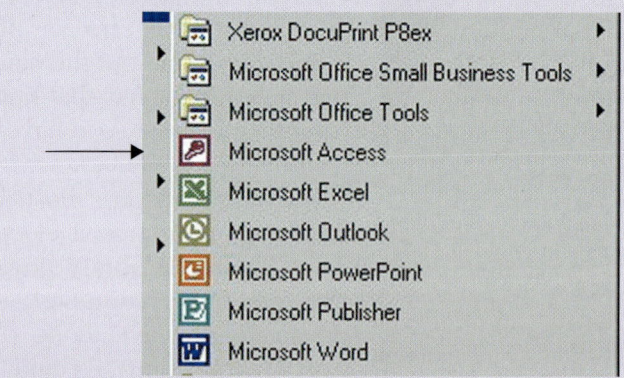

1. Click on the icon and Access will open. If it starts with a box asking whether you want to *Open an existing file*, click on *Blank Access database*, then click *OK*.

   You will then see a box which prompts you to give your new database file a name. Call the file 'Planets.mdb' and click *Create*. Save it somewhere that you'll remember.

   (continued)

Screen A

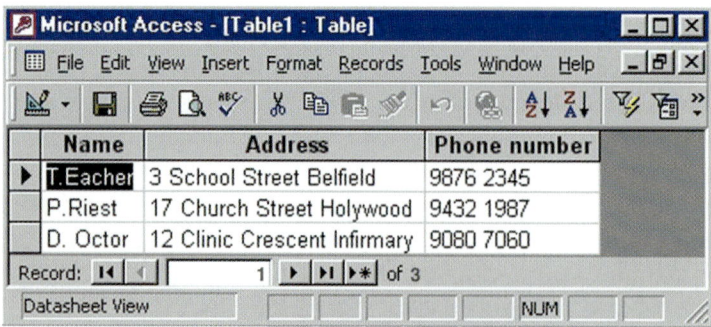

2. Now another dialogue box will give you several alternatives for creating the table which the database will rely on for information. Double click *Create table in Design View*.

   Your screen should look like screen B below.

3. What you see is called a **table**. It's time to enter the names of the fields. This is just like writing the headings for the columns in a table in your exercise book. For convenience we will let the **data type** be *Text* even though most of our information will be numbers. It is a good idea to write a brief **description** of the field. Enter your field information so that it looks like screen C below.

4. You are in what Access calls Design View. You now need to be in Datasheet View. Click on the arrow next to the *View* icon under the *File* menu. It looks like this:

Click on *Datasheet View*. You will be asked to save the table. Give it a meaningful name like 'Planet info'. You may be asked to nominate a **primary key**. At this stage just click *No*.

5. You are now ready to enter the relevant information about the planets. The complete row of information is called a record. In Datasheet View just type in the information and press the *'Right arrow'* to go to the next field and press *'Enter'* to go to the next record. When you have finished entering data, your datasheet should look like screen D below.

Congratulations! You have successfully created your first database. It is what we call a **flat file database**. Don't forget to save it and remember where it is because you can use it and add to it later.

Just as an example of the power of a database and the sort of things you can do with it, let's ask the planets database to sort some information for us.

Screen B

Screen C

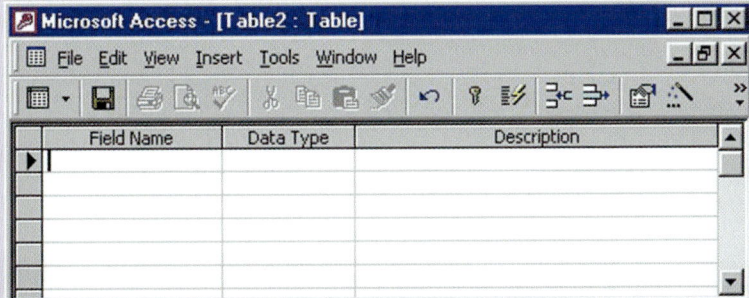

Screen D

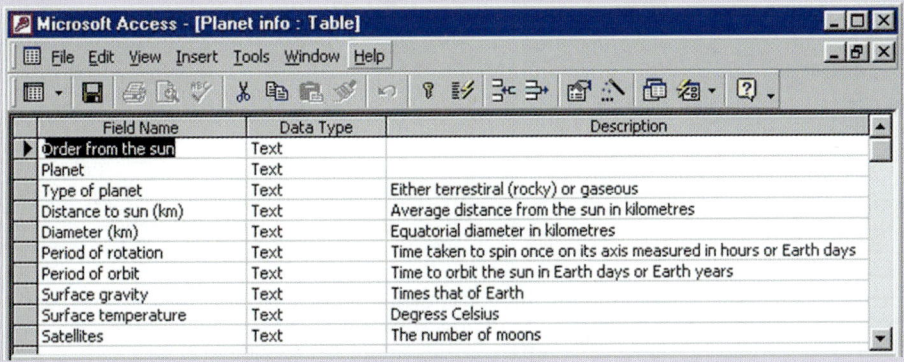

Order	Planet	Type of planet	Distance to sun	Diameter	Period of rotation	Period of orbit	Surface gravity
1	Mercury	Terrestrial	58 000 000	4 900	59 Earth days	88 Earth days	0.38
2	Venus	Terrestrial	108 000 000	12 100	243 Earth days	225 Earth days	0.91
3	Earth	Terrestrial	150 000 000	12 700	1 Earth day	365 Earth days	1
4	Mars	Terrestrial	228 000 000	6 800	24.5 hours	687 Earth days	0.38
5	Jupiter	Gaseous	778 000 000	142 700	10 hours	12 Earth years	2.9
6	Saturn	Gaseous	1 425 000 000	120 000	10.7 hours	29.5 Earth years	1.3
7	Uranus	Gaseous	2 867 000 000	50 800	16 hours	84 Earth years	0.93
8	Neptune	Gaseous	4 486 000 000	48 600	16 hours	165 Earth years	1.2

(continued)

We'll run a **query** to find out which planets are terrestrial and their distance from the sun.

6. With your table of planets on the screen, click on the arrow next to the *New object: Autoform icon*. It looks like this:

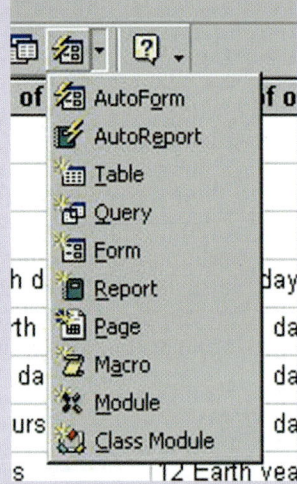

7. Now click on *Query*. Then click on *OK* to open the query in *Design View*, which should look like the screen below. Notice that your planet table fields are visible in a small box.

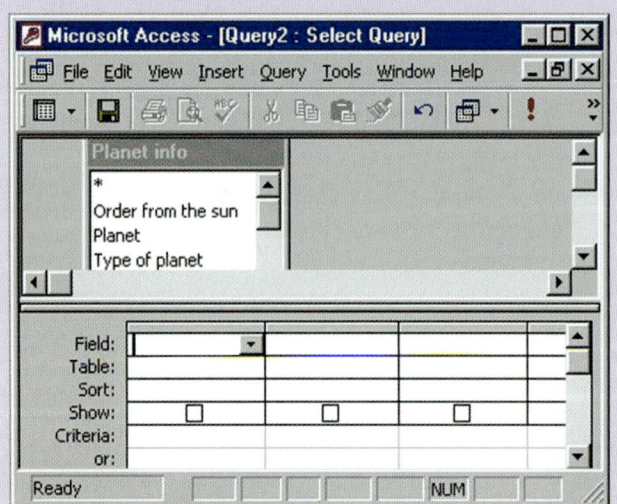

8. Click in the blank box next to *Field*. Click on the arrow to select *Type of planet* from the drop-down list of your field names.
9. Now go down to the blank box next to **Criteria** and type in 'Terrestrial'. Don't tick the little box next to **Show**.
10. Now go back up to the next *Field* box and select *Planet*. Tick the box so that it will *Show*.
11. Finally, select *Distance to Sun* in the next *Field* box and tick the box so that it will *Show*.

You should have a query that looks like the screen below.

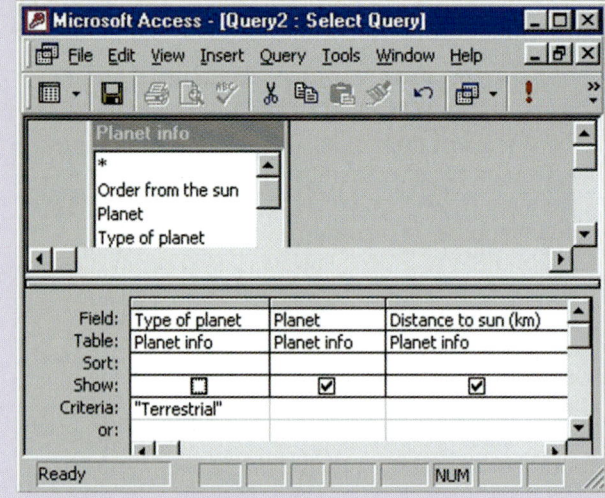

Let's get some answers to our query.

12. Click on the RUN icon in the tool bar. It looks like this:

You should see a little table of the terrestrial planets which looks like the screen below.

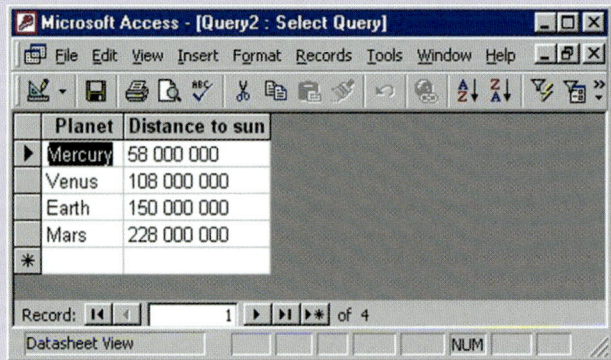

You can save your query if you wish to.

Think

In making the planets database, you may have seen a few patterns or connections between things. Use your database to help you answer the following questions.
1. How does the temperature of a planet vary with its distance from the sun?
2. How does the time it takes a planet to orbit the sun vary with its distance from the sun?
3. How does the gravity of the terrestrial planets vary with their diameter?
4. Is there any connection between the size of a planet and the number of moons that it has?

S.10
Surveys

What *is a* survey?

A survey is a collection of data usually obtained by interviewing people or asking them to write answers on a questionnaire. The questions asked are either about facts, such as the types of sport they play, or opinions, such as the brand of toothpaste they prefer.

Why *use* surveys?

Surveys can provide useful information about the lifestyle, opinions and views of a population. The largest survey in Australia is the Census, which takes place every five years. Every household on the night of the survey completes a questionnaire about the occupation, age, and lifestyle of the people in the house at that time (whether they live there or not). The Census is useful in determining trends in the population

and detecting changes that may have an impact on business, health, politics and other aspects of society.

In business a survey can be used to determine a suitable product for a market or how people feel about an existing product.

In science, surveys are used to determine the social aspects of science — what impact science has on people's lives or how people feel about certain science-based issues, such as space travel or the environment. Science surveys are also widely used to collect factual data and are especially important in the collection of medical data, such as the diseases people have had, immunisation rates and the usage of medication.

Business people, scientists and educators often take action based on the results of surveys. It is therefore important that surveys are performed accurately.

When *should* *we* conduct a survey?

Surveys are conducted when we need to collect information about some aspect of life that involves human opinion or practices.

How *do we* conduct a survey?

The choice of people to be surveyed is very important. For example, in the survey activity

at the end of chapter 8 *The solar system* (page 177) you were to ask people about their memories of the first moon landing in 1969. It is important that the people surveyed were in a suitable age group. (They would need to have been over five-years-old in 1969.) Care should also be taken to interview both males and females from different backgrounds. In other surveys about general issues, it might be important to survey a wide cross-section of the population; that is, people of all ages, occupations and ethnic origins. This is done so that a sample representation of the entire population is obtained. Otherwise, the survey may contain information from a small group that may think differently from the majority of the population.

Designing and carrying out a survey

In designing and carrying out a survey, you will need to do the following:

1. Carefully design your survey questions and conduct a trial run on about five people. This will provide enough feedback to make any necessary adjustments before starting the real survey.
2. At the top of the survey sheet leave spaces for the respondents' sex, age bracket (e.g. 0–20 years, 21–30 years, 31–40 years etc.) and perhaps occupation. Do not ask for the respondents' names and explain that the survey is part of your science project.

3. Make sure that your sample size (number of people surveyed) is not too small. Survey at least 20–30 people. This is because the results for small populations are not statistically valid.

4. Leave spaces after the questions for you or the respondent to write in the responses. You may prefer to complete the survey sheet while talking to the respondent or allow the person to write in his or her own responses. If you want spontaneous opinions, make sure that the answers are written in while you are present, rather than leaving the survey sheet with the respondent. Other surveys may require longer consideration and the survey can be left with the respondent and collected later.

5. If your survey is about a general question, try to interview a cross-section of people, both male and female and across different age brackets.

6. Thank the respondents at the end of the survey.

Analysing *the* results

Now that you have collected the data, you can set up an analysis sheet with spaces for the responses to each question. For example, a question you may have asked for the survey activity on the first moon landing could have been 'In what year was the first moon landing?' The answer is 1969. A possible structure to organise the respondents' answers is a tally system like the one below.

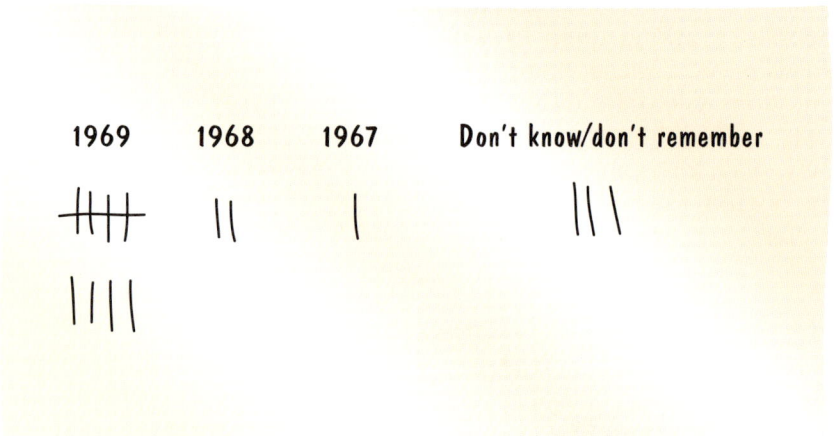

You could then look at the details of the respondents who answered correctly and see if there is any pattern in terms of sex, age group, ethnic origin or type of occupation, and compare them to the respondents who did not answer correctly.

Finally, you could make some conclusions and share your findings with your friends and teacher. You could now discuss the lifestyles and views of the population using the evidence that you have collected.

Topics for science surveys

1. How do aspects of science impact on people's lives? (e.g. 'What effect does the measles vaccination have on people's lives?' or 'What is the impact of water pollution?')

2. Do people know the meaning of scientific words? (e.g. 'Do you know what a solution is?')

3. What do people know about the history of science? (e.g. 'When was electricity discovered?' or 'When was the first heart transplant?')

There are many more questions that you could ask about science. You might like to think up some of your own.

Activities

1. Design a survey to find out the 'big ideas' that people associate with the following famous scientists.

   Galileo Galilei
   Howard Florey
   Louis Pasteur
   Albert Einstein
   Charles Darwin
   John Tebbutt
   Joseph Lister

   James Watson, Francis Crick and Maurice Wilkins
   Isaac Newton
   Peter Doherty
   Marie Curie
   Sir Macfarlane Burnet

   Describe the sample you will use, your survey outline and questions and how you will analyse your results. If you do carry out the survey, you could share or pool the results with other students. How would this be an advantage?

2. Design a survey to find out the diet patterns in the population. Because this is a large and complex area, you may decide to concentrate on a particular aspect of a diet, such as whether all food groups are covered in the diet, or concentrate on the diet of a particular group in the population, such as teenagers. Brainstorm survey ideas in your class or group and then choose one or two areas for your survey. When you have designed the survey, describe the sample, questions and method of analysis.

Drawing and describing

What is drawing and describing?

This is a technique that will enable you to express your views or ideas. It involves drawing a sketch or diagram which shows what you think about an object or event and then adding a short description to explain what you have drawn.

Why draw and describe?

There are a few reasons why drawing and describing helps you to learn.

- It helps you to clarify your thoughts, feelings and ideas about something.
- It may lead to a discussion with classmates so that you can share ideas and perhaps gain more understanding from the discussion.
- Sometimes it helps your teacher to see what you are thinking so that he or she can plan lessons more effectively for you.

When should you draw and describe?

Whenever you come across material that is not easy to visualise or understand.

How do you draw and describe?

Draw the ideas that are in your mind as clearly as you can. Above right is an example to show how drawing and describing works.

What happens when water is heated?

A student, Jim, was asked to draw and describe what happens when water is heated. He knew that water contains particles that consist of two hydrogens and one oxygen. Here is what he did.

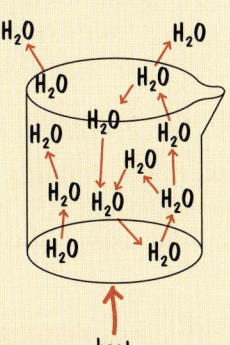

I think the water particles get extra energy when they are heated. I have shown this by the arrows which give the direction of the water movement. The particles can bounce off each other, and some escape from the beaker as a gas.

Activities

1. Try to visualise what's in a grain of sand. Draw and describe it, and share your ideas with your group. You may now like to look up what actually is in a grain of sand at the library or on the Internet.
2. When a can of air freshener is sprayed in one corner of a room, a person in another part of the room can quickly smell it. How does this happen? Do a 'draw and describe' activity to give your explanations, then share your ideas in the class.
   For any 'draw and describe' activities designed by yourself or your teacher, you may wish to pin your completed exercises up in the classroom. These can be reviewed later and you may then wish to change your ideas as you learn more.
3. Draw and describe the following objects.
   (a) A bar of iron, imagining that you can see inside it with 'microscopic' eyes.

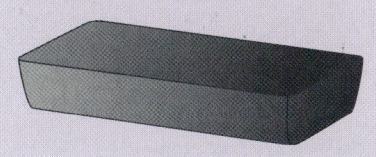

   (b) A beaker of salty water, as if you could see its particles. Salt is sodium chloride. You may want to research its particles before starting.
4. Using the illustrations below draw and describe the forces that you think act on:
   (a) the falling leaf
   (b) the parachutist.

Share your drawings and descriptions with your group. You could also discuss them with your teacher.

Mind and concept maps

What are mind and concept maps?

A mind map or concept map allows you to make connections between ideas or words. A concept map tends to have words in boxes with lines connecting them, while mind maps can include words, images, feelings and much more.

Why use mind and concept maps?

Mind maps and concept maps:
- are useful for making summaries and revision notes
- help you to link what you already know with what you are about to learn
- allow you to graphically display a lot of information
- allow you to be creative
- are an easy way to share ideas when you make one in a group
- let your teacher know what you already know or have learnt
- help you to clarify your ideas and identify any misconceptions you might have
- allow you to think about the connection between concepts and ideas.

When should we use mind maps and concept maps?

Use them anytime that suits you, but always make one at the end of a topic or for revision before a test. They are also useful before you start a topic to clarify what you already know. You can then keep your pre-topic mind map (displaying it where you learn best) and add to it as you are working through the topic.

How to make a concept map

Concept maps connect ideas or concepts. The main concept is usually written in the centre of the space. To get started, try to make connections between the following words:

force   **magnetism**   **iron**

attracts   **magnetic field**

electromagnet

1. Write each word on a square of paper and draw a box around each word.
2. Find any two words that you feel link together. Place them beside each other on a large sheet of paper and draw a line between the words. On the line, write why they are linked.
   For example, one possible linkage could be:

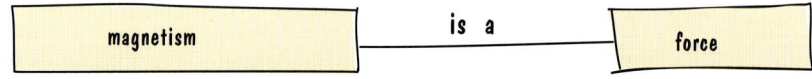

3. Now connect all the words, making as many connections as possible and decide which is the main concept that should be placed in the centre. Remember there are many ways to build connections. With practise, you will get better at knowing which word will be best placed in the centre. This helps to avoid too many cross-over links. Below is an example of a finished concept map.

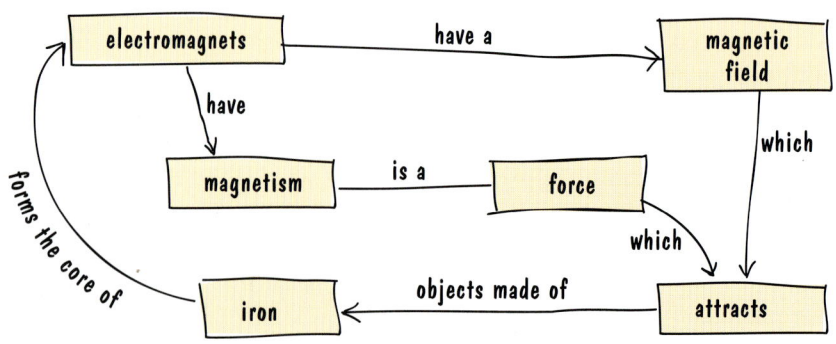

A finished concept map

How to make a mind map

Rule number 1 — Be creative! Use colour, symbols, shapes, locations, feelings — anything that helps you remember. Think of this as mapping what's in your brain and develop your own personal style of mind map. Mind maps can be made by groups of people contributing ideas. This is when mind maps can become really wild and creative.

An example of a mind map is shown below.

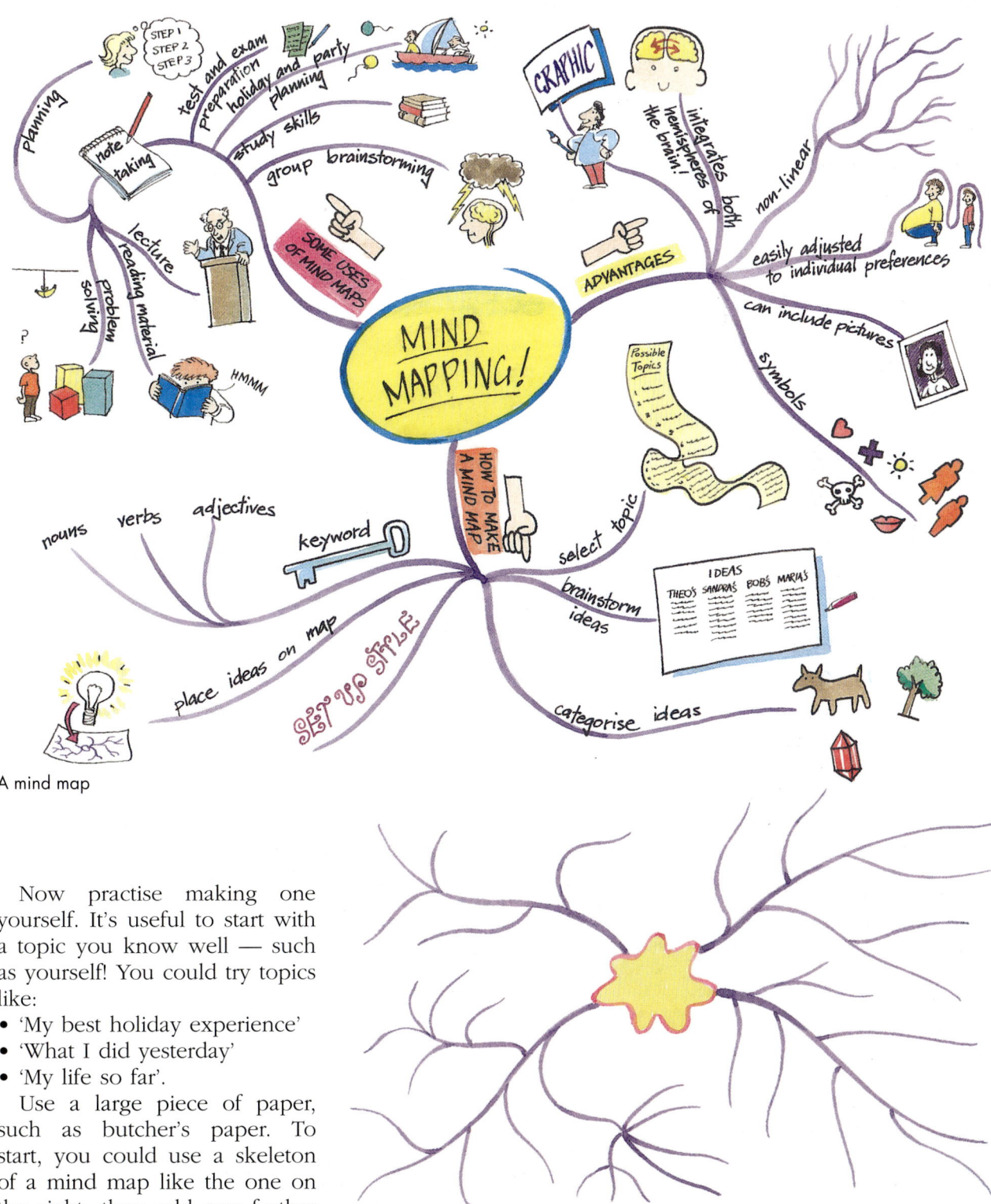

A mind map

Now practise making one yourself. It's useful to start with a topic you know well — such as yourself! You could try topics like:

- 'My best holiday experience'
- 'What I did yesterday'
- 'My life so far'.

Use a large piece of paper, such as butcher's paper. To start, you could use a skeleton of a mind map like the one on the right, then add any further branches that suit you.

The skeleton of a mind map

When you complete activity 3 below, compare this mind map about science with your group's mind map. Write down any similarities and differences. Science is so vast it would be hard to fit it all on a single mind map. You can always add to your mind map as your ideas change.

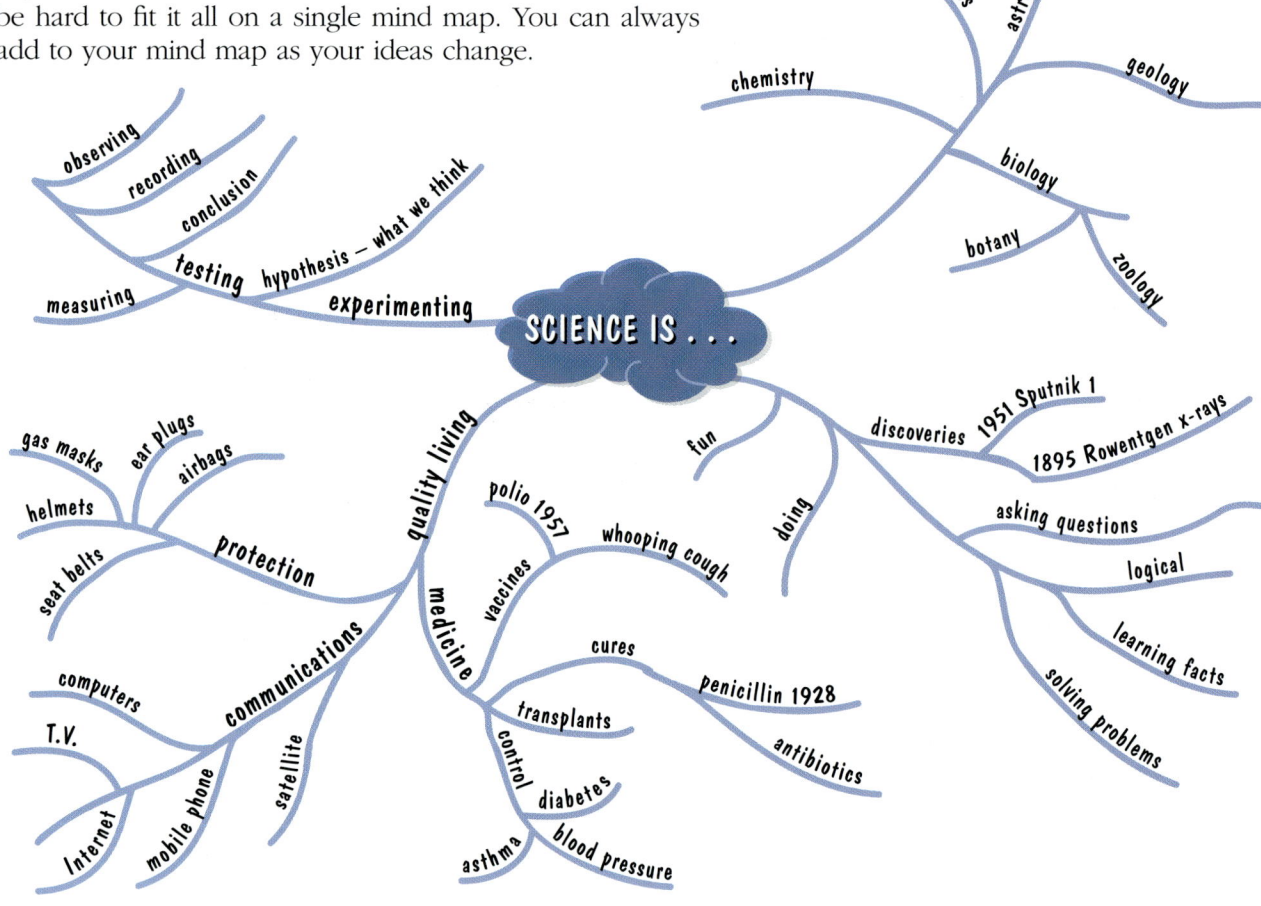

A mind map about science

Activities

1. Make a concept map about a topic you have recently learnt in science. Work with a partner to start off the concept map. Look back over your notes to help you remember the important words.
2. Now make a concept map for another subject that you enjoy.
3. In a group, make a mind map about science.
   (a) Choose a group leader who will say the word 'science' several times. (Say it slowly and using a different voice each time.)
   (b) Close your eyes and see what images come into your mind when you hear the word 'science'. Your group leader will need to say the word several times to give you time to get strong images.
   (c) Take turns adding your images to a group mind map. Put all your ideas down, then stand back and see if they make sense. Discuss what seems odd or incorrect. Make changes — you do not have to be neat.

4. Now that you have experience at making both a concept map and a mind map, fill in a table like the one below to explain the similarities and differences between these two learning tools.

Mind mapping and concept mapping

Similarities	Differences

Group work

What is group work?

Group work is working together to achieve a common goal. Group work gives you the opportunity to discuss and share your ideas, learn from others and, as a team, solve a problem or complete a task. Every member of the group has a role and contributes to the success of the group.

Why work in groups?

In real life people work in groups in many jobs. A team working together can achieve more than the sum of its individuals. You can bounce ideas off each other, clarify your understandings and gain self-confidence. Learning is easier when you can enjoy yourself while staying on task.

When should we work in groups?

You can work in groups at any time. It is especially good when the task is large and the time is short. Everyone in the group contributes to get the job done.

How do we work in groups?

Group work is about working effectively as a team. However, there are some things you should watch out for, such as the following:

- one person taking over
- leaving someone out
- giving too much work to one person
- getting distracted from the task
- having too large a group (four is best for most activities)
- criticising without offering your own suggestions.

Rules for successful group work

1. Work as a team — for all to succeed each person needs to contribute.
2. Make sure everyone gets to share their ideas. If this is not happening, take turns.
3. Divide the task into 'bits' and give each person their own 'bit' — and a deadline.
4. Respect all ideas.
5. Every so often, evaluate how you are going. Help others if you finish quickly.
6. Once the task is completed, talk about what you did well as a group and what needs to be improved.

Jigsaw technique

The jigsaw technique is a special way to do group work. It works well when you need to learn a lot in a short time. You do it by forming Home Teams and Expert Teams. You learn the new material in your Expert Team and then take it back and teach it to your Home Team.

The following steps tell you how to start.

1. Form Home Teams of four people. Give each person in each team a number from 1–4.
2. All the number 1s from the Home Teams then form Expert Team 1, all the number 2s form Expert Team 2 and so on.
3. When all the Expert Teams get together, there could be six or seven people in each team. They solve the problem or challenge assigned to them. Here are some Expert Team challenges to try. (While the following Expert Team activities are unconnected, the activities will usually be related to the topic you are studying.)

Expert Team 1 challenge
In pairs, work out how to separate a mixture of pepper, salt and iron filings so that you have three separate substances.

Expert Team 2 challenge
Find out how far away you have to place a mirror before you are able to see your whole image in the mirror.

Look into the mirror at an angle. What objects can you see? Choose one and see what happens to this object as you change your position. Write some rules for using a mirror to spy on others.

Expert Team 3 challenge
Each member is to research a different scientist. (See page 26 for a list of Nobel Prize-winning scientists.) Find out six facts about each scientist and share this with the rest of your Expert Team.

Expert Team 4 challenge
Use a microscope to watch what happens when you place a drop of silver nitrate solution on a piece of copper wire. Make as many observations as possible and then share them with your Expert Team.

4. Once each Expert Team has completed their challenge and discussed the results, then it's time to return to your Home Team. Once in your Home Team, explain what you did and share your results. You can either tell your team or show your team what you learnt. You do this in the way that you feel will help them to learn best.

Try this — **WALKING STEPS**

- Break up into groups of four. You need to complete this activity in five minutes.
- Write a set of instructions that will tell someone (from another group) how to walk using only your instructions. Decide who will keep track of time, who will write the instructions, who will read the instructions to the person from another group and who will be the person to perform the instructions of another group.

- As a group think and talk about the instructions, and discuss whether they will work. Then write down the instructions.
- When all groups have finished and your teacher gives the signal, read your instructions to the person from another group.

How well did you work as a group? Give each person a score out of ten for their efforts.

S.14
Role-playing

What is *role-playing?*

Role-playing is a bit like acting, but you are not always a character. In 'scientific' role-playing, you imagine that you are a process, an object or a living thing. You need to think about what you understand and then find a way to explain using props. It's best to talk about your ideas first because this will help you clarify your thinking and ask useful questions.

Why *role-play?*

You can get a clearer understanding of difficult ideas by role-playing. In fact, you are modelling how you think the concept or process works using your body as well as objects. You also get to see what other students believe. It is a fun, creative way to express yourself and learn new concepts.

When *do* you *role-play?*

Role-playing is a useful skill to use when a concept is new and the meaning is difficult to understand.

How *do* you *role-play?*

To role-play a process, you need to think of all the smaller parts that make up the whole process. This sort of role-play is ideal to do in groups. Decide how you will perform the process and give each member a role. Practise and then perform for the class.

Activities

1. Role-play the process of boiling water, using two students as the beaker, one student as the water and another student as the Bunsen burner.

As the Bunsen burner heats the beaker, the water starts to move around until it leaves the beaker as steam. By role-playing this process, you are showing that you understand that water takes in energy and changes from a liquid to a gas (evaporation) as it boils.

2. Role-play some of these ideas either alone or in groups.
   - day, night and the seasons
   - a space mission to the farther edges of the solar system
   - the greenhouse effect
   - plant and animal cells
   - static electricity
   - the journey of a piece of food from fork to flush
   - any separation technique, such as evaporation, filtration, floatation, chromatography or centrifugation.

   (continued)

3. Role-play moving molecules.
In chapter 3 you learnt about solids, liquids and gases. You already know water exists as ice, water and steam. Water is made up of molecules that contain two atoms of hydrogen and one atom of oxygen called H_2O. Whether water exists as ice, water or steam, it is still made up of lots of molecules of H_2O. So what is it that makes each one look so different? Answer: the temperature at which each one is stored.

You know that ice has to be kept in the freezer or it will turn into water. If you want steam, you know you have to heat water until it boils to 100°C. If you could see the molecules of H_2O in ice, water and steam, you would see they move at different speeds. In ice they vibrate, in water they move about but in steam they zip around quickly. Molecules of most substances exist as solid, liquid and gas and the movement of their molecules is related to the surrounding temperature.

If your class were to role-play the molecules of H_2O in an ice cube, you would all stand close together and vibrate on the spot.

If you then imagined you were left on the counter overnight, you would start to move slowly around the room as the ice melted and turned into water.

However, if you were zapped in the microwave for five minutes, you would all start to move more quickly. Some of you would turn into steam and leave your container so quickly you would bounce off the microwave walls. If the walls were cold you might turn back into water.

4. Role-play an electromagnet.
Two students act as an electromagnet. They each have a tennis ball to represent electrons. The rest of the class act as substances that are either attracted or not attracted by a magnet. The challenge is for the electromagnet to turn on and off while seeking out the students in the room who represent magnetic substances and separating them from the students who represent non-magnetic substances.

While the two students in the electromagnet work out how to show when their power is turned on and off, everyone else decides whether they will be magnetic or non-magnetic (see pages 120–1). Write the name of the substance you are role-playing on a card and stand up so everyone can see whether you are magnetic or non-magnetic. When the electromagnet comes close, you must show your card. If you are attracted to a magnet, you go where the electromagnet directs you providing it has power flowing through it. If you are non-magnetic, you sit down after the challenge by the electromagnet.

Once the electromagnet has found all the magnetic materials, each group should explain why they moved as they did during the role-play.

STUDENT RESEARCH PROJECT

Your student research project may be about one of the topics studied in class or any other topic that interests you. By doing your own research, you will gain valuable skills in making a hypothesis from observations and then designing a controlled experiment to test your hypothesis. In other words, you become a scientist, following in the footsteps of the many scientists who have followed their own curiosity.

KEY CONTENT

Identify a question that can be researched.

Make a hypothesis from observations.

Choose appropriate equipment and use it safely to test a hypothesis.

Control variables in an experiment to test a hypothesis.

Record and process data.

Make conclusions based on evidence.

KEY QUESTIONS

What approach does a scientist take to solve problems?

Which type of ball bounces highest — a tennis ball or a cricket ball?

What is the connection between a pendulum and a playground swing?

Are you wasting energy and water in your home?

Does an athlete perform better with or without an audience?

What type of soil do earthworms prefer?

SRP.1
Investigations

Formulating *your* question

Before you define your question in detail you need to find a topic that interests you. Selecting your topic is the first, and one of the most crucial steps in conducting your research project. Keep a record of your progress in a logbook.

Selecting your topic is a very important step in conducting your research project.

Finding a topic

1. Start by searching for a general area of interest. List your hobbies and other interests.

2. Do you have a friend or relative who might be able to help you in a scientific investigation? Write down the topic areas in which you could get help.

3. Discuss the possible research topics you have already written down with a group of fellow students. Listen carefully to their ideas. They might help you to decide on your own topic. Write down your ideas.

Discuss your ideas with others.

4. Start each entry in your logbook with the date, for example:

   15 April — went to the library to search the Internet.

5. Read through the summaries of student research on pages 250 and 251. Then read through the list of ideas for investigation topics in the adjacent box. Even if none of the suggested topics appeals to you, they may help you to think of other ideas. For example, 'The strength of sticky tape' could lead you to consider topics such as the strength of glass, wood, paper, plastics or some other material. 'Brainstorm' possible topics with your friends and make your own list of suggested investigations.

Some ideas for topics

How do fertilisers affect the growth of plants?
Does talking to plants improve their growth?
Can plants grow without soil?
What makes algae grow in an aquarium?
The behaviour of slaters (or snails, worms etc.)
Whirlpools in the bath
What is the best shape for a boomerang?
What type of wood gives off the most heat while burning?
Which material makes the best insulator?
What makes iron rust?
Which paint weathers best?
Which battery lasts longest?
The strength of sticky tape
Which type of glue is best?
How much weight can a plastic garbage bag hold?
Which food wrap keeps food fresher?
The effectiveness of pre-wash stain removers
Which fabrics burn faster?
Comparing fabrics for warmth
How can the growth of mould on fruit be slowed down?
Which concrete mixture is strongest?
Comparing the strength of fishing lines

Comparing the strength of fishing lines

6. Search in a library or at home for books or newspaper articles about the topic areas that you have already written down. You might also find magazines or journals that include articles about these topic areas. Conduct an Internet search. Use a table like the one below to organise your ideas.

Topic area	Name of book, magazine, web site etc.	Chapter or article	Topic ideas

You do not need to record detailed information yet. At this stage you are only searching for a good topic.

Defining the question

Once you have decided on your topic, you need to determine exactly what it is you would like to investigate. It is better to start with a fairly simple question. For example, rather than investigate 'The growth of plants', you need to focus on a small part of the topic. Here are some questions relating to the growth of plants:

- What is the effect of different fertilisers on the growth of peas?
- Does talking to plants improve their growth?
- How does light affect the growth of plants?
- What is the effect of caffeine on the growth of grasses?
- How does salt affect the growth of plants?

Investigating the effect of caffeine on the growth of grasses

When you have defined your own question, make sure that it is realistic. You should be able to answer 'yes' to each of the questions below. Complete the checklist.

Is my question simple and clear enough? .... Yes/No

Do I know where to get the background
information I need? .... Yes/No

Is the equipment I may need for experiments
available or able to be made? .... Yes/No

Is the problem a safe one to investigate? .... Yes/No

Researching *your* topic

Before you start your own experiments, you should find out more about your topic.

As well as increasing your general knowledge of the topic, you need to find out whether your problem has been investigated by others. Information already available about your topic might help you to design your experiments. It might also help you in explaining your results.

Make notes on your topic as you find information. You may be able to include some relevant background information in your report.

Make notes on your topic.

Using the library

The best place to start is the school library. There are several different types of information sources in the library. They usually include the following.

Non-fiction books

Use the subject index catalogue to find out where to find books with information about your topic. Your library catalogue is most likely to be stored in a computer database. You might need to ask the librarian to help you use the catalogue at first. It is a good idea to browse through the contents list of science textbooks. Your topic may appear.

Reference books

These include encyclopaedias, atlases and yearbooks. The index of a good encyclopaedia is a great place to start looking for information.

Journals and magazines

There are quite a few scientific journals that are suitable for use by school students. They provide up-to-date information. Your library may have an index for journals, such as 'Guidelines', which you can use to find articles on your topic. You may, however, need to browse. Some journals to look for are: *New Scientist*, *Australasian Science*, *Ecos*, *Habitat*, *Popular Science*, *Choice* and *Helix*.

Information file

Many school libraries keep information files of newspaper articles on topics of interest or even collections of articles on CD-ROM. Ask your school librarian if you don't know how to use these resources.

Audio-visual resources

The library may have slides, videos, CD-ROMs and audio tapes that can be used or borrowed. These resources can be located using the subject index catalogue.

Beyond the library

Information on your topic may be available from the following sources.

Your science teacher

This may seem obvious, but many people don't even think to ask. Your science teacher may also be able to direct you to other sources of information.

Government departments and agencies

Federal, State and local government departments and agencies may be able to provide you with information or advice on your topic. Try searching through the government listing at the front of Telstra's White Pages. Addresses to write to are usually listed. A polite letter to the appropriate department or agency is the best way to ask for help.

The Internet

The World Wide Web provides a wealth of information on almost every topic imaginable. Use a search engine such as Google, AltaVista, Excite, Lycos, Yahoo! or Infoseek. The success of your search will depend on a thoughtful choice of key words. Take the time to find out how to take full advantage of the search engine before you use it.

Industry

Information on some topics can be obtained from certain industries. For example, if you were testing glues for strength, or batteries to find which ones last longest, the manufacturers might have useful information. Use Telstra's Yellow or White Pages to find addresses. A polite letter or e-mail is often the best way to ask for help.

Relatives or friends

Perhaps you or a relative know somebody who works in your area of interest. Let your friends and relatives know about your intended research.

Look for information beyond the library.

In your logbook complete a checklist like the one below to see if you have thoroughly searched sources of information.

School library:	• non-fiction books	☐
	• reference books	☐
	• journals and magazines	☐
	• information file	☐
	• audio-visual resources	☐
Beyond the library:	• your science teacher	☐
	• government departments and agencies	☐
	• the Internet	☐
	• industry	☐
	• relatives or friends	☐
	• other sources	☐

How to use information

Make notes on information that is *relevant* to your research topic. Think about what you really need to know. You need information that will help you to:

• plan your experiments
• understand your results later on
• show in your report how your research relates to everyday life or why your research is important.

You will need to keep an accurate list in your logbook of the steps you have taken and the resources that you have used.

Keep an accurate list in your logbook of resources that you have used.

How to list your resources

Library sources

Non-fiction books: author, title, publisher, place of publication, date of publication, relevant page numbers and, of course, the Dewey number so that you can locate the source again.

Reference books: title, volume, publisher, place of publication, date of publication, relevant pages and the Dewey number.

Journals, magazines or newspaper articles: author of article, title of article, name of journal or magazine, volume and number or date of issue and relevant page numbers.

Audio-visual resources: title, date of production and Dewey number.

Non-library printed material

Record title, source of material and date produced. If you are unable to print out a hard copy of Internet material, quote the URL (Uniform Resource Locator; for example, http://www.csiro.au/). Make sure you keep copies of letters written and received for your report.

Verbal information

If you have received information verbally, record the name of the person spoken to, their position or occupation if relevant, the date and a summary of what was said.

Designing *and performing* experiments

In order to reach sound conclusions you need to make sure that your experiments are well controlled. The factors that can change in an experiment are called **variables**. If you are trying to find the effect of one variable on another, all other variables must be kept constant. The process of changing only one variable at a time is called **controlling variables** (see page 246).

When you are investigating the effect of the presence of some factor on a variable, a **control** is needed for comparison. For example, if you were investigating the effect of the presence of certain chemicals in water on the growth of plants, a control group of plants would be needed — that is, a group of plants given water with none of those chemicals present. Remember that controlled variables are kept constant in both the control group and the test group. The experimental variable is the factor being tested and it will be different in both groups.

In designing your own experiments you need to ensure that:

• you will have enough time to complete your observations
• the equipment you need is available
• variables in the experiment are controlled (Sometimes it is impossible to control all variables. Do the best you can!)
• a control group is used if necessary
• you have taken all necessary safety precautions.

Writing your plan

You should now be ready to write a plan for your investigation. You should not commence any experiments until your plan has been approved by your teacher. Your plan should include:

1. Title

The likely title — you may decide to change it before your work is completed.

2. The aim or problem

Briefly state what you intend to investigate or the question you intend to answer.

Aim: To study the behaviour of slaters
Problem: What makes algae grow in an aquarium?

3. Hypothesis

An educated guess about the answer to your problem or what you expect to find out. It is important to be creative and objective and to use logical reasoning when devising a hypothesis and testing it.

4. Outline of experiment

Explain how you intend to test your hypothesis, and briefly outline the experiments that you intend to conduct.

5. Equipment

List any equipment that you will need for your experiments.

6. Resources

List the sources of information that you have used or intend to use. This list should include library resources, organisations and people.

Write out a plan for your investigation.

Performing your experiments

Once your plan has been approved by your teacher, you may begin your experiments. Detail how you conducted your experiments in your logbook. All observations and measurements should be recorded. Use tables where possible to record your data.

Where appropriate, measurements should be repeated and an average value determined. All measurements — not just the averages — should be recorded in your logbook.

Photographs should be taken if appropriate.

You might need to change your experiments if you get results you don't expect. If things go wrong, record what happened. Knowing what went wrong allows you to improve your experiment and technique. Any major changes should be checked with your teacher.

All observations and measurements should be recorded

Writing *your* report

You can begin writing your report as soon as you have planned your investigation, but it cannot be completed until your observations are complete. Your report should be typed or neatly written on A4 paper. It should begin with a 'table of contents', and the pages should be numbered. Your report should include the following headings (unless they are inappropriate for your investigation):

Abstract

Briefly describe your experiments and your main conclusions. Even though this appears at the beginning of your report, it is best not to write it until after you have completed the rest of your report.

Introduction

Present all relevant background information. Include a statement of the problem that you are investigating, saying why it is relevant or important. You could also explain why you became interested in the topic.

Aim or problem

State the purpose of your investigation; that is, what you are trying to find out.

Hypothesis

Using the knowledge you already have about your topic, make a guess about what you will find out by doing your investigation.

Materials and methods

Describe in detail how you carried out your experiments. Begin with a list of the equipment used and include photographs of your equipment if appropriate. The description of your method must be detailed enough to allow somebody else to repeat your experiments. It should also convince the reader that your investigation is well controlled. Labelled diagrams can be used to make your description clear. Using a step-by-step outline makes your method easier to follow.

Results

Observations and measurements (data) are presented here. Wherever possible, present data in table form so that they are easy to read. Graphs can be used to help you and the reader interpret data. Each table and graph should have a title. Make sure that you use the most appropriate type of graph for your data (see pages 211–12).

Discussion

Discuss your results here. Begin with a statement of what your results indicate about the answer to your question. Explain how your results might be useful. Any weaknesses in your design or difficulties in measuring could be outlined here. Explain how you could have improved your experiments. What further experiments are suggested by your results?

Conclusion

This is a brief statement of what you found out and may link with the final paragraph of your 'Discussion'. It is a good idea to read your 'Aim' again before you write your conclusion. Your conclusion should also state whether your hypothesis was supported. Don't be disappointed if it is *not* supported. Some scientists deliberately set out to reject hypotheses!

Bibliography

Make a list of books and other printed or audio-visual material to which you have referred. The list should include enough information to allow the source of information to be easily found by the reader. Arrange the sources in alphabetical order.

For each resource, list the following information in the order shown.
- author(s) (if known)
- title of book or article
- publisher or name of journal/magazine (if not in title)
- place of publication (if given)
- date of publication
- chapter or pages used.

Some examples are listed below.

Breidahl, H. Australia's Southern Shores, Lothian, Melbourne, 1997, Chapter 2.

World Book Encyclopaedia, **Volume 4**, 1991, pp. 234–236.

'The Battle of the Bathroom', Choice, Sydney, November 1990, pp. 34–37.

Acknowledgements

List the people and organisations who gave you help or advice. You should state how each person or organisation assisted you.

Acknowledge the help you received.

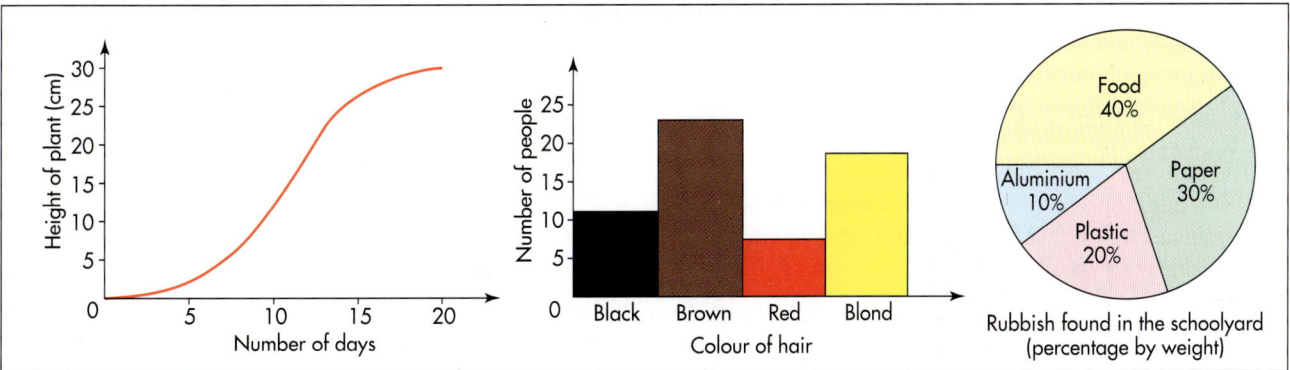

(*Left to right*) A line graph, a bar graph and a pie chart. Choose the type of graph that is appropriate to your data.

It's all under control

Which type of ball bounces the highest after being dropped onto the ground?

This seems like a simple question to answer. However, in order to answer it scientifically, some care must be taken.

Factors that change in a scientific test are called variables. The variable that has to be deliberately changed to answer the question above is the type of ball. This is called the **independent variable**; it is what the researcher changes. There is also a **dependent variable** which follows from or depends on the independent variable. This is what you measure.

The independent variable is usually graphed on the x-axis and the dependent variable on the y-axis.

In the bouncing balls investigation, the type of ball is the independent variable and the height to which the ball bounces is the dependent variable. That is, the height to which the ball bounces (the dependent variable)

Bouncing balls — which ball will bounce the highest?

depends on the type of ball (the independent variable). The data from these variables are often graphed.

There are, however, other variables that could affect the bounce height of a ball. Two of those variables are:

- the height from which the ball is dropped
- the type of surface onto which the ball is dropped.

If you want to find out which type of ball bounces the highest, these other variables must be kept constant. These are called the **controlled variables**. If the question is to be answered scientifically, the only variable that can

be changed is the type of ball, otherwise different bounce heights could be due to other factors.

The technique of changing only one variable at a time is called fair testing or controlling variables.

Some variables are difficult to keep constant. For example, the surface on which the balls are bounced might not be uniform. An uneven surface would produce unreliable **data**. To minimise the effect of this problem you need to:

- try to bounce the balls in exactly the same place each time
- repeat measurements several times and find the average bounce height for each ball.

Experiment SRP.1 BOUNCING BALLS

YOU WILL NEED
tennis ball
rubber ball (about the size of the tennis ball)
cricket ball
baseball
any other ball that is about the same size as a tennis ball
one-metre ruler

- The question you are trying to answer is 'Which ball bounces the highest?'. Prepare a table in which to record your results.

1. Write down your **hypothesis**. A hypothesis is a sensible prediction of the answer to your question.

- Take care not to introduce unwanted variables. Make sure that the balls are *dropped* each time. Don't throw them down. Also, think about which part of each ball you will measure the height of the bounce from.

2. Make a list of all the variables that you can think of that need to be kept constant (other than dropping height and type of surface).

- Drop each ball from the same height and measure how high each one bounces. Now go ahead and answer the question — scientifically!

3. Write a brief report about your experiment. Ensure that you explain your procedure in detail and include a brief statement of the answer to the question.

It is usually necessary to prepare a control. The test results are compared with the control. The control and the test set-ups differ only in the independent variable. The test set-up contains the independent variable; the control does not. This means that, at the end of the experiment, you can say that any difference in results between the test and the control are due to the independent variable. The table to the right shows which variables are present in the control and test set-ups when carrying out a controlled experiment.

The hypothetical investigation on the effect of chemicals on plant growth mentioned on page 243 is an example showing the absence of the independent variable (the chemicals) from the control. The amount of chemical (independent variable) is decided at the start of the experiment. The height (dependent variable) of the plants is measured as the experiment progresses.

Controlled experiment

	Control	Test
Controlled variables	constant	constant
Independent variable	not present	present

Activities

Remember

1. What is a variable? Describe the different types of variable.
2. What is a hypothesis? How would you test it?

Using data

Simon and Jessie performed an experiment to find out how effectively two plastic cups maintain the temperature of near boiling water. Their data are shown below.

Comparing plastic cups

Time (min)	Temperature (°C) Simon's cup	Temperature (°C) Jessie's cup
0	90	90
10	47	58
20	29	39
30	22	31
40	20	26
50	20	23

1. Draw a graph to display the data in the table.
2. Which cup maintained the temperature of the water more effectively?
3. Estimate the temperature of the water in Simon's cup 15 minutes after timing commenced.
4. Use your graph to estimate how long it would have taken the water in Jessie's cup to drop to a temperature of 20°C.

Think

Amy and Nguyen are trying to find out whether stoneware or glass cups are better for keeping water hot. The illustration below shows their experiment in progress.

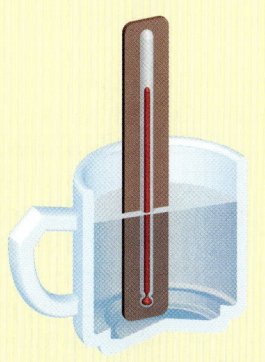 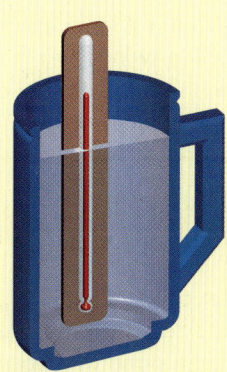

Amy and Nguyen's experiment in progress

(a) List at least two weaknesses in their experiment design.
(b) Make a list of all the variables that could affect the results of Amy and Nguyen's experiment.
(c) List any variables that Amy and Nguyen do not need to control.
(d) Write a step-by-step outline of the procedure that they could use to find out which cups keep water hot.

Investigate

How is the bounce height of a tennis ball affected:
(a) when it is damp?
(b) when it is hot?
(c) as it gets old and worn?
(d) by different tennis court surfaces?
Design and perform an investigation to answer one or more of these questions.

SRP.3
In the swing of things

A playground swing is simply a large **pendulum**. Pendulums are mainly used as measuring instruments. Their most well-known use is in clocks. The following experiment using a pendulum will help to develop your skills in devising and testing a hypothesis.

A pendulum is a suspended object that is free to swing to and fro. Each complete swing is called an **oscillation**. The time taken for one complete oscillation of a pendulum is called its **period**.

A playground swing is simply a large pendulum.

Experiment SRP.2   SWING HIGH, SWING LOW

What is it that determines the period of the swing? Is it the size of the push? Is it the mass of the person sitting on the swing? Is it the length of the swing?

YOU WILL NEED
length of light string (at least 80 cm long)
set of slotted masses (or various sized pendulum bobs)
retort stand with bosshead (or a high structure from which to suspend the pendulum)
pair of scissors and a one-metre ruler
stopwatch or clock with a second hand or display

A. Does the push make a difference?
1. Write down your hypothesis about the size of the push.

- Set up your pendulum so it can swing freely. Start with the largest possible length and the smallest mass.
- Copy the table on the right in your workbook and record the mass and the length of the pendulum in it. The length should be measured from the top of the

pendulum to the bottom of the swinging mass, as shown in the diagram.
- Pull the mass aside so that the angle of release is about 20°. Take note of the height from which the mass is released so that this angle of release is used throughout the experiment.
- Release the pendulum. Measure the time taken for ten complete swings of the pendulum. Repeat your measurement at least twice so that you can find the average time for ten swings. Use this average to calculate the time taken for one complete swing (the period). Record all the measurements in your table.

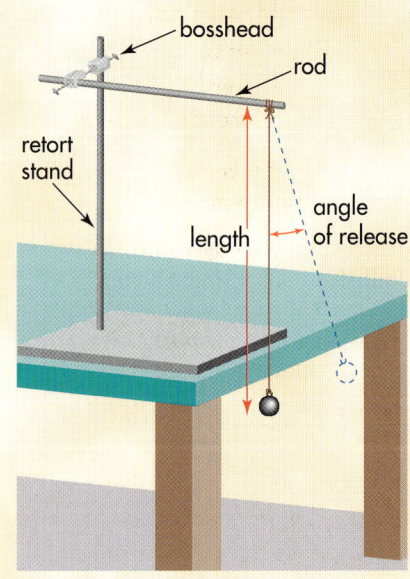

Setting up a swinging pendulum

The effect of different pushing forces on a pendulum

Mass of pendulum = _____ g   Length of pendulum = _____ cm

Size of push	Time taken for 10 complete swings (s)			Average (s)	Period (s)
	Trial 1	Trial 2	Trial 3		
no push					
small push					
larger push					

Activities

Remember

1. What is a pendulum?
2. What does the period of a pendulum measure?
3. List three uses of pendulums.
4. How is the period of a pendulum affected by:
   (a) the size of the push applied to start its motion?
   (b) its mass?
   (c) its length?

Think

1. In the experiment, you were required to repeat each measurement three times. When you do this, the time taken for ten complete swings is not always the same.

   (a) Suggest two or more reasons for this.
   (b) Suggest why the differences between measurements are usually greater for shorter pendulums.
2. A metronome is an 'upside-down' pendulum. To make the period of the metronome longer, should you move the sliding mass up or down? Explain your answer.
3. List the variables that affect the period of a pendulum including at least one variable that wasn't considered in experiment SRP.2.
4. List the controlled variables in parts A and B of the experiment.

A metronome's period is changed by sliding the mass up or down.

- Repeat this procedure, this time giving the mass a small push.
- Repeat the procedure once more, giving the mass a larger push.

2. How does the size of the push affect the pendulum's period?

B. Do mass or length make a difference?

3. Write down your hypothesis about the effect of mass and length.

- Make a copy of the table below in your workbook and transfer the data corresponding to no push into the first row of your new table.
- Using the same angle of release and pendulum length as before, determine the period of the pendulum for several different

masses. Use three trials for each mass. Record all data in your table.
- Halve the length of the string and repeat your measurements for the different masses. Record the mass and length of the pendulum as well as the average times and period.
- Halve the length of the string again and repeat your measurements, ensuring that all of the necessary data are recorded in the table.

4. How does the mass affect the period of the pendulum?
5. Draw a line graph to show how the period is affected by the length of the pendulum. You need to graph data for only one mass.
6. How does the length of the pendulum affect its period?

Draw a line graph showing how the period is affected by the length of your pendulum.

7. The period of most standard clock pendulums is one second. Use your graph to predict the length of a standard clock pendulum.
8. Why is it a good idea to measure the time for ten swings rather than just one?
9. Which variables must be kept constant when determining the effect of mass on the period of a pendulum?
10. Predict whether the angle of release affects the period of a pendulum. Perform a simple experiment to check your prediction.

Varying the mass and length

Mass (g)	Length (cm)	Time taken for 10 complete swings (s)			Average (s)	Period (s)
		Trial 1	Trial 2	Trial 3		

Students as scientists

Does *an* athlete *need an* audience?

Catherine Pippos, 15, a year 10 student, was interested in what motivated athletes to strive to win. She wondered whether a cheering audience actually made athletes perform better.

Catherine set about answering her own question with a research investigation. She persuaded twelve amateur, but competent, athletes to be her subjects. Six subjects were male and six were female. Her subjects were required to complete three tasks on three separate occasions, one week apart. The tasks were as follows:

1. Basketball goal shooting — the number of successful attempts out of 20 was recorded.

2. Sit-ups — the number completed in 30 seconds was recorded.

3. Shot put — the distance thrown in metres was recorded.

On the first occasion, only Catherine and the athlete were present. On the second occasion, a quiet audience of twenty-seven year 10 students was present. On the third occasion, there was a loudly cheering audience of twenty-seven year 10 students.

Catherine's research investigation resulted from her own curiosity. She chose a topic based on her interests. The question she asked was very simple to begin with (see page 251 for her results).

Think about this HOUSEHOLD CONSERVATION

Nathan Morsillo, 13, was a year 8 student when he decided to do something about his concern about the Earth's dwindling energy resources. With the cooperation of his parents, he performed an experiment in which he compared the amount of energy and water used in a normal week with the amount used when efforts were made to conserve these resources. Nathan was also able to show that money can be saved when efforts are made to conserve energy and water.

Nathan took readings from the water, gas and electricity meters each day at 5.00 pm for two weeks.

During the first week, his household followed its normal routine. During the second week, the household made some changes to its routine in order to save energy and water. The changes are listed in the table below.

Nathan's results are shown in the diagram to the right. They showed a 10 per cent saving in gas, a 62 per cent saving in electricity and a 33.7 per cent saving in water!

Nathan also found the savings in money terms to be quite worthwhile. The changes made in the household routine would lead to savings of about $40 on a quarterly electricity bill, about $14 on a

two-monthly gas bill and about $45 on the annual excess water bill.

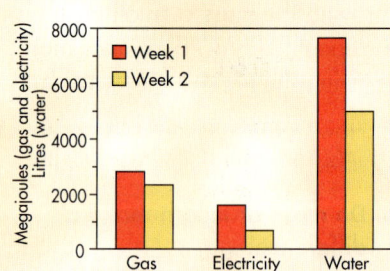

Savings in energy and water (Source: Nathan Morsillo)

1. Nathan was unable to control all of the variables that he would have liked to control. Which variables are difficult to control? Which variables cannot be controlled at all?

2. How could Nathan improve his experiment?

3. In Nathan's experiment a number of changes were made to the household routine at once. How would you go about finding the effect of just one change? Give an example.

4. Suggest an experiment on energy conservation that you might be able to undertake at home or school.

Changes to household routines

Week 1	Week 2
incandescent light globes	three low-wattage fluorescent globes to replace most used incandescents
standard shower rose	low pressure shower rose
baths for children	showers for children
warm water used for clothes washing	cold water used for clothes washing
hot dry and normal dishwasher cycle	cool dry and short dishwasher cycle
full use of clothes dryer	use of clothes line when possible
full flush toilets	reduced flush toilets

Think about this GO, GO, GO!

You will find Catherine's results in the table below.

Effect of an audience on the performance of athletes

Task	Result (average)					
	No audience		Quiet audience		Loud audience	
	M	F	M	F	M	F
basketball shots (out of 20)	4.7	6.0	4.3	8.0	6.3	5.7
sit-ups (in 30 seconds)	23.7	17.3	20.0	18.0	21.0	19.7
shot put (distance in metres)	7.2	5.4	8.4	5.9	9.1	7.1

(Source: Catherine Pippos)

1. What conclusions can be reached from Catherine's results?
2. How do the results compare with what you would expect?
3. What variables, apart from the audience type, are difficult or impossible to control in this experiment?
4. How could Catherine's experiments be improved?
5. Catherine's basic question was, 'Does an audience affect the performance of an athlete?'. Was her question successfully answered?
6. Write a list of other questions that could be answered as a result of Catherine's experiments.

Think about this WHERE DID THE EARTHWORMS GO?

Liam Newman, 14, a year 9 student, enjoys fishing on weekends and during the holidays. He often found it difficult to find earthworms for bait, so he planned and completed an experiment designed to show what type of soil earthworms preferred to live in.

Liam created five different earthworm environments in a large box. The environments were:

- compost
- potting mixture
- soil with fertiliser
- soil with manure
- untreated garden soil.

He put twenty earthworms into each environment (100 worms in all). The earthworms were given a six-week period during which they could migrate freely to their preferred environment.

The chart on the far right shows how the worms were distributed after the six-week period. Unfortunately, four worms were unaccounted for.

1. What would Liam's conclusion have been?
2. What should Liam do to make sure that he has an adequate supply of bait for fishing?
3. Liam was trying to observe the effect of soil type on the population of earthworms. Were there any other variables that might affect the number of earthworms present?
4. Liam counted the worms after six weeks. How conclusive were his results? What could he have done to make his results more reliable?

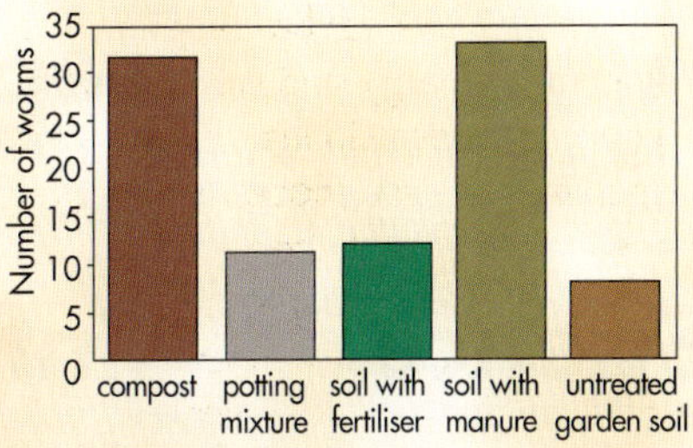

Distribution of worms after six weeks
(Source: Liam Newman)

Fishing can be relaxing and enjoyable, but finding earthworms for bait is not always easy.

Ways and means

The way you present your scientific investigation can take a number of forms — a scientific report, using information and communication technologies (ICT), a working model or a piece of creative expression. The subject of the investigation, your creative ability and whom you choose as your audience will suggest the most suitable presentation method.

No matter how you choose to present your results, you start off by conducting a scientific investigation. Use the information on pages 244–5 to get under way. Devise a hypothesis based on observations and test that hypothesis using a controlled experiment. Clearly present and label your data, draw conclusions that are consistent with your data and relate your conclusions to your hypothesis. Use the checklists on pages 253 and 254 to ensure you have included all aspects of a scientific investigation somewhere in your report.

Problem: How quickly does a car heat up on a hot day?

A *scientific* report

This is the formal scientific way to present your scientific investigation. Generally your audience would be the scientific community.

Science *and* Information and *Communication Technologies (ICT)*

Choose this format if your audience is part of the general public. You want to make the investigation easier to understand and wish to use a technology as a means of communication. You will still need to have a written report explaining your work.

If you recorded your observations or experiments on video or took photographs, then you may wish to include this as part of your presentation. If you obtained and used material from the Internet or made or used any computer software, then this may also be presented.

If you do want to use video in your presentation, make sure you take more video footage than you need and edit it so that it is

clear and concise. The same holds for photographs. Refine your computer programs too, and provide brief instructions on the disk on how to open your entry and the type of computer that should be used.

Science and *technological* design

Sometimes you need to design and build something to assist you with your scientific investigation. This could be a model or a piece of technology. A model that performs a simple task is an excellent way of explaining a scientific idea. It can be a useful means of attracting and assisting your audience to understand your investigation. Once they see how it works, they often ask lots of questions that will be answered in your accompanying report. This report still needs to explain what it was you were trying to achieve and how you designed and built your piece of technology.

Science and creative *expression*

Creative expression allows you to present a scientific investigation in a creative and entertaining way. Choose an appropriate text style to present your information most effectively to your chosen audience. Examples of text styles are:

- a **report**, which classifies and describes things, both generally and specifically

- an **exposition**, which presents all sides of an issue but argues in favour of one side
- a **narrative**, which is a written account of something that has happened, i.e. a story
- a **recount**, which is similar to a narrative, except that it does not build up to a climax
- an **explanation**, which describes how and why things happen.

Sometimes the most effective style is a mixture of text styles. For example, your narrative could also contain a scientific report.

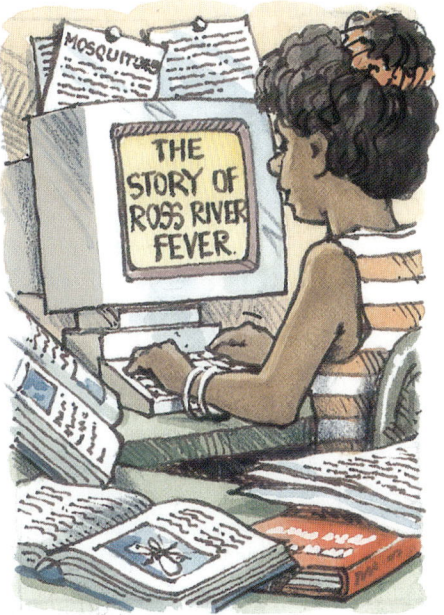

Scientific *investigation* checklist

A scientific investigation is a series of tests or experiments. An excellent scientific report describes your work, explains your thinking and clearly and logically leads the reader to valid conclusions. Use the following checklist to ensure that you modify and improve your work.

CHECKLIST

Planning your topic

☐ 1. A problem, question or hypothesis clearly stated in an unambiguous way.

☐ 2. A summary of the key points from relevant background research related to your investigation.

☐ 3. An explanation of the science related to your investigation.

Experimental design

☐ 4. Relevant variables clearly identified as dependent, independent or controlled with an explanation of why they were chosen.

☐ 5. Clear identification of what's being measured and an explanation of why these measurements will be useful to your investigation.

☐ 6. Repeat trials to validate results.

☐ 7. Repeat test with changed variables.

☐ 8. Appropriate equipment, which will provide you with meaningful results.

☐ 9. Evidence that safety has been considered during the planning stages.

Displaying your results

☐ 10. Data or results from observations recorded using correct units.

☐ 11. Measurements organised clearly in a manner that allows the reader to see trends and patterns easily.

Interpreting your results

☐ 12. Identification of patterns and trends and relationships.

☐ 13. Explanation and discussion of the results in the context of the problem, question or hypothesis.

☐ 14. Conclusions stating what each test or experiment proved.

☐ 15. Overall conclusion which sums up all the available evidence provided by the investigation.

☐ 16. A logbook that outlines your preparation and planning, any problems you experienced and your thinking throughout the investigation.

Checklist *for presenting your* student research *project*

Make a copy of this checklist, and tick off each part before submitting your student research project. If you have not completed each part, make a note to do it or explain why it has not been done.

CHECKLIST

FINAL PRESENTATION

- ❏ 1. Has your report been typed or neatly written so that it is legible?
- ❏ 2. Is there a table of contents with page numbers?
- ❏ 3. Have the pages been numbered?
- ❏ 4. Is the grammar and spelling correct?

SCIENTIFIC REPORTS

Introduction

- ❏ 5. Does your report follow the format of a scientific report?
- ❏ 6. Does your introduction provide background information, including:
  - an explanation of the scientific ideas?
  - a statement explaining why the investigation is important to you and your audience?

Aim or problem

- ❏ 7. Have you clearly stated the aim or purpose of the investigation; that is, what you are trying to find out?

Hypothesis

- ❏ 8. Has your hypothesis been clearly stated, including details of the observations on which your hypothesis is based?

Materials and methods

- ❏ 9. Have you clearly listed the materials and equipment you used? You may wish to include photographs or diagrams.
- ❏ 10. Is the description of the method you used in your experiment clear enough for somebody else to repeat the experiment easily?
- ❏ 11. Have you shown how you controlled the variables in your experiment? Has a control been used?
- ❏ 12. Where possible, did you give a clear outline of the procedure, showing the steps you took in your experiment?

Results

- ❏ 13. Are your results recorded in tables and graphs where possible?
- ❏ 14. Have tables and graphs been labelled and given a title?
- ❏ 15. If graphs have been included, have you chosen the most appropriate types of graph to present your data?

Discussion

- ❏ 16. Does your discussion make a general statement about what your results show? Is the statement a logical interpretation of your results?
- ❏ 17. Did you discuss possible human errors and weaknesses in experimental design?
- ❏ 18. Have you suggested how you could improve your experiment?
- ❏ 19. If further experiments have been suggested by your results, have you briefly described them?

Conclusion

- ❏ 20. Does your conclusion relate to your aim? Does your conclusion state if your hypothesis was supported or not?

Bibliography and acknowledgements

- ❏ 21. Have you provided a bibliography that includes all the reference material that you have used?
- ❏ 22. Have your references been arranged in alphabetical order and according to the format on page 245.
- ❏ 23. Have you acknowledged the people and organisations that gave you assistance and advice, and stated how they have assisted you?

OTHER FORMS OF PRESENTATION

- ❏ 24. If making an ICT presentation, do the media you have chosen enhance your scientific message and findings?
- ❏ 25. If designing a technology model, check that the model works as you hand it in.
- ❏ 26. If presenting a piece of creative writing, does it hold the attention of the reader? (Give it to your friends and family to check.)
- ❏ 27. If presenting a piece of writing, is the text style that you chose appropriate for the scientific concepts and findings that you are presenting?

LOGBOOK

- ❏ 28. Is there evidence of scientific thinking in your logbook?
- ❏ 29. Does your logbook provide evidence that you persisted with a task to a reasonable end point?
- ❏ 30. Have your logbook entries been dated?

SRP.6
Hear ye, hear ye!

There's not much point conducting scientific research if you are unable to tell anyone about it. You can write a report for school, but it will probably be read only by your teacher. However, there are opportunities to present your findings to a much wider audience.

Striving for gold

The CREST awards, run by CSIRO, are a series of awards for primary and secondary school students who complete projects in science or technology. They comprise Bronze, Silver and Gold awards. CREST stands for Creativity in Science and Technology. CREST is not a competition. In order to receive a CREST award, you must carry out experimental research into a topic that has useful applications, such as developing a way of reducing water pollution in a local stream or creating a better mouse-trap. In other words, you must solve a problem for the benefit of individuals, the community or the environment. The type of award received depends on the amount of time involved and the level of difficulty of the project. Secondary school students who are working towards Silver or Gold awards are encouraged to work with scientists or engineers as well as their teachers.

You can work on your own or in small groups. Your progress is monitored by your teacher or supervisor. You will need to follow procedures similar to those described on pages 244–5 and submit a report.

To apply for CREST awards your school, college or science club must be registered as a CREST centre. Ask your teacher for details, phone (02) 6276 6567 or e-mail education@csiro.au.

Some examples of CREST award projects can be found on the Internet at:
http://www.csiro.au/

Double Helix — science with a twist

Joining the CSIRO's Double Helix Club is another way of putting on the shoes of the scientist. It provides you with opportunities to take part in science excursions, nationwide experiments and competitions. It also allows you to keep up to date with scientific research in Australia through the *Helix* or *Scientriffic* magazines, which are issued six times a year.

Application forms can be obtained by writing to:
Double Helix Club
PO Box 225
Dickson ACT 2602
Phone (02) 6276 6643 or further information can also be found on the Internet at: http://www.csiro.au/helix or try e-mailing: education@csiro.au

Everyone has talent

The Young Scientist award scheme, run by the Science Teachers' Association of New South Wales, is an annual event. Prizes are cash, trophies and certificates of participation. You can present the results of your student research project creatively through one of four categories. Categories include scientific report, science and technological design, science and ICT, and science and creative expression. Information about Young Scientist can be obtained from your science teacher. Winners' entries are displayed at the Powerhouse Museum in Sydney, and are also shown in major country centres throughout New South Wales.

Activities

Think

1. Why is it important that scientists publish their findings in scientific journals?
2. Make a list of some ideas for inventions, such as a better mouse-trap, a supermarket trolley that can be pushed in a straight line, a hot-weather lunch box or bath plug that can be easily pulled out of a full bath.

Investigate

1. What is a helix?
2. Which important molecule has a double helix structure?

PRONUNCIATION GUIDE

amphibian (am-*fib*-ee-uhn)

angiosperm (*an*-ji-oh-sperm)

annelid (*an*-il-id)

arachnid (uh-*rak*-nid)

arthropod (*arth*-ruh-pod)

asthenosphere (as-*theen*-uhs-fear)

auricle (*or*-ik-uhl)

batholith (*ba*-thuh-lith)

bioluminescent (*buy*-oh-looh-muh-nes-uhnt)

bryophyte (*bri*-uh-fyt)

buoyancy (*boy*-uhnt-see)

centrifuging (*sen*-truh-fyooh-jing)

Cenozoic (see-nuh-*zoh*-ik)

chilopod (*kuy*-le-pod)

chlorophyll (*klo*-ruh-fil)

chromatography (kroh-ma-*tog*-grafy)

cnidarian (ni-*dar*-ian)

cochlea (*kok*-lee-uh)

cornea (*kaw*-nee-uh *or* kaw-*nee*-uh)

crustacean (krus-*tay*-shuhn)

dichotomous (duy-*kot*-uh-mus)

diffuse (duh-*fyoohz*)

diplopod (*dip*-lo-pod)

diprotodon di-*pro*-to-don)

distillation (dis-tuh-*lay*-shuhn)

echinoderm (eh-*ky*-neh-derm)

echolocation (eko-lo-*kay*-shuhn)

ectothermic (ecto-*ther*-mik)

electromagnetic (uh-lek-troh-mag-*net*-ik)

ellipse (uh-*lips*)

endothermic (endo-*ther*-mik)

Eocene (*ee*-oh-seen)

epoch (*ee*-pok)

Eustachian (yooh-*stay*-shuhn)

eutherian (yooh-*thear*-ree-uhn)

extrusive (ek-*strooh*-siv)

flotation (floh-*tay*-shuhn)

fungi (*fung*-gee)

ganglion (*gang*-lee-uhn)

gymnosperm (*jim*-noh-sperm)

Holocene (*hol*-uh-seen)

hydrosphere (*huy*-druhs-fear)

incandescent (in-kan-*dess*-uhnt)

insoluble (in-*sol*-yooh-buhl)

insulator (*in*-shuh-layt-or)

intrusive (*in*-troo-siv)

inversion (in-*ver*-shuhn)

ionosphere (uy-*on*-uhs-fear)

lichen (*luy*-kuhn)

lithosphere (*lith*-uhs-fear)

lubricant (*looh*-bruh-kant)

luminous (*looh*-muh-nuhs)

Martian (*mah*-shuhn)

mesosphere (*mes*-o-sfear)

Mesozoic (*mes*-uh-*zoh*-ik)

meteor (*mee*-tee-uh *or mee*-tee-aw)

meteoroid (*meet*-ee-uh-royd)

Miocene (*muy*-uh-seen)

mollusc (*mol*-uhsk)

nematode (*nem*-uh-tohd)

nocturnal (nok-*ter*-nuhl)

nucleus (*nyooh*-klee-uhs)

olfactory (ol-*fak*-tuh-ree)

Oligocene (o-*lig*-oh-seen)

opaque (oh-*payk*)

ossicle (*oss*-ik-uhl)

Palaeocene (*pal*-ee-uh-seen)

Palaeozoic (pal-ee-oh-*zoh*-ik)

parallax (*pa*-ruh-laks)

peripheral (puh-*rif*-uh-ruhl)

pharyngeal (*fa*-rin-jee-al)

photokeratitis (foh-toh-keh-rah-*tuy*-tuhs)

phloem (*flo*-em)

placenta (pluh-*sen*-tuh)

platyhelminths (plat-i-*hel*-minths)

Pleistocene (*pluys*-toh-seen)

Pliocene   (*pluy*-oh-seen)

porifera   (por-*if*-era)

precipitate   (pruh-*sip*-uh-tayt)

presbyopia   (prez-bee-*oh*-pee-uh)

proboscis   (pruh-*bos*-kuhs)

Procoptodon   (pro-*cop*-to-don)

pteridophyte   (*te*-ri-do-fyt)

receptor   (ruh-*sep*-tuh)

retina   (*ret*-uh-nuh)

revolution   (rev-uh-*loo*-shuhn)

Richter scale   (*rik*-tuh *skayl*)

seismology   (suyz-*mol*-uh-jee)

soluble   (*sol*-yuh-buhl)

stimulus   (*stim*-yuh-luhs)

stratosphere   (*strat*-uhs-fear)

submersible   (sub-*mer*-sa-bl)

temperature   (*temp*-ruh-chuh)

terrestrial   (tuh-*res*-tree-al)

Thylacinus   (thy-la-*sin*-us)

Thylacoleo   (thy-le-*col*-eo)

tracheophyte   (*tra*-kee-o-fyt)

translucent   (tranz-*looh*-suhnt)

troposphere   (*trop*-uhs-fear)

tsunami   (tsoo-*nah*-mi)

vacuole   (*vak*-yooh-ohl)

vascular   (*vas*-kyuh-luh)

xylem   (*zy*-lem)

INDEX